Musical Structure and Cognition

Musical Structure and Cognition

Edited by

PETER HOWELL
Department of Psychology
University College London
London

IAN CROSS
Department of Music
The City University
London

ROBERT WEST
Institute of Psychiatry
De Crespigny Park
London

1985

ACADEMIC PRESS

(Harcourt Brace Jovanovich, Publishers)

London Orlando San Diego New York
Toronto Montreal Sydney Tokyo

ACADEMIC PRESS INC. (LONDON) LTD.
24–28 Oval Road
LONDON NW1 7DX

United States Edition published by
ACADEMIC PRESS, INC.
Orlando, Florida 32887

British Library Cataloguing in Publication Data

Musical structure and cognition.
   1. Music----Psychology
   I. Howell, Peter   II. Cross, Ian   III. West, Robert
   781'.15   ML3830

Library of Congress Cataloging in Publication Data

Main entry under title:

Musical structure and cognition.

   Includes index.
   Contents: Music and change--on the establishment of
rules / I. Cross -- Modelling perceived musical structure /
R. West, P. Howell, and I. Cross -- The rhythmic interpre-
tation of simple musical sequences / C.S. Lee -- [etc.]
   1. Music--Psychology--Addresses, essays, lectures.
I. Howell, Peter. II. Cross, Ian. III. West, Robert.
ML3830.M985 1985   781'.15   84-24346
ISBN 0-12-357170-7 (alk. paper)

PRINTED IN THE UNITED STATES OF AMERICA

85 86 87 88   9 8 7 6 5 4 3 2 1

Contents

Contributors   ix

Foreword   xi

Preface   xiii

1.   **Music and Change: On the Establishment of Rules**
     IAN CROSS

     Introduction   1
     Pitch in Western Music: A Brief Historical Review   5
     The Naked Diatonic Scale   9
     The Prototypical Tonic   13
     References   19

2.   **Modelling Perceived Musical Structure**
     ROBERT WEST, PETER HOWELL, AND IAN CROSS

     Introduction   21
     The Basics of Music Modelling   21
     Models as Descriptions   23
     Natural Language Grammars and Music Modelling   31
     Developing a Model of Musical Structure   44
     Conclusions   50
     References   51

3.   **The Rhythmic Interpretation of Simple Musical
     Sequences: Towards a Perceptual Model**
     C. S. LEE

     Introduction   53
     Existing Theories   56
     A Model   62

Conclusions   67
References   68

4. **On the Perceptual Organisation of Tone Sequences
    and Melodies**
    ANTHONY J. WATKINS AND MARY C. DYSON

    Melody and Perception   71
    A Rudimentary Analysis of Melody   74
    The Synthesis of Melody Approximations   87
    Melodious Scaling   90
    Recognition Memory   92
    Tuning and Mistuning   96
    Contour and Contour Features   103
    New Music?   110
    References   114

5. **Structural Relationships in the Perception of Musical Pitch**
    IAN CROSS, PETER HOWELL, AND ROBERT WEST

    Introduction   121
    Psychoacoustic Approaches to Pitch Perception   122
    Structural Approaches to Pitch Perception   123
    Pitch Organisation and the Circle of Fifths   126
    Perception of Note Sequences Ranging in Approximation
       to Scalar Conformance   130
    Deriving a Sense of Scalar Conformance   132
    Conclusions   139
    References   140

6. **Immediate Recall of Melodies**
    JOHN A. SLOBODA AND DAVID H. H. PARKER

    Introduction   143
    Method   147
    Results of Data Analyses   149
    Conclusions   159
    Appendix   162
    References   166

7. **Melodic Contour and Musical Structure**
    JUDY EDWORTHY

    Introduction   169
    Contour   170
    Methodology   172
    Experimental Results   175
    Contour in Music Perception   183
    References   187

8. **The Relativity of Absolute Pitch**
    ALAN COSTALL

    Introduction   189
    The Relativity of Musical Pitch   190
    Relational Strategies in Pitch Identification   191
    The Training of Pitch Identification   199
    Conclusion   205
    References   206

9. **Structure and Expression in Rhythmic Performance**
    ERIC F. CLARKE

    Introduction   209
    Rhythmic Structures   211
    Expressive Transformations of Rhythmic Structures   227
    Concluding Remarks: Structure and Expression   233
    References   235

10. **Music Structure and Human Movement**
    JOHN BAILY

    Introduction   237
    Movement Patterns in African Music   238
    A Study of the Herati Dutār and the Afghan Rubāb   242
    Spatial Representations of Music Structure   256
    References   258

11. Auditory Feedback of the Voice in Singing
     PETER HOWELL

     Introduction   259
     Properties of Airborne Vocalisation and Transduction of
        Sound by the Peripheral Auditory System   259
     Factors Affecting the Sound of the Singer's Own Voice   270
     Altered Auditory Feedback and Vocal Control   282
     Conclusions   285
     References   285

12. Vocal Control in Singing: A Cognitive Approach
     NIGEL HARVEY

     Introduction   287
     The Processes Involved in Singing   289
     Application of Schema Theory to Singing   290
     Exhalation   291
     Phonation   305
     Articulation of Vowels   313
     Coordination   320
     Implications   321
     Queries   322
     References   328

Index   333

Contributors

Numbers in parentheses indicate the pages on which the authors' contributions begin.

JOHN BAILY[1] (237), Department of Social Anthropology, The Queen's University of Belfast, Belfast BT7 1NN, Northern Ireland

ERIC F. CLARKE (209), Department of Music, The City University, London EC1V OHB, England

ALAN COSTALL (189), Department of Psychology, The University of Southampton, Southampton SO9 5NH, England

IAN CROSS (1, 21, 121), Centre for Arts and Related Studies, The City University, London EC1V OHB, England

MARY C. DYSON (71), Department of Psychology, University of Reading, Reading RG6 2AL, England

JUDY EDWORTHY (169), Medical Research Council Applied Psychology Unit, Cambridge CB2 2EF, England

NIGEL HARVEY (287), Department of Psychology, University College London, London WC1E 6BT, England

PETER HOWELL (21, 121, 259), Department of Psychology, University College London, London WC1E 6BT, England

C. S. LEE (53), Laboratory of Experimental Psychology, University of Sussex, Brighton BN1 9QG, England

DAVID H. H. PARKER (143), Department of Psychology, City of Liverpool College of Higher Education, Merseyside L34 1NP, England

JOHN A. SLOBODA (143), Department of Psychology, University of Keele, Newcastle Under Lyme, Staffordshire ST5 5BG, England

ANTHONY J. WATKINS (71), Department of Psychology, University of Reading, Reading RG6 2AL, England

ROBERT WEST (21, 121), Institute of Psychiatry, De Crespigny Park, London SE5 8AF, England

[1]Present address: National Film and Television School, Beaconsfield Studios, Station Road, Beaconsfield, Buckinghamshire, England

Foreword

Music is perhaps the most mysterious of all the arts, being at the same time so remote from reality and so faithful to experience. It has long been the subject of scholarly examination and will doubtless continue to fascinate the psychologist for as long as performers play and listeners attend. Musical cognition involves the creation of elaborate rhythmic and tonal structures, which may be formally described in grammatical terms; but the realisation of these structures in sound and their recreation by the listener involve skills and sensibilities of a delicacy that the psychologist of music is only beginning to appreciate. It is in this spirit that the reader is invited to approach these thought-provoking essays on the cognitive psychology of music.

Christopher Longuet-Higgins

Laboratory of Experimental Psychology and
Centre for Research on Perception and Cognition
University of Sussex

Preface

Music plays an important part in the lives of people of many cultures, serving as a component of ritual and as a source of recreation. The forms it may take vary from culture to culture and change over time. One integral feature of music that remains constant is that it involves the patterning or structuring of sound. Music theory provides ways of describing structure in music, but to comprehend musical structure fully we must focus on the human activities and capacities that give rise to and respond to it. The chapters in this volume describe recent advances in our understanding of musical structure as it exists in perception and performance.

The scope of the volume is intended to be broad. The content ranges from an analysis of systems of pitch organisation in music theory to an account of the constraints on musical structure that may be imposed by the human motor system. The emphasis is on empirical investigation, and the need to base theoretical accounts of musical structure on extramusical principles relating to human cognition. Though the primary purpose of this volume is to convey the ''state of the art'' in the study of musical cognition, many of the chapters should be accessible to undergraduate students of music and psychology, and contain sufficient background material to provide an introduction to important topics within the field.

Chapter 1 sets the remainder of the volume in historical context by analysing the implications for the cognitive study of pitch provided by Western musical theory (the rules that constrain the composition, performance, and analysis of music within the Western style or idiom). Chapters 2–8 are principally concerned with the perceptual organisation of music in terms of melodic, harmonic, and rhythmic properties. Chapter 2 reviews current models of musical structure and proposes a scheme for a more broadly based approach, while Chapter 3 considers formal models of metric and rhythmic groupings. Chapter 4 shows how probalistic rules based on theoretical principles of tonal organisation can capture significant details of melodic perception. Chapter 5 takes a more abstract, formal level of pitch organisation as its basis in seeking to describe how listeners arrive at a sense of scale in the course of listening to a melody. Chapter 6 presents data from recalls of a folk tune that provide striking insights into what information we have access to from melodies to which we have recently listened. Chapter 7 describes an empirical investigation into the role of pitch contour in the perception and recognition of melodies. Chapter 8 takes us away from the perception of pitch sequences to the perception of pitch in isolation—the thorny problem of absolute pitch identification.

The final four chapters focus primarily on production of music. Chapter 9 examines the relationship between structural and expressive cognitive representations of rhythm in musical performances, while Chapter 10 examines how motor control in human movement may influence the structure of instrumental repertoire and performance. Chapters 11 and 12 are intended to be read as a pair and take the reader through a basic introduction to principles governing voice production and feedback, to an account of how singers may regulate their vocal output.

We would like to thank Kathy Maloney and Jane Woods for help with typing, Jonathan Hunwick and Andrew Vores for their technical assistance, and Stuart Rosen for reading and commenting on several chapters. Our own collaboration in this area developed out of a series of seminars on the psychology of music organised by Cathy Weir at University College London, and we are grateful to her and other participants, in particular Natasha Spender and Ian Morin.

1

Music and Change:
On the Establishment of Rules

Ian Cross

INTRODUCTION

Music is a participatory art. Participation demands structure. Two proposals are implicit in these aphoristic assertions. The first is that music is essentially a social activity. Its existence, function, and form are determined by the nature and values of the culture that enfold it. Even the seemingly private activity of listening to a sequence of sounds as music is partially rooted in cultural norms, in the form of a listener's previous experience of music and the role of that experience in the constructive and predictive perception of a sequence of sounds as music. The second proposal is that any social activity—particularly when it takes the form of the transmission or communication of skills, ideas, and values—requires rules for its conduct, together with a means of ordering and systematising its constituents.

If these proposals are accepted (founded, as they are, on the ideas and observations of contemporary psychology and ethnomusicology), then structure can be thought of as inherent in music. At a low level, this can arise as a simple naming of parts; at a higher level, the description of musical structure can entail an attempt to outline the systems involved in the creation, performance, and perception of music. This chapter examines some of the problems that confront any empirical investigation of the perception of musical structure and makes some suggestions for the revaluation or resolution of those problems. It is argued that, as music-theoretic descriptions of musical structure are, by and large, tied to the particular music they seek to elucidate (Bent, 1980), their usage in the study of the cognition of musical structure should be limited by the extent to which those music-theoretic descriptions can be defined in terms extrinsic to music theory or, perhaps, to music. The argument is undertaken in the context of the study of musical pitch perception and examines historical Western (i.e., European) pitch usages and the music-theoretic descriptions that sought to systematise them in an attempt to find ways of expressing these systematisations in formal terms.

MUSICAL STRUCTURE AND COGNITION

1

To quantify, qualify, and comprehend the cognition of musical structure, we must have a working definition of music. Given the vast range of sets of sounds and activities which different cultures consider to be music, this task is not easy. It scarcely seems possible to define music unless the culture in which it occurs is narrowly defined. Even then, music may be regarded as dissociable from its cultural context only in a highly abstract form (Blacking, 1981; see also Baily, Chapter 10, this volume), and then, only on the basis of a complete description of the context within which it occurs (Geertz, 1973). Perhaps the only situation where music explicitly may be defined (Nattiez, 1976) is where a musical corpus has, unchanged, outlived the culture which formed it, a situation found in relationship to Japanese *gagaku* (court) music (Stanton, 1981) and certain liturgical musics such as Byzantine cantillation (Sachs, 1943). Moreover, in addition to the wide range of forms in which music co-exists across cultures, those forms are subject to change in time; this phenomenon occurs in both Western and non-Western cultures (Becker, 1982; Treibitz, 1983.) For a definition of music to serve as a basis for the study of the cognition of music structure, that definition must be expressed in terms that enable the factors of divergence in the music of different cultures and change in time of the music of each culture to be taken into account.

Even if the field is narrowed, and a definition of music that may only be appropriate to the Western cultural tradition is adopted, difficulties arise. First, can the music of even one culture, in all its changing forms over a millenium, be regarded as one music? Second, if music is defined and described in terms pertinent only to music, studying musical cognition by means of such a description risks being both self-referential and overly cultural-specific. These problems are treated as interlinked in this chapter. An account is given of ways in which Western music theory and musicology offer only partial solutions to these problems, particularly insofar as the problems arise in the domain of the study of musical pitch perception. Initially, it is shown that the use of music-theoretic concepts or music-specific means of representing structure (such as musical notation) in the empirical study of musical cognition might act to overdetermine the hypotheses underlying such study. This is followed by a brief outline of the historical changes in pitch usages within the Western musical tradition. The systems of organisation, modality, and tonality used in music theory to account for and define these usages are described. Finally, a method of describing a historically stable music-theoretic system of pitch organisation (the diatonic scale) in terms extrinsic to music theory are outlined; some of its implications for the bases of modality and tonality, and the study of their operation in musical cognition are explored.

Currently, the study of musical cognition tends to focus on the cognition of traditional Western music largely by force of circumstance (bases of cognitive psychology in Western empiricism, availability of acculturated subjects, and pre-formed music-theoretic concepts). Western music theory seems to indicate that common features extend over the entire historical range of Western music, that, to some extent, Western musical history may be viewed as evolutionary, and that well-defined principles may be applied to, or drawn from music of the last 400 years more or less equally. Thus, some basis does exist in music-theoretic terms for treating Western music (up to a point) as a unity. That unity, however, is not a static phenomenon in music theory. The form that Western music takes changes gradually over time, music of one period being differentiable from music of other periods by sets of features which constitute their different styles (La Rue, 1970).

Nonetheless, certain factors or principles do seem to remain constant as styles change, particularly in music circa 1600–1900. The study of musical cognition must, therefore, in forming its operational definition of Western musical structure, follow music theory in differentiating between those elements that change in time from style to style and those elements that remain constant or stable across styles and centuries. However, the study of musical cognition should not necessarily follow music theory in its criteria for identifying and differentiating between style-transcending and style-linked elements; music theory, as a codificatory body of knowledge and procedures, should form part of the object of the study of musical cognition (e.g., Dowling, 1978; Burns and Ward, 1982).

However, to provide a basis for its procedures, the psychology of music has relied on music theory to provide an initial musical morphology which may, in some instances, cloud rather than clarify a cognitive view of the constituents of music. For example, many (indeed, most) music-theoretic approaches to the analysis of music adopt as their object of study music as manifested in notation. Musical notation is, essentially, functional for cultural participants: for codification, teaching prescription, transmission, and performance of music. It embodies particular aspects of music, and an accurate usage of musical notation will only occur if the user is aware of the context of the notation. That is, notation is selective. As much information again as is explicitly derivable from the notation may be required to produce an accurate interpretation of the music that the notation is intended to represent (see, e.g., Ferguson, 1975; Tyler, 1980). The selectivity of notation is well recognised in current musicology, not only at the level of performance practice (Boretz and Cone, 1972; Cole, 1974), but also as indicative of notation's codificatory function. Notation, like theory, tends to follow practice. Awareness of this selectivity and the ways in which it may condition and shape musical concepts at a very basic level is as important in the cognitive study of music. It might be expected, for example, that a culture or period in which musical notation consists of tablature (representation of sequence of actions in time) would have access to a somewhat different set of intuitions as to the form and nature of music from a culture or period of which the primary form of notation is traditional Western staff notation (pitch/time grid). Figure 1 shows the same fragment of music in both forms.

(a)

(b)

Figure 1. Gavotte II from J. S. Bach's Lute Suite No. 3. (a) Tablature notation; (b) staff notation.

Note that the dimension of pitch height appears explicitly as vertical displacement in staff notation, and as a complex correlate of symbol type and vertical displacement in tablature. Whereas the concept of height—as applied to pitch—is well established in the psychological literature (Shepard, 1964), there is some evidence to show that childrens' differentiation between pitches may be expressed preferentially in terms such as dull-bright rather than low–high (Crowther and Durkin, 1982). To some extent, the acceptability of the application of the application of some spatial basis in the study of pitch differentiation and ordering may be conditioned by traditional notational usages. However, it is likely that some aspects of musical notation do reflect strategies and structures that are important in musical cognition (Sloboda, 1982) at the level of perception. In particular, it is to be expected that the relative perceptual importance of different aspects of music may be reflected in their relative saliences in notation.

An aspect of music that Western music theory and Western notation have accorded considerable salience is pitch (a situation mirrored in the study of musical cognition). The pitch of a musical event is (and generally, has been) notatable independent of any other musical characteristics of that event, and abstract schemes by which pitches may be differentiated and ordered always have constituted an important part of Western musical theories. These theoretical schemes have had to accommodate and adapt to a wide range of conceptions and usages of pitch over the course of Western musical history. First, those usages will be described, followed by an outline of the schemes which accommodated and accommodate them.

PITCH IN WESTERN MUSIC: A BRIEF
HISTORICAL REVIEW

Usages

As Powers says, "Medieval Christian music of the West is the oldest musical style from which theory and repertory survive in sufficient quantity for comparative examination over time" (1980, p. 378). The earliest body of that music was more or less fully formed by the ninth century and consisted of monophonic (single melody) liturgical music: each melody characterisable as restricted in pitch range and made up of a series of simple melodic fragments (ordered pitch sets). In this monophonic context, a system of rules exists (codified in the ninth century Scholia Enchiriadis—Strunk, 1950) for improvising melodies to be sung together with pre-established melodies. These polyphonic (multiple, simultaneous melodies) practices were extended and formalised through the Middle Ages, so that by the thirteenth century, polyphony could be said to be a predominant feature of Western liturgical (and, increasingly, secular) music. Through the thirteenth and fourteenth centuries, polyphonic practice was further extended; melodic pitch ranges increased with simultaneous melodies usually overlapping in range or sharing the same range (e.g., de Machaut, "S'il estoit nulz" in Davis and Apel, 1949). Composition, in this period was generally carried out part by part, a melody being taken or adapted and further melodies individually composed to fit the initial melody. Through the fifteenth century, this compositional process gradually changed. Simultaneous melodies tended to occupy adjacent non-overlapping pitch ranges (e.g. Obrecht's *Missa Sine Nomine* in Davis and Apel, 1949) and individual melodies of a polyphonic composition were composed simultaneously, a practice formalised by the early sixteenth century (see Aron in Strunk, 1950).

This change in compositional practice prefigures many late developments in Western music. It represents a change from a consideration of melodic succession of individual pitches (or pitch sets) as being the primary determinant of pitch structure in music to a consideration of the succession of pitch simultaneities (chords) across melodies as the dominant factor. This dominance, formalised in terms of figured bass (a method of notating chords by scale-step distance from the lowest note; Palisca, 1968) by the end of the sixteenth century, led to the predominance of chordal succession in the late seventeenth century in the guise of tonality in the works of Corelli and Lully (Blume, 1975). Tonality is an elusive musical concept, perhaps best described (in its typical Western usage) by Rosen (1976) as "a system with a central perfect triad [e.g., the notes C, E, G] all the other triads, major and minor are arranged around the central one" (p. 36). So chords and their relationships to one another come to dominate consideration of successivity.

Tonality may be thought of as the primary determinant of pitch structure in Western music during the eighteenth and nineteenth centuries (Dahlhaus, 1980) and in Western popular music throughout the twentieth century. However, the musical structures it has "generated" changed in this period to the extent that a broad catch-all definition such as Rosen's (1976) is as explicit as is commensurate with bare accuracy in its applicability.

The range of pitch usages across Western musical history is, to some extent, reflected in changes in its notation. Early Christian chant notation is composed of series of symbols, each indicating a particular melodic fragment. Pitch in this neumatic notation is not a series of discrete, differentiable equivalent single events, but a series of articulated and differentiable shapes or gestures in the pitch continuum (Reese, 1941). Pitch levels were gradually differentiated by placement of neumatic symbols on horizontal staff lines, and the symbols (with the advent of "measured" polyphony) split into component equivalent single pitches. This system of pitch representation, with minor changes such as fluctuating numbers of staff lines, has persisted to the present day.

Schemes of Organisation

Underlying—or perhaps, accompanying—these different Western pitch usages are the abstract schemes by which pitches may be differentiated and ordered. The earliest of these schemes may be said to have had at least three different bases for its form, those bases being pre-existent theoretical schemes, the need to differentiate between melodies and between sets of melodies, and the need to describe and differentiate between the functions of melodic components such as pitches and pitch sets. One particularly important pre-existing scheme was the Hellenistic scheme, transmitted to music theorists of the early Middle Ages by the writings of Boethius (Powers, 1980). This scheme provided a basis for generating seven octave-spanning sets of eight pitches—each a different arrangement of tones and semitones across the octave (called the "octave species")—but all capable of being derived—in practice—from an underlying diatonic major scale. Medieval theorists selected different octave species, attached particular absolute pitch ranges, identified particular pitches within each octave species as privileged, and used these conglomerate concepts, called "modes," to classify melodies and to assist in their teaching of Christian chant. Thus, the Western concept of mode served an equivocal double function from its inception onwards; as a classificatory system; and as a practical, working tool, sometimes assuming different forms in each domain. Its underlying diatonic scale, however, remained remarkably stable, particularly in the form of the gamut, or Guidonian hand (Strunk, 1950) when mode was used as a working tool.

Throughout its medieval usage, the concept of mode was partially determined by the different intervallic contexts afforded to structurally equivalent notes in different modes. That is, for example, in the first mode of octave species D to D′, the final (or note in which melodies in the first mode should end) which is D has notes E, F, G, and A above it, constituting intervals tone, semitone, tone, tone; in the second (authentic) mode, (octave species E to E′), E, the final, has the interval arrangement semitone, tone, tone, tone above it. Thus, structurally equivalent notes (finals) in different modes are differentiated by the intervals they may form with their surrounding notes.

The concept of mode survived (in various forms) through to the seventeenth century when it was gradually supplanted by the concepts of major and minor keys, more or less synchronously with the rise of the use of tonality as a primary organising principle. In its later days, during the late Renaissance (circa sixteenth century), the concept of mode was, for all practical purposes, a means of differentiating between and identifying intervallic contexts of notes, having more or less shed its implications of absolute pitch range but not of functional differentiation between member pitches. The concept of functional differentiation between member pitches continued in the use of major and minor key (Zuckerkandl, 1971), although altered by the dichotomy inherent in a basic precept of tonality, that an individual pitch may be considered as part of a melody or as part of a chord (Dahlhaus, 1980).

Tonality can be said to have supplanted modality as the primary framework for pitch organisation in Western music: It should be clear, however, that the two terms are not equatable. Tonality, in particular, is an ambiguous concept; part of its ambiguity derives from the tendency of theorists to use the term to denote different aspects of different bodies of music. If Rosen's (1976) definition is adopted, the term may properly be applied only to Western music from about 1600. Its usage implies that, in this body of music, particular pitches may be differentiated weakly by intervallic context but more strongly by the relationships that chords using those pitches may have with a central, tonic chord and the relationship that those pitches have with the root note of the central triad, the tonic note. Although tonality and modality have been shown here to share the principle of using a reference element, the factors which may act to establish them are different in each system, as indeed are the reference elements themselves. In modality, melodic succession and the intervallic context of each pitch act to determine which pitch should be accorded referential status; in tonality, both these factors may be operational, but they are generally subordinated to considerations of chordal succession and chord-constituent interrelationships in defining the tonic or tonic triad. Apart from the use of reference elements, perhaps the *only* constant across modality and tonality is the use of the diatonic scale as a background structure of pitch differentiation.

From the foregoing, it can be seen that the definitions of tonality and (to a lesser extent) modality tend to be pragmatically based; the terms and concepts have been developed for the purpose of describing particular, limited bodies of music and for pedagogical ends. Several proposals for formalising the concept of tonality have been made (see West *et al.*, Chapter 2, this volume). However, these tend either to suffer from an openendedness which limits their ability to generate strong hypotheses about the cognition of musical structure or to be based upon axiomatic premises which themselves should be the objects of empirical study.

Despite these caveats, the experimental study of musical pitch perception has tended to rely on the concepts of modality and tonality both to describe its experimental material and to provide a framework for its results. The concept of mode has been used by Dowling (1978) to represent the most concrete level of musical scale representation in melodic perception; Krumhansl (1979) found some evidence to indicate the use of the tonic (and weakly, the tonic triad) as a reference element within the diatonic major scale: Cuddy (1982) used the concept of tonality to differentiate between melodic sequences; Bharucha and Krumhansl (1983) tested an aspect of tonality, chord-relatedness, in demonstrating differential degrees of stability accorded different, but related, chords in perception. Similarly, Deutsch and Feroe (1981) and Deutsch (1982) make use of aspects of tonality (triads, keys) in constructing alphabets held to underlie representation of melodic pitch succession (see West et al., Chapter 2, this volume). As stated, a difficulty in using aspects of these abstract music-theoretic schemes for pitch organisation in the study of musical cognition is their nebulous status in music theory itself. Although both modality and tonality have been briefly described, either term can be used to denote a wide range of types (and levels) of pitch organisation. Powers (1980) indicates that mode may refer to any level of abstract melodic organisation other than to a scale or a specific melody; Dahlhaus (1980) similarly gives seven partially overlapping definitions of tonality, some, in fact, coterminous with mode. The term "tonality" may also be used legitimately to refer to aspects of certain contemporary Western music that is neither modally nor triadically based (Perle, 1977). Moreover, experimental research has indicated that certain aspects of pitch organisation such as contour (Davies, 1979; Dowling, 1978; Edworthy, Chapter 7, this volume) may be operational in melodic pitch perception; the concept of pitch contour is not immediately referrable to any well-formulated concept within modality or tonality (though see Reti, 1951; Rosner and Meyer, 1982).

Given the relative informality of these music-theoretic descriptions of pitch organisation, it would seem best to seek a more stable and more formal pitch scheme on which to base investigations into the cognition of pitch. One historically stable scheme seems to be the diatonic scale, which, as shown previously, can be said to underlie Western concepts of both modality and tonality. From the historical evidence, neither term is reducible to scale alone, but, in general, neither term has or has had a usage in Western music theory which is not at least partially reliant on scale. Again, it might be objected that scale, even in Western music, has not acted as a stable form but has taken on a variety of physical forms in accordance with different tuning methods (Strunk, 1950). However, as Burns and Ward (1982) point out, "the standards of intonation for a given culture are the learned interval categories of the scales of that culture" (p. 264). Those interval categories have remained remarkably stable in terms of their scale-step size (though not, theoretically, in terms of frequency ratios) through Western musical history. An outline will accordingly be given of ways of expressing diatonic scale structure in *formal* rather than music-theoretic or frequency-ratio based terms.

THE NAKED DIATONIC SCALE

Currently, Western music tends to use—as a superordinate method of pitch differentiation—a system having twelve different pitches to the octave, each interval between adjacent pitches, in theory, equal (each a semitone) and octave-related pitches being regarded as more or less equivalent. This constitutes the equally tempered chromatic set of available pitches (Figure 2a and b). From this set, within which all smallest intervals are equal, the diatonic major scale may be formed by selecting out seven of the available twelve pitches within an octave; the scale may be formed by applying the series of intervals 2 (semitones), 2, 1, 2, 2, 2, 1 in any rotational form (e.g., 2, 1, 2, 2, 2, 1, 2). The diatonic scale is regarded here as an abstract intervallically based structure having no functional differentiation between constituent notes on any basis other than intervallic context.

Recent formulations of Western pitch structure treat the chromatic set as analogous to a cyclic group of order 12 (that is, they collapse pitch range into a

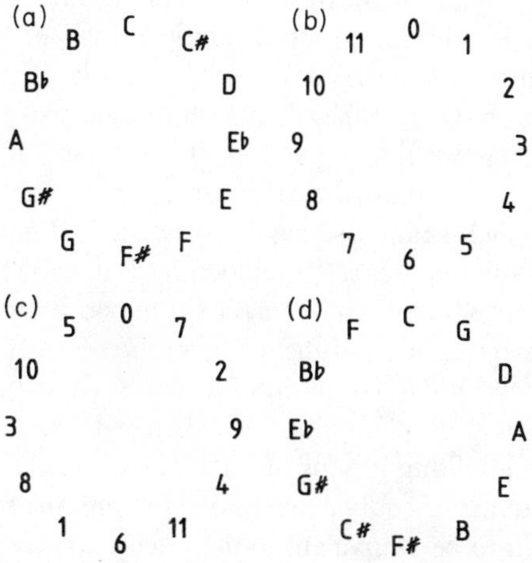

Figure 2. The chroma circle and the circle of fifths, represented as note names and as numbers.

cyclic group of 12 different pitch chroma levels by treating octave-related notes as exactly equivalent). This has certain advantages as it enables the representation of pitches—Figure 2a—or more properly, pitch-classes—as each pitch now represents a class of octave-related pitches—to be presented numerically, as in Figure 2b. Figure 2b has certain obvious properties: in mod 12 arithmetic, all 12 possible pitch-classes (numbers) occur, and the intervals between adjacent pitches are all equal (in mod 12 arithmetic, only 1 step separates 11 and 0 as 0 is equivalent to 12). A particular advantage is gained by retaining those properties (complete group representation and interval equality) while rearranging the order in which elements occur. The one way in which this can be done is as shown in Figure 2c. In this formulation, which is analagous to the musical circle of fifths, a major diatonic scale occurs (reordered) as any collection of 7 adjacent pitch-classes on the circle as in Figure 2d (Balzano, 1980). In the circle-of-fifths representation, each pair of adjacent notes is separated by (7) mod 12 minimum intervals (semitones); an interval of seven semitones is equivalent to a musical interval of a perfect fifth (e.g., the interval between the notes C and G). In representing the chromatic set as a cyclic group, certain assumptions are made: It is assumed that octave equivalence between pitches is a complete equivalence (Attneave and Olson, 1971); it is not, at least at the extremes of the usable musical pitch range. Despite the group representation's lack of certain features of musical pitch that are operational in music and musical perception, it has the advantage of being formally definable and, to a certain extent, empirically neutral; the relationships between and within its constituent parts (pitch-class sets or collections of pitch-class sets) and between its whole and its parts can be completely described formally, and clearly formulated hypotheses and predictions about the perceptual status of those relationships can be empirically tested.

There now exists a large body of music-theoretic literature that seeks to explain pitch structure in music in group-theoretic terms (see Rahn 1980, p. 120). Most of this literature is concerned with the analysis of pitch organisation in recent notated Western music rather than with the study of perception, although this limited scope of application is rarely made clear (see, however, Rahn 1980, p. 31). However, at least one particular use of group-theoretic terms in relationship to musical pitch is directed explicitly at accounting for aspects of musical pitch perception: the approach developed by Balzano (1980, 1982).

One of Balzano's (1982) primary concerns is the position of the diatonic scale when viewed as a manifestation of the cyclic group of order 12 rather than as an ordering of frequency ratios. To outline Balzano's view, certain aspects of the group representation(s) of pitch must be sketched. As has been said, relationships between and within groups of pitch-class sets can be formally characterised, initially in terms of equivalence. For example, the set of pitch-class sets (0, 1, 2) can be said to be equivalent to the pitch-class set (1, 2, 3) in that the same relationships are formable within each set, and one set may be mapped onto the other by one operation, termed "transposition" (i.e., in reference to a pitch-class set, transposition consists of the addition or subtraction of the same mod 12 number to or from all members of the pitch-class set). Thus, pitch-class sets having the same number of elements and the same layout on the circle of fifths or chroma circle, are equivalent under transposition. Transposition has, more or less, its strict musical usage whereby a melody played in two different keys can be said to be the same melody—transposed—in the second, as in the first, key. The difference here is that transpositional equivalence between pitch-class sets is order-independent and (0, 1, 2) and (1, 2, 3) are equivalent; then (1, 0, 2) is here still equivalent transpositionally to (3, 2, 1) even though the order of the elements of the pitch-class sets are rearranged.

Taking transposition as the basis for equivalence, the total number of different sets of pitch-class sets which may be formed from the chromatic set, 4095, may be reduced to 351 pitch-class sets by treating transpositionally related sets having the same number of members (e.g., [0, 1, 2] and [1, 2, 3]) as "the same" pitch-class set. From this range of 351 non-transpositionally equivalent pitch-class sets, Balzano describes particular, singular characteristics of the pitch-class set that represents the diatonic scale (0, 2, 4, 5, 7, 9, 11). First, the scale has the property of *uniqueness,* i.e., as mentioned earlier, each scale note may be differentiated from another scale note by the set of intervals which it may form with all other scale notes. This property is common to a range of pitch-class sets; however, the diatonic scale possesses not only uniqueness but also *coherence.* Coherence is the property that the sum of any two consecutive intervals formed within a set in normal order (roughly, arranged so that pitch-class numbers increase from left to right; see Forte, 1973) will be greater than any single interval occurring in a pitch-class set so ordered. Although the diatonic scale has unequal-sized, single scale-step intervals (as it must, to possess uniqueness), the sum of any two consecutive scale-step intervals is always larger than any single scale-step interval. Coherence (together with uniqueness) confers perceptual advantages on the diatonic major scale, in that any interval occurring in a scalar melody may be characterised as constituted of a fixed number of scale steps (the one exception is the tritone, the interval between the notes B and F, for example).

In addition to coherence and uniqueness, the diatonic major scale has the property of *simplicity.* Simplicity is used here to indicate that each diatonic major scale may be transformed into a transpositionally equivalent diatonic scale with a different pitch-class content by changing one element, and that the relationship between the initial scale and the element that transforms it is the same for all equivalent forms of the diatonic scale. This can be seen most simply in Figure 2c. Given that 7 adjacent pitch-class sets here form a diatonic scale, any scale can be transformed (in terms of pitch-class context) simply by shifting the connected region around one step, for example, the marked region (5, 0, 7, 2, 9, 4,

11; (scale of C in Figure 2d) can be shifted around to produce the region (0, 7, 2, 9, 4, 11, 6; scale of G). All diatonic major scales have similarly adjacent neighbours with which they share all but one of their pitch-class content. Only one other pitch-class set of cardinality 7, the pitch-class set (0, 1, 2, 3, 4, 5, 6) has the property of simplicity, and although it has the property of uniqueness, it lacks that of coherence.

Balzano (1980, 1982) derives these three properties of the diatonic scale from a group-theoretic representation in which equivalence between pitch-class sets is based solely on set cardinality (number of set members) and transposition. In current music theory, a more widespread usage of group-theoretic formulations of pitch (Forte, 1973; Rahn, 1980) uses equivalence relationships between pitch-class sets founded on cardinality, transposition, and inversion. Inversion is best defined as complementation; inversion of a pitch-class number would entail subtracting it from the modulo number (here, 12) so that the inversion of 8 would be 4, of 7 would be 5. Inversional equivalence between pitch-class sets is usually defined in terms of transposition taken together with inversion (Rahn, 1980); that is, equivalence in Forte's system is a compound of transpositional and inversional equivalence. This makes certain facts clearer; for instance, if the set (0, 1, 2) is inverted to become (1, 11, 10), then reordered (10, 11, 0) and transposed upwards by 2, the set (0, 1, 2) reappears; (0, 1, 2) can, by using inversion together with transposition, be seen to be inversionally symmetrical.

Using a form of equivalence based on transposition and inversion does raise apparent problems. For instance, the set (0, 4, 7), if inverted, produced the set (0, 8, 5). Reordered to (5, 8, 0) and transposed upwards by 7, this becomes the set (0, 3, 7); therefore, the set (0, 4, 7) is equivalent to the set (0, 3, 7). However, the set (0, 4, 7) could be written as (C, E, G), the major triad, and the set (0, 3, 7) as (C, E♭, G), the minor; so the major triad is equivalent to the minor. Structurally in music, this may be so, but to equate major with minor absolutely (Forte, 1973) does not seem to make complete perceptual sense.

That aside, the use of inversional equivalence does permit a further property to be assigned to the diatonic major scale, that of *complete and unique interval multiplicity*. That is, all inversionally equivalent interval types formable within the chromatic set may be formed with the diatonic scale and each interval type is formable a unique number of times. This means that intervals are specifiable as more common or more rare than other intervals within the diatonic scale, and thus, intervals may serve differentially in perception of a melody to indicate position within scale or act as a cue to underlying scale structure (Browne 1981). As Gamer (1981) points out, unique interval multiplicity is not solely a property of the diatonic scale, being possessed by other pitch-class sets within the chromatic set and associable with the property of uniqueness. However, taken together, the possession of the properties of uniqueness, coherence, simplicity, and complete unique interval multiplicity by the diatonic scale, and only by the diatonic scale (out of all the pitch-class sets formable within the chromatic set), marks out the diatonic scale as being in possession of singular structural characteristics.

The fact that these characteristics may be described—in terms of formal structure—means that strong hypotheses and predictions about the perception of pitch organisation in music can be generated and tested. Moreover, the use of group-theoretic formulations appears to offer an approach to the study of musical pitch perception consonant with some aspects of the structure of the music of non-Western cultures. Group-theoretic formulations such as outlined previously do not rely on any particular tuning (frequency ratio) system; they assume only octave equivalence—which generalises across several musical cultures (see Burns and Ward, 1982)—and a minimum equivalent interval size for the construction of a superordinate set (in Western usage, the chromatic set). Moreover, many of the features differentiating the diatonic scale from other subsets of the chromatic set are common to formulations based on cyclic groups of orders other than 12 (although see Balzano, 1980; Gamer, 1981).

However, the question of how the special properties of the diatonic scale outlined might be operational in perception is still, by and large, unanswered (although see Balzano, 1982; Browne, 1981; Cross, Howell, and West, Chapter 5, this volume; Watkins and Dyson, Chapter 4, this volume). Also, questions concerning central features of both modal and tonal usages, and identification and use of a reference element seem to be out with group-theoretic formulation. As Balzano writes, "There is nothing in the theory of sets that provides for individuating a particular element of a set as a reference element" (1982, p. 325). Even given this, it might be possible to use the group-theoretic formulation of musical pitch as a starting point for such an individuation.

THE PROTOTYPICAL TONIC

Scale notes, as we have seen, may be structurally differentiated from one another by the intervals they form with other scale notes. In any actual melody, to this differentiation may be added some order-dependent differentiation. That is, a particular scale note may be used as the last note of sets of melodies, or particular inter-note transitions may occur more frequently than others, or in particular temporal positions (beginning, end) in a melody. The particular scale notes used, for example, to end melodies, do not remain constant in Western musical history; the referential value of different scale notes is different as music (and theory) changes in time—even within very abstract schemes of music-theoretic pitch organisation such as modality and tonality. For example, taking C as the underlying scale, the final of the first-classified mode (Boethius's hypodorian, church mode *protus authenticus*) would be D. In tonality, the primary scale note would be C (as can be seen from the way the scale is specified at the beginning of the sentence). Therefore, an explication of referential value in pitch organisation must be flexible enough to account for such a change within actual usages of melodic organisation. It may seem, intuitively, that order-dependent factors are sufficient to account for the referential status of particular notes. But given that structural, order-independent factors have been shown to operate in the perception of sequences of pitches (Brown and Butler, 1981; Howell, West, and Cross, 1984), it seems presumptuous not to seek out possible structural influences on referential value so that those possible structural influences can be tested. A means of elucidating those structural factors can be found by using the concept of similarity.

All scale notes have different intervallic contexts (Balzano's "uniqueness"); the intervallic context of different notes might be expected to show degrees of similarity with each other. For example, Table 1 shows the intervals (counting upwards) that can be formed with other scale notes by C, D, and G in the scale of C. C's interval context has one point of difference from that of G and two points of difference with that of D; G's interval context has one point of difference with both C and D. It can be shown that in the scale of C, C is more similar (in terms of interval context) to G than to D, D is more similar to G than to C, and (if differences are accounted of equivalent value, irrespective of what constitutes them) G is equally similar to C and to D. It might be that the scale notes' different degrees of similarity to one another can produce some hierarchy of similarity, or perhaps, account for tendencies of one note or another to act prototypically.

The prototypicality of members of a category (in respect of that category) can be assessed by measuring the similarities or differences between the category members. One formal method of assessing prototypicality is that developed as a means of assessing similarity without having to make the "distance metric" assumptions implicit in geometric methods of similarity scaling (Tversky, 1977). Although this method generally has been applied to empirical data in behavioural decision theory (Einhorn and Hogarth, 1981), it may be applied in the present instance. Tversky's method assesses similarity by applying a metric function to

Table 1

INTERVALLIC CONTEXT OF THE NOTES C, D, AND G
IN THE SCALE OF C[a]

	1	2	3	4	5	6	7	8	9	10	11
C		x		x	x		x		x		x
D		x	x		x		x		x	x	
G		x		x	x		x		x	x	

[a]Intervals are shown in terms of the number of semitone steps that constitute them, counting upwards from the note of which the context is being described.

both the features shared by two elements and the features which are proper only to one or the other element.

Thus, elements would be represented by features, and the similarity between objects a and b, $s(a, b)$ is defined in terms of sets of features here denoted by A and B, respectively:

$$s(a, b) = \theta f (A \cap B) - \alpha f (A - B) - \beta f (B - A), \qquad (1)$$

where $A \cap B$ are the features common to A and B, $A - B$ and $B - A$ are the distinctive features of a and b, respectively, f is the salience of the features, and θ, α, and β are weighting factors. In other words, the similarity between a and b is equal to some weighting of their common factors ($A \cap B$), less some weighting of the features a has and b does not ($A - B$), less some weighting of the features b has and a does not ($B - A$). Prototypicality of an element a with respect to a category, $P(a, \wedge)$ would be determined similarly:

$$P(a, \wedge) = pn(\lambda \Sigma f(\wedge \cap B) - \Sigma(\alpha f(A - B) + \beta f(B - A))), \qquad (2)$$

where the summations are over all the not-a members of $\wedge$. So $P(a, \wedge)$ is a linear combination of the measure of all features of element a that are shared with the other elements of $\wedge$; less the measure of all features of a which are not shared with elements of $\wedge$; if $P(a, \wedge)$ is maximal (i.e., greater than $P(n, \wedge)$ where n is any element of /3 other than a), then a is a prototype of $\wedge$. Tversky (1977) points out that it is probable that common features are more heavily weighted in prototypicality judgments than in similarity judgments.

If this formal model is to be applied informally to the question of referentiality or prototypicality of scale notes in respect of intervallic contexts, the first step is the selection of the features to represent the notes. These will be the intervals that may be formed with all other scale notes (as in Table 1). Each note may form only six intervals with other scale notes, that is, intervals common to note a and note b, will be summed for note a over all instances where note a and another scale note can form that interval. The results of this process carried out on the members of the scale of C are shown in Table 2. C has the Interval 2 in common with four other notes, the Interval 4 in common with 2 other notes, 5 in common with 5 other notes, 7 in common with 5 other notes, 9 in common with 3 other notes, and 11 in common with 1 other note, making a total of 20. Distinctive features are not considered as, in the absence of empirical data, weighting factors may have any value (except that to maintain symmetry of similarity relationships ($\alpha = \beta$); if common features are weighted more heavily than distinctive ones, (Tversky, 1977) then irrespective of the actual value chosen for λ (common feature weighting) the same ordinal ranking of prototypicality holds as shown in Table 2. As can be seen, if diatonic major scale notes are equated for their interval contexts, then the prototype of the scale of C is, in fact, the note D, the final or most important note of the first-classified church mode on that scale.

Table 2

RANKING OF PROTOTYPICALITY DERIVED FROM INTERVAL CONTEXTS OF SCALE NOTES[a]

	1	2	3	4	5	6	7	8	9	10	11	Common features	Ordinal prototypicality
C		x		x	x		x		x		x	20	4
D		x	x		x		x		x	x		24	1
E	x		x		x		x	x		x		20	4
F		x		x		x	x		x		x	16	6
G		x		x	x		x		x	x		23	2
A			x		x		x	x		x		23	2
B	x	x	x		x	x		x		x		16	6

[a]Intervals are taken as being transpositionally equivalent.

However, a different result can be obtained by treating intervals as inversionally equivalent. For example, this would mean treating the interval from C to A upwards (9 semitone steps) as identical to the interval from that A upwards to the next C (3 semitone steps); thus, intervals would be equivalent to their mod 12 complements (11–1, 10–2, 9–3, etc). If intervals are taken as possessing inversional equivalence, only six different interval types may be formed; this has consequences for the similarities of the intervallic contexts of different scale notes, as may be seen in Table 3. Here, prototypicality is assessed as in Table 2 (only common features are considered) with one difference: The number of same-sized intervals that a note may form with other scale notes is used to help characterise the features of that note. For example, D can form 2 intervals of two semitones (Size 2); it shares that feature with the notes G and A, but not with the notes C, E, F, or B, each of which may form only one interval of two semitones. This method of accounting for features and for the different degrees to which scale notes share features means that if intervals are taken as inversionally equivalent, the diatonic major scale of C has two prototypes, the notes C and E, the notes occupying two of the most "privileged" scale-degrees in most theories of *melodic* tonality (Zuckerkandl, 1971).

The fact that some bases for enhanced referential value of particular scale notes can be derived from structural considerations alone does not imply (and is not intended to imply) that those structural considerations are necessarily determining factors in the use of referential values in musical cognition. This outline simply offers a means of describing musical (or music-theoretical) relationships in terms that are extrinsic to music theory. Moreover, although the outline of prototype formation is expressed (and carried out) in relatively informal terms, it has its bases in formal logical principles and procedures. These can be defined precisely, and the properties of systems based in them predicted (the modulo 12

Table 3

RANKING OF PROTOTYPICALITY DERIVED FROM INTERVAL CONTEXTS OF SCALE NOTES[a]

	1	2	3	4	5	6	Common features	Ordinal prototypicality
C	x	x	x	x	xx		20	1
D		xx	xx		xx		6	7
E	x	x	x	x	xx		20	1
F	x	x	x	x	x	x	18	3
G		xx	x	x	xx		16	5
A		xx	x	x	xx		16	5
B	x	x	x	x	x	x	18	3

[a]Intervals are taken as being transpositionally and inversionally equivalent.

pitch formulations of Balzano, 1982 and Forte, 1973 or the set-theoretic usages of Tversky, 1977).

The corollary—that formal systems can serve, by virtue of the rigorous characterisation of their constituent elements and relationships, as the bases for equally rigorous characterisations of the possible cognitive usage of such systems—does, however, have considerable implications for the study of musical cognition. Many approaches to musical cognition which make use of music-theoretic definitions of musical elements and musical structures, are implicitly making use of formal properties embodied by, or embedded in, those definitions. To be effective, such approaches must clarify and explore all the consequences of these implicit formal properties. For example, both Jones (1981) and Deutsch and Feroe (1981) make use of the diatonic scale as a cyclic alphabet, i,e., as a system of cyclic order 7 in its own right ("flattening out" the differences between scale-step sizes). A cyclic system of order 7 has (in common with all other prime-order cyclic systems) the property that the complete set of seven elements may be generated by using any set member and recursively applying a successor operator that can be of any interval class formable within the set. Thus, in representing a serial pattern, a run—or succession of same-size intervals between elements—is representable as a sequence of steps between proximate elements in some isomorphic form of the cyclic group of order 7; that is, any element of the cyclic set may be immediately next to any other element. This property of potential importance in serial-pattern representation of pitch structure is not recognised in either of the previously mentioned approaches.

Music is a social activity and must—ultimately—be referred to in its cultural context, The ways in which it exists are many and complex, and it may be that in seeking to dissect it by determinate, formal methods, we kill off our ostensible object of study: namely, living musical experience. Perhaps we should approach an understanding of the cognition of musical structure by relying on the intuitions and observations of musicians and music theorists (Randall, 1972) rather than try to account for music in extramusical terms.

As we have seen, music and music theory change in time. If we are to rely on music theory to provide basic concepts for the study of musical cognition, we must be wary of accepting concepts which may apply only to an historically or culturally limited body of music. Moreover, as Blacking (1981) points out, the study of language is conducted in terms of the judgments and discourses of ordinary, rather than expert, users; to study the cognition of musical structure by means of the observations and intuitions of expert users may be to miss some more common grain of musical experience.

Given the vast range of currently available musical structures and music theories and the potential circularity of attempts to explore the cognition of musical structure by means of concepts appropriate only to that structure, it seems that formal accounts of structure have much to offer the study of musical cognition.

Formal accounts are not complete explications of musical cognition; they simply offer ways of characterising relationships between the potential elements of musical structure in terms that are relatively free from, or a completion of, the assumptions underlying music-theoretic terms, these having been developed to fulfill culturally specific codificatory and pedagogic functions.

Formal accounts of musical structure may ultimately provide explications of the cognition of musical structure by providing a computational basis for theory and experiment broad enough to encompass our cognition of the different music of the world. To explain the cognition of musical structure may not explain the cognition of music; to take effective steps towards that explication is to begin to understand how much more there is left to explain.

REFERENCES

Attneave, F., and Olson, R. K. Pitch as a medium: A new approach to psychological scaling. *American Journal of Psychology,* 1971, *84,* 147–166.

Balzano, G. J. The group-theoretic description of twelvefold and microtonal pitch systems. *Computer Music Journal,* 1980, *4*(4), 66–84.

Balzano, G. J. The pitch set as a level of description for studying musical pitch perception. In M. Clynes (Ed.), *Music, mind and brain.* New York: Plenum, 1982.

Becker, J. *Traditional music in modern Jave.* Honolulu: University of Hawaii Press, 1982.

Bent, I. Analysis. In *Grove's dictionary of music.* London: Macmillan, 1980.

Bharucha, J. and Krumhansl, C. L. The representation of harmonic structure in music: Hierarchies of stability as a function of context. *Cognition,* 1983, *13,* 63–102.

Blacking, J. The problem of "ethnic" perception in the semiotics of music. In W. Steiner (Ed.), *The sign in music and literature.* Austin: University of Texas, 1981.

Blume, F. *Renaissance and baroque music* (M. D. H. Norton, Trans.) London: Faber and Faber, 1975.

Boretz, B. and Cone, E. T. (Eds.), *Perspectives on notation and performance.* New York: Norton, 1972.

Brown, H. and Butler, D. Diatonic trichords, as minimal tonal cue-cells. *In Theory Only,* 1981, *5,* 37–55.

Browne, R. Tonal implications of the diatonic set. *In Theory Only,* 1981, *5,* 3–21.

Burns, E. M. and Ward, W. D. Intervals, scales and tuning. In D. Deutsch (Ed.), *The psychology of music.* London: Academic Press, 1982.

Cole, H. *Sounds and signs.* London: Oxford University Press, 1974.

Crowther, R. and Durkin, K. Towards an applied psycholinguistic study of musical concept development. Special issue: Proceedings of the Ninth International Seminar on Research in Music Education. *Psychology of Music,* 1982.

Cuddy, L. L. On hearing pattern in melody. *Psychology of Music,* 1982, *10*(1), 3–10.

Dahlhaus, C. Tonality. In *Groves' dictionary of music.* London: Macmillan, 1980.

Davies, J. B. Memory for melodies and tonal sequences: A theoretical note. *British Journal of Psychology,* 1979, *70,* 205–210.

Davies, A. T. and Apel, W. *Historical anthology of music.* Cambridge, MA: Harvard University Press, 1949.

Deutsch, D. The processing of pitch combinations. In D. Deutsch (Ed.), *The psychology of music.* London: Academic Press, 1982.

Deutsch, D., and Feroe, J. The internal representation of pitch sequences in tonal music. *Psychological Review*, 1981, *88*, 510–522.

Dowling, W. J. Scale and contour: Two components of a theory of memory for melodies. *Psychological Review*, 1978, *85*, 341–354.

Einhorn, H. J. and Hogarth, R. M. Behavioural decision theory: Processes of judgment and choice. *Annual Review of Psychology*, 1981, *32*, 53–88.

Ferguson, H. *Keyboard interpretation*. London: Oxford University Press, 1975.

Forte, A. *The structure of atonal music*. New Haven: Yale University Press, 1973.

Gamer, C. Et setera: Some temperamental speculations. In R. Browne (Ed.), *Music theory: Special topics*. London: Academic Press, 1981, pp. 59–82.

Geertz, C. *The interpretation of cultures*. New York: Basic Books, 1973.

Howell, P., West, R., and Cross, I. The detection of notes incompatible with scalar structure. *Journal of the Acoustic Society of America*, 1984, *76*, 1682–1689.

Jones, M. R. A tutorial on some issues and methods in serial pattern research. *Perception and Psychophysics*, 1981, *30*, 493–504.

Krumhansl, C. L. The psychological representation of pitch in a tonal context. *Cognitive Psychology*, 1979, *11*, 346–374.

La Rue, J. *Guidelines for style analysis*. New York: Norton, 1970.

Nattiez, J.-J. *Fondements d'une semiologie de la musique:* Paris: Union Générale d'Editions, 1976

Palisca, C. V. *Baroque music*. Englewood Cliffs, NJ: Prentice-Hall, 1968.

Perle, G. *Twelve-tone tonality*. Berkeley: University of California Press, 1977.

Powers, H. Mode. In *Groves' Dictionary of Music*. London: Macmillan, 1980.

Rahn, J. *Basic Atonal Theory,* New York: Longmans, Green: 1980.

Randall, J. K. Two lectures to scientists. In B. Boretz and E. Cone (Eds.), *Perspectives on Contemporary Music Theory*. New York: W. W. Norton & Co., 1972.

Reese, G. *Music in the Middle Ages*. London: Dent, 1941.

Reti, R. *The thematic process in music*. London: Macmillan, 1951.

Rosen, C. *Schoenberg*. Glasgow: Fontana, 1976.

Rosner, B., and Meyer, L. Melodic processes and the perception of music. In D. Deutsch (Ed.), *The psychology of music*. London: Academic Press, 1982.

Sachs, C. *The rise of music in the ancient world*. New York: Norton, 1943.

Shepard, R. N. Circularity in judgments of relative pitch. *Journal of the Acoustical Society of America*. 1964, *36*, 2346–2353.

Sloboda, J. Music performance. In D. Deutsch (Ed.), *The psychology of music*. London: Academic Press, 1982.

Stanton, S. ''*The structural analysis of Japanese* gagaku'' Paper presented at the Conference on Music Semiotics, The City University, London, May 1981.

Strunk, O. *Source readings in music history*. London: Faber and Faber, 1950.

Treibitz, C. H. Substance and function in concepts of musical structure. *Musical Quarterly*, 1983, *69*, 209–226.

Tversky, A. Features of similarity. *Psychological Review*, 1977, *84*, 327–352.

Tyler, J. *The early guitar*. London: Oxford University Press, 1980.

Zuckerkandl, V. *The sense of music*. Princeton, NJ: Princeton University Press, 1971.

2

Modelling Perceived Musical Structure

Robert West, Peter Howell, and Ian Cross

INTRODUCTION

Our comprehension of music and the pleasure we derive from it depend on our ability to perceive patterns. In principle, a given piece of music may be patterned in numerous ways. However, as listeners, we share common perceptual processes which composers and performers can take into account to lead us to perceive one set of patterns rather than another. The extent to which we share a common experience of a piece depends on the piece itself, the way it is performed, and its audience. Modelling musical structure requires that all three of these factors be taken into account.

To date, no attempts have been made to produce a generally applicable model of perceived musical structure. Current models are concerned with limited aspects of music and music of particular kinds. Only a few are explicitly concerned with music perception; others focus on analysis according to music-theoretic principles. Those explicitly oriented towards music perception are, to a large extent, divorced from present-day understanding of psychological processes.

This chapter reviews several of these attempts to model specific facets of music (e.g., pitch relations or chord progressions), and the contribution these could make towards a more general modelling system. The chapter concludes with a look at the form such a modelling system might take. Before reviewing specific models, it would be well to consider some principles of modelling as they might be applied to music.

In this chapter the portrayal of musical sequences in the figures is generally by an approximation to stave notation. However, the intent is only to show the pitch and timing values of the notes concerned. Bar lines and other notational devices are normally omitted, as these suggest a structuring that may not be present in the listener's experience.

THE BASICS OF MUSIC MODELLING

A model is an analogue. It portrays important features of the thing being modelled. It may take the form of a mathematical equation, a pictorial representation, a sentence, a chart, or any of a number of representational devices. A model of a piece of music may choose to focus on one or more facets of music perception. A conventional musical score clearly constitutes such a model. For example, it shows notes which vary in pitch, indicates stresses and phrasing, and shows which notes are heard together and in what order. With a little training, it is not difficult to follow a piece of music from the score. On the other hand, the score is not intended as a model for the listener but rather a set of instructions for the performer, and, as such, it may indicate relationships that a listener could not hear and fail to portray patterns and relationships that the listener does hear.

With many models, there is no difficulty conceptualising the thing being modelled. The same is not the case for models of music perception. At the level of physical events, perception is, presumably, a series of nerve impulses. Yet, it would not be very satisfactory to seek to model music perception in those terms. A more reasonable approach is to focus on the subjective experience of sound in our senses and our imagination. We can only do so by making inferences about how that experience will affect our musical judgments or other behaviour. It must be remembered that we are always working one step removed from the thing we are trying to model. The portrayal of musical experience can only say it is "as though" music were perceived in this or that way.

With this in mind, let us consider a very simple modelling system. It applies only to single-line melodies and recognizes only two types of components: "notes" and "motifs." Notes are characterised in terms of the number of semitones (the interval) between them (e.g., the sequence C, D, E, C may be represented by C, +2, +2, −4). A motif is a set of three or more notes with the intervals between repeated. Thus, in the note sequence, C–D–E–C–F–G–A–F, we see a representation at note level of: C, +2, +2, +2, −4, +5, +2, +2, −4. It is clear from this that the interval pattern, +2, +2, −4, is repeated and constitutes a motif which is denoted by parentheses. Thus, the model of the preceding sequence would be: (C, +2, +2, −4)(+5, +2, +2, −4).

This simple model system fails to encapsulate well-recognized features of musical intuition. However, it is unambiguous both in terminology and in application. As a psychological statement, it makes claims about the nature of pitch encoding and the subjective partitioning of melodic sequences. These are necessary although not sufficient conditions for a psychological model of music.

We now consider a range of models that have been proposed and examine their strengths and limitations. First we look at some models that seek to describe aspects of music without regard to any particular rule system. This contrasts with models that attempt to relate music to grammatical systems such as those found in natural languages like (English).

MODELS AS DESCRIPTIONS

Deutsch and Feroe

The most fully articulated model system of this type comes from Deutsch and Feroe (1981) who have proposed a model of pitch relations which attempts to describe how melodic sequences are represented in memory. The model concerns only single-line melodic sequences. It is explicitly hierarchical—larger components are assumed to encompass subcomponents, which themselves encompass subcomponents, and so on down to the level of the note.

The model makes use of the concept of an overlearnt alphabet. Alphabets are ordered sets of musical pitches (or chromas—a chroma is denoted by a note name such as ''A'' without regard to octave) in which successive elements are related to each other in some specified way (e.g., the chromatic alphabet is simply the semitone series). In formal notation, an alphabet x is defined as follows:

$$x = [e(1),\ e(2),\ e(3),\ \ldots],$$

where $e(k)$ is the kth element in the set.

This simply means that x is made up of a series of pitches $e(1)$, $e(2)$, and so on in that order, just as the English alphabet is made up of the letters A, B, C, . . . in that order.

Thus, the chromatic alphabet is

$$Chr = [C,\ C\sharp,\ D,\ E\flat,\ E,\ F,\ F\sharp,\ G,\ A\flat,\ A,\ B\flat,\ B],$$

where the elements are defined in terms of their conventional note names. A set of elementary operators are defined as follows:

$$s[e(k)] = e(k)$$
$$n[e(k)] = e(k + 1)$$
$$n.i[e(k)] = e(k + i)$$
$$p[e(k)] = e(k - 1)$$
$$p.i[e(k)] = e(k - i)$$

The operator s produces a note that is the same as the one on which it operates. For example, $s[e(1)]$ gives $e(1)$. The operator n produces a note which is *next* in the alphabet to the operational note. So, $n[e(1)]$ gives $e(2)$. The operator, $n.i$, is similar to the next operator except that one has to go i elements further. For example, $n.4[e(1)]$ gives $e(5)$ and $n.1[e(1)]$ is the same as $n[e(1)]$, that is, $e(2)$. The p operators are similar to the n operators except that they invoke previous elements rather than next ones. Thus, $p[e(3)]$ gives $e(2)$, and $p.4[e(5)]$ gives $e(1)$.

These elementary operators, when put together in a given order, make up a structure. Therefore, a structure, A, consisting of n elementary operators is given by:

$$A = [A(0), A(1), \ldots, A(l - 1),*, A(l + 1), \ldots, A(n - 1)]$$

where $A(0)$ to $A(l - 1)$ and $A(l + 1)$ to $A(n - 1)$ are elementary operators and where $*$ is the reference point, that is, the unit on which the operators work. Operators to the left of the reference point are assumed to operate on those immediately on their right, and those on the right of the reference point operate on those immediately to their left. An example of a simple structure is

$$[s, s, n.4, p.4, *, p]$$

In terms of steps up and down the alphabet, this is equivalent to

$$[+0, +0, +4, -4, *, -1]$$

Thus, if the reference element is $e(5)$ of some alphabet, then the structure is

$$[e(5), e(5), e(5), e(1), \mathbf{e(5)}, e(4)]$$

The structure needs two things to establish a relationship to a melodic sequence: a specific alphabet and a specific reference element. A sequence of notes (S) is defined in terms of the structure and information about the alphabet and the reference element:

$$S = \{A;x\}r,$$

where A is the structure and x is the alphabet and r is the reference element.

Thus, the structure given could be turned into a sequence of notes, as follows:

$$S = \{[s, s, n.4, p.4, *, p]; \text{Chr}\}E,$$

which gives

$$E, E, E, C, E, E\flat$$

For convenience, repeated occurrences of an operator in a structure are given a number, then the operator. For example, $4n[e(k)]$ means $n[n[n[n[e(k)]]]]$. An example of a structural description given by Deutsch and Feroe (p. 506) is

$$\{[*, 4n]; \text{C major}\}C$$

where C major is the alphabet of the C major scale and C is the reference element. This gives the sequence of notes C–D–E–F–G. If the C-major triad is substituted as the alphabet the sequence of notes becomes C–E–G–C–E. Alternatively, the reference element might be the note E, in which case the sequence would be E–F–G–A–B.

Of course, any given sequence of notes may be represented in a variety of ways. Thus, the sequence C–D–E–F–G could also be represented

$$\{[p, *, 3n]; \text{C major }\}D,$$

or even

$$\{[*, 2n.2, n, n.2]; \text{Chr}\}C,$$

where Chr is the chromatic alphabet. Deutsch and Feroe (1981) propose that adding an assumption that music is represented in an hierarchical fashion will greatly reduce the number of plausible alternative representations.

In addition to the elementary operators a number of *sequence operators* are introduced. These, as the name suggests, operate on sequences such as those already described. The action of sequence operators on two or more sequences produces *compound sequences,* which are the basis for the hierarchical nature of the model.

The first sequence operator is called *prime* (or ''pr''), and it allows a sequence X to operate on another sequence, Y. Thus, if

$$X = \{[*, 3n]; \text{Ctr}\},$$

where Ctr is the C-major triad (i.e., [C, E, G]), and

$$Y = \{[p, *]; \text{Chr}\},$$

then

$$\{X \text{ pr } Y\}C$$

gives B–C–E♭–E–F♯–G–B–C (Figure 1) because the reference element C is introduced into X to give C, E, G, C, then, each of these notes becomes a reference element for Y so that four pairs of notes are created: B–C, E♭–E, F♯–G, and B–C.

The other sequence operators are *retrograde* and *inversion.* The retrograde operator, ''ret,'' operates similarly to prime but with the elements in the right-hand operator in reverse order. Thus,

$$\{X \text{ ret } Y\}C$$

would give C–B–E–E♭–G–F#–C–B.

Figure 1. The note sequence can be construed as four pairs of notes, each pair having the same internal relationships (succession in the chromatic scale) and the same interpair relationships (successive notes of the C major triad). Deutsch and Feroe (1981) have provided a compact method of describing this hierarchical organisation.

The inversion operator, "inv," acts like prime but with the meaning of the elementary operators in the right-hand sequence reversed (e.g. *n* becomes *p*). Thus,

$$\{X \text{ inv } Y\}C$$

as shown would give C♯–C–F–E–G♯–G–C♯–C.

The model also allows different alphabets to be applied to the same structure in a compound sequence so that each occurrence of that structure is based on similar next and previous operations, but using a different alphabet. If sequence *Y* in the previous example is changed to:

$$Y = \{[p, *]; \text{ Chr, Ctriad, Cmajor, Chr}\},$$

then {*X* pr *Y*}C would give B–C, C–E, F–G, B–C. As mentioned, sequence *X* produces the notes C–E–G–C, which act as reference elements for sequence *Y*. But each operation of the structure in *Y* is on a different alphabet. The chromatic alphabet is first, so C becomes B–C. Then comes the C-triad alphabet so E becomes C–E. Then there is the C-major alphabet so G becomes F–G, and finally, we arrive back at the chromatic alphabet so that C becomes B–C again.

Further complexities are incorporated into the model such as rules to enable sequence operators to act on strings of sequences and specific provision for alternations between two or more streams of notes (see Deutsch and Feroe, 1981).

The alphabets, which lie at the heart of this model, can, it is argued, be reduced to a small number (the major scale, the various forms of the minor scale, the triad, the seventh chord, and the chromatic scale form the core). These can be applied to different reference elements (e.g., in the case of the scales, to different key notes) to produce the great variety of note sets seen in practice. Although the model deals primarily with single-tune melodies, the authors consider that it can, in principle, be generalised to chord progressions.

Deutsch and Feroe (1981) state that in *regenerating* (presumably, this means remembering) a tune, listeners work from the top down. That is, they take the highest-order structure and use it to create reference elements for successively lower-order structures. Thus, higher-order notes should be remembered best. Recall that higher-order elements act as reference elements for lower-order elements and, therefore, are represented at all lower levels as well.

Deutsch and Feroe (1981) argue for the use of the Gestalt principles of proximity and good continuation to establish the most probable structural realizations of a given piece. It is suggested that perceptual groupings are made on the basis of proximity in pitch, timbre, loudness, location, and proximity in time. They also are likely to depend on obvious continuity in terms of pitch change (e.g, continued ascent) or contour. Also assumed to be important are key attribution, the dominance of certain notes within a key, and within-key notes versus chromatic notes.

It is not suggested that listeners necessarily assign only one structure to a piece as it progresses. Ambiguity in structural description, and retrospective changes in description are allowed, a major factor being information load. Deutsch and Feroe (1981) cite Restle's (1979) argument that observers actualize interpretations that have the minimum information load.

A great deal is made of the benefits that would occur if pitch information were encoded according to this model. For example, there is redundancy of representation with structurally significant notes represented at many levels serving to cement a piece together. However, many of these benefits seem to derive, not from the model itself, but rather from the particular manifestation of the model which it is assumed the listener would adopt; for example, using the Gestalt principles of proximity or good continuation to derive a given representation of a piece of music within the language of the model. Yet, Deutsch and Feroe (1981) are far from explicit about how these principles would apply, and what areas of application would receive priority.

Deutsch and Feroe's (1981) model is limited solely to pitch information and does not attempt to consider rhythm or meter or the interaction between these and pitch information. Its use of prelearned alphabets gives it considerable encoding power and the ability to treat almost any piece in terms of hierarchical groupings of small chunks of proximate elements. The authors find that this provides processing advantages—particularly given evidence that people find it difficult to chunk sequential information in groups larger than three or four (Estes, 1972). However, it could equally be argued that this transfers the information processing burden to the organisation of those chunks.

This model is intended to be psychological, but scant evidence is provided to support the underlying assumptions. Such evidence as exists relates only tangentially to the model and equally could support a range of alternative approaches bearing little or no relationship to it. The postulated alphabets are derived from simple music-theoretic considerations, and it is possible that other alphabets such as the circle of fifths (Cross *et al.*, 1983; Chapter 5, this volume) or a matrix of major and minor thirds (Balzano, 1980) could play an equal, if not more important, role. For example, it may make sense to consider the interval between successive notes in terms of movement clockwise or anticlockwise in the circle of fifths rather than up or down the scale.

A major weakness of the model must be its failure to consider rhythmic and metric structure as it is clear that these must play a crucial role in determining groupings of notes within melodies that may override or modify groupings in terms of tonal hierarchies (Chapter 6, this volume).

The choice of hierarchical principles in the model appears to be gratuitous. Although, as the authors rightly point out, there is evidence for improved memory for structures that lend themselves to hierarchical encoding, this does not mean that we attempt to impose hierarchical structures on sequences not describable in hierarchical terms. Also, the model fails to make provision for the application of a single alphabet at different hierarchical levels. The alphabets need to be specified separately. Thus, for example, there is no economic method of capturing the fact that a whole piece is written and perceived in one key.

Finally, the most basic feature of the model is its assumption that pitch is encoded as a difference function from an adjacent note. Another possibility is that pitch is encoded as a difference from a tonal or pitch centre that may not be presented but merely inferred from the notes presented (Brown and Butler, 1981).

Simon and Sumner

Many of the ideas and much of the notation adopted in Deutsch and Feroe's (1981) model derive from an attempt by Simon and Sumner (1968) to define a symbolic system by which means pattern in music can be understood. The system is based on the notion of alphabets and same/next relationships with reference to these alphabets. It is intended to apply, not only to pitch, but to melody, harmony, rhythm, and form. The description of the model provided here differs slightly from the original only in that we attempt to clarify the exposition and rationalize the symbolism.

Elements are defined in terms of their position in hierarchically organized groups. Consider the number sequence: 1, 2, 1, 2, 1, 2, 1, 2. This is simply a fourfold repetition of the numbers 1 and 2. Thus, the sequence can be represented as

$$x(i, 1) = 1$$

$$x(i, 2) = 2,$$

where $i = 1$ to 4. The elements cycle through the numbers in brackets in right-to-left order. We get $x(1, 1)$; $x(1, 2)$; $x(2, 1)$; $x(2, 2)$; $x(3, 1)$; and so on, rather than $x(1, 1)$; $x(2, 1)$; $x(3, 1)$; $x(4, 1)$; $x(1, 2)$; $x(2, 2)$; $x(3, 2)$; and so on.

In the preceding example, there are two levels in the hierarchy. Of course, there can be any number of levels. For example, the sequence,

$$1, 2, 3, 1, 2, 3, 3, 4, 5, 3, 4, 5$$

can be structured as follows:

$$((1, 2, 3)(1, 2, 3))((3, 4, 5)(3, 4, 5))$$

and would be represented by the following (i and j go from 1 to 2, and k goes from 1 to 3):

Rule 1. $x(1, 1, 1) = 1$

Rule 2. $x(2, 1, 1) = x(1, 1, 1) + 2$

Rule 3. $x(i, 2, 1) = x(i, 1, 1)$ for $i = 1$ to 2

Rule 4. $x(i, j, k) = x(i, j, k-1)$ for $k = 2$ to 3 and $j = 1$ to 2

Thus,

$$x(1, 1, 1) = 1 \quad \text{by Rule 1}$$

$$x(1, 1, 2) = 2 \quad \text{by Rule 4}$$

$$x(1, 1, 3) = 3 \quad \text{by Rule 4}$$

$$x(1, 2, 1) = 1 \quad \text{by Rule 3}$$

and so on.

One can apply exactly the same system to notes but, instead of adding or subtracting, one invokes the same, or next relationships with reference to an alphabet. Consider the alphabet "DIAT," the diatonic major scale. This can be represented as a set of semitone intervals from the key note:

$$[0, +2, +2, +1, +2, +2, +2, +1]$$

If one starts with C, then this gives the standard C-major scale, C–D–E, and so on. The next relationship (n) simply indicates that a note is the next one in the alphabet as in Deutsch and Feroe's (1981) model and $n.i$ means that the note is the ith element on. The note sequence, C–F–B–E–A–D–G would be represented as follows:

Rule 1: $x(1) = $ "C"

Rule 2: $x(i) = n.3[\text{DIAT}; x(i\text{-}1)]$ for $i = 2$ to 7

The circle of fifths would be represented by

Rule 1: $x(1) = $ "C"

Rule 2: $x(i) = n.7[\text{CHROM}; x(i - 1)]$ for $i = 2$ to 11,

where CHROM is the chromatic scale.

The note sequence C–D–E–D–E–F–E–F–G–F–G–A (Figure 2) could be represented by a two-level hierarchy:

Rule 1: $x(1, 1) = $ "C"

Rule 2: $x(i, 1) = n[\text{DIAT}; x(i - 1, 1)]$ for $i = 1$ to 4

Rule 3: $x(i, j) = n[\text{DIAT}; x(i, j - 1)]$ for $j = 2$ to 3

This, in fact, breaks the sequence down into four groups of three notes with the first note of each group being next one up in the scale to the first note in the previous group, and the second and third notes of each group being next in the scale to their predecessors in their group.

Figure 2.　This note sequence breaks down into a two-level hierarchy: At the lower level, are three consecutive notes moving up the scale of C; at the higher level are four groups starting on consecutive notes and moving up the scale of C. Simon and Sumner, 1968, describe these relationships as a set of rules.

The elements can be—among other things—notes, rhythmic patterns, melodic or harmonic groupings, or even patterns of melodic contour. The operators also may operate on elements that are themselves the product of the operations on smaller elements. Thus, notes C–D–D–E–E–E–F–F–F–F. . . could be given by

$$\text{Rule 1:}\quad x(i) = n[\text{DIAT}; x(i - 1)] \qquad \text{for } i = 1 \text{ to infinity,}$$

where

$$\text{Rule 2:}\quad z(1) = \text{``C''} \text{ and}$$

$$\text{Rule 3:}\quad x(i) = z(i).i$$

Note that the final i gives the number of times an element or a function is to be repeated.

Alphabets are classified into those that are common—inherent in a particular musical style—(e.g., scales, the chromatic set, and triads) and those that are ad hoc; i.e., specifically constructed for the purposes of the piece (a tone row in 12-tone or serial music). Ad hoc alphabets are generated from common alphabets by selection operators (for example, one arbitrary operator may be "take every other element from the circle of fifths"). In fact, all alphabets can be derived from the chromatic alphabet.

It is theoretically, possible for many musical dimensions (e.g., rhythm and melody) to be represented concurrently, using this formal language. However, it would be cumbersome and pose considerable encoding difficulties. More plausible is the representation of multiple musical lines (melody and chordal structures or counterpoint), except that there does not seem to be any way of integrating the lines.

The encoding benefits of Simon and Sumner's (1968) system depend crucially on the extent to which periodicity and symmetry exist within (or can be extracted from) the music itself. There is no particular reason to assign psychological validity to the model, and its highly abstract structure makes it difficult to construct specific hypotheses about music perception. Nevertheless, it does provide, a potentially useful way of describing certain kinds of music which, with the addition of certain assumptions, could form the basis for a formal system of musical analysis and a way of approaching the problem of musical cognition.

One of its great strengths is its generality. It is derived from and relatable to non-musical pattern-description techniques.

Other Descriptive Models

There are numerous possible approaches to what we have called the "descriptive modelling" of music. For example, it is possible to view melodies in terms of a set of transitional probabilities, where the value of note n depends on the value of note $n-1$. Alternatively, the value of note n could depend on both $n-1$ and $n-2$, and so on. Thus, the structure of a musical sequence could be encapsulated, not in a string of symbols representing the notes and note combinations as in Deutsch and Feroe's (1981) model or in a set of assignments as in Simon and Sumner's (1968) model, but in a transition matrix that gives the probability of moving from one note to another or from one group of notes to another. This kind of approach may be applicable in a limited way to serial music—(based on 12-tone rows; see Wuorinen, 1979)—and to root progressions in modern music (Youngblood, 1970), but is unlikely to capture important elements of a listener's musical experience as we are not good at discerning probabilistic dependencies.

Another approach has been suggested by Jones, Kidd, and Wetzel (1981). They have proposed a model describing listeners' expectancies in which musical sequences are represented as vectors on a two-dimensional chart—showing both pitch and time. However, this form of representation appears too literal (i.e., too close to the physical musical signal itself) to be very informative about cognition. Longuet-Higgins (1976) has proposed a system by which listeners may arrive at a representation of a melody which is analogous to a musical score, including derivation of meter and identification of a tonal centre. The psychological validity of this model largely depends on how good an approximation to musical cognition the conventional score is. Steedman (1977) has proposed an account of the perception of rhythmic structure. Theoretical accounts of the derivation and perception of rhythmic structure are examined in detail in Chapter 3 (this volume) and will not be considered further here. Also, Chapter 9 of this volume looks at rhythmic structure both in perception and performance.

In the next section, we look at models that attempt to apply principles of natural language grammars to musical modelling.

NATURAL LANGUAGE GRAMMARS AND MUSIC MODELLING

Over the years, there has been considerable interest expressed in possible analogies between music and natural language (Powers, 1980; Roads, 1979). Both are temporally patterned, and both appear to be circumscribed and differentiable from non-linguistic or non-musical noise. Indeed, much music is intended to express ideas or portray events, although how far it succeeds in doing this in any fashion other than by direct resemblance is open to question. Several musical models make explicit links between structural principles in music and natural language grammars. Thus, to understand some of the musical models, it is necessary to know a little of the terminology of natural language grammars.

A natural language grammar identifies classes of words (e.g. nouns, transitive verbs, adjectives) and ways of combining members of those classes to produce well-formed sentences. A well-formed sentence is one recognizable as being within the corpus of a given language. For example, "The dog the man bit," is not well formed, whereas "The dog bit the man" is. In music, a well-formed set of sounds or notes is one recognizably within the corpus of the music concerned. Almost any string of notes could be considered well formed in relationship to the corpus of all possible musical sounds. However, there are stricter limitations on note strings within the corpus of "tonal" music. For example, the note sequence shown in Figure 3*a* is recognizably within the corpus of tonal music (all the notes come from the key of C major); whereas, the note sequence shown in Figure 3*b* would not be a well-formed tonal melody because it does not suggest any particular key. The concept of generative grammars, sets of rules that produce only well-formed sentences, can be applied to music so that generative procedures create only pieces of music within a given idiom or style (La Rue, 1970). It can also be applied in a graduated way so that pieces of music closest to a stylistic prototype are more likely. By the reverse process, judgments can be made about how far existing pieces of music conform to a given idiom or style. A computer language for both creation and analysis of music according to principles of generative grammar has been proposed (Holtzman, 1980).

An important point must be made at this stage about the concept of well-formedness in music and natural language. In natural language, well-formedness is a basic prerequisite for conveying meaning. Although we often speak and understand ungrammatical utterances, we do so by implicitly transforming them into grammatical ones. Thus, the rules that determine well-formedness in natural grammar are rules for the conveyance of meaning, and judgments about well-

Figure 3. Note sequences that are (a) well-formed (although not perhaps very interesting) since all the notes are within the key of C and the sequence starts and ends on the key note; and (b) not well-formed since the notes do not suggest any particular key and seem to possess no tonal structure.

formedness can be made on the basis of whether utterances convey meaning. Music does not exist to convey meaning in the same way. It exists to provide listening satisfaction, to accompany rituals, and so on. The criterion of enabling the conveyance of meaning cannot be applied to judgements of musical well-formedness. In the case of music, we are in a similar position to someone who is attempting to judge the grammatic correctness of a language he or she does not understand.

Another concept basic to natural language grammars is that of the rewriting rule. Sentences can be broken down (or parsed) in stages into smaller and smaller components in such a way that each successive stage involves rewriting components in terms of their constituents. Thus, in Figure 4a, S (the sentence) is rewritten into NP (noun phrase) plus VP (verb phrase). NP is rewritten to A (article) plus N (noun). VP is rewritten to V (verb) plus NP, which is then rewritten to A plus N. In music, a rewrite rule would link a lower-order component to a higher-order one according to a specified rule. With the chord progression given in Figure 4b, a G-major harmony (a higher-order component) is broken down as three successive chords: G-major 7th, G-major 6th, and G-major 7th.

In the course of studying natural language, it became clear that rewrite rules were insufficient to account for many grammatical constructions. In an attempt overcome this problem, Chomsky (1957) developed what was known as a transformational grammar for English. Rather than simply breaking down sentences

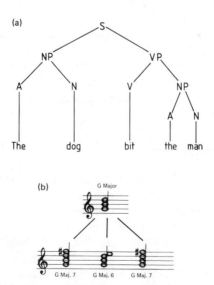

Figure 4. (a) The phrase structure of a simple, active, declarative sentence in English. Units at higher levels are rewritten as units at lower levels. (b) A possible rewriting operation in music.

as described previously, he proposed a distinction between the surface structure of a sentence and its deep structure. The surface structure was the word sequence encountered, whereas, the deep structure was a word sequence corresponding to a simple, active, declarative kernel sentence. The deep structure mapped onto the surface structure by means of a set of transformational rules, which had the effect of reordering, substituting, or omitting words or phrases. Thus, the sentences, "Did the dog bite the man?" and "The dog bit the man" could derive from a common kernel, which is, in fact, the second of these two sentences. Transformational rules inserting the word "did" and changing "bit" to "bite" produce the first sentence.

Transformational rules act to reorder words or phrases, to omit them, or to substitute word combinations for others. The result is that many surface structures can be derived from a common, deep structure. Similarly, in music, one could use transformational rules to reorder notes or note strings, or to enable their omission, or even to substitute different note strings. For example, the last three notes of the sequence in Figure 3a could be conceived as a product of a transformational rule: A tonic-dominant tonic-deep structure could be realized by a middle note that was any member of the V chord (dominant). However, in natural language, it seems that many transformational rules are ad hoc and have no intrinsic validity but appear to be necessary to account for grammatical constructions. It is harder to justify ad hoc transformational rules on the grounds that they are necessary to explain intuitions regarding whether a given piece of music falls within a musical corpus. This is because, as explained earlier, musical grammaticality is much more ambiguous. Nevertheless, the concept of a kernel, which is, in some sense, a prototype and to which actual musical examples can be related, can be usefully applied to music (Jones, Kidd, and Wetzel, 1981).

It is not our intention to dwell heavily on possible connections between natural language and musical structure. However, with this in mind, the reader should be in a position to understand the models described, and to see how, in some cases, they derive from linguistic analyses.

Lerdahl and Jackendoff

Lerdahl and Jackendoff (1977; 1983) have produced one of the best-known attempts at a structural description of tonal music. They set themselves the goal of developing a formal description of the musical intuitions of the idealized educated listener. Although they explicitly limit their analysis to tonal music, they also seek to make claims regarding musical universals that should transcend cultural boundaries.

Lerdahl and Jackendoff's (1977, 1983) model deals with four kinds of structural analysis called "grouping analysis," "metrical analysis," "time-span reduction," and "prolongational reduction." Each analysis is based on a strong assumption that a piece of music can be partitioned into discrete regions organised hierarchically. It is further assumed that the processes of organisation are the same at each hierarchical level and are recursive. That is, organisational principles apply to notes to form groups, and to groups to form higher-order groups, and so on. Within each domain of structural analysis, two kinds of rules are proposed: well-formedness rules and preference rules. Well-formedness rules enable the assignment of structures that are *permissable,* whereas preference rules determine the several permissible structures that are most stable or *likely* to occur.

Grouping and metrical analyses are concerned with the rhythmic structure of a piece of music. The grouping analysis identifies perceptual units such as motives, themes, and so on. The grouping well-formedness rules allow only hierarchical group structures. The preference rules work on the basis of three classes of criteria: (1) articulation of boundaries is determined by distance between attack points, rests, slurs, changes in register, texture, dynamics or timbre, and cadences that signify the end of groups. Thus, a sudden change in loudness, tempo or instrumentation, or a pause, would tend to be perceived as a disjunction; (2) parallelism in structure involves a repetition or near repetition of a motive, sequence, and so forth. Thus, repetition of a simple rhythmic or melodic fragment would tend to identify that fragment as a coherent group; and (3) symmetry involves the degree to which the subdivision produces equal-length groups, which are more likely.

Occasionally, the principle of hierarchic organisation is broken when there is some overlap between groups. A transformational rule is proposed that relates an overlap to an underlying hierarchical grouping. Thus, a given note may serve as both the end of one group and the beginning of another.

Figure 5 shows a grouping analysis based primarily on the repetition of rhythmic, melodic, and harmonic patterns (parallelism). The excerpt is divisible into two equal-length groups, involving a repetition of a rhythmic and melodic pattern; these groups are composed of subgroups having similar metrical structure. Finally, the first of each of these subgroups is divided into two groups.

Metrical analysis assigns to a piece a pattern of strong and weak beats in a

Figure 5. A grouping analysis constructed by Lerdahl and Jackendoff (1977) based on repetition of rhythmic, melodic, and harmonic patterns. (The extract is from Beethoven's Sonata op. 2, no. 2, Scherzo. The figure is reproduced from the *Journal of Music Theory* by permission).

hierarchical manner. The strength of a beat is denoted by associating with it a certain number of dots below the musical score—the more dots, the stronger the beat. The well-formedness rule assumes a hierarchical organisation and equal spacing of beats. At each hierarchical level, the distance between beats must be either two or three times that of the immediately lower level. The metrical preference rules takes into account cues for strong beats (e.g., accent), parallelism with grouping structure, and regularity of pattern. Figure 6 gives an example of a metrical analysis. The first beat of quadruple crotchet group gets most stress; then, the first beat of each crotchet pair; then, each crotchet beat; and finally, each quaver beat.

The two further forms of analysis, time-span reduction and prolongational reduction, both concern the pitch organisation of a piece. They use a tree notation in which two or more branches join to produce a branch at a higher level. The lower-order branches may refer to units: one is a dominating unit and others are subordinated to it. The subordinated units can be thought of as ornamental to the main unit or elaborations of it. The rules for determining which tree structures to apply are, to some extent, dependent on music-theoretic considerations and cannot necessarily be applied as an algorithm.

With time-span analysis, one needs to identify more or less equally spaced regions that normally correspond to groupings from the grouping analysis. Within each region, a dominating event of which all other events are elaborations must be found. The well-formedness rules insist there be no crossing of branches, and no event may be assigned more than one branch. This means that elaborations of dominant events can relate only to the most adjacent dominant event in a given direction, and can only be elaborations of one dominant event at the next level up in the hierarchy. With time-span reduction, elaboration concerns the temporal succession of a piece (e.g., whether a given set of notes implies a subsequent dominant event or is implied by one).

The preference rules favour interpretations in which the tonic is apparent and where there is a hierarchy of relative stability in relationship to the tonic. Sta-

Figure 6. A metric analysis by Lerdahl and Jackendoff (1977), with assignment of strong beats indicating a quadruple meter. (The extract is from Bach's "O Haupt voll blut und Wunden." The figure is reproduced from the *Journal of Music Theory* by permission).

Figure 7. A time-span reduction by Lerdahl and Jackendoff (1977). Offshoots from main branches represent elaborations. Note that the time-span reduction follows closely from the grouping and metric analyses. (The extract is a simplified form of part of Mozart's Sonata K. 331, I. The figure is reproduced in modified form from the *Journal of Music Theory* by permission).

bility depends on such factors as consonance, triads in root rather than inverted position, coincidence of root and melodic notes of chords, proximity in the circle of fifths to the tonic and so forth. Figure 7 gives an example of a time-span reduction. The most dominant event in the excerpt is the first note. This is elaborated at the highest level in the hierarchy by the last note; then each of these notes is elaborated in successive stages as indicated. Note that the time-span reduction follows the grouping and metrical structures very closely. Time-span reduction also involves determination of what are referred to as "structural beginnings and endings." Structural endings are cadences (e.g., V–I progressions) that occur at the end of groups. Structural beginnings are the most stable (dominating) events within groups which have structural endings. Normally there must be some intervening events between structural beginnings and endings, thus they do not normally apply to the lowest level groups.

The final domain of analysis treated by Lerdahl and Jackendoff (1977, 1983) is prolongational reduction. This is closely related to a form of musical analysis developed by Heinrich Schenker that continues to be highly influential in music theory. According to Schenker, there is a difference between harmonic, structural chords (defined by the restricted set of progressions within which they may occur) and contrapuntal, directional chords (definable as the products of voice leading or contrapuntal motion). The prolongation of a harmonic chord is shown when a (succession of) contrapuntal chord(s) intervenes between two forms of the same harmonic chord (e.g., I, VII_5^6, I_6), or when the progression from one harmonic chord to another is elaborated contrapuntally (e.g., V, $II_\sharp^6$, $II_{\flat 3}^6$, I_6). For Lerdahl and Jackendoff (1977, 1983), prolongational reduction derives from the associated time-span reduction and undertakes to show the primarily harmonic articulation of tension and relaxation embodied in the unfolding of a piece of tonal music. In prolongational reduction, also, there are two types of progression—elaboration and contrast. Elaboration involves the repetition of an event. Both the original pitch event and its repetition(s) possess the same weight. Contrast involves the introduction of a different, relatively ornamental, pitch event.

Prolongational-reduction analysis is represented by a tree structure similar to that of time-span reduction. The well-formedness rules of prolongational reduction are identical to those for time-span reduction. The preference rules select a hierarchy on the basis of stability and principles of harmonic progression derived from music-theoretic considerations as indicated. Figure 8 shows a prolongation reduction for the same sequence shown in Figure 7. Events formed by two branches extending from a small circular node are assumed to have the same weight (note that they involve repetition). Events that are marked by branches coming off another branch are subordinate. (Note that the prolongational reduction and time-span reduction of this extract do not follow each other exactly.)

A number of general points should be made about this model. It is by way of an addition to, rather than a replacement of, standard musical notation. It does not seek to cover the same ground as stave notation, and whereas pitch information is critical in determining the structures arrived at, it is not represented in the model itself. In fact, the model describes only two aspects of musical structure—boundaries and hierarchical relationships between components. It does not attempt to deal explicitly with the nature of the transformations and symmetries that give a piece its coherence and unique quality.

The model goes further than those of Deutsch and Feroe (1981) or Simon and Sumner (1968) in defining the rules by which a particular structural description is arrived at from a piece of music. The well-formedness rules and preference rules allow a two-tier system, which gives, at the same time, an indication of the types of structures never encountered and a degree of flexibility to take account of individual differences in musical perception. The formulation of the well-formedness and preference rules give this model its grammatical flavour by relating the structures specifically to tonal music. Music that fell outside this corpus could not be accommodated.

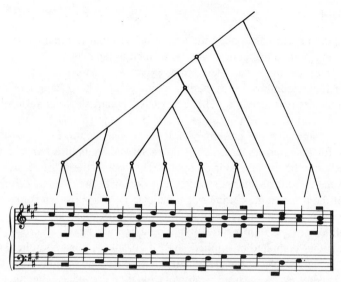

Figure 8. A prolongation reduction by Lerdahl and Jackendoff (1977). Branches from small circular nodes are prolongations (i.e., repetitions) and receive the same structural weight. Offshoots are contrasts and receive less weight. (The extract is a simplified form of part of Mozart's Sonata K. 331, I. The figure is reproduced in modified form from the *Journal of Music Theory* by permission).

An unfortunate facet of the model from our point of view is that, despite having a formal output, the structural descriptions must be derived intuitively and, therefore, depend on the analytical capabilities and propensities of the model builder. However, there are principles embodied in the model; they can be examined and may apply equally to music that does not fall within the classical tonal tradition, for example, hierarchical organisation, and existence of tonal centres.

Lerdahl and Jackendoff's (1977, 1983) model attempts to provide a symbolic representation of music that elucidates its structure as perceived by a listener. Other systems of analysis exist which attempt to identify structural relationships within music, which are assumed to reside in the music itself, and which a listener should strive to hear. Most notable of these is the system of Schenkerian analysis (see Salzer, 1962) taught in some form in most college music courses. This system is based on the principle that tonal music (which, as far as Schenker was concerned, is the only music) is ultimately a prolongation of the ursatz which is itself an arpeggiation of the tonic-major triad. The product of Schenkerian analysis is an annotated and precised score that describes how notes and chords prolong other notes or chords in an hierarchical fashion according to principles of harmonic and melodic progression. Understanding it depends on an understanding of traditional harmony and counterpoint and it will not be discussed here. Forte (1982) provides a comprehensive introduction with additions.

Winograd

Winograd (1968) has applied the notion of grammar to tonal harmony taking as a starting point a systemic grammar of natural language.

Harmonic structure is considered to be expressible in terms of five hierarchical levels or ranks: composition, tonality, chord group, chord, and note with each level having its own network. This consists of a chart showing various features associated with the rank concerned, Sets of alternative features are known as ''systems'' and give the grammar its name. For example, Figure 9 shows the network for a composition, which is characterized by both a mode and a root. The mode can be either major or minor. The root is the tonal centre, and the mode is the pattern of intervals which, together with the root, make up the key (*K*) of the piece (e.g., C minor or F major). The composition is made up of a concatenation of tonalities (i.e., tonalities joined together in series).

Tonalities possess four features: type, relative root, mode, and root. The type must be either complete or implied; and, if complete, must be either simple or modulating. A simple, complete tonality must always go from dominant to tonic and end there. A modulating, complete tonality continues after the tonic to another tonality or chord group. An implied tonality goes from dominant preparation (the chord group II, IV, or VI) to dominant (in this case, chord group V or VII). The relative root of the tonality is connected via its mode and root to produce a key (*K*). The various features of tonalities are shown in Figure 10.

The next lowest level is the chord group, which has a single root and type, and functions as a unit within the harmonic structure. The chord has the classic features: root, type, inversion, and linear function (the latter necessarily being context-dependent, but only within a local context). The note is defined in terms of its diatonic position, its chromatic position, and its octave position.

The networks associated with each rank provide a means of describing a chord sequence in terms of conventional music theory. The charts show what the

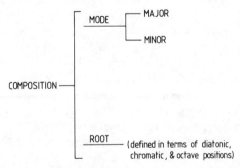

Figure 9.   A system network for a composition devised by Winograd (1968). The root is defined in terms of diatonic position, chromatic position, and octave position.

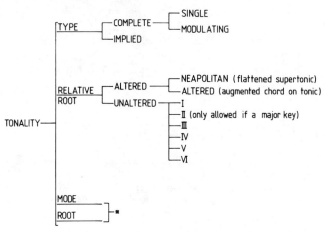

Figure 10.   A system network for a tonality devised by Winograd (1968). The choice of mode and root depend on relative root and *K* (e.g., if the relative root is III, and if the superordinate rank is in the major mode, then the mode of the tonality must be minor and the root must be a major third from the keynote of *K*).

possibilities are, and the realization rules (akin to Lerdahl and Jackendoff's, 1977, 1983, well-formedness rules) determine how a particular piece may be related to a specific set of these possibilities. However, Winograd (1968) recognizes that tonal harmony is a highly ambiguous language by which he means that it admits of any number of structural descriptions. The example is cited of the VI–V–I progression in C major, which could be viewed instead, as a II–I–IV, progression in G major or any number of other possibilities. Context obviously should play an important role in disambiguating a structural description, but even the context of the complete composition may still leave ambiguity. The process of disambiguation relies heavily on music-theoretic principles such as the pre-eminence of the dominant-tonic cadence and the interval of the fifth more generally. Three basic principles are used by Winograd (1968) to produce an intelligent parsing: sequence progression, clarity of function, and complexity of parsing.

Sequence progression and clarity of function are combined to give the main parameter of plausibility value, the extent to which a piece or part of a piece, as specified in a given structural description, adheres to certain music-theoretic principles. Given two or more structural descriptions of the same piece, the one with the greatest plausibility value is selected. For example, an authentic cadence (V–I) has a higher value than a fifth progression (e.g., VI–II) or a plagal cadence (IV–I).

The output of the process can be represented most simply as a set of chord names and their associated tonalities which, while fulfilling the definition of a

Figure 11. Part of the results of a computer implementation of Winograd's (1968) analysis of tonal harmony. Roman numerals denote the scale degree of the chord concerned (e.g., I is the tonic, II is the supertonic, and so on), in relationship to the next highest rank. Subscripts are conventional notations for inversions of chords and whether the chord is a seventh, and so on. (The extract is reproduced from the *Journal of Music Theory* by permission).

formal model, are within the bounds of conventional musical description. Indeed, the purpose of Winograd's (1968) efforts was not to provide a new system for the description of musical structure, but to provide a set of principles and procedures that would enable one to derive the structure from simple knowledge of the notes. He has successfully implemented these procedures on a computer. Figure 11 shows part of the results of one such computer implementation.

Winograd's (1968) model does not attempt explicitly to describe how a listener parses a piece of music. Rather, he talks in terms of elucidating the logical structure of the piece itself. Of course, this structure is only logical in terms of assumptions derived from music theory that may or may not bear some relationship to the listener's faculties.

Generative Grammars Applied to Jazz and Nursery Tunes

Jazz is a musical genre that had its roots firmly in tonal music but since has fragmented into diverse musical forms, some of which are far from tonal. Traditional jazz or blues music is particularly susceptible to the grammatical approach because it is fairly well circumscribed and derived from a relatively few harmonic patterns (e.g., the 12-bar blues). Perlman and Greenblatt (1981) have put forward a set of principles to provide the basis for a system for modelling improvised solos. They argue that jazz-improvised solos (within the mainstream tradition) can be seen as analogous to surface structure in natural language (i.e., the words and word order used in a given sentence). They should bear a definite relationship to the underlying harmonic structure of the piece, which is itself regarded as analogous to deep structure in natural language (i.e., the kernel that embodies the meaning of a sentence before optional grammatical transformations have been applied to create the surface structure). Between the deep and surface structure is the shallow structure. This is the "array of possibilities that the musician may choose from at a given point," (see also the implication/realization analytic approach—Meyer, 1956; Narmour, 1977). The shallow structure is a cluster of notes upon which improvisation may be built, including the notes of the underlying chord or a scale based on the notes of the triad forming the basis of the chord and in the key of the root of the chord.

It should be pointed out that the concept of deep structure in this approach differs fundamentally from that seen in linguistics. In linguistics, deep structure is a non-temporally organized, irreducible entity, whereas in Perlman and Greenblatt's (1981) analysis, the deep structure of jazz solos is an underlying harmonic progression with a clear temporal dimension and is reducible as described by Winograd (1968).

Perlman and Greenblatt (1981) point out that basic harmonic patterns (such as the standard cadence II, V, I), like noun and verb phrases, can be embedded and conjoined to create new deep structures of greater interest and complexity. It is also a major feature of jazz harmony that certain chords are substituted for others—serving the same harmonic function but implying a different progression. Thus, a seventh chord may be replaced by a diminished chord one scale step below the original. This and other substitutions only make sense, however, when the seventh chord is one which is about to resolve, not a structural chord. Perlman and Greenblatt (1981) make the point that most jazz improvizations are based on a relatively few melodic patterns ("licks"), which achieve variety by the fact that they can be played over different chords, on different scale degrees, and with different degrees of repetition. Another standard device is to use "quotes," which are short phrases lifted wholesale from other tunes.

A formal model based on these principles would consist of identifying the three levels of structure and the relationships among them. The surface structure would be described in terms of: (1) a selection from the set of notes available from the shallow structure at a given point in a piece, and (2) a grouping of notes according to their correspondence to standard licks, or developments of these. The shallow structure would be defined as sets of notes permissible, given the underlying harmonic state of the piece at a given moment. The deep structure would be described in terms of the application of a set of phrase-structure (rewriting) rules and permissable substitutions on a relatively few harmonic patterns. Steedman (1983) makes explicit the rewriting rules that produce chord sequences recognisably within the jazz idiom from the standard, I, IV, V combination that forms the basis of much popular music.

Even more constrained than traditional jazz are the sets of nursery tunes found in different countries. Sundberg and Lindblom (1976) have proposed a generative grammar for a set of Swedish nursery tunes written by the composer, Alice Tegner. They adapted a set of rules for determining the emphasis to be given to particular words in a sentence in spoken English and applied it to these tunes to determine the emphasis and structural role attaching to certain notes. They proposed further sets of rules, which translated this information into actual note values, including both rhythmic and pitch information. We briefly consider just the first generative rule system which was derived from natural language grammar.

Chomsky and Halle (1968) proposed a set of rules for relating prosody (i.e., emphasis attaching to certain words or syllables in spoken language) to phrase structure. The primary rule is that additional stress is given to the last word of each constituent in the phrase structure (e.g., noun phrase). Thus, in the noun phrase *the man, man* gets extra emphasis. In the verb phrase, *bit the man, man* gets even more emphasis. Finally, in the other noun phrase *the dog, dog* gets emphasis. In the whole sentence, *man* gets greatest emphasis, followed by *dog*.

Sundberg and Lindblom (1976) noticed that the eight-bar tunes with which they were concerned could be successively bifurcated into two phrases, each of which had two subphrases which were composed of two bars, and so on to note level. They proposed that the tree so formed could be viewed as analogous to the phrase-structure tree in English. The rules for emphasis differed from those proposed by Chomsky and Halle (1968). At lower than bar level, greater emphasis was given to rightmost elements and above-bar level to leftmost elements. This produced a set of weights that formed the basis for generating rhythmic and pitch values (see Sundberg and Lindblom, 1976, for details).

The link between the musical analysis of Sundberg and Lindblom (1976) and linguistic analysis appears tenuous as it is necessary to make the rather arbitrary distinction between sub- and suprabar level rules. Moreover, the analysis is very much tied to tunes of a particular type.

DEVELOPING A MODEL OF MUSICAL STRUCTURE

None of the models described could be adopted wholesale as a characterization of perceived musical structure, but each can point to principles that could be used in such a model.

It is not practicable to model all perceptible facets of musical experience. One must decide the most important features to look at and define those sufficiently well understood to be included in a model. Patterning of music involves, at the very least, an identification of what elements go together, where disjunctions occur, and inclusion of elements and groups of elements in superordinate groups. It also requires identification of elements perceived as structurally important, as opposed to those which are, in some sense, embellishments. Having satisfied these basic requirements, a model may seek to go further and explicate how pitch, rhythm, and timbre may be represented in experience and/or memory. We limit ourselves only to the basic requirements. Thus, the output of the model is a specification of notes perceived as belonging together, points of disjunction between notes or groups of notes, and subordinate and superordinate relationships.

A number of principles can be adduced, and lessons learned from the foregoing models which need to be taken into account in a more general model. First we outline some general principles that need to be taken into account formulating a model of musical structure. Then, we look at specific rule systems that could be employed in such a model.

General Observations

1. Perceptible dimensions of musical experience should be involved in the creation of structures even if they do not appear in the final output. For example, Deutsch and Feroe (1981) were concerned only with pitch relationships and assumed that sequences of pitches would be grouped only by reference to pitch values. Yet it is clear that metric information is a highly salient grouping factor (Sloboda and Parker, Chapter 6, this volume) even in equitone sequences (Povel and Okkerman, 1981). Therefore, it is not possible to look solely at one feature or another to determine perceived groupings. Any perceptible feature of a sequence may play a role. Indeed, competing cues towards groupings and boundaries may interact to produce different effects. Metric information may suggest a different grouping from pitch information, and the resulting conflict may produce its own perceptual effect. The sequence in Figure 12, for example, conflicts metric groupings of four beats in a bar (indicated by stresses attached to every fourth beat) with pitch groupings (by virtue of repetition) of five.

2. The listener brings to a piece of music a history of musical experience, which is itself a product of the musical history of his or her culture. Therefore, a model must be able to frame musical structure in terms of components and relationships that form part of the listener's musical competence. This may mean attaching precedence to interval sets such as diatonic scales (Deutsch and Feroe, 1981; Simon and Sumner, 1968), as well as prototypical musical event combinations within a given style or idiom (Jones, 1981; Perlmann and Greenblatt, 1981; Sundberg and Lindblom, 1976). However, it should also be appreciated that musical components and dimensions that seem fundamental to the Western ear

Figure 12. A note sequence in which metric and melodic groupings conflict. The question arises as to which, if either, is most salient, or whether a compound effect is produced.

may not have general applicability. The concept of a note possessing determinate pitch and rhythmic properties is not necessarily universal (Serafine, 1983).

3. Listeners do not necessarily perceive music in terms of a fully coordinated structure (Sloboda and Parker, Chapter 6, this volume). The extent to which they are able to do so is likely to depend on the music itself, their previous experience of it, and their experience with music of the same style or idiom, as well as their aptitudes. For example, familiar nursery tunes tend to exhibit a simple symmetry and clear hierarchical relationships that most adults would recognise. However, a listener unfamiliar with a Chopin sonata or a Mozart symphony may not perceive fully articulated phrases—let alone how these combine to produce larger structures. The stream of musical events may be left unstructured in places, and patterns detected may not be related coherently to each other. Thus, Lerdahl and Jackendoff's (1977, 1983) model may overestimate the perceptual and cognitive propensities as well as powers of even musically educated listeners. In fact, the features used to pattern a piece of music on a single hearing may well differ from those used if the listener is given time to study a piece (Cuddy and Lyons, 1981).

4. The output of the model should be related to some aspect or aspects of judgement or behaviour relating to music. For example, Winograd's (1968) model can produce analyses of tonal harmony not unlike those performed by music undergraduates. Performance in judgement tasks must provide potential criteria against which to test assumptions of the model, and from which to derive parameters. Winograd's model also illustrates another desirable feature of a music model: It should be possible to determine unambiguously the patterning expected in a given situation with a given listener. Lerdahl and Jackendoff's (1977, 1983) preference rules are too flexible in that they do not specify when less preferred structures will be found. For pieces of music believed to be perceived in the same way, for a set of listeners, structural descriptions should be unambiguously derivable from the piece (not necessarily the score). If it is expected that different listeners will hear the piece in a different way, then, their characteristics will also need to be specified.

5. Structure often can be understood, at least partly, by reference to an extra-musical or historical context. For example, a considerable amount of present-day music is associated with, or has developed from, music for dancing. Other music involves, or has developed out of, songs that require phrasing which makes linguistic sense and permits breaths at particular points. Similarly, music written for, or played on, particular instruments is constrained by the ergonomic possibilities of those instruments.

Specific Modelling Principles

6. All music is serial; patterning occurs over time. However, much of it also involves simultaneous or concurrent musical events. Therefore, it is necessary to

Figure 13. (a) Two concurrent melodic lines that may be separated because they operate in different pitch regions. (b) A single line that may perceptually appear as two concurrent lines, as in (c).

model both horizontal and vertical structure. None of the models described have attempted to do this despite the fact that a considerable amount of evidence has accumulated to suggest how it might be done (Macadams and Bregman, 1979). For example, there is clear evidence of division of music into attentional streams, which may stand in figure/ground relationships similar to those found in vision. Figure 13 shows two musical excerpts that may be partitioned into vertical streams. Figure 13a shows two concurrent sets of notes distinguishable by the fact that they operate in different pitch regions. Figures 13b and 13c show how a single series of notes may be partitioned into two streams operating in different pitch regions. This separation of consecutive notes into attentional streams need not arise solely because of pitch differences. Streaming occurs between stressed notes (Cross, Howell and West, 1983), by timbre, and by notes coming from different locations.

7. It is possible to identify a few global factors, whose operation could account for much of the patterning of musical sound. Deutsch and Feroe (1981) believe that Gestalt principles, considered at length in relationship to vision, could prove useful. These factors could form the core of a system of music modelling, and indeed, have been applied in an incomplete way to certain existing models.

Good continuation. This means we tend to consider as belonging together notes that follow a common rule, such as continued ascent of a scale, repetition of a single note, or alternation.

Proximity. We view as belonging together things close to each other. In music, this might be proximity in time or in pitch. This principle forms the basis for the most fundamental grouping factor in music perception—the grouping of contiguous elements within a given attentional stream. This grouping factor, so basic to our perception of music that it is easy to overlook, also, accounts for the tendency to perceive disjunctions where rests or pauses occur.

Similarity. This is conceptually related to good continuation and proximity, but operates where there is no obvious dimension on which to measure proximity, and no obvious rule to be observed. For example, a succession of sounds with similar timbres will be considered as belonging, whereas sudden changes in timbre would create a discontinuity.

Regularity. We are more likely to group things into regular bundles than irregular ones. This tendency underlies the derivation of both a beat and a meter. It also accounts for more global groupings into phrases.

Symmetry. Symmetrical groups are preferred to asymmetrical groups. One of the commonest themes in Western music is movement away from some point of departure (say, a tonal centre), followed by a return to that point. The symmetry also could be rhythmic or in relationship to the group structure itself. For example, part of the perceived simplicity of nursery tunes derives from the fact that they are divisible successively and symmetrically into even numbers of groups.

Common fate. Visual object perception is facilitated by the fact that bits of objects seem consistently to go together, and although their relationships may change, the nature of that change is predictable. Similarly, with music. Repetition of a sequence of notes can make the listener hear those notes as a group. The repetition need not be exact; it could be under transposition, or simply repetition of rhythm.

These general principles operate in the context of cultural expectations and overlearned combinations of musical ideas. Such cultural considerations provide the substrate on which the perceptual principles may operate. They also produce specific meanings in their own right. For example, cadences are a culturally established way of indicating the closure of a group.

8. Groups formed by the operation of these factors may be assigned features such as pitch and rhythm, and may combine to form higher-order groups. One means by which assignment of features to groups may be undertaken is by reference to dominant elements within those groups. Dominant events are identifiable by: (1) location, i.e., whether they occur at points of stress (e.g., beats), and (2) quality, that is, whether they are themselves indicative of stress by virtue of their dynamics, pitch, or timing (see Thomassen, 1982, for an account of how stress may be imparted to notes). These dominant events could transfer their pitch values to the group to which they belong. However, it also seems possible that features associated with groups could be derived by an integration of information from more than one member of the group. For example, a triplet of notes (e.g., tritone plus one note) may imply a certain tonal centre different from all three (Brown and Butler, 1981). The rhythmic properties of groups are determined by their own timings in relationship to each other.

The above considerations suggest a model of musical structure that takes into account pitch, timing, stress, and timbre to produce a description of how musical events are grouped both in the attentional domain and over time. The output of the model could be a kind of score in which separate attentional streams are denoted by joining together notes heard as forming a coherent horizontal line. (This is, of course, predicated on being able to identify pitched events and timing relationships.) Horizontal structure could be denoted by bracketing groups of musical events. An open bracket would represent the perception of a start of a group, and a close bracket a perceived end. Open and closed brackets need not cancel each other out. Groups could be nested to whatever level necessary; there would be no a priori requirement for groups not to overlap; and structurally important notes or groups could be denoted by a symbol.

A number of elaborations of this simple scheme are possible. Relative salience of attentional streams could be represented by numbers attaching to the different staves at particular points. Pitch information could be encoded as a deviation (according to whatever alphabet was assumed to be operating) from the pitch centre of the group to which it belongs. Rhythmic information could be represented as deviation from an assumed regular beat, and so on.

Figure 14 shows a set of notes and their relative timings in a form that is readable like a musical score, and it shows how the perception of these notes might be modelled. In this example, it is assumed that a listener immediately will pick up a four-beat meter and will perceive two concurrent streams comprising two perceptually distinct melody lines. The pitch organization of the sequence reinforces the metric and rhythmic organisation (e.g., inverted repetition of pitch patterns is mirrored by repetition of rhythmic patterns). In fact, the principles of good continuation, common fate, and regularity appear to be working towards a single interpretation in both the pitch and rhythmic domains.

The appearance of the basic model is quite simple and reflects the relatively unambitious nature of the project in terms of what one would be attempting to

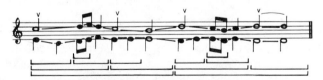

Figure 14. A possible modelling of basic aspects of perceived musical structure. Notes joined together are assumed to be heard as separate streams and are separable by distance (the opposite of proximity) in the pitch dimension. By the same token, it is the proximity within the streams that gives those streams their internal coherence. Repetition of metric, rhythmic, and (inverted) melodic patterns suggests a particular grouping pattern (by the principle of common fate). This is strengthened by the fact that the groups thus formed are of equal length (by the principle of regularity) and by the fact that group boundaries are also suggested by violation of good continuation, both in rhythmic and melodic dimensions.

encode. The crucial feature is the set of rules enabling us to derive a specific structural description. We have already outlined the broad principles we believe could form the basis for this set of rules. In simple cases, they actually serve as the rules themselves. For example, where all features of pitch, timing, stress, timbre, and the six basic principles work towards the same structural description, it should be obvious what that description should be. The difficulty appears when one or more of these features come into conflict. In that event, there is a need to determine the relative priorities attaching to each one. This is a task that cannot be done in an empirical vacuum; the only way to resolve such issues is by experimentation.

One crucial issue is the relative importance of the different grouping principles described, and the relative impact of these grouping factors on different dimensions. For example, in music with strong cues towards a regular metric structure, does this metric structure override groupings by reference to pitch structure? Is repetition of a rhythmic pattern more important in establishing that pattern as a coherent group than repetition of a melodic pattern? Research into the memorability of different aspects of musical structure and different musical dimensions may provide clues to the answers. The use of data from recalls of pieces of music could prove of considerable value (Sloboda and Parker, Chapter 6, this volume).

Other techniques for investigating these issues include getting listeners to indicate as they listen to a piece where they feel groups begin and end, ending pieces at different points and finding out whether listeners regard the piece as complete, probing for recognition of parts of musical sequences that are presumed to fall within, or to cross, perceptual grouping boundaries, and asking listeners to judge the complexity of musical sequences. Another approach that has been adopted is to examine performances of pieces of music to see to what extent these can tell us how the performer structured the piece (see Clarke, Chapter 9, this volume).

CONCLUSIONS

This chapter has reviewed some of the more influential models of musical structure, noting that none could provide a comprehensive account of how listeners pattern musical sequences. However, they do provide pointers for the construction of such an account. We have drawn together what we feel are the important lessons that may be learned from these previous attempts. Instead of an alternative model, the result has been a schema on which we feel a model could be built. To flesh out this schema, it will be necessary to expand the data base on the perception of musical structure, and we have suggested a number of ways in which this might be done.

REFERENCES

Balzano, G. J. The group-theoretic description of twelve-fold and microtonal pitch systems. *Computer Music Journal*, 1980, *4*, 66–84.

Brown, H., and Butler, D. Diatonic trichords as minimal tonal cue-cells. *In Theory Only*, 1981, *5*, 39–55.

Chomsky, N. Syntactic structures. The Hague: Mouton, 1957.

Chomsky, N., and Halle, M. *Sound pattern of English*, New York: Harper & Row, 1968.

Cross, I., Howell, P., and West, R. Preferences for scale structure in melodic sequences. *Journal of Experimental Psychology: Human Perception and Performance*, 1983, *9*, 444–460.

Cross, I., West, R., and Howell, P. Pitch relations and the formation of scalar structure. *Music Perception*, in press.

Cuddy, L. L., and Lyons, H. I. Musical pattern recognition: A comparison of listening to and studying tonal structures and tonal ambiguities. *Psychomusicology*, 1981, *1*, 15–33.

Deutsch, D. and Feroe, J. The internal representation of pitch sequences in tonal music. *Psychological Review*, 1981, *88*, 503–522.

Estes, W. K. An associative basis for coding and organization in memory. In A. W. Melton and E. Martin (Eds.), *Coding processes in human memory*. Washington, DC: Winston, 1972.

Forte, A. *Introduction to Schenkerian analysis: Form and content in tonal music*. New York: Norton, 1983.

Holtzman, S. R. *Generative grammar definitional language* (Internal Report CSR–56–80). Edinburgh, Scotland: Edinburgh University, Department of Computer Science, 1980.

Jones, M. R., Kidd, G., and Wetzel, R. Evidence for rhythmic attention. *Journal of Experimental Psychology: Human Perception and Performance*, 1981, *7*, 1059–1073.

LaRue J. *Guidelines for style analysis*. New York: Norton, 1970.

Lerdahl, F., and Jackendoff, R. Toward a formal theory of tonal music. *Journal of Music Theory*, 1977, *21*, 111–171.

Lerdahl, F. and Jackendoff, R. *A generative theory of tonal music*. Cambridge, MA.: MIT Press, 1983.

Longuet-Higgins, H. C. The perception of melodies. *Nature*, 1976, *263*, 646–653.

Macadams, S., and Bregman, A. Hearing musical streams. *Computer Music Journal*, 1979, *3*, 26–44.

Meyer, L. B. Toward a theory of style. In B. Lang (Ed.), *The concept of style*. Philadelphia: University of Pennsylvania Press; 1979.

Narmour, E. *Beyond Schenkerism*. Chicago: University of Chicago Press, 1977.

Perlman, A. M., and Greenblatt, D. Miles Davis meets Noam Chomsky: Some observations on jazz improvisation and language structure. In W. Steiner (Ed.), *The sign in music and literature*. Austin, Texas: University of Texas Press, 1981.

Povel, D., and Okkerman, H. Accents in equitone sequences. *Perception and Psychophysics*, 1981, *30*, 565–572.

Powers, H. S. Language models and musical analysis. *Ethnomusicology*, 1980, *24*, 1–61.

Restle, F. Coding theory of the perception of motion configurations, *Psychological Review*, 1979, *86*, 1–24.

Roads, C. Grammars as representations for music. *Computer Music Journal*, 1979, *111*, 48–55.

Salzer, F. *Structural hearing*. New York: Dover, 1962.

Serafine, M. L. Cognition in music. *Cognition*, 1983, 119–183.

Simon, H. A., and Sumner, R. K. Pattern in music. In B. Kleinmuntz (Ed.), *Formal representation of human judgement*. New York: Wiley, 1968.

Steedman, M. J. The perception of musical rhythm and meter. *Perception*, 1977, *6*, 555–569.

Steedman, M. *The blues and the abstract truth: A generative grammar for jazz chord sequences.* Paper presented to BPS Conference on Psychology and The Arts, Cardiff, 1983.

Sundberg, J., and Lindblom, B. Generative theories in language and music descriptions. *Cognition,* 1976, *4,* 99–122.

Thomassen, J. M. Melodic accent: Experiments and a tentative model. *Journal of the Acoustic Society of America,* 1982, *71,* 1596–1605.

Winograd, T. Linguistics and the computer analysis of tonal harmony. *Journal of Music Theory,* 1968, *12,* 3–49.

Wuorinen, C. *Simple composition.* New York: Longman, 1979.

Youngblood, J. Root progression and composer identification. In H. B. Lincoln (Ed.), *The computer and music.* Ithaca: Cornell University Press, 1970.

3

The Rhythmic Interpretation of Simple Musical Sequences: Towards a Perceptual Model

C. S. Lee

INTRODUCTION

One of the most obvious facts about the experience of listening to practically any piece of music is that one perceives not merely an arbitrary sequence of note durations, but some sort of temporal structure in which the notes are grouped into various kinds of units. There seem to be two ways in which the notes of a piece may be temporally organised: They may be grouped into what a musician calls *phrases,* and they may also be grouped into *metrical* units, known in musical parlance as bars and beats. These two types of temporal organisation are distinct and obey different restrictions; thus, metrical units at the same level are normally all of the same length, whereas this is not true of phrases. In this chapter, I am concerned with the metrical structure, or *rhythm* of musical sequences, and I address the question of how a listener, when presented with a particular sequence, interprets it as the realisation of a particular rhythm. There are many factors that determine how a listener accomplishes this task, but I deal here only with the metrical inferences the listener bases on information about the relative lengths of the notes. Although this avoids the important problem of how other factors affect the perception of rhythm, it seems essential to first come to an understanding of the influence of this most basic of factors in isolation, as it is necessarily present in any musical sequence that admits of a rhythmic interpretation. Accordingly, all the data and predictions refer to sequences in which all the notes have the same pitch, dynamic, and articulation.

I begin by considering what a rhythm is and what a listener has to do to interpret a sequence of notes as the realisation of a particular rhythm. It has been recognised for some time that rhythms are hierarchical structures, closely akin to the syntactic structures of sentences. This insight has been most fully developed by Longuet-Higgins (1978), although Martin (1972) and Sundberg and Lindblom

(1976) present similar views. According to Longuet-Higgins, a rhythm can be regarded as a tree structure generated by a phrase-structure grammar: The grammar is what musicians call the metre, which, in standard musical notation, is partially specified by the time signature. The grammars for 4/4 and 3/4 are shown below in (1) and (2), respectively; the symbols 4/4, 3/4, and so on designate metrical units and may be realised as notes or rests (or in certain cases, tied notes).

$$4/4 \longrightarrow \circ \text{ or } \quad \text{ or } \quad 2/4 + 2/4 \tag{1}$$

$$2/4 \longrightarrow \text{\textomega} \text{ or } \quad \text{ or } \quad 1/4 + 1/4$$

$$1/4 \longrightarrow \text{\textquarter} \text{ or } \text{\textrest} \text{ or } 1/8 + 1/8$$

$$1/8 \longrightarrow \text{\texteighth} \text{ or } \text{\textrest} \text{ or } \bullet\bullet\bullet$$

$$3/4 \longrightarrow \text{\textdotted} \text{ or } \quad \text{ or } \quad 1/4 + 1/4 + 1/4 \tag{2}$$

$$1/4 \longrightarrow \text{\textquarter} \text{ or } \text{\textrest} \text{ or } 1/8 + 1/8$$

$$1/8 \longrightarrow \text{\texteighth} \text{ or } \text{\textrest} \text{ or } \bullet\bullet\bullet$$

One of the rhythms generated by (1) is that of the first two bars of "Auld Lang Syne," (6), whereas (2) generates the rhythm of "Oh dear, what can the matter be," whose first four bars are shown in (3).

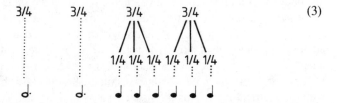

We assume that when a listener perceives the rhythm of a sequence, he or she identifies the rules that generate it and represents the sequence as a tree structure (or series of tree structures) that accommodates all the notes and rests as terminal symbols.

The accomplishment of this task is not a straightforward matter. Although most sequences are perceived as rhythmically unambiguous (that is, there is just one interpretation that is obvious to the listener), all sequences have, in principle, an indefinite number of possible rhythmic interpretations, as Longuet-Higgins and Lee (1984), among others, have pointed out. For example, if a listener were presented with the sequences of notes in (4) without any preceding context, he or she would probably interpret it to be in 4/4 as in example (5) to give the rhythm

$$\text{♩ ♩. ▐♩♩ ♩ . . .} \qquad (4)$$

$$\tfrac{4}{4} \text{– } \xi \text{ ♩ |♩. ▐♩♩ ♩ |. . .} \qquad (5)$$

of "Auld Lang Syne" with the tree structure in (6). But (5) is not the only possible interpretation of (4). There is no reason in principle, why (4) should not be assigned the interpretation in (7) or (8) or any of a whole set of implausible interpretations. The even more innocuous-looking sequence in (9) would normally receive a 3/4 interpretation, as in the rhythm of "Oh dear, what can the matter be," shown in (10). But again, it could be assigned any of a large number of implausible interpretations, such as (11) or (12). The central question, then, is: How does a listener arrive at a particular interpretation of a sequence, given that any sequence could be the realisation of an indefinite number of rhythms?

(6)

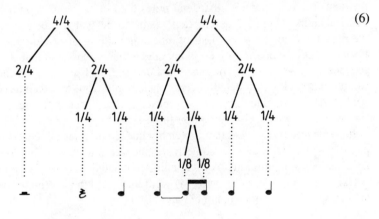

$$\tfrac{4}{4} \text{♩ ♩▁♩♩♩ |♩ . . .} \qquad (7)$$

$$\tfrac{3}{4} \text{♩ ♩▁♩♩|♩ ♩ . . .} \qquad (8)$$

$$\text{♩. ♩. ♩♩♩♩♩♩ . . .} \qquad (9)$$

$$\tfrac{3}{4} \text{♩. |♩. |♩♩♩|♩♩♩|. . .} \qquad (10)$$

$$\tfrac{4}{4} \text{♩. ♩▁|♩ ♩ ♩|♩ ♩ ♩ ♩|. . .} \qquad (11)$$

$$\frac{3}{4} - \quad \text{♩|♩} \quad \text{♩|♩} \quad \text{♩|♩♩♩♩|♩♩.}\ldots \qquad (12)$$

EXISTING THEORIES

There have been a number of attempts over the last few years to give some account of the process of rhythmic perception. Simon (1968), Longuet-Higgins and Steedman (1971), Steedman (1977), and Longuet-Higgins and Lee (1982, 1984) suggest various rules that the listener might use to infer the most natural interpretation of a given sequence, and they implement the rules in algorithmic models. Lerdahl and Jackendoff (1983) also suggest rules for the inference of metrical structure, although they do not implement them in an algorithm. In spite of the differences between these accounts, it is possible to discern an assumption underlying all of them (except Simon's) about the way in which note length cues metrical structure; namely, that long notes tend to be heard as initiating major metrical units. (Simon's assumption seems to be that the listener establishes metrical units merely on the basis of repeating patterns of note durations, but his theory makes counterintuitive claims about the interpretation of a number of sequences—see Longuet-Higgins and Lee, 1982). The way in which the assumption is spelt out in detail differs considerably from one account to another, but before we examine the various proposals, let us consider the general grounds for believing some such assumption to be true.

It seems intuitively clear that, given a sequence of notes of equal duration and pitch in which every note at some fixed interval is accented, one will hear the accented notes as initiating metrical units that include the following unaccented notes. Thus, sequences (13) and (14) would normally be interpreted as (15) and (16), respectively, rather than (17) and (18).

$$\text{♩ ♩ ♩ ♩ ♩ ♩ ♩ } \ldots \qquad (13)$$

$$\text{♩ ♩ ♩ ♩ ♩ ♩ ♩ } \ldots \qquad (14)$$

$$\frac{2}{4} \text{ ≳ ♩|♩ ♩|♩ ♩|♩ ♩|.}\ldots \qquad (15)$$

$$\frac{3}{4} - \quad \text{♩|♩ ♩ ♩|♩ ♩ ♩|.}\ldots \qquad (16)$$

$$\frac{2}{4} \text{♩ ♩|♩ ♩|♩ ♩|♩ } \ldots \qquad (17)$$

$$\frac{3}{4} \text{♩ ♩ ♩|♩ ♩ ♩|♩ } \ldots \qquad (18)$$

The objective intensity of a note, however, is not the only determinant of its perceptual salience. Woodrow (1909) found that long sounds tend to be heard louder than short sounds, while Povel and Okkerman (1982) found that sounds followed by a long silent interval were perceived as accented with respect to sounds followed by a short silent interval. In musical terms, then, this means that—other things being equal—a long note is perceptually more salient than a short note, regardless of whether the absolute duration of the long note (measured from its time of onset to its time of offset) is greater than that of the short note. It seems reasonable to conclude that long notes and accented notes cue metrical structure in the same way: They tend to be heard as initiating higher-level metrical units than notes which are short or unaccented.[1]

The question still remains as to how far the listener might try to ensure that long notes are metrically prominent. One possibility is that the listener will try to interpret a sequence in such a way that the first note of every metrical unit is the longest. This appears to be the view taken by Lerdahl and Jackendoff (1983) (see their metrical preference rule MPR5)[2], while Longuet-Higgins and Lee (1982) make a similar assumption. They present an algorithmic model which, within certain limits, groups the notes of a sequence into high-level units in such a way that the longest notes occur at the beginning of units. (An earlier model in Longuet-Higgins and Steedman, 1971, also yields interpretations in which long notes occur at the beginning of major metrical units, but it suffers from a number of limitations; Longuet-Higgins and Lee, 1982). According to both accounts, if the listener were presented with the sequences in (19)–(21), he or she would bar them in the way indicated in the interpretations in (22)–(24).

(19)

(20)

(21)

[1]Povel and Okkerman (1982) do not present any evidence that bears on the question of perceived grouping. Woodrow (1909) presents evidence that seems to contradict the assumption that long notes tend to be heard as metrically prominent; thus, he finds that long sounds are more likely to be heard as group-ending than short sounds. However, many of the sequences which he presented to his subjects would not be easily amenable to metrical interpretation, given the complex interval ratios of the durations. It is thus conceivable that his subjects resorted to "figural" interpretations (Bamberger, 1978) of the sequences; that is, they simply grouped the tones according to the proximity of their onsets, thus yielding units which were terminated by the long tone.

[2]The metrical preference rule MPR5 seems only to apply, however, in cases where the absolute duration of one note (from time of onset to time of offset) is longer than that of another.

$\frac{4}{4}$ 𝅗𝅥 𝅘𝅥 𝅘𝅥 |𝅗𝅥 𝅘𝅥 𝅘𝅥 |𝅗𝅥 𝅘𝅥 𝅘𝅥 |𝅗𝅥 . . . (22)

$\frac{9}{8}$ 𝅘𝅥. ♫♫♫ ♫♫♫|𝅘𝅥. ♫♫♫ ♫♫♫|𝅘𝅥. . . . (23)

$\frac{4}{4}$ 𝅗𝅥 𝅘𝅥. ♪|𝅗𝅥 𝅘𝅥 ♫|𝅗𝅥 ♫♫♫|𝅗𝅥 . . . (24)

These are, indeed, the most plausible interpretations of the sequences, and the fact that the listener bars them in this way might be taken as evidence that he or she does try to find interpretations in which the longest note in any unit is the first. However, consider the sequences in (25) and (26). The model and the preference rule predict that the listener would bar them in the way indicated in interpretations (27) and (28), respectively, rather than (29) and (30), but it simply is not clear whether this is true.

𝅘𝅥 𝅘𝅥 𝅗𝅥   𝅘𝅥 𝅘𝅥 𝅗𝅥   𝅘𝅥 𝅘𝅥 𝅗𝅥   . . . . (25)

𝅘𝅥. 𝅘𝅥. ♫♫♫. ♫♫♫♫♫. . . . (26)

$\frac{4}{4}$ 𝄽 𝅘𝅥 𝅘𝅥 |𝅗𝅥 𝅘𝅥 𝅘𝅥 |𝅗𝅥 𝅘𝅥 𝅘𝅥 |𝅗𝅥 . . . . (27)

$\frac{9}{8}$ 𝅘𝅥. 𝅘𝅥. ♫♫♫|𝅘𝅥. ♫♫♫ ♫♫♫|𝅘𝅥. . . . (28)

$\frac{4}{4}$ 𝅘𝅥 𝅘𝅥 𝅗𝅥 |𝅗𝅥 𝅘𝅥 𝅗𝅥 |𝅗𝅥 𝅘𝅥 𝅗𝅥 |. . . (29)

$\frac{6}{8}$ 𝅘𝅥. 𝅘𝅥. |♫♫♫ 𝅘𝅥. |♫♫♫ ♫♫♫|𝅘𝅥. . . . (30)

Further doubts arise when one considers whether other factors might not be at work in the sequences in (19)–(21). It is generally recognised that repetition is probably an important factor even in the interpretation of impoverished sequences of the sort under consideration (see Longuet-Higgins and Lee, 1982; Lerdahl and Jackendoff, 1983), although no one has made any specific proposals in this respect. Steedman (1977) considers the way in which melodic repetition—the repetition of one or more fragments in a melody—may cause the listener to change his metrical hypothesis in various ways, and presents some rules (which he implements in an algorithm) that would account for this: He proposes that, if the listener perceives a melodic fragment as a copy of an earlier figure, then he takes the distance between their starting points as a metrical unit. We might, therefore, by analogy, suppose that the listener makes the same sort of inferences on the basis of identical patterns of note durations. If this is so, then, in the case of the sequences in (19) and (20), the interpretations he or she would assign them are the very ones picked out by the model and the preference rule. Furthermore, since it is quite possible that repeats may not have to be exactly identical copies of figures—as appears to be the case with melodic repetition (see Steedman, 1977)—repetition may well account for how the listener interprets the sequence in (21) as well.

The implication of the evidence presented seems to be that the listener does not base inferences about higher metrical levels so much on relative note length as on other factors such as repetition, and that, in the absence of such factors, judgments are correspondingly ambiguous. A recent model, which bases fewer predictions about high-level metrical structure on relative note length (and would not, in the case of the sequences in (25)–(26), yield the high-level groupings of either the interpretations in (27)–(28) or (29)–(30), is presented in Longuet-Higgins and Lee (1984). It is based on the assumption that the listener, where possible, will try to interpret a sequence as the realisation of an unsyncopated rhythm. In accordance with musical intuition, they define a syncopation as the occurrence, on a rest or tied note, of a beat that is stronger than the one occurring on the immediately preceding sounded note. (In some cases, the two need only be equally strong). Thus, there are syncopations (arrowed) on every other crotchet beat in (31), since there are tied notes at each of these points and the previously sounded notes occur on quaver beats (as the notation makes clear).

$$\begin{array}{c} \frac{2}{4} \, \musicnotation \quad | \musicnotation \quad | \musicnotation \quad | \cdots \\ \qquad \uparrow \qquad\qquad \uparrow \qquad\qquad \uparrow \end{array} \qquad\qquad (31)$$

Longuet-Higgins and Lee's (1984) assumption can be related easily to the general idea that long notes tend to be placed on strong beats. A note on a strong beat initiates a longer metrical unit than one on a weak beat; thus, a note occurring on the first beat of a 2/4 bar initiates a minim unit (the whole bar), whereas one occurring on the second beat initiates only a crotchet unit (the half bar). Longuet-Higgins and Lee have shown that a syncopation occurs if and only if a (sounded) note outlasts the highest-level metrical unit it initiates: In (31), for example, the highest-level units initiated by the long notes (which have the notional length of dotted crotchets) are only quaver units (as the notation makes clear). Thus, given the general assumption that the listener tends to place long notes on strong beats, it would not be surprising to discover that he or she favoured unsyncopated interpretations where possible. And indeed, Longuet-Higgins and Lee's claim seems to be borne out over a large range of cases: What distinguishes the natural from the unnatural interpretations is the fact that the former are unsyncopated whereas the latter are not. While the natural interpretations—(6) and (11)—of the sequences in (5) and (9), respectively, are unsyncopated, all the unnatural interpretations—(7), (8), (11), and (12)—contain syncopations (arrowed).

(7a)

(8a)

(11a)

(12a)

A general problem with both the proposals in Longuet-Higgins and Lee (1984) and Lerdahl and Jackendoff (1983) is that little or no account is taken of the way in which the listener's hypotheses about earlier parts of a sequence can affect his hypotheses about later parts. It seems to be the case, as Longuet-Higgins and Steedman (1971) and Steedman (1977) have proposed, that metrical evidence early on in a sequence counts for more than later evidence. The most plausible explanation for this is that the listener establishes metrical hypotheses as he or she works through the notes of a sequence from left to right and is conservative about his or her hypotheses in the sense of being reluctant to abandon one he or she has already established. Consider the sequence in (32) and two possible interpretations, (33) and (34).

(32)

(33)

(34)

The sequence in (34) is clearly the more plausible interpretation. The most obvious explanation of this is that the listener tries to find a natural interpretation of notes 1–4 before considering the rest of the sequence; and since these four notes alone compel (under just about any assumption) an interpretation in which the quavers are grouped into crotchet units as in (34), this is the one that is chosen. Lerdahl and Jackendoff's (1983) rule system, however, even though it would pick out an interpretation of the first four notes alone in which the quavers are grouped in twos, allows no way of deciding between (33) and (34) because it takes no account of where metrical evidence occurs in a sequence. Longuet-Higgins and Lee's (most recent) model fares no better, for the same reason, although it, too, would choose an interpretation of the first four notes alone in which the quavers are grouped in twos, since an interpretation in which they were grouped in threes would contain a syncopation, arrowed in example (35).

$$\text{(35)}$$

This failure to allow for the way in which the perceptual process may affect the listener's interpretation of a given sequence follows from a general assumption that seems to underlie both Longuet-Higgins and Lee's (1984) approach and, to a lesser extent, that of Lerdahl and Jackendoff (1983); namely, that the constraints governing the listener's choice of interpretation are stateable in terms of some general property (or set of properties) of rhythms. The assumption entails the claim that the listener possesses an algorithm that enables him or her to discover an interpretation of the appropriate sort for any sequence which admits of such an interpretation. Longuet-Higgins and Lee's proposal requires that the listener has an algorithm that yields an unsyncopated interpretation for any sequence that is the realisation of an unsyncopated rhythm. However, there are general grounds for thinking that the assumption may be too simple. It is well known, for example, in linguistic research that the native speaker does not have an algorithm for discovering grammatical interpretations for any word string that is the realisation of a grammatical sentence. The evidence for this comes, in large part, from the existence of what are termed "gardenpath" sentences (Kimball, 1973), which have a grammatical interpretation but are difficult or impossible to interpret grammatically because of misleading cues in the earlier part of the sentence (a famous example is the sentence *the horse raced past the barn fell,* where one tends to interpret the words up to *barn* as constituting a sentence and then not be able to fit *fell* into this interpretation). We might therefore, by analogy, argue as follows: Even if the listener does, in general, prefer unsyncopated to syncopated interpretations, it is, nevertheless, quite possible that he or she does not have an algorithm for finding unsyncopated interpretations; therefore, he or she does not always choose an unsyncopated interpretation of a sequence even if this is, in principle, possible.

The question arises as to whether there is any evidence in support of this view, in the form, perhaps, of musical equivalents of gardenpath sentences. Sequences (36) and (37) are possible cases in point. These have the (unique) unsyncopated interpretations (38) and (39), respectively.

$$\text{(36)}$$

$$\text{(37)}$$

$$\text{(38)}$$

$$\text{(39)}$$

It seems intuitively unlikely, however, that the listener would easily discover these interpretations; it seems, rather, that the first long note in each case causes him or her to infer an incorrect grouping of the quavers (binary in (38), ternary, in (39)) so that the resulting interpretations of the whole sequences contain syncopations, arrowed in (40) and (41). (The listener might nevertheless succeed in discovering the interpretations in (38) and (39) if the sequences are repeated one or more times, by inferring metrical units of the same length and phase as the repeating figure and then subdividing, but I do not consider this possibility here).

(40)

(41)

If these claims are correct, then the sequences in (36) and (37) constitute counterexamples to Longuet-Higgins and Lee's (1984) claim (and to Lerdahl and Jackendoff's, 1983, preference rule) since the listener chooses interpretations that are syncopated (and in which the first note in some metrical units is not the longest), even though alternative interpretations are, in principle, possible. It seems that what is required in order to account for the listener's choice of interpretations here is an explanation in procedural terms. Some of the earlier proposals discussed in this section—such as the one presented in Longuet-Higgins and Steedman (1971)—would yield such an account. In the next section I sketch a new proposal, based on the earlier models, that overcomes some of their limitations.

A MODEL

We have already remarked that the listener seems to be misled in the sequences in (36) and (37) by the first long notes. In each case, the listener seems to hypothesise that the long note defines a metrical unit and to confirm the hypothesis as soon as he or she notices that the first note in the next unit of his or her provisional grouping is no shorter than any of the other notes in the unit. Having thus established a metrical grouping, he or she does not abandon it, even though it results in a later syncopation. These observations suggest the following generalisation: As soon as a series of notes can be interpreted as constituting two consecutive metrical units containing one or more notes each, in which the first note of each is no shorter than any of the others, the listener infers a metrical grouping containing these units. Thus, in the case of (36) and (37), the first point at which the listener can interpret what he or she has heard as constituting two units meeting the above conditions is on reaching the third note in (36) and the fourth in (37); in (36) the units are crotchets and in (37), dotted crotchets, which are the units in incorrect interpretations (40) and (41), respectively.

Let us now consider how the listener might aggregate metrical units he or she has already established into higher-level units. Since he or she has already established one or more lower levels of grouping, he or she can count and can ensure that any higher-level grouping he or she hypothesises is consonant with the lower-level grouping in the sense that the onset of every higher-level unit coincides with the onset of a lower-level unit. This means he or she only need compare the lengths of notes which actually occur on successive beats of the lower-level grouping (where a beat marks the onset of a unit) since no other notes could initiate a metrical unit at a higher level. Thus, consider again the sequence in (37) and suppose that there is a crotchet preceding the first dotted crotchet, as in (42):

$$\text{♩ ♩ ♫ ♫ ♫ ♩ ♫ ♫ ...} \tag{42}$$

Let us assume that the listener has already established a crotchet metrical level, with the phase as indicated by the dotted lines, and that on the basis of the dotted crotchet, he or she is trying to find a higher-level grouping. The units at the next level cannot be smaller than a minim, so if the dotted crotchet initiates one such unit, the next unit will be initiated by the second quaver. These two putative units meet the required conditions, so a minim grouping is inferred, resulting in the interpretation in (43).

$$\text{♩ ♩ |♩. ♩|♫♫|♩. ♩|♫ ...} \tag{43}$$

There seems to be a further condition on the inference of higher-level groupings. Given the proposal so far, we would predict that in the case of the sequences in (25) and (26), the listener will assign them the interpretations in (27) and (28), respectively, as would Lerdahl and Jackendoff (1983) and Longuet-Higgins and Lee (1982). But as we have seen, (29) and (30) are also perfectly plausible interpretations.

$$\text{♩ ♩ |♩ ♩ ♩ |♩ ♩ ♩ |♩ ...} \tag{27a}$$

$$\text{♩. ♩. ♫♫|♩. ♫♫ ♫♫|♩. ...} \tag{28a}$$

$$\text{♩ ♩ ♩ |♩ ♩ ♩ |♩ ♩ ♩ |... } \tag{29a}$$

$$\text{♩. ♩. |♫♫ ♩. |♫♫ ♫♫|♩. ...} \tag{30a}$$

Why, then, are the interpretations in (29) and (30) apparently not ruled out by the listener? The crucial factor appears to be that the rival interpretations differ only in how they group units (crotchets in the case of (25) and dotted crotchets in the case of (26)) that are already large enough to accommodate the longest notes. It seems to be the case, then, that what causes the listener to infer a particular higher level of grouping is the occurrence of a note that initiates and outlasts a unit at the lower level. If there are no such notes (and in the absence of other factors such as repetition), the listener does not infer any one particular higher level.

These proposals can be illustrated by describing a simple procedure that implements them. It is based on the assumption, proposed in Longuet-Higgins and Lee (1982) that the listener establishes metrical groupings by a process of trial and error. More precisely, it calculates times, $t1$, $t2$, and $t3$, which mark the onset of three hypothetical consecutive units, and it adjusts $t2$ and $t3$ until there are no notes between $t2$ and $t3$ longer than the note on $t2$. At this point, $t1$–$t2$ and $t2$–$t3$ are established as metrical units. The procedure is repeated in the course of working through a sequence if there is a note that is longer than the longest metrical unit so far established. Consider how the procedure would work with the sequence in (47). We start, as in every case, by placing $t1$ on the first note and $t2$ on the second, since this is clearly the smallest putative unit that would accommodate the first note; $t3$ is then calculated such that $t2$–$t3$ is equal to $t1$–$t2$, giving (44). There is a note (the first dotted crotchet) between $t2$ and $t3$ that is longer than the note on $t2$, so $t2$ is moved onto this note, and $t3$ recalculated accordingly, giving (45). There is now no note between $t2$ and $t3$ longer than the note on $t2$, so $t1$–$t2$ and $t2$–$t3$ are taken as consecutive metrical units. We then look for notes on successive beats of the implied grouping that outlast the unit they initiate at this level, giving (46).

(44)

(45)

(46)

The first such note is the first dotted crotchet, so we now try to find a metrical unit that will accommodate this note. We place $t1$ on the dotted crotchet and $t2$ on the first note after the dotted crotchet that occurs on a crotchet beat; $t3$ is recalculated in the usual way, giving (47). There is now a note between $t2$ and $t3$

that is longer than the note on $t2$ and occurs on a crotchet beat (namely, the second dotted crotchet), so $t2$ is moved onto this note and $t3$ recalculated, as in (48).

(47)

(48)

Since there are no notes between $t2$ and $t3$ longer than the dotted crotchet, $t1-t2$ and $t2-t3$ are confirmed as metrical units, thus establishing a dotted-minim metrical level; furthermore, as there are no notes in the remainder of the sequence that are longer than a dotted minim (and occur on a dotted minim beat), we do not infer any higher levels of grouping. The resulting interpretation of the sequence is shown in (49).

(49)

Let us now consider how the procedure would work with some of the sequences presented earlier. In the case of sequences in (9), (19), (20), (21) and (26), the procedure would establish that the first note in each case defined a metrical unit (since the note on $t2$ in each case would be no shorter than any of the notes occurring before $t3$), thus yielding the groupings indicated by the dotted lines.

(9a)

(19a)

(20a)

(21a)

(26a)

The procedure would not yield a higher level of grouping for any of these sequences since none contain notes longer than the units at the level already established. Thus, it would fail in the case of sequences in (19), (20), and (21) to yield the higher-level grouping the listener undoubtedly perceives; but, as we have argued, repetition and not relative note length seems to be the factor at work here. As for the sequences in (5), (25) and (32), the procedure again would establish that the first note in each case defined a metrical unit, resulting in the following groupings:

(5a)

(25a)

(32a)

It would then encounter a later note that is longer than the unit just established, so it would place $t1$ on this note and calculate $t2$ and $t3$ in the usual way. The resulting groupings are indicated by the dotted lines:

(5b)

(25b)

(32b)

Neither (5) nor (25) contains any notes that outlast the units at the level just established, so the procedure would not yield any higher level of metrical structure. In the case of (32), there *is* such a note (arrowed), but as it does not initiate one of the crotchet units already established, the procedure would ignore it.

It should be noted from the preceding examples that the procedure as described does not supply the time of the first downbeat (the onset time of the first top-level unit that is initiated by a note). This can be calculated, however, as follows: If the highest-level unit established for a particular sequence is of length D, then we can find the downbeat by counting back in multiples of D from $t1$. In the following sequence, the procedure will establish a minim unit, but only on reaching the last note, since none of the notes preceding the first minim outlasts the previously established crotchet units, as in (50). The downbeat can be determined by counting back in minims from $t1$: it turns out to fall on the second crotchet, arrowed in (51).

(50)

(51)

There are problems, however, with this account since it is not certain that the listener would easily discover the interpretation in (50). Indeed, he or she might even be unable to interpret the sequence at all. The reason may be that before the listener reaches the first minim, he or she groups the crotchets into twos or threes, starting on the first crotchet, but on encountering the implied syncopations (arrowed), abandons the hypothesis and is unable to establish an alternative hypothesis for the whole sequence because of the amount of backtracking involved, as in (52) and (53).

$$\text{(52)}$$

$$\text{(53)}$$

The implication of these claims is that the listener will infer metrical structure in the absence of specific rhythmic cues, although he or she may have no particular preference for either binary or ternary groupings. More precisely, in the absence of contradictory evidence, the listener will establish one or more higher levels of grouping, starting on the first unit of the highest level already established; there will thus be no need to determine the downbeat for any sequence by counting back from the onset of a later top-level unit. If these claims turn out to be true, the procedure will require modification, although the preceding account is not sufficient for the specification of a revised algorithm.

CONCLUSIONS

The proposal sketched in the previous section is a speculative (and somewhat partial) attempt to account for the way in which the listener interprets a particular sequence as the realisation of a particular rhythm. It is founded on two main assumptions. The first assumption, which, in some form, underlies nearly every proposal we have discussed, is that the listener will attempt to place long notes on strong beats, although it seems that this ceases to be true once a metrical structure has been established in which the units are long enough to accommodate the longest notes. The second assumption is that the listener tries to establish a metrical analysis as soon as possible; that is, as soon as he or she can interpret a sequence of notes as constituting two consecutive metrical units that meet certain conditions, that is how he or she will interpret them.

The scope of the proposed model is obviously very limited. It has nothing to say about most of the factors that determine the listener's rhythmic interpretation of real music. It also has nothing to say about how the listener copes with the deviations from strict time and changes of tempo that are a feature of live music (see Longuet-Higgins, 1976, for an account of how the listener might do this). One consequence of this limitation (shared in varying degrees by every proposal discussed) is that where the model makes a prediction about a real musical example that does not agree with intuition, it may be quite difficult to decide whether the example constitutes a counterexample or an exception to the theory. Thus, the model makes the wrong prediction about how the listener would interpret the well-known C-minor fugue subject from Book 1 of Bach's *Well-Tempered Clavier*. The correct interpretation (54) contains a syncopation (arrowed) on the crotchet, but the model takes this note as defining a metrical unit—to give the interpretation in (55)—since it has not previously established a sufficiently high level of metrical grouping to yield a syncopation. However, are the relative durations of the notes sufficient on their own to establish the interpretation (54) and exclude the one in (55)? It is not obvious that they are, given the evidence of examples such as (25); it may well turn out that melodic factors are responsible. It remains to be seen whether this and other predictions of the model can be experimentally corroborated.

(54)

(55)

ACKNOWLEDGEMENTS

I am deeply indebted to Christopher Longuet-Higgins and Mark Steedman; their ideas on music have fundamentally shaped my thinking. They and Ian Cross, Chris Darwin, Pete Howell, and Rob West read earlier versions of the chapter and made many helpful comments and suggestions. None of them, of course, necessarily subscribes to any of my conclusions.

REFERENCES

Bamberger, J. Intuitive and formal musical knowing: Parables of cognitive dissonance. In S. S. Madeja (Ed.), *The arts, cognition and basic skills*. New Brunswick, NJ: Transaction Books, 1978.

Kimball, J. Seven principles of surface structure parsing in natural language. *Cognition*, 1973, *2*(1), 15–47.

Lerdahl, F., and Jackendoff, R. *A generative theory of tonal music*. Cambridge, MA: MIT Press, 1983.

Longuet-Higgins, H. C. The perception of melodies. *Nature*, 1976, *263*, 646–653.

Longuet-Higgins, H. C. The perception of music. *Interdisciplinary Science Review*, 1978, *3*, 148–156.

Longuet-Higgins, H. C., and Lee, C. S. The perception of musical rhythms. *Perception*, 1982, *11*, 115–128.

Longuet-Higgins, H. C., and Lee, C. S. The rhythmic interpretation of monophonic music. *Music Perception*, 1984, *1*(4), 424–441.

Longuet-Higgins, H. C., and Steedman, M. J. On interpreting Bach. In B. Meltzer and D. Michie (Eds.), *Machine intelligence 6*. Edinburgh: Edinburgh University Press, 1971.

Martin, J. G. Rhythmic (hierarchical) versus serial structure in speech and other behaviour. *Psychological Review,* 1972, *79,* 487–509.

Povel, D. J., and Okkerman, H. Accents in equitone sequences. *Perception and Psychophysics,* 1981, *30*(6), 565–572.

Simon, H. A. Perception du pattern musical par AUDITEUR. *Sciences de l'Art,* 1968, *5*(2), 28–34.

Steedman, M. J. The perception of musical rhythm and metre. *Perception,* 1968, *6,* 555–569.

Sundberg, J., and Lindblom, B. Generative theories in language and music descriptions. *Cognition,* 1976, *4,* 99–122.

Woodrow, H. A quantitative study of rhythm. In R. S. Woodworth (Ed.), *Archives of psychology 14.* New York: Science Press, 1909.

4

On the Perceptual Organisation of Tone Sequences and Melodies

Anthony J. Watkins and Mary C. Dyson

MELODY AND PERCEPTION

The auditory system provides us with an extremely accurate representation of the frequency of tones, a frequency difference that corresponds to only 5% of a semitone can be reliably discriminated by a practiced subject who is listening for differences between successive tones (see Schubert, 1980). Even if the sound is made more complicated by embedding the target tone within a longer sequence of tones, frequency discrimination is of comparable accuracy as long as there is no uncertainty about the temporal location and frequency range of the target tone (Watson and Kelly, 1981; Watson, Kelly, and Wroton, 1976). However, when there is such uncertainty, for listeners comparing short but novel tone sequences presented successively, then the picture changes dramatically; differences between the component tones of each sequence that amount to a number of semitones can often go unnoticed. If the task is made still more complicated—by asking the listener to compare different transpositions of a tone sequence (where "same" is the correct answer if each tone of one melody has been shifted by a constant number of semitones)—then, under certain circumstances, performance can deteriorate to guessing level, even for musically sophisticated listeners trying to detect differences of the order of semitones. In this type of task, it has been found that accuracy does not depend on the degree of change of any one tone, but is crucially dependent on the relationships between tones. This is because, in attempting to resolve this type of uncertainty, the auditory system draws on certain principles of perceptual organisation that interact with the interrelationships or structure of the input.

In a recent discussion of current thinking on the topic of perceptual organisation, Attneave (1981) maintains that a confluence of much of the opinion in this area might be possible. He proposes a form of "Pragnanz" principle by which the perceptual system seeks parsimonious descriptions of the perceptual array. These descriptions are arrived at by way of a hill-climbing progression (Turvey,

Shaw and Mace, 1978). This is a sort of general purpose problem-solving procedure, which uses feedback about its current state of solution approximation, in order to direct and redirect its search towards the areas that promise the closer approximations. In perceptual problem solving, according to Attneave, the search involves two-way communication between an analogue image system and a languagelike or propositional system. It is aided by certain intrinsic stimulus properties such as redundancy or homogeneity, and is also aided if the input is brought into conformity with the schemata of familiar environmental events. This proposal attributes what might be described as "intelligence" to perception, but this has been distinguished from the sort of intelligence that characterises our thinking and linguistic skills. Rock (1975) points out that many behaviour patterns found in lower organisms might, similarly, be described as intelligent but that there are important differences. Some of the hallmarks of perceptual intelligence are that it is fast, unconscious, non-verbal, but above all, inflexible. So although certain organisations that our perceptions readily achieve may seem to be elegant solutions of seemingly complex problems, the system is incapable of adapting these procedures if problems of comparable complexity are presented in different terms. Similarly, having arrived at an organisational solution, perceivers more or less have to accept it, even if they know that their percepts are illusory. Nevertheless, thinking and reasoning often display some specificity and a certain amount of inflexibility, so perhaps the distinction is better stated as one of degree. Indeed, Shepard (1981) attributes these and other similarities to the fact that linguistic skills are built on the more basic perceptual structures that have evolutionary precedence.

Our present aim is to capture and characterise the perceptual skills engaged when a listener hears and recognises a familiar melody. We are not referring to the analytic skills of music scholars, but to the everyday perceptions of the untutored native of the pervading musical idiom. We propose to demonstrate that this sort of melody perception exhibits properties similar to those discussed. That is, the perceptual organisation of tone sequences is facilitated if they are structured to approximate the schemata of melodies belonging to the musical idiom with which our listeners are familiar. Specifically, we will demonstrate that tone sequences that obey the constraints imposed by the system of Western scales and keys are more easily organised, learned, and discriminated than control sequences of comparable complexity. Thus, in perceiving a melody, the perceptual problems that are solved might be analagous to those involved in transcription: For example, assigning a keynote, properly labelling accidentals, and so on. If the tone sequence is a plausible approximation to a sensible melody then this task will be relatively easy, perceptual organisation will be efficient. However, if the tones do not easily fit in with our expectations about melodies, then this strategy would not be of much use in arriving at a useful organisation, and we would be left only with those organisational strategies afforded by intrinsic stimulus properties, which operate for all tone sequences regardless of whether they are melodies or not.

Our study of melody perception is quite distinct from a study of the aesthetics of music, and should, perhaps, also be distinguished from certain linguistic analogues (e.g., Winograd, 1968; Lerdahl and Jackendoff, 1977). The relationship between our perceptual studies and music is more akin to the relationship between the perception of visual perspective and visual art. Just as visual artists build on the perceptual predispositions engaged by perspective (and often tease us with them as in surrealist painting or the impossible worlds depicted by Escher), so musicians create auditory worlds within perceptual structures such as scale and key. Similarly, just as many visual artists reject perspective and prefer to express themselves in terms of radically different constraints (as in the work of Jackson Pollock), so some musicians (such as Stockhausen) have rejected musical constraints that reflect an obsession with the interval and express themselves in quite different terms.

So, how does one discover the nature of the relationships between tones that have perceptual relevance? As Hochberg (1981) points out, the notion of perceptual problem solving is not much use unless one also knows the premises and the inference rules used to solve the problems. One promising approach has been proposed by workers in the area of timbre perception (Null and Young, 1981; Risset and Wessel, 1982) and by speech researchers (Bailey and Summerfield, 1980). This research strategy is called analysis-resynthesis and is itself a sort of hill climbing. The general idea is that constraints that hold some promise are selected, on the basis of empirical observation and/or theoretical initiative, and formalised so as to allow a resynthesis of suitably constrained artifices. These are then used in perception experiments to establish the perceptual relevance (or otherwise) of the constraints. The results of such tests are then used to reshape the original formulations into forms more closely approaching perceptual validity. One attractive aspect of such an approach is to allow the design of powerful experiments, with research materials generated using constrained randomness. In the investigation of melody, this would mean an essentially random selection of sequences of notes and intervals, but with certain biases in favour of those that clearly reflect the constraints in operation. The result will be some degree of approximation to a *real* melody. It is then possible to devise equal-and-opposite forms of the constraints to generate control melodies of comparable complexity and to compare the perception of these and experimental melodies. In this way, any effects due to constraint per se (e.g., Watson and Kelly, 1981) may be distinguished from effects due to the perceptually meaningful nature of the experimental constraints.

An objection to such an approach is that veridical musical structure can be found only in existing melodies. This is because the full musical intuitions of a composer are not embodied in the synthesis process from the outset, and such schemata are not readily constructed by hill climbing. However, the use of existing melodies does create a number of problems in the design and interpretation of experiments. There may be some unwitting bias in the selection of experimental and control melodies; the melodies or melody features examined may be idiosyncratic and unrepresentative of the general population of melodies; and the effects attributed to specific melody variables may be confounded with non-explicit properties of the melodies used. Our compromise is to employ the constrained randomness technique to generate large numbers of melodies; experimental melody constraints are systematically varied, whereas other aspects are either fixed or randomised on a trial-by-trial basis. We therefore, obtain experimental power, but must be content to work with only a partial description of the framework in which a composer might operate. Thus, the constraints we study might be perceived rather differently in more realistically structured environments. Indeed, the same may be said about, for example, the use of line drawings to study the perception of visual perspective and other partially structured stimuli frequently used by perceptual psychologists. This conundrum is essentially the ecological validity issue (see Hochberg, 1981, and Shaw and Turvey, 1981, for more extensive debate on the matter). In subsequent sections, we describe some of our work with melody approximations and discuss its implications for a more general picture of the way melodies are perceived. We offer some clues about the nature of the perception of real melodies, while bearing in mind the caveats concerning the generality of our findings. Before describing our techniques, we briefly review some of the prerequisites for a description of our melodic constraints.

A RUDIMENTARY ANALYSIS OF MELODY

Pitch and Frequency

Musicians use a physical unit, Hertz (Hz), in the specification of instrument tunings and speak of the frequency of a note (e.g., A = 440 Hz). However, any one musical note may be realised by a large number of sounds differing widely in their (Fourier) frequency composition, although they all generate the same pitch percept. This situation may be clarified by considering pitch-perception research. Here, we find that the clearest and least ambiguous pitch percepts are generated by harmonic complex sounds having several low, successive harmonics (deBoer, 1976) such as trains of periodic short impulses (Schouten, 1940/1969; Seebeck, 1841). The frequencies of such a complex are at integer multiples of some fundamental frequency; thus, if the latter is f Hz, then the harmonics or overtones are at $2f$, $3f$, $4f$, $5f$ . . . nf Hz. The pitch of a sound is often operationally specified by the fundamental frequency of such a harmonic complex, that is, the complex that the listener judges to be of equal pitch (Warren and Wrightson,

1981). Indeed, currently successful models used to predict perceived pitch embody some form of matching of the incoming sound to harmonic-complex templates (Goldstein, 1973; Terhardt, 1974; Wightman, 1973). This view of pitch perception accounts for the finding that a range of different sounds will give rise to the same pitch, as all belong to the same harmonic series. For example, a sound composed of the components $3f + 4f + 5f$ will generally match the pitch of the sound $6f + 7f + 8f$, and both sounds will have the same pitch as a tone of frequency f presented alone. What all these sounds have in common is that they are members of the same harmonic series, based on the frequency f. So if $f = 261.6$ Hz, then all these sounds will be said to have a pitch of middle C. Thus, the frequency of a note may be taken to represent perceived pitch in the sense of the fundamental frequency of the appropriately matched harmonic complex. This means that it is unnecessary for a sound to possess energy at the frequency corresponding to its note frequency, but it does mean that it should contain some low successive harmonics of the note frequency if the fundamental is absent (Schouten, Ritsma, and Cardozo, 1962; Wightman and Green, 1974). Schouten et al. also showed that the auditory system does not readily adapt itself to sounds that are not simple successions of overtones. This sort of sound can be produced by adding a constant number of Hertz to the components of a successive overtone series. The pitch of such a sound is ambiguous, and each of the pitches heard corresponds to an harmonic complex having successive overtones that nearly match those of the sound presented. Thus, it is only possible to understand the nature of pitch perception if we realise that the auditory system is predisposed to hear sounds comprising successive harmonics of a series. These appear to be a basic unit of perceptual sound analysis and are in many senses "fundamental" to perception.

Octave Equivalence and Pitch Class; Pitch Chroma and Pitch Height

Notes whose frequencies form a 2:1 ratio (i.e., an octave) bear a close similarity to one another and are given the same note names (e.g., C, G, etc.). These constitute what Babbitt (1960) calls "pitch classes with class membership defined by octave equivalence" (p. 247). Members of the same pitch class are said to generate the same percept of chroma, whereas the perceptual differences between members of the same class are called pitch height variations. Evidence for perceptual dimensions of chroma and height comes from three main sources: Shepard (1964) discusses his pitch paradox in terms of a spiral representation of pitch, in which vertical height represents pitch height, and the angle of rotation around the spiral represents chroma. Thus, a continuous increase in the frequency of a pure tone will be heard as a continuous increase in pitch height, along with repetitions of perceived chroma with each octave traversed. The sounds used by Shepard consisted of a very low fundamental frequency f along with harmonics at octaves above the fundamental, i.e., $2f$, $4f$, $8f$, $16f$, and so on. According to Shepard, this procedure saturates the height representation so that pitch can be judged only in terms of chroma. In this way, the illusion of continuous upward pitch motion can be generated by gradually moving all the components upward until they have risen an octave, then skipping back to the starting point and continuing. However, this interpretation of the pitch paradox has been called into question because Burns (1982) has shown that it is not necessary to separate the components by octaves to generate this illusion; other logarithmic spacings produce similar effects. In fact, Wilson (1967) was able to demonstrate that certain sounds, having components equally separated on a linear scale, can be manipulated to generate this sort of illusion.

Other evidence for a chroma dimension comes from the multidimensional scaling work of Krumhansl (1979) and Krumhansl and Shepard (1979) who show that octave equivalents are judged to be perceptually similar in certain contexts, although not all paradigms reveal this sort of relationship (Kallman, 1982).

The role of chroma in melody perception has been investigated by scattering the notes of familiar melodies across octaves. This procedure does not entirely destroy the ability to identify the melody, as long as the contour of the original is preserved. Recognition is better for scatterings that preserve the original chroma (Idson and Massaro, 1978).

Tuning, Scale, and Key

The equal temperament tuning system (see Young, 1960) consists of 12 pitch classes produced by dividing the octave into 12 logarithmically equal steps (semitones). These pitch classes are collectively known as the chromatic scale. Within a given musical idiom, certain subsets of the chromatic set are assigned differential importance, and the determinants of these subsets have been the focus of much recent theory (e.g., Balzano, 1980, 1982b; Bernstein, 1976; Deutsch and Feroe, 1981; Dowling, 1978; Jackendoff and Lerdahl, 1982; Lerdahl and Jackendoff, 1977; Terhardt, 1977, 1978; von Hoerner, 1974, 1976). Here, we are concerned with the notions of tonic, diatonic scale, and key prevalent in much Western music (Burns and Ward, 1982). A diatonic scale is obtained by dividing an octave into seven pitch classes separated by the following successive semitone steps (see Young, 1960): 2, 2, 1, 2, 2, 2, 1. Key refers to the fact that, in many Western tonal melodies, one note acts as a tonal centre (Lerdahl and Jackendoff, 1977) called the keynote. For the major mode, the keynote or tonic is the first pitch-class. Other modes may be generated by taking other pitch-classes as the keynote. For example, the melodic descending minor mode takes the sixth pitch-class as the tonic (see Helmholtz, 1885/1954, for a full historical account of other modes and their vicissitudes).

Longuet-Higgins (1976, 1978) describes a succinct and precise notation for expressing tonal relationships, which captures many of the classical ideas about key, scale, and mode such as those of Helmholtz (1885/1954). An adapted form of this notation is used here. A central idea is that every note may be assigned a sharpness value represented by the letter q. This is the number of fifths between any note and the keynote, (a fifth being seven semitones in the equal-temperament tuning system). To understand this idea, it is helpful to recall the cycle of fifths. Here, the 12 notes of the octave are arranged so that adjacent notes are one fifth apart. The q value of each note may then be found by counting along from the keynote. The following shows this arrangement, together with the associated value of q for the case where the keynote is C.

$$\text{note:} \quad D\flat \ A\flat \ E\flat \ B\flat \ F \ C \ G \ D \ A \ E \ B \ F\sharp$$
$$q \text{ value:} \ -5 \ -4 \ -3 \ -2 \ -1 \ 0 \ 1 \ 2 \ 3 \ 4 \ 5 \ 6$$

Notice that in a cyclical form of this progression, the value of q is ambiguous, being either the value shown or 12 minus this value. Here, this ambiguity is avoided by restricting q to the integer range -5 through $+6$.

We can express the relationship between the frequency of a note and its q value in the following way: The first step is to select a keynote from the equal temperament range, for example, C = 261.6 Hz. This frequency is represented by f_0. We may then define a signed integer p, which is the number of semitones between a note and the keynote (see Hahn and Jones, 1981). If f is the frequency of this note then

$$f/f_0 = 2^{p/12}, \tag{1}$$

The relationship between p and q may then be stated using a third signed integer, r:

$$p = 7q - 12r. \tag{2}$$

To solve this equation, a value of r is chosen, which gives integer values for p and q.

In this way, the 12 q values are derived, each denoting one of the 12 pitch classes of equal-temperament tuning (Balzano, 1982b). Moreover, it is easy to show that any seven adjacent q values constitute a diatonic scale (Balzano, 1980, 1982b). For example, the 7 q values -1 through $+5$ are a diatonic major scale, and the 7 q values -4 through $+2$ are a melodic descending minor scale. More generally, the mode of a diatonic scale is determined by the choice of keynote. Thus, in the example shown, if the scale consists of the seven adjacent white notes, then keynote equals C tells us that we are in the major mode. If we wish to change modes preserving the same scale, we might change the keynote to A. Our scale would now be a melodic descending minor in A, the relative minor of C.

Longuet-Higgins (1976, 1978) observed that large numbers of Western melodies are constrained as long as they remain within a single key. These constraints refer to the intervals of a melody; each interval is described by the separation of its notes measured along a progression of fifths, that is, the difference between their q values. This will be called the "fifth span" of the interval. In this analysis, the progression is not cyclical, but is restricted to the range of notes between 5 fifths below the keynote through 6 fifths above the keynote. The number of fifths from the keynote is represented by an integer, q; and the fifth span of an interval is represented by delta q. The latter is computed by calculating the q values for each note, subtracting one from the other, and taking the absolute value of the result. An important consequence of the restrictions on this fifth progression is that the fifth span of intervals—other than the tritone—will depend upon the choice of keynote. For example, the interval G to D is 1 fifth in some keys (such as F), but 11 fifths in others (such as D flat). Similarly, C to D is 2 fifths or 10 fifths; and so on.

Analysis of a large number of existing melodies showed that successive fifth spans tended to be less than 6 fifths. Fifth spans larger than this were rare. Any large fifth spans that did occur were not found in adjacent intervals. These observations suggested that such constraints may provide listeners with information about the key of the melody: Each interval will suggest a range of likely keynotes, for which the fifth span of the interval is less than 6. Each interval will also suggest a range of unlikely keynotes, for which the fifth span of the interval is greater than 6. In this way, if the listener looks at the melody in terms of this progression of fifths, then the keynote will appear as an orienting influence amidst the dancing note patterns.

This type of information might be especially useful when other indicators of key (e.g., harmony) are ambiguous or absent. The potential effectiveness of this information was demonstrated with a computer program that operated with these constraints: It was able to establish the key of a range of existing melodies given only information about the succession of note frequencies. There was one additional constraint that this program needed to take into account, and this concerned the interpretation of ascending semitones that end on notes between 2 and 5 fifths above the keynote. According to these constraints, such an interval would be considered unlikely—having a fifth span, or delta q, of 7—and should encourage the listener to perceive modulation to a key consistent with the smaller value of delta q, that is, 5. However, these intervals appear to be special cases and fulfill an ornamental role that is not designed to change the key. To accommodate this, the q value of the initial note is here adjusted to a value 5 fifths above the second note. Therefore, the adjusted fifth span is 5 and so is consistent with the original key.

Intervals having a fifth span of 5 or less are traditionally called "diatonic" intervals, whereas those with a fifth span greater than 5 are called "non-diatonic" (Longuet-Higgins, 1976). Nevertheless, it should be noted that these constraints do not restrict the melody to any particular diatonic scale, not even at a local level. This is because adjacent diatonic intervals (with a low fifth span, or delta q of less than 6) need not be compatible with the same diatonic scale. It is possible, in principle at least, for these delta q restrictions to indicate any one of the 12 keynotes, regardless of the diatonic scale of the melody, although, in Western music, the keynote is also a member of the scale (Helmholtz, 1885/1954).

The reasons for the pervasiveness of diatonic scales have been widely debated (see Burns and Ward, 1982). One line of reasoning is based on the fact that the sounds used in music are made up of frequency components that are members of harmonic series, which, as we have seen, form basic units or templates in the perceptual assessment of pitch. But authors such as Helmholtz (1885/1954) and Jeans (1937/1968) see the mathematical properties of such series as having much wider implications. They emphasise the importance of simultaneously sounded harmonic series in the development of music and point out that there will be a certain amount of overlap between the lower harmonics for small whole-number ratios of fundamental frequencies. For example, in the octave interval, the frequency ratio of the fundamentals is 2:1, so that every even numbered overtone of the lower series will correspond to the fundamental or an overtone of the higher series. Similarly for the 3:2 ratio of the fifth, there will be a correspondence for every third component of the lower series with every second component of the higher. The idea of consonance is related to the extent of this overlap, and the argument is that the diatonic scale arose in order to maximise the number of consonant note pairs, thereby facilitating harmony. A related idea is that overlaps between subharmonics of the note frequencies are responsible. These are components at $f/2$, $f/3$, $f/4$, and so on; so again, two notes whose frequencies form a simple whole-number ratio will have a number of subharmonics in common. Terhardt (1977, 1978) and van Noorden (1982) speculate about different perceptual processes that might give rise to such subharmonics. These simple-ratio ideas apparently stumble on the fact that the 2:1 ratio of the octave is incommensurable with other simple ratios (notably the 3:2 ratio of the fifth) so that the pervasive equal temperament tuning system lacks simple-ratio intervals. More recently, psychoacousticians have pointed out that the frequency-resolving power of the ear is limited, so that a slight mistuning preserves differences between psychoacoustically consonant and dissonant note pairs. These differences serve to distinguish the diatonic scale of the equal temperament system (Kameoka and Kuriyagawa, 1969; Plomp, 1976; Terhardt, 1977, 1978). In other words, the scale is simply a best fit to a system based on small whole-number ratios (von Hoerner, 1974, 1976).

Jackendoff (1977) rejects these ideas. He states that, "tonality is not simply man's reaction to the physical facts about sound . . . tonality in music provides evidence for a cognitive organisation with a logic all its own" (p. 890). Subsequently, Lerdahl and Jackendoff (1977) and Jackendoff and Lerdahl (1982) showed the elements of a structural description of music more closely akin to a linguistic theory. Here the notions of diatonic scale, key, and mode are seen as idiomatic examples of preference rules that "ascertain the most stable structure (the tonic) . . . and the hierarchy of relative stability in relation to the most stable structure" (Lerdahl and Jackendoff, 1977, p. 130). A related formalism (Deutsch and Feroe, 1981) is similar in that tonal constraints are treated as specific examples of more general concepts, that is, as a hierarchy of overlearned alphabets (e.g., diatonic scale, chromatic scale) with certain proximal relationships operating at the different levels. An example of the latter is a restriction on the semitone span of intervals to facilitate certain types of perceptual grouping, a proximal relationship operating at the chromatic level. One further example might be the fifth-span restrictions of Longuet-Higgins (1976) simultaneously operating at some other level. An advantage of this type of analysis is that it provides a theoretical framework for describing quite diverse tonal idioms.

Other authors (Dowling, 1978; Krumhansl and Shepard, 1979) seek to explain scale in terms of cognitive-psychological constraints on information-processing capacity. These authors point out that the number of scale notes (seven) corresponds to limitations found in some other information-processing tasks, for example, absolute judgment tasks using unidimensional continua. However, Miller (1956), who originally pointed to these correspondences, was less certain that they reflected such a basic limitation, because the tasks involve a diversity of cognitive processes. Also, this view requires that the notes within an octave constitute a unidimensional continuum; whereas the results reported by Krumhansl and Shepard (1979) show that more than one dimension is perceived. It is worth restating Miller's (1956) conclusions at this point.

> What about the seven wonders of the world, the seven seas, the seven deadly sins, the seven daughters of Atlas in Pleiades, the seven ages of man, the seven levels of hell, the seven primary colours, the seven notes of the musical scale, and the seven days of the week? . . . Perhaps there is something deep and profound behind all these sevens, something just calling out for us to discover it. But I suspect that it is only a pernicious, Pythagorean coincidence. (p. 95)

One attractive aspect of the simple-ratio approach remains: It explains the pervasiveness of the diatonic scale. However, Balzano (1980, 1982) has recently attempted to account for the prevalence of diatonic scales independently of the simple ratio ideas. He points out that the system of scales and keys used in Western music has unique properties when viewed in terms of Group Theory: The fifth and the semitone are the only single intervals that will generate the 12 chromatic-scale notes. The only other generator is a combination of major and minor thirds, and this leads to a two-dimensional space with the tonic notes of the major and minor modes centrally placed among the tightly grouped notes of the major and minor triads. The diatonic scale contains at least one example of every interval. The number of ways that an interval may be formed by taking different note pairs is unique to that interval. Thus, in the scale of C major, the tritone may be formed once (B to F), the semitone twice (B to C and E to F), and so on. In fact, the number of intervals that may be formed in this way is equal to 7 minus the delta q value of the interval. Diatonic scales are also coherent, meaning that the size of an interval measured in scale steps is a monotonically increasing function of the semitone span of the interval. Finally, the number of notes that two major scales have in common is the fifth span of the interval between their tonic notes, and transposition to an adjacent scale results in a minimal change (one semitone) of just one member of the set. Other divisions of the octave will have these properties (e.g., a system based on 20 divisions) but the 12-fold scale is the only one that also provides a good fit to a simple ratio type of system.

The perceptual implications of such group structure are probably best understood in terms of ideas such as Shepard's (1981) psychophysical complementarity, meaning that these environmental constraints, if useful, should somehow be represented internally. The demonstration of this structure and its usefulness are an essential step in such an approach. In addition, some demonstration that this structure is in fact engaged in perception and a description of how this is done are also necessary for a satisfactory understanding of perception. The description of tonality used in our work has much in common with these ideas. However, the fifth-span constraints of Longuet-Higgins (1976) go further in that they provide an explicit account of how such Group Structure might be communicated to the listener.

There have been experiments that indicate that the diatonic scale is important in perception: The multidimensional scaling experiments of Krumhansl and Shepard (1979) and Krumhansl (1979) show that the diatonic notes form a group based on perceptual similarity as long as a suitable musical context is provided. Krumhansl (1979) also demonstrated that the initial note of melodies based on diatonic notes was more easily recognised than that of non-diatonic melodies. In a melody discrimination study, Dowling (1978) found that exact transpositions of two different melodies were perceptually confused if they were based on a common scale.

There have also been some studies of how the constraints of key might relate to perception. Bartlett and Dowling (1980) have shown that transpositions of two different melodies tend to be confused if their keynotes are closely related, although a similar effect reported by Cuddy, Cohen, and Miller (1979) depended upon the nature of the melodies and the differences between them. Here, key proximity is measured by the separation of the keynotes along the circle of fifths (Balzano, 1980).

Perceptual Grouping

According to Kubovy and Pomerantz (1981), perceptual organisation has previously been taken as synonymous with Gestalt psychology. However, this influential approach was not originally elaborated beyond classification and description. It remains for the experimental psychologist to use these writings to guide them in the direction of useful research.

Gestalt principles of perceptual organisation have been applied to both auditory and visual events, although the original expositions of their rules or organisational principles were almost always demonstrated with visual examples. The Gestalt psychologists believe that objects or scenes are organised in terms of general grouping principles that provide the simplest or most economical fit to the sensory pattern. However, there are problems with this approach (see Hochberg, 1981). A major concern is the need to attach a measure of simplicity to an overall unit. That is, in attempting to predict the appearance of the environment, one must somehow decide on the relative salience of various wholes in their determination of the appearance of the parts. Furthermore, there are certain (visual) examples where local properties of the figure appear to determine what one sees, in that changes in the fixation point change its appearance. Finally, Hochberg argues that there never was a satisfactory explanation for the figure–ground distinction nor for the laws of organisation themselves. He proposes a view closer to that of Helmholtz (1885/1954) and others, who see perceptual groupings as reflecting ecological likelihood rather than simplicity.

Nevertheless, the ideas of the Gestalt psychologists have influenced many recent writings on auditory perception. For example, Julesz and Hirsh (1972) discuss how the Gestalt principles of organisation might prove useful in drawing analogies between sound and visual-form perception and how these principles might suitably be translated; they suggest that some rules are more suited to translation than others. Principles of proximity, similarity, and good continuation can be applied in both domains, whereas closedness and symmetry are seen as more problematic. Similarly, Moore (1982) discusses how Gestalt principles might usefully be applied in audition, but only to the extent that a grouping of events reflects some common source of origin in the environment. Gestalt ideas also have provided the general framework for a large body of recent experimental work, especially experiments on the perception of tone sequences.

Divenyi and Hirsh (1978) compared the perceptual characteristics of visual patterns and melodic fragments, maintaining that tone sequences possess three of the properties of visual figures; namely, translation, distortion, and figure–ground relationships. In other experiments, Divenyi and Hirsh (1974, 1975) drew upon the principle of good continuation to account for the superior identification of unidirectional pitch changes. In a study by Balch (1981), listeners were asked to judge the degree of good continuation they perceived in a tone sequence. The judgments were influenced by perceived symmetry, with listeners preferring the more symmetrical sequences.

An auditory equivalent of closure or closedness has also been demonstrated (Dannenbring, 1976). An alternation of tones and gaps is heard to be continuous if suitable noise bursts are inserted in the gaps. It is as though the auditory system fills in the gaps with a suitable tone. Furthermore, suitable filling in also occurs if the tonal segments are part of a longer frequency glide, so that illusory glides are heard in the gaps. The closure idea accounts for this by attributing the physical absence of the tones to masking by the louder noise. A different use of the term "closure" is offered by Meyer (1973) in the context of music. Here, it refers to arrival at a point of relative stability (for example, in a cadence), and this can be articulated via rhythm or melody.

Some form of principle of proximity appears to operate in rapidly presented tone sequences. Listeners report a perceptual separation of tones into groups having a similar pitch range. Various examples of this phenomenon have been reported, (e.g., Miller and Heise, 1950; van Noorden, 1975). Bregman and Campbell (1971) showed that this sort of grouping is associated with distortions in judgments of temporal order, and called the phenomenon "primary auditory stream segregation" (PASS). Deutsch (1978a) reports that pitch identification is better if the intervening distractor tones are proximally related by pitch, and Dowling (1973) demonstrates how the interleaving of voices, together with a fast tempo, can lead to the illusory perception of two instruments when both melodies are played by one. The speed of the tone sequence is an important influence on this type of grouping: Van Noorden (1975) has shown that rate of presentation interacts with the size of frequency differences in two-tone sequences. As rate decreases, a sequence with large frequency separations between the tones is likely to be perceived as a single coherent group, but at faster rates, the sequence perceptually separates into a number of pitch groups. One might suppose that such grouping reflects environmental likelihood, for example, when allocating notes to singers (bass, contralto, etc.), although such organisations seem to be engaged regardless of the type of events being perceived, since they are an intrinsic property of all tone sequences.

Bregman (1981) points out that these principles of grouping can be applied to both auditory and visual events (see Bregman and Achim, 1973). They may override physical proximities and form organised groups or auditory streams on the basis of homogeneous features. This position is close to the traditional Gestalt view; Bregman sees his aim as describing "the role of smaller perceptual phenomena in the larger process of perceiving and understanding a natural environment" (p. 117). Two possible explanations for the observed phenomena are proposed. The first regards segregation as the breakdown of a mechanism that normally follows the order of a sequence. However, it was demonstrated that a pair of tones of fixed frequency separation and rate of presentation could be heard in the same or in different streams, and this depended entirely on the nature of the context of temporally adjoining tones. The alternative view is that segregation is an achievement of perception that allows the listener to untangle the complex of intermingled sounds, which constitute the auditory environment. The result is the formation of orderly and appropriate groupings of events. The sounds are organised using heuristic rules which capitalise on the common origin of certain features. In other words, streaming organises acoustic events into an auditory scene, which is simultaneously populated by various auditory objects. An ideal stream is formed from homogeneous features such as similar pitch height or timbre. But some latitude is necessary to select the most parsimonious guess about the environment. If a set of acoustic features do not possess sufficiently similar properties, then another stream must be formed. Therefore, stream membership is dependent on competition between alternative methods of grouping and not just the degree of frequency separation, for example.

These and other studies have provided considerable insight into the perception of auditory sequences. They demonstrate that tone sequences are not perceived as a series of separate events but are perceptually organised into forms variously described as single patterns, Gestalts, streams, or auditory figures. However, it should be emphasised that, because these are general grouping principles, we would expect them to operate with equal effectiveness in both melodic and non-melodic tone sequences.

Contour

Contour refers to an ordinal representation (Stevens, 1946) of the intervals of a melody, which indicates whether adjacent notes are higher or lower than one another (Jones, 1976). The melody "Three Blind Mice" would be reduced to the representation down, down, up, down, down. Dowling and Fujitani (1971) have shown that exact transpositions of slightly different novel melodies that share the same contour tend to sound like transpositions of the same melody. Other workers demonstrate that contour information can aid melody identification (Idson and Massaro, 1978; Kallman and Massaro, 1979; Massaro, Kallman, and Kelly, 1980) although this is limited by the fact that different melodies often share the same contour. It has been suggested that different aspects of the contour are important for the communication of structure in music (M. R. Jones, 1981; Rosner and Meyer, 1982) and that contour is an important component in our memory for music (Dowling, 1978). There is also much discussion of melodic contour in terms of general perceptual notions, notably those of Gestalt psychology (e.g., Ortmann, 1926; Heise and Miller, 1951; Divenyi and Hirsh, 1974, 1978; Deutsch, 1978a, b), on the assumption that various visual and auditory contours are perceived in broadly similar ways.

Such a discussion of tone sequences as auditory figures requires some form of translation between the visual and auditory domains. This may be achieved by regarding the visual abscissa as auditory time and the visual ordinate as the pitch height of the note. This idea has intuitive appeal, especially in view of its similarity to the traditional method of music notation. Davies and Jennings

(1977) have shown that this intuitive appeal also extends to musically unsophisticated listeners who can make fairly accurate drawings of the contours of melodies they have just heard.

A theory governing the perceptual organisation of visual figures may therefore prove useful in the investigation of figural aspects of melody, such as melodic contour. A basic question appropriate to both modalities concerns the identification of perceptual characteristics important for the recognition of a figure. One view of the theory of visual pattern recognition is that it should be able to specify distinctive attributes or features (Ward and Wexler, 1976). Some workers have attempted to identify those properties of features contributing to their selection. If features enhance perceptually important differences between environmental events, then feature extraction makes for economical information processing (Howard and Ballas, 1981). The important features may therefore differ from task to task, which means that the perceiver must select and employ the most efficient perceptual strategy. However, Howard and Ballas do not provide general guidelines for identifying the important features in a given situation. Attneave (1954) attempted to do this by using Gestalt principles of organisation and putting them into the more quantitative framework of information theory. The points of information value are said to be the angles or points of intersection, and these are thought to provide the most economical description of a figure. When subjects are required to represent figures with a series of dots, these tend to be placed at changes in direction. Common objects are represented quite well by points at these contour reversals.

Applications of information theory in this area are problematic (Green and Courtis, 1966). One difficulty lies in objectively defining the elements of the figure to which the informational values are attached. Nevertheless, a study by Baker and Loeb (1973) provides some support for the importance of corners in visual perception. They made recordings of eye movements and found that their observers fixated for longer periods on corners of patterns than other parts. These parts of the figure were also rated as most important for the purposes of identification.

In investigating the figural properties of melody, it is appropriate to make comparisons between visual and auditory contours. Findings from visual-form perception suggest that some elements of the overall contour may be more salient than others. A useful approach would be to break down contour into a series of elements or components. Here, we can circumvent the problem of defining elements by referring to visual work. Thus, we divide melodic contour into reversals in pitch (auditory corners) and non-reversals.

These features of melodic contour have not received a great deal of attention by researchers: Most of the work has looked at the contribution of the overall contour to melody recognition. Some exceptions are the observations of Ortmann (1926) and the experimental work of Thomassen (1982). Ortmann discusses absolute and relative factors that determine the salience of notes in a melody, with highest and lowest tones included among the absolute factors. Their salience is attributed to the absence of notes beyond the extremes, so that they take on the character of *first* and *last*. This salience also was extended to local pitch extremes, that is, contour reversals or corners.

Thomassen (1982) provides a more experimental approach to this issue in looking at the factors responsible for melodic accentuation. This is defined as the prominence given by the succession of frequency intervals of the tone sequence. In three- or four-note motifs, the accent comes on the note following a frequency change. In cases where a further change in frequency in the opposite direction occurs, the accent falls on a corner. Two intervals moving in the same direction (non-reversals) are equally accented, whereas the first of two intervals in opposite directions receives the strongest accentuation.

These results have been taken as representative of the perceptual consequences of pitch vicissitudes. For example, Thomassen (1982) draws comparisons between melody and the pitch contour of speech. Changes in the fundamental frequency of the voice (f_0) provides this pitch contour, or intonation pattern. Aspects of these fluctuations have been shown to be powerful cues for accent perception in Dutch speech (Cohen and t'Hart, 1967). Similar work in English has looked at cues to the location of stressed syllables. Various workers have demonstrated that pitch is a sufficient cue for the perception of stress (Bolinger, 1958; Fry, 1958; Lieberman, 1960; Morton and Jassem, 1965; Fourcin et al., 1979; Faure, Hirst, and Chafcouloff, 1980). Given the use of these changes in speech, Thomassen argues there is no reason they should be less effective in music.

The way intonation is used to convey this type of information meets differences of opinion (see Lehiste, 1970). The debate centres on whether it is the pitch level or pitch contour that is important. Thomassen (1982) might side with the pitch contour proponents as his results suggest that pitch movement is a salient factor. Within this school of thought, linguists tend to agree that changes in the direction of pitch are functionally important. Pitch prominence has been associated with sharp points or corners in the pitch contour and these are heard as stressed (Bolinger, 1958; Cooper, Soares, Ham, and Damon, 1983; O'Connor and Arnold, 1961). It also has been shown that the boundary between main and embedded clauses is often characterised by a fall-rise pitch movement (Cooper and Sorenson, 1977). So in speech, as in visual figures, the corners of the contour seem to be perceptually important. Some workers have attributed a differential salience to the downward and upward *pointing* corners of the pitch contour (Bolinger, 1958). These and other studies demonstrate the function of changes in the fundamental frequency contour of speech. The changes appear to direct attention to perceptually important or more informative parts of the sentence.

Comparisons such as these may be used to explore general principles of perceptual organisation. These observations imply that certain perceptual properties of the tone sequences which occur in music may be shared by a wide variety of sounds (and perhaps also by certain visual figures). These common properties are presumably the result of perceptual operations which proceed regardless of whether the sound fits in with our expectations or schemata.

THE SYNTHESIS OF MELODY APPROXIMATIONS

Having formalised the results of our rudimentary analysis, it is now possible to enter the resynthesis stage of the procedure. To this end, a range of tone sequences was generated by using a random-number selector in conjunction with probability weightings. In this way, it was possible to synthesise large numbers of novel tone sequences in which certain notes and intervals could be made more likely than others. These weightings were chosen to emphasise likely occurrences in real melodies (as described in the preceding sections) or unlikely occurrences (for the control sequences). These techniques were pioneered by Hiller and Isaacson (1959), whose machines were able to construct entirely original pieces, notably the "Illiac Suite." However, since the work of Xenakis (1971) the trend in this area has been toward the use of the computer as a composer's aid, rather than as a substitute for human creativity. Subsequent developments are described by Lorrain (1980), Hiller (1981), and K. Jones (1981).

The first step in our procedure was to select a keynote at random from the range C = 261.6 Hz plus or minus five semitones. This note was used as the initial and final note of the sequence. The remaining notes were selected from a two-octave range around the keynote according to different types of probability weightings that reflected combinations of different types of constraint (henceforward referred to as factors). Each factor has two values: a melodic form and a less melodic or control form.

Scale

As discussed previously, it is common for the melodies of Western tonal music to be based on scales that are subsets of the 12-note chromatic scale. Here, we will be concerned with the 7-note diatonic scale, the pervasiveness of which is widely acknowledged (e.g., Helmholtz, 1885/1956; Jeans, 1937/1968; von Hoerner, 1974, 1976; Plomp, 1976; Bernstein, 1976; Terhardt, 1977, 1978; Dowling, 1978; Balzano, 1980, 1982a, b).

When the scale factor is in its melodic form the seven q values of the diatonic major scale (-1 through $+5$) are more likely to occur. When this factor is in its control form, a control scale was emphasised, based on the semitone subdivisions of an octave: 2, 2, 1, 2, 1, 2, 1, 1.

These eight notes were reduced to seven by exclusion of the keynote; this control is comparable to the melodic form, having notes fairly evenly spread over the octave. The crucial difference is that there is no one diatonic scale that encompasses these notes, because the notes are well scattered over the cycle of fifths (Balzano, 1980, 1982a). They have the following q values: -4, -2, -1, 1, 2, 4, 5.

Key and Fifth Span of Intervals

To clarify the key of a melody, the constraints described by Longuet-Higgins (1976, 1978) were implemented. These refer to the intervals of a melody described by the separation of their notes around a progression of fifths, that is, the fifth span of the interval. (The translation of notes represented as semitones from the keynote to a representation as fifths from the keynote has been described previously.) This may be calculated by finding the number of fifths from the keynote for each of its notes, then subtracting these values and taking the absolute value of the result. The melodic form of the key factor makes intervals having a fifth span of less than six more likely than others. For the control form, these probability weightings are reversed. It is also necessary to implement two rules. First, intervals having a fifth span greater than five must not occur in adjacent intervals. Second, the perception of continuous modulation associated with certain sequences of ascending semitones must be avoided. If the second note of such an interval is 2, 3, 4, or 5 fifths from the keynote, then the first note of the interval is considered to be 7, 8, 9, or 10 fifths from the keynote, respectively. The control forms of these rules constrain the sequence to the same degree, but the values of fifths from the keynote are incorrect and not correlated with the true values. In this way, systematic differences in pattern uncertainty between the two values of the factor are avoided.

Semitone Span of Intervals

The rationale for this factor is not concerned with tonality but derives from work on perceptual grouping as described previously. When this factor is positive, the probability of intervals greater than five semitones is made less probable than those of five semitones or less (vice versa for the control form).

Probability Weightings

The probability weightings reflect combinations of the factors so that it is possible to produce a tone sequence that is constrained in three ways simultaneously. This was done by computing the tone sequence note by note (left to right) so that, at each stage, there is a particular current note and a range of 25 possible next notes (i.e., the two-octave range around the keynote). To determine the probability of any one note, all three constraints must be considered. Two of the constraints govern interval sizes, so the previous note affects the probability of the next. For each note of the melody, the probabilities of all possible next notes are calculated. This is done by cross-multiplying three numbers that represent the probability of the note with respect to scale, the interval with respect to its fifth span, and the interval with respect to its semitone span. Having performed this calculation for all possible next notes, the random-number selector picks the next note with the appropriate biases. This note is appended to the sequence unless it violates the rules associated with the key factor or if it is simply a repetition of the previous note. Such failures require the random-number selector to try again. In this way, numerous examples of eight different types of melody can be synthesised (i.e., from the combination of three factors with each in either their melodic or control form).

The resulting melodies that emerge incorporate numerous instances of events likely in a real Western melody. For example, when the keynote equals C, then the intervals B to C and F♯ to G are given a relatively high probability, but only if all factors are in their melodic form. These particular events are specifically referred to by Cuddy et. al. (1979), who call them tonal rules, that is, leading note to tonic root and dominant leading note to dominant root, respectively.

The probability distributions governing the selection of the next note allow us to measure the pattern uncertainty of the resulting sequences: According to Watson and Kelly (1981) this may be defined as "the size of the set of patterns from which samples are drawn" (p. 45). A closely related measure is redundancy as defined in information theory (Attneave, 1959); if the patterns are derived from a relatively small set, then their redundancy is high, and vice versa. The index used here is the mean redundancy per note, which is low if the probabilities are evenly divided among all 25 alternatives but increases as these probabilities become unevenly spread. Thus, our index calculated for the different types of sequence measures the degree of constraint per se, regardless of the particular form of the constraint. The results show that there are no reliable differences between the redundancy indices for all combinations of factor values, so we can be reasonably sure that any observed perceptual differences cannot be attributed to differences in pattern uncertainty.

Redundancy

This factor was designed to check whether redundancy differences affected performance in our perceptual tasks and to emphasise the influence of the key factor. When the redundancy factor is applied, the mean redundancy per note is increased by approximately 8%. This was done by taking the cube of the appropriate fifth-span weightings, which emphasise the differences between the higher and lower probabilities, resulting in a reduction of the overall pattern uncertainty.

MELODIOUS SCALING

Although constraints may be involved in the production of melodies, they may not be sufficient to synthesise a plausible melody. There is, clearly, much more to melodies than has been discussed here; one glaring omission is rhythm and its possible interactions with the constraints described. So, although our experimental melodies may contain many events likely in a real melody, they may not be heard as such, and our perceptual tests become meaningless. That is, if the listeners' musical knowledge is not adequately engaged by our melodic sequences, then we cannot expect them to take advantage of this knowledge in their perceptual processing, and no superiority will be observed. We need to check whether different combinations of the factors generate different degrees of approximation to real melodies.

Paired Comparisons Scaling of Melodies

A psychophysical scaling procedure was used by observers to indicate the relative melodiousness of different types of tone sequence. This attribute label was chosen because it was found that listeners readily understand this term as indicating the degree of similarity to musical melody. Unfortunately, there is no way of establishing, on a priori grounds, whether there are differences between the listeners in their interpretation of this term. However, the method and analysis technique give a clear indication of the degree of consensus, and disentangle systematic effects from individual idiosyncrasies.

Each tone sequence was 21 notes long, played at an even tempo of four notes per second. The set of sequence types comprised the eight possible trios of factor values together with a short melody from Bach (the king's theme from *A Musical Offering*, with all notes given the same duration) and a random type of sequence. The latter were produced by randomly selecting notes from a two-octave range in which all notes were equally probable. Each member of this set of 10 was paired with every other member and comparisons were made between successively presented sequences in both orders. Each of the 20 listeners was asked which member of each pair was the more melodious. Thus, each listener made 90 such judgments. The data were analysed according to Thurstone's method of paired comparisons (see d'Amato, 1970), whereby the scale score is the overall probability of a sequence type being judged the more melodious.

With the exception of the Bach piece, no sequence was used more than once:

Whenever possible, a new melody was generated, so that any one factor combination was represented by a large number of examples. Furthermore, no two listeners heard the same melodies or ordering of the trial types. Thus, variables such as contour, overall note range, absolute note values, and so on were completely randomised, and their contribution to any systematic effects may be discounted. Similarly, problems associated with the selection of possibly idiosyncratic melodies were avoided.

Results of Melodious Scaling

The mean scale scores extended from Z values of approximately $+1.0$ for the Bach melody down to Z values of approximately -1.0 for the random notes. Thus, the Bach piece was consistently judged to be the best melody. The remaining eight experimental melody types obtained values extending over this range. The most melodious occurred when all the factors were in their melodic form; here, the scale score approached that for the Bach. The factor combination judged least melodious was that in which all three factors were in their control form.

The results showed that the melodic value of each factor always produced more melodious types of melody with the exception of the key factor, for which the superiority was clearer when the scale factor was also in its melodic form. This pattern of results indicates a close perceptual relationship between scale and key with tonal factors appearing to operate independently of the non-tonal melody variable that governs the semitone span of the intervals.

We may, therefore, reject the hypothesis of no perceptual differences over and above pattern uncertainty. Furthermore, intersubject differences in the use of the attribute label appear to be small. If these were a serious problem, there would be no systematic differences between the scale scores for the different factors, all of which would approach zero.

Melodiousness and Redundancy

The results of the scaling experiment cannot be explained in terms of pattern uncertainty. This raises the question of whether any effect of this variable can be demonstrated with this paradigm. Therefore, in this experiment, melodious scales were obtained for sequences varying in pattern uncertainty, scale, and key factors. The pattern uncertainty of sequences was decreased by taking the cube of the probabilities associated with the key factor. This raised the mean redundancy per note by approximately 8%. The paired comparisons set comprised the Bach and random sequences as before, together with the eight possible trios of redundancy, scale, and key. All sequences were synthesised with a bias towards melodic (low) semitone spans. Other aspects were as described previously.

Once again, the melodies generated by the melodic values of the scale and key factors were judged the most melodious, with the effect of the key factor clearest when the scale-factor was in its melodic form. Increasing the pattern uncertainty of the sequences produced a marked effect on the melodious scores; that is, a sharp reduction in melodiousness for the more redundant sequences. Again, the factors based on tonality are perceptually related but seem to operate independently of the non-tonal factor, pattern uncertainty. Notice that reduction of the latter reduces melodiousness. This may mean that perceived melodiousness is not a simple index of the listener's ability to perceptually organise a tone sequence. A simple (highly redundant) tone sequence will be easy to organise perceptually and to remember (Watson and Kelly, 1981), but a melodious melody should not be too predictable. Although our melodiousness scales might provide some indication of what Attneave (1981) calls goodness of fit to schemata of familiar events, they do not give an accurate view of other intrinsic stimulus properties that aid perceptual organisation.

These two experiments have shown that it is possible to synthesise degrees of approximation to real melodies from a formal representation of the rather general constraints described. We are now in a position to investigate the extent to which the closer approximations to melody are easier to organise and remember.

RECOGNITION MEMORY

Well-known melodies such as nursery rhymes or folk tunes are readily named by unsophisticated listeners. This is, therefore, an example of a musical skill that requires no formal musical training. The following experiments attempt to capture this ability, using the novel melody approximations previously described. Because our listeners were not musically sophisticated, the test had to obviate the need for transcription skills. Our solution was to use an adapted form of Dowling and Fujitani's (1971) melody discrimination paradigm: Listeners were presented a pair of melodies and asked to judge whether the second was an exact transposition of the first or whether it was an exact transposition of a slightly different melody.

Each melody of the pair was 14 notes long and was presented at an even tempo of 4 notes per second. The transposition factor was randomly selected from trial to trial, being between three and five semitones up or down. When novel melodies appeared on each trial, this task is extremely difficult even for musically sophisticated listeners. Indeed, Dowling and Fujitani (1971) found this to be the case for their relatively short 5-note sequences. However, we have found that performance levels improve considerably if the first melody of the pair is held constant over a series of trials, allowing the listener to become familiar with, or to learn, the melody. In these experiments, 12 successive trials contained the same initial melody, and immediate feedback was provided for the listener after his or her response to a pair of melodies.

Care must be exercised in generating the different-melodies; if the differences are too gross then little musical skill will be engaged by the task. An example of such a difference concerns the contour of the melody as described previously: Knowledge of the size of the intervals is unnecessary for discrimination between contours but is crucial for understanding the tonality of the piece. In these experiments, the different-melodies preserve the contour of the original.

An additional problem concerns the distinction between perceptual sensitivity and the decisions made on the basis of perceptual information. Workers in the area of signal detection have shown that it is possible to influence the decision-making aspects of discrimination independently of the listener's sensitivity to differences. The danger here is that the degree of perceived melodiousness may bias decision making, so we want to be sure that such biases do not influence our assessment of recognition performance. To this end, non-parametric assessments of the areas under the receiver operating characteristics were calculated for each listener, giving the discrimination index $p(A)$, which runs from 0.5 at chance level up to a perfect score of 1.0 and is insensitive to any changes in the decision biases of the listener. An arcsin transform of these values preceded further data reduction. The reader is referred to McNicol (1972) for an explanation of these and other aspects of the theory of signal detection.

The experiments asked whether the different factors affect performance in such a task and how these results relate to the melodiousness judgments.

Scale and Key

In this section, we pay particular attention to the role of the tonal factors, that is, scale and key.

The first melody of a pair was synthesised from one of the four combinations of the scale and key factor values, whereas the semitone span of intervals was biased towards the lower values throughout. The melodies were generated by randomly selecting and altering between 3 and 6 notes, making sure that the contour of the first melody was preserved. The initial and final notes were excluded from this selection as were changes of adjacent notes and changes at contour reversals. We hoped that these precautions would encourage the listener to pay close attention to the tonal relationships of both melodies. Other aspects of melody synthesis were as previously described.

Results for Scale and Key

The results show that the melodic form of one of the tonal factors—scale— gives rise to melodies that are reliably easier to discriminate than control-scale melodies. However, there was no difference between the discrimination indices for the melodic and control forms of the key factor. Once again, this indicates a difference between the variables important for the melodiousness judgment and those influencing recognition memory; melodies that are judged to be more melodious (i.e., those generated using the melodic form of the key factor) are not necessarily easier to remember. This would appear to reflect a difference in the perceptual processes involved in the two tasks: A melodiousness judgment requires the listeners to indicate only degree of similarity. But for optimal use of tonal constraints in the recognition memory task, listeners must perceptually understand the reasons for the similarity. Alternatively, it might be argued that the fifth-span constraint (key) is inherently less restrictive than the scale constraint because, in our formalisation, there are more opportunities for a melody to go off scale than there are to go off key. In either case, one would expect an enhancement of any key effect using simpler (more redundant) melodies in which the fifth-span constraints are made more restrictive. Therefore, the following experiment was performed.

Key and Redundancy

In this section, we examine the effect of implementing the redundancy factor, which emphasises the contrast between higher and lower fifth-span probabilities and increases the mean redundancy per note by approximately 8%. If recognition memory is dictated by the melodiousness of the sequences, then the less melodious (more redundant) melodies should be more difficult to remember. This would seem to be an unlikely outcome for two reasons: (1) Many studies have shown that decreases in pattern uncertainty give rise to improvements in perception and memory (e.g., Watson and Kelly, 1981); and (2) the results of the previous experiment indicate qualitative differences between melodiousness judgments and recognition memory. It is suggested that increases in redundancy are more likely to lead to an overall improvement in recognition memory. Also, increasing redundancy in this way might improve recognition memory for the melodic form of the key factor because of the greater emphasis of the fifth-span constraints.

The four combinations of the redundancy and key factor values controlled the synthesis of different melody types, and the listeners learned three of each type. The key and semitone span constraints were in their melodic forms throughout; other aspects were identical to those described for the previous experiment.

Results for Key and Redundancy

We found a reliable discrimination advantage for melodies generated from the melodic form of the key constraint but no differences in performance on the more and less redundant melodies. The pattern of results indicates that the differences found for the key factor when the melodies are more redundant are the clearest. However, other aspects of the analysis indicate that the corresponding differences for the less melodious melodies are not qualitatively different.

We conclude that the key factor does give rise to melodies that are easier to learn and recognise–remember in the context of simpler (more redundant) melodies. Again, we see a pattern of results that indicates differences between melodiousness judgments and recognition performance. Pattern uncertainty variations of the magnitude used here have little or no overall effect on recognition memory performance. This is not necessarily inconsistent with the results of other researchers; larger increases in the mean redundancy per note would almost certainly generate highly memorable tone sequences (e.g., repetition of the same interval in the extreme).

Conclusions

The experiments described so far have demonstrated that a handful of general constraints are sufficient for the synthesis of varying degrees of perceptual approximation to melody. To a certain extent, the closer approximations can be said to make more sense to our listeners in that they are easier to remember in the recognition memory paradigm. However, this relationship is subtle for two main reasons: (1) There appears to be a disparity between the ability to perceive the melodiousness generated by the fifth-span constraint and the ability to use this constraint to improve recognition memory. This may be because the key constraint is inherently less restrictive than scale; and (2) the simpler, more redundant sequences are not particularly melodious, but this does not make them more difficult to recognise.

Nevertheless, the two tonal constraints governing the occurrence of scale notes and the fifth span of intervals and clarifying the key and mode of the melody give rise to demonstrable recognition memory advantages. Furthermore, these constraints are specifically musical in their origins.

The results of the experiments reported here support the view that the perception of melody involves perceptual knowledge that is quite specific to music. The alternative is an account of melody perception in terms of simpler component processes governed by general perceptual principles. If such an analysis were entirely correct, then our control melodies, being of equal complexity, should be equally easy to learn and discriminate, but they are not. These results do not deny a role for such processes in the perception of melodies; indeed, recent general theory of perceptual organisation, such as that of Attneave (1981) embraces various organisational strategies. The tonal constraints described here are therefore seen as improving the goodness of fit to melody schemata, hence, the perceptual advantages.

TUNING AND MISTUNING

In this section, we are concerned with the effects that mistuning has on the discrimination of melodies, that is, where the note frequencies are based on equal temperament values or where these note frequencies are either expanded or contracted. Physical discrepancies between melody pairs are a linear function of the size of the semitone, but as we have seen, any perceptual effects are more likely to depend upon note relationships and the way in which these are perceived. Three organisational factors are considered: melodic contour, scale, and key. All three influence melody discrimination in some way, and the present aim is to discover the fate of these factors when melodies are mistuned.

Mistuning

There have been some previous studies on the effects of distorting the absolute sizes of the intervals of a melody: Werner (1940) reduced the semitone to 16.5% of its usual size and reported that the resulting melodies seemed to take on the perceptual characteristics of undistorted melodies. This happened only after a good deal of familiarisation with the novel tuning. Other authors report a dramatic reduction in melody-identification performance when melodies are mistuned (Idson and Massaro, 1978; Moore and Rosen, 1979; White, 1960). Moore and Rosen reported that listeners found that the mistuned melodies became almost acceptable as music, and all three studies showed that, despite the reduction in performance, the mistuned intervals did seem to be conveying some information. Idson and Massaro were able to demonstrate that most of this information was simply the contour of the melody, but the results also showed some advantage for mistuning over other distortions that preserved contour but changed the relative sizes of the intervals. Is it possible that mistuning preserves some sense of scale and key as Werner suggested?

This conclusion is compatible with some views on the nature of scale: Theories that argue that scale can be understood in terms of general perceptual principles (e.g., Dowling, 1978; Krumhansl and Shepard, 1979) are not necessarily constrained by the tuning system adopted. Others (e.g., Deutsch and Feroe, 1981) who argue that scales are overlearned alphabets are not specific as to the nature of the learning process or the degree of plasticity, but one might expect some new learning to be possible. Werner's (1940) conclusions run contrary to theories of scale that have the frequency ratio of the octave as their cornerstone. These include the various versions of the simple-ratio hypothesis, that is, that tuning systems evolved to maximise sets of notes related by small whole-number frequency ratios. Other theories are constrained by an immutable octave but derive their explanations of scale independently of simple-ratio ideas (Balzano, 1980, 1982a).

Two theorists have considered tuning systems based on intervals smaller than a semitone. One is Balzano; the other, von Hoerner (1974, 1976), who based his work on simple-ratio formalism. Neither of their theories envisages that the new scale be a simple condensed version of the correctly tuned scale notes; quite different sets of notes are predicted to emerge in each case, and these depend upon the degree of semitone contraction. Both theories lead one to expect that a mistuned melody will encourage perception in terms of a more finely divided octave, and so the scale and key of the original should be destroyed. This prediction is supported by the findings of Idson and Massaro (1978), who were able to show that the perception of octave equivalence (chroma) does influence melody identification; when this is destroyed by mistuning, perception suffers.

However, the identification paradigm will only illuminate those factors that mediate the naming of particular melodies. Indeed, it might be argued that the key and scale of mistuned melodies are perfectly clear to the listener but that the novel tuning generates new music, which the listener does not relate to the names of conventional melodies. This interpretation remains tenable in the absence of information on the factors influencing the perception of mistuned melodies. The following experiments are designed to investigate some of these and to discover how their influence varies with the type of tuning.

The task employed is the melody discrimination paradigm previously described, so the listener is not required to name melodies. Three factors are of current interest. Two of them are the scale and key factors previously described. A third factor determines whether contour is changed within a pair of different melodies. The effects that these factors have in correctly tuned melodies have already been discussed. That is, both the scale and key factors give rise to melodies that are easier to remember when they are in their melodic forms. Also, contour differences between pairs of melodies aid discrimination in this type of task. How are these effects influenced by the type of tuning?

Listeners learned novel melodies and performed discriminations between similarly tuned melodies. If there was sufficient flexibility of the melody schemata as Werner (1940) suggested, then it would be possible that scale and key effects would emerge for mistuned melodies. Such a result would be compatible with the theoretical positions of Dowling (1978), Krumhansl and Shepard (1979), and Deutsch and Feroe (1981) as discussed previously. Theories based on the frequency ratio of the octave would therefore need to be revised. One other possibility is that the constraints used to clarify scale and key produce their effects by way of some non-musical artifact (e.g., by generating contours easier to learn or by generating smaller intervals). Mistuning would not be expected to disrupt such effects.

Because contour tends to be discussed in terms of general perceptual principles, it is expected that the discrimination advantage for different contour melodies should be found for all types of tuning. However, the literature is not unanimous on this point: Idson and Massaro (1976) raised the possibility that exaggerated contours, generated by expanding intervals, might be easier to perceive than those generated by smaller intervals (see also Ortmann, 1926). Also, the theoretical positions of Rosner and Meyer (1982) and M. R. Jones (1981) raise the possibility that melodic contours are perceived in a way that is fundamentally different from the way non-melodic contours are perceived. Examples of non-melodic contours include those generated by the fundamental-frequency vicissitudes of sounds such as speech and even machinery noise.

The results of two experiments are reported. The first examines the scale, contour, and tuning factors; the second looks at key, contour, and tuning.

Contour

When it is required that the second melody of a pair be different from the first, the following procedure is adopted: The first step is to define a region of permissible variation around each note of the first melody. In the simplest case, this has boundaries four semitones above and below the note. To keep both melodies within a two-octave range around the initial note, boundaries that lie outside this range are suitably contracted. Also, if a note in the first melody is above the keynote, then the boundaries for the corresponding note in the second melody must also be above the keynote, and vice versa. A new melody is then synthesised by selecting notes at random from each of these regions in turn. At each step, it is necessary to decide whether it is possible to change the contour of the original. If it is, then the regions are further restricted so that the contour of the original is either preserved or violated, depending upon the value of the contour factor, that is, contour-same or contour-different. For the former, a final check ensures that the resulting melody is, in fact, different from the first; for the latter, a check is made to ensure that there are some contour differences. The only other restrictions are that the initial and final notes remain the same as the keynote and that there be no successive repetitions. The second melody is then transposed as before.

Micro- and Macromelodies

In the equal temperament tuning system, there is a constant-frequency ratio relating the notes of adjacent semitones. This means that it is possible to define an integer for each note, which represents the number of semitone steps from some reference-note frequency as shown in Equation 1 above. If we wish to vary the frequency ratio of the semitone by a constant amount, then a scaling factor c may be introduced into the equation so that

(3) $$f/f_0 = 2^{cp/12},$$

where $c = 1.0$ for the usual equal temperament notes. If $c < 1.0$, then all semitones are contracted, giving *micromelodies*. Similarly, if $c > 1.0$, then *macromelodies* result. Here, the value of the reference note is defined as $f_0 = 261.6$ Hz (middle C).

The tuning factor has three values, where $c = 0.6$ (micro), $c = 1.0$ (12-tone equal temperament), and $c = 1.4$ (macro). To avoid confusion, the semitones of these tunings are referred to as "pitch units," and the number of 12-tone equal-temperament cents per pitch unit is simply the appropriate value of c multiplied by 100. The tuning factor is implemented after the melody approximations have been computed and has no effect on the method of computation.

Experiments

In one experiment, the key factor is held constant in its melodic form, whereas scale, contour, and tuning are varied. Three groups of 20 listeners each were given one type of tuning and learned melodies differing in scale, either with same or different contours for the pairs of different melodies. The other experiment was similar, except that scale was kept constant in its melodic form whereas key was either in its melodic form or its control form. In addition, the key factor was emphasised by increasing the difference between the probability weightings for more and less probable fifth-span intervals. As we have seen, the key factor needed to be emphasised to obtain discrimination advantages for the melodic form of the factor.

Findings

In the scale-with-contour experiment, discrimination scores were well above the chance level for all combinations of factor values but below the performance ceiling for all listeners. There was an overall superiority for different-contour trials over same-contour trials, and this did not vary with the tuning or the scale of the melodies. The data also show that the melodies based on a diatonic scale are much easier to learn and discriminate than their controls, but only when the melodies are correctly tuned to the equal-temperament values. This superiority is not found when the melodies are mistuned, as the effects of scale are negligible.

In the key-with-contour experiment, performance was again well above chance but below ceiling. Here again the contour effect appears as an overall superiority for different-contour over same-contour trials, and this effect does not vary with the key or tuning of the melodies. There is an overall superiority for equal temperament over both micro- and macrotunings. However, the tuning effect is more subtle because of an interaction between tuning and key. This shows up as a marked superiority for the discrimination of melodies based on a clear key over controls, but only when the melodies are correctly tuned. Mistuning destroys this superiority.

Conclusions

These experiments show that the discrimination of complex tone sequences is not solely governed by physical discrepancies between them (i.e., as measured by differences in note frequencies). Rather, the effects of mistuning depend on more subtle interactions with factors concerned with perceptual organisation. Contour differences between a pair of melodies, as well as the scale and key of the initial melody, have been shown to influence the discrimination of correctly tuned melodies. Expansions or contractions of the semitone lead to comparable effects on performance levels, and both destroy the perceptual advantages for scale and key. However, the perception of contour differences is unaffected by this sort of mistuning.

Why is it that listeners can adapt to mistuned contours but not to mistuned scales or keys? One possibility is that mistuning destroys the relationships between the frequency ratios of intervals and the harmonics of note frequencies. This is the basis of simple-ratio hypotheses about the origin of scales, rooted in psychoacoustical aspects of consonance (e.g., Plomp, 1976; Terhardt, 1977, 1978).

Such a view finds some support from Werner's (1940) report that harmonic aspects tended to be absent from his micromelodies, although he did claim that his condensed octaves and fifths acquired the perceptual characteristics of their correctly tuned counterparts. It is possible to restore this relationship between intervals and harmonics while preserving the mistuning. This could be done by employing notes where the partials are appropriately stretched or condensed (Cohen, 1979; Mathews and Pierce, 1980; McAdams, 1982; Slaymaker, 1970). An alternative proposal derives from von Hoerner's (1974, 1976) concept of microtonal pitch systems. The idea is that condensed semitones are derived from a correctly tuned octave with more than 12 divisions, with scale notes selected from this range so that psychoacoustic consonance is preserved. This system therefore, envisages that the scale and key of micro- and macromelodies should be based on quite different notes than those used in the present study. A different hypothesis about the origins of scale notes underlies the microtonal systems proposed by Balzano (1980). These Group Theory ideas predict different micro-scales for a multiply-divided octave; once again, these are not a simple expansion or contraction of the correctly tuned scale. It is therefore possible that there is more flexibility in scale and key perception than is presently apparent, and this might be revealed by the use of different note frequencies for the mistuned scales or by the use of different sounds.

Other ideas about the origin of scales are inherently more adaptable, for example, the view that scales derive from a need to reduce the information content of melodies to within psychologically acceptable limits (Dowling, 1978; Krumhansl and Shepard, 1979) or that they are learned through contact with the pervasive musical idiom (Deutsch and Feroe, 1981). However, the present results show that any potential for adapting to different scales and tunings has been lost by the present group of listeners. Indeed, Deutsch and Feroe (1981) stress the robust nature of their alphabets (scales) by describing them as overlearned. Also, a developmental study (Krumhansl and Keil, 1982) found that the perceptual distinctiveness of the diatonic notes was present at a very early age. It is therefore, not too surprising that little flexibility in scale and key perception is found for the present group of listeners; and, although this seems at variance with many of Werner's (1940) observations, there are numerous procedural differences that might account for the disparity: Perhaps the most significant of these is that Werner's listeners were slowly introduced to the new scales on an interval-by-interval basis over a period of weeks. Here, listeners had only one session—lasting approximately 45 minutes—in which they heard just 288 presentations of the 14-note melodies.

Nevertheless, this amount of exposure was sufficient to generate introspections comparable to those reported by Moore and Rosen (1979), our listeners rapidly found that the novel tunings "didn't seem too bad really," (indeed, some found they had lost all awareness of any mistuning. Such reports are not too surprising as all tunings led to high performance levels, so that listeners were able to remember, transpose, and compare the tone sequences relatively well. It is difficult to believe that listeners can perform such a complex feat when the tone sequences remain entirely devoid of meaning. However, the present experiments show that this ability does not require the perception of tonality for the sounds and is therefore unlikely to be a unique property of melody perception. Indeed, there are other sounds for which such abilities are useful, notably in the perception of the fundamental-frequency contours of speech. Here, contour similarities need to be recognised in various frequency ranges (transpositions) and across varying degrees of frequency excursion (tunings). It has been argued that speech and melodic contours have similar perceptual properties (Thomassen, 1982). This argument is reinforced by the present findings; that is, that the discrimination of contour differences in both melodic and non-melodic tone sequences is quantitatively similar, as no reliable differences in the size of the contour effect across the different tunings are found. So the idea that exaggerated contours might be easier to discriminate (Idson and Massaro, 1976) is not tenable. This does not necessarily mean that the perceptual representation of contour is merely ordinal, because the relative degrees of contour (Idson and Massaro, 1978) are comparable across tunings. It may be that contour discrimination is generally similar for a variety of sounds. This may be due to the operation of rudimentary organisational principles governing the perception of all contours (e.g., Ortmann, 1926; Heise and Miller, 1951; Divenyi and Hirsh, 1974, 1978; Deutsch, 1978a, 1978b), but it might also be explained by listeners drawing on perceptual strategies normally used in perceiving the pitch of the voice.

One caveat should be noted: The design of these and other discrimination experiments does not allow us to decide whether some contours are more easily remembered than others. Nor does it illuminate possible interactions between tonality and contour. This is also true of identification experiments to the extent that contour is used merely to discriminate between possible answers. So the idea that contour is used in the communication of musical structure (Jones, 1981; Rosner and Meyer, 1982) needs to be investigated in other ways, especially in view of the finding that contour discrimination is not uniquely melodic. A more appropriate test of these views would require the construction of sequences with structurally good contours and a comparison of the learning of these with appropriate control melodies (i.e., an approach similar to that adopted for the key and scale factors in this study).

The lack of flexibility associated with the perception of tonality is apparent for the perception of other complex sounds, notably those of speech. Sounds that might plausibly have been produced by a human vocal apparatus are perceived differently from sounds of comparable complexity that are not perceived as speech (e.g., Best, Morrongiello, and Robson, 1981). There is also a learning superiority for speech over other complex sounds (House, Stevens, Sandel, and Arnold, 1962). Some authors (e.g., Repp, 1982; Liberman, 1982) argue that this is evidence for a mode of perception for speech that exhibits unique properties. However, the present findings for melody are, in many ways, analogous to the speech perception results of House et. al. (1962). This raises the possibility that this general class of effects might be observable for other complex sounds that have environmental significance and that a variety of specialisations are part and parcel of perceptual organisation. Indeed, the notion that the efficiency of perceptual problem solving is bought at the cost of specificity and inflexibility has wide currency in discussions of visual perception (see, e.g., Rock, 1975).

The present experiments indicate two independent kinds of influence on the perception of melodies. There are factors that interact with the listeners' knowledge of the pervasive musical idiom, in this case, the tonality of the melody as communicated by the scale and key constraints of these melody approximations. The listeners appear to be able to take advantage of these constraints in order to build a more accurate perceptual representation of the melodic melodies, possibly in the manner suggested by Attneave (1981). This results in better learning of such melodies and less confusion with exact transpositions presented soon afterwards. However, these factors are influential only if the tones are correctly tuned to the 12-tone equal-temperament values. If the tones are badly mistuned, as is the case for the present micro- and macromelodies, the perceptual system is unable to adapt its problem-solving strategies appropriately, even though the nature of the problem is similar when expressed in terms of a physical description of the sounds. A similar lack of adaptability would also explain the poor performance for correctly tuned control melodies.

Other factors involved in the discrimination task are more general in nature. This is illustrated by the detection of similarities and differences in the contours of transposed melodies. Listeners were able to perceive these differences regardless of the tuning of the tones, which contrasts sharply with the effects found for the tonal factors. This may be because listeners were "importing" organisational strategies developed for the perception of the pitch contours of speech or of other sounds, although perceptual similarities between the contours of other sounds and melodic contour may have a common origin in a more rudimentary organisational principle. These ideas are elaborated in the following section.

CONTOUR AND CONTOUR FEATURES

A distinction has been made between contour in the global sense and components of contour. Here we discuss work that indicates that these two aspects of contour may be perceived in different ways. The literature on the use of contour information in melody recognition and identification suggests that contour is important in novel transposed melodies and in more familiar melodies. This has been shown to be true also for melodies the listener learns during the course of an experiment. In the case of untransposed melodies, the situation is somewhat different: Listeners seem to remember specific pitches and global contour effects are negligible (Dowling and Fujitani, 1971).

To look at the details of contour, the overall pattern of ups and downs is divided into overlapping sequences of three notes. These form contour reversals if the final note of the three-note sequence moves towards the first, and they form non-reversals if the third note moves away from the first. Thus, contour reversals are a change in the direction of pitch, whereas non-reversals preserve the direction of pitch movement. Although each note (excluding the first and last of a sequence) can be labelled either "reversal" or "non-reversal," the immediate context of each note must be taken into account in the definition of the contour component.

The following experiments examine the relative salience of specific contour components in a short-term recognition memory paradigm. A number of physical parameters, such as note range and stimulus wave form, are varied to test the generality of the results. We also try to isolate factors responsible for any perceptual salience by considering a range of possible confounding influences, such as the absolute pitches associated with the different components. Finally, we introduce tuning as a factor and compare the contour effects with those found in micro- and macromelodies. If the pattern of results is similar across a range of conditions, it is reasonable to suppose that certain contour features are common to a range of sounds, including the pitch contour of speech, in which case, we may be dealing with a general perceptual principle or organisational strategy rather than a perceptual skill specific to music.

Our experiments employed the recognition memory paradigm previously described. Novel melody approximations were synthesised as before, using the melodic forms of the scale, key, and semitone span constraints throughout. Each melody was 15 notes long. Listeners were required to say whether the second melody of the pair was identical to or different from the first, and a comparison was made between transposed and untransposed tasks. Also, tasks that allowed the listener some familiarity with the melody (by repeating the first melody of the pair over a series of trials) were compared with tasks in which novel melodies appeared on every trial.

Contour constraints were implemented using two methods. One method entailed the construction of the overall contour from combinations of three types of elements and their inversions. These were a *V*, a *W*, and a lazy *Z*, (i.e., a *Z* rotated 45°). Each contour contained an example of each type. In the other method, a complete sequence was generated and then checked for a criterion number of contour reversals and non-reversals. If the sequence failed to meet these requirements, then the program tried again. Comparisons between these two methods revealed no perceptual differences with respect to feature salience.

In generating pairs of different melodies, changes were made at either reversals or non-reversals, but the same overall contour was always preserved. Upper and lower limits were set for possible new notes based on the old note (the candidate for change) and the notes on either side. The limits for non-reversals were based on the position of the intervals in relationship to the old note. For reversals, the size of intervals was taken into account to ensure a comparable degree of change with trials in which non-reversals were changed. The difference in semitones between the old and the new note varied. However, by judiciously prescribing limits for such changes, we avoided systematic differences in the number of semitones altered for the different types of contour component.

Feature Salience in Untransposed Contours

In this section, we examine the proposal that pitch reversals (auditory corners) are perceived as more salient than the intervening notes (slopes). We divided these corners into both upper reversals or peaks (upward followed by downward pitch movement) and compared them with the reverse, troughs. We also examined the possibility that salience is attributable to some form of auditory stream segregation. This is important because any differences between, for example, peaks and troughs may be attributable to a streaming within their respective pitch ranges, which are generally different. Another possibility is that the feature that drives stream formation is the contour reversal itself. So streaming, along with some attentional bias towards a particular stream, may give the false impression of differentially salient features. We can investigate these possibilities by manipulating the rate of presentation: If salience is due to some form of streaming, then it should be enhanced at the faster rates (see Dowling, 1973; van Noorden, 1975).

The second melody of each trial was not transposed in these experiments. Also, novel melodies appeared on every trial. Different-melodies contained changes to either four reversals or four non-reversals. Where a comparison was made between upper and lower reversals, the number of changes was reduced to three. Melodies were played at rates of either 15, 25, or 35 csecs per note.

The results showed that changes at contour reversals are more discriminable than changes at non-reversals. When the reversals are further divided into upper and lower, we find that peaks are more salient than troughs. Rate of presentation did not differentially affect the relative salience of the different contour components. Thus, it is unlikely that auditory stream segregation can account for the differences between contour reversals and non-reversals.

However, superiority of upper reversals over lower might be attributable to the greater salience of upper reversals alone. If so, it is possible to account for the results with the hypothesis that relatively higher-pitched notes are more salient because upper reversals are generally higher in pitch than non-reversals, which are, in turn, usually higher in pitch than the lower reversals. If this explanation is correct, then non-reversals should be more salient than lower reversals. The following experiment was designed to check this possibility.

Feature Generality in Untransposed Contours

In this section, we look at the relative salience of the three components: upper and lower contour reversals and non-reversals. If the salience of corners is due to inherent properties of reversals, then we expect to find that both types of reversals are more discriminable than non-reversals. Alternatively, the results may be attributable to the greater salience of upper reversals alone or simply to differences in relative pitch height.

In order to extend the generality of these results, a variety of conditions were included. Two types of waveforms were compared—pulse trains and square waves; these sounds show different changes of intensity with fundamental frequency. Absolute pitch height and relative pitch differences were varied by generating melodies from either a one- or two-octave range. The larger note range allows us to investigate a number of potentially significant variables: The absolute pitch of upper reversals is generally higher, there are greater relative pitch differences between upper and lower reversals, and larger intervals between adjacent notes are more probable. Therefore, if the size of the note range interacts with contour component effects, then relative and/or absolute pitch height must be a factor influencing perceptual salience. This also implicates a role for some form of auditory stream segregation on the basis of pitch proximity because larger frequency differences between the extremes would be likely to promote such an effect.

We found a systematic pattern of results across all conditions. Performance on upper reversals is better than on lower reversals, which, in turn, is better than performance on non-reversals. The consistency of these results points to a general (feature) notion of the role of reversals of contour. The pitch-height hypothesis cannot account for the superiority of lower reversals over non-reversals. Similarly, differences in intensity and relative and absolute pitch are not responsible for perceived salience. Again, we obtain no evidence that auditory streaming is involved.

The experiments reported thus far support a figural approach to the definition of contour features (i.e., the reversals or corners are the perceptually salient aspects of the figure). These features seem to be common to melodic contours over a range of conditions, although we have restricted our investigation so far to novel, untransposed melodies. Next we investigate whether the same contour features are important in transposed comparisons and with more familiar sequences.

Transposed Contours

To investigate the effect of transposition on the contour features, it is necessary to modify the method of testing recognition memory. As discussed previously, such a task is extremely difficult unless the listener is given some familiarisation with the melody. Therefore, we use the learning paradigm, where the first tune of each trial is held constant through 10 successive trials.

The effects of learning were separated from those of transposition by including familiar but untransposed melodies in one condition. We anticipated higher scores with the untransposed melodies than with the transposed. However, we are interested primarily in differences between contour components to see if contour features are differentially salient in familiar melodies.

As expected, the learning paradigm gave rise to a higher level of performance. However, the most interesting finding was a different pattern of relative feature salience from that obtained with novel untransposed melodies. Although upper reversals are again more easily discriminated than the other components, lower reversals appear to lose their perceptual significance and give rise to the lowest discrimination scores.

Thus, we find that contour features are not a property of the perceptual organisation of transposed and more familiar melodies. Unfortunately, it is not possible to disentangle the individual effects of transposition and learning, because the difficulty of the transposition task precludes the inclusion of a transposed-with-novel-melodies condition.

Microcontours and Macrocontours

Our experiments have shown that components of contour are salient with novel tone sequences in 12-tone equal-temperament tuning. We now look at the effects of mistuning on these contour features by varying the tuning factor. If these features can be accounted for by fairly general perceptual principles, then we would expect to find evidence of these features in the recognition of micro- and macromelodies. These unusual tone sequences provide a means of establishing whether the results obtained so far are truly representative of tone sequences in general, as suggested by Thomassen (1982).

We returned to using untransposed melody pairs, with novel melodies on each trial. Each melody was 12 notes long. Melodies based on the micro- and macrotunings outlined previously were compared with the correct tuning for 12-tone equal temperament.

Our results illustrate the generality of contour features. The three tunings produced the familiar pattern of reversal over non-reversal superiority with upper reversals more salient than lower ones. There was no overall difference in the level of performance across tunings. There was a reliable difference between the different contour features, and this effect did not vary with tuning. We conclude that the ability to perform this type of task does not require the tone sequence to be heard as a melody. Furthermore, the differential salience of these contour features appears to be a general property of tone sequences: it is not confined to melodies.

Conclusions

These experiments have revealed perceptually salient aspects of contour, which can be interpreted as features. Here we discuss this result in terms of the analogies pursued earlier and offer our speculations concerning possible underlying mechanisms.

The comparison of transposed and untransposed sequences underlines the distinction between the overall contour and contour features. Whereas the overall contour is useful in recognising transposed melodies, contour features are only salient with untransposed comparisons. In addition, although familiar melodies demonstrate global contour effects, they do not show differential salience of specific contour features.

The general nature of these contour features suggests that we may make comparisons with other perceptual tasks. It has been suggested that untransposed melodies are recognised on the basis of a memory for specific pitches (Dowling and Fujitani, 1971; cf. Davies, 1978). Some of the properties of pitch memory have been investigated by Deutsch (e.g., 1970, 1972, 1973). By looking at how memory for a tone is disrupted by subsequent events, we gain some idea of the way in which pitch may be represented. Deutsch (1972) used these results to arrive at a model of pitch memory in which both the pitch and time of arrival of a note are stored in an array, thus capturing the two-dimensional aspect of tone sequences. A third dimension is used to represent the distribution of activity at a particular point in the array. This creates a bell-shaped distribution that spreads along the spatial and temporal dimensions with time. Errors in pitch discrimination may be attributed to this spread of activity: The distributions of notes close together in frequency and time tend to overlap; consequently, when the array is accessed at a particular time, a number of different notes will have contributed to the excitation pattern found.

This type of representation may account for the salience of reversals over non-reversals, given that reversals may be subject to greater interference from adjacent notes. As non-reversals lie between both higher and lower pitches, the pattern of activity at this time may be spread over a fairly large area. As reversals reflect a local extreme of pitch, interference is restricted to one direction along the pitch dimension (see Ortmann, 1926). This type of explanation holds that the differential salience of the features is a necessary consequence of the particular context. If this is so, the effects should not be affected by reducing the uncertainty in the manner described by Watson et al. (1976) and Watson and Kelly (1981). We have not, as yet, investigated this possibility.

Alternatively, these effects might be a consequence of perceptual strategies used in resolving uncertainty. Given that the kind of representation that Deutsch suggests is like a blurred visual figure, listeners may be importing a perceptual strategy that has proved effective in the recognition of visual figures. As we have seen, the theory of visual processing proposed by Attneave (1954) holds that angles and points of intersection are features of high information value. Thus, the volatile nature of the auditory representation after just one presentation might encourage listeners to extract whatever information they can by aiming for the corners or reversals. We would not expect mistuning to affect such a strategy.

A similar type of strategy may also account for the superiority of upper over lower reversals, as well as the minor differences between contour components with familiar transposed and untransposed melodies. These results are characterised by a greater salience for the higher pitches. Such an effect was reported by Watson and Kelly (1981), who ascribe these differences to a "major attentional emphasis toward relatively high frequency . . . sounds" (p. 56).

The reduction in the salience of these contour features as the melodies become more familiar and are also transposed has parallels with other findings in the area of visual figure perception. It has been suggested that global structure is available earlier than local features, a process labelled "global precedence" by Navon (1977). Furthermore, a two-stage model poposed by Kroll and Hershenson (1980) begins with a global comparison. Such comparisons are followed by additional analytic processing if necessary, given that sufficient time is available. Whereas this model is essentially congruent with the notion of global precedence, Navon (1977) eagerly points out that local processing need not wait for the termination of global analysis. Nevertheless, the observed perceptual salience of our contour reversals or corners may be attributable to some such global comparison that compares the outlines of the figures, because perceptual resources will be limited after just one presentation. As listeners are familiarised with a melody, finer details may be filled in. Consequently, listeners need not rely on these global characteristics to such an extent if the melody is more familiar. Repetition of the melody provides resources for the additional analytic processing and so provides the details in-between the outline of contour reversals.

The extent to which global precedence may adhere to either one interpretation or the other of the auditory–visual analogy is under debate; there are both perceptual and postperceptual interpretations of the global over local superiority effects. This approach has been adopted (Attneave, 1954; Miller, 1981) for the role of selective attention to global features. Attention may be driven by many factors, including knowledge of visual figures. By contrast, Navon (1977) favours a perceptual explanation that regards the salience of global features as a necessary consequence of the form of representation. This view is supported by findings that the global-precedence effect may be manipulated by other perceptual variables such as types of distortion (Hoffman, 1980) and certainty of location (Grice, Canham, and Boroughs, 1983). These authors report that global precedence depends upon the greater degradation of local features compared with the relative robustness of global features, and this occurs in peripheral viewing. For tone sequences, a comparable form of degradation may be the blurring believed to occur in pitch memory; this might explain our analogous findings.

The consistency of our results across different tunings lends support to a more general notion of contour, which encompasses both melodic contour and the pitch contours of speech and other sounds. The perceptual significance of changes in the pitch of the voice has been discussed with reference to perceived stress and phrase boundaries. The similarity of the two contours suggests that the pitch reversals, which are perceived as salient in the context of melody (for whatever reason), may have similar consequences when they occur in the intonation pattern of speech. (see Thomassen, 1982)

In keeping with the earlier treatment of analogies, an alternative interpretation is offered: that listeners may capitalise on their knowledge of intonation in speech in dealing with melodic contours. Listeners may learn, through prior experience with speech, that the parts of the message providing important information, (e.g., the phrase boundary) are signaled by changes in pitch. What has proved fruitful with novel speech may therefore be applied to novel tone sequences.

These experiments have demonstrated perceptually salient aspects of contour in novel tone sequences. These features, though obviously related to the overall contour, have distinct properties: They are found with untransposed melodies but not with transposed and more familiar sequences. However, we have shown that both types of contour effects are due to properties intrinsic to tone sequences in general and are not influenced by the degree to which the sound conforms to the schemata of tonality.

The generality of these features encourages discussion of the general principles appropriate for the description of certain aspects of tone sequence perception. We have drawn upon examples from visual figure perception to highlight possible similarities between the organisational strategies applied to visual and auditory figures. Similarities between the pitch contour of speech and melodic contours have also been discussed. These two areas are possible sources of perceptual knowledge that may be applied to the recognition memory tasks because listeners may be using strategies developed for other purposes to interpret the sounds. Alternatively, the apparent similarities may be due to the operation of a more basic organisational principle: The representation of tones in pitch memory may account for the salience of reversals in tone sequences, in melodies, and in speech. This representation is reminiscent of a two-dimensional visual display, which may be sufficient to account for the various analogies.

NEW MUSIC?

We return to our discussion of the tonal constraints, scale, and key. These factors, when they are in their melodic forms, give rise to melodies that are easier to learn and discriminate than their appropriate controls. It has been shown that these effects seem to be specific to correctly tuned 12-tone equal temperament and are not found when the notes are mistuned by condensing or expanding the semitone by a constant (log) amount. There appears to be little flexibility associated with the schemata of melody, in that the perceptual system does not seem prepared to adapt them by appropriately scaling its semitone. So, it is unlikely that new music generated in this way will take on the full richness of correctly tuned melodies; it appears to be at odds with perceptual constraints. However, there may be more appropriate transformations that extend these constraints along more perceptually relevant dimensions. In other words, the possibility of new types of perceptually salient tonality will depend upon the nature of the perceptual invariants underlying scale and key and upon whether these are pre-served under transformation (see Cutting, 1983). For example, we know that the appropriate invariant is not simply the number of scale notes. If it were, then the transformation from the melodic to the control form of the scale factor, which is invariant with respect to number of scale notes, should not lead to the observed performance differences. Similarly, we may discount related ideas such as the information reduction incurred by basing melodies on a limited subset of the chromatic scale. Again, the mistuning experiments allow us to reject candidates for tonal invariants based on relative frequency spacing, although contour effects are invariant here. For contour effects, the analogy with visual shape–distance invariance is tempting, but as we have seen, this will not do for tonality. A number of other candidates for the perceptual invariants underlying scale and key have been suggested, and a variety of microtonal systems have been proposed (Chalmers, 1979; Glasier, 1978; Partch, 1974; Rothenberg, 1978a, 1978b; Schafer and Piehl, 1947; Yunik and Swift, 1980). Two formalisms will be considered here: The first is von Hoerner's (1974, 1976) derivation from simple ratio ideas, where the invariant is the relationship between interval size and the overtones of the note frequencies; and the second is based on certain invariants of Group Structure as described by Balzano (1980, 1982b). Both theorists have proposed scale and key systems based on more than 12 divisions of the octave, and both make diverse predictions about the microscales appropriate for octaves which are divided into a similar number of steps.

Von Hoerner's Microtonal System

This formulation indicates that the overtones of the frequencies of lower notes should overlap with the fundamentals of higher notes, so that the new scale is "compatible with our concepts of harmony" (von Hoerner, 1976, p. 12). The important parameters are the number of overtones considered and the degree of tolerance allowed in deciding whether frequency components overlap. Von Hoerner goes on to derive a variety of scales, and their precise form depends on the number of divisions of the octave (N), the number of scale notes (n), and the number of major (or minor) chords that can be formed without accidentals (H). $H = 3$ for correctly tuned tonal music, corresponding to the tonic, dominant, and subdominant major triads. It is convenient to illustrate these ideas with one particular scale—based on a 19-fold division of the octave, 9 scale notes, and 5 major chords—and to express it in terms of the formalism previously described for 12-tone equal temperament. To find the note frequencies of such a scale, we need to express equation 1 more generally:

$$f/f_0 = 2^{p/N}, \tag{4}$$

where $N = 12$ for 12-tone equal temperament, and $N = 19$ here. For $N = 19$, p

represents the separation from the keynote in semitones, which are nineteenths of an octave.

To define the scale and key with our terminology, we can express equation 2 more generally:

$$(5) \qquad\qquad\qquad p = Fq - Nr,$$

where F is the number of semitones corresponding to the interval of a fifth. So, $F = 7$ for 12-tone equal temperament, and $F = 11$ here. As one might expect, the frequency ratios of these 2 "fifths" are quite similar because von Hoerner's system aims for intervals with simple frequency ratios. Similarly, the scale of such a tuning system consists of notes that are adjacent along the new q dimension. If the range of q is restricted to -9 through $+9$, then the diatonic major scale consists of the q values -2 through $+6$. This scale can also be expressed in terms of successive intervals along a 19-fold octave. These intervals are: 3, 3, 2, 1, 2, 3, 2, 1, 2. This new q dimension also permits a similar description of the key of a micromelody to that previously described, that is, in terms of constraints on the (new) fifth span.

Balzano's Microtonal System

Balzano describes a number of properties a scale and key system must possess in order to conform to the constraints of the Group Structure he describes. One of these concerns the idea of a generator. This means that progressions of single intervals other than the smallest will produce all of the pitch classes. Furthermore, the notes of any one scale should be adjacent along such a progression, and the number of notes shared by two scales should be proportional to their separation along the progression. So, in changing from one scale to another, the number of scale notes that are changed is the number of steps along the generator progression. A further constraint is that such changes of scale notes should be minimal (i.e., by an increase or decrease corresponding to the smallest interval). Finally, the scales should possess a property called coherence; the number of diatonic scale steps spanned by an interval should be a monotonically increasing function of the number of chromatic scale-steps that it spans.

Notice that some of these properties are shared by von Hoerner's scale. This is because the series of q values is a generator progression, the interval of the fifth being the generator. However, there are two group properties not shared by von Hoerner's scales: (1) There is not a minimal change of one scale note for each step of the keynote along the q progression; although only one note changes, the amount by which it changes varies; and (2) The scales are not coherent.

A number of proposed scale and key systems incorporate the important group properties. The one called C20 is of particular interest in the present context. It is based on an octave divided into 20 steps; thus these semitones are similar to those of von Hoerner's 19-fold octave. The frequencies of the notes of this system are given by substituting $N = 20$ into equation 4. The generator used here is quite different; C20 uses an interval of nine; so, in order to form the appropriate q dimension, a value of $F = 9$ should be substituted in equation 5. If q is also restricted to the range -9 through $+10$, then the new diatonic scale consists of the q values -2 through $+6$. In terms of successive intervals along a 20-fold octave, this scale is 2, 3, 2, 2, 2, 3, 2, 2, 2. Although such a scale possesses the important properties of Group Structure, there is no simple-ratio relationship between the intervals and the overtone series of its notes.

An Experimental Comparison

It appears that microtonal music offers a convenient testbed for theories about the underlying structure of tonal music. The generalisation of these ideas to different pitch systems has revealed that, although they are quite comparable in some respects (e.g., number of divisions of the octave or number of scale notes), other predictions are divergent. Thus, von Hoerner's scale embodies the relationship between intervals and the overtone series, but does not obey the group constraints regarding transposition, and is not coherent; whereas, the opposite is true for Balzano's C20.

We adapted the experimental procedures previously described to investigate the learning and discrimination of melodies derived from the constraints of the two different systems. That is, listeners were required to discriminate same-transposed from different-transposed pairs of 14-note melodies, the first melody of the pair being the same over a series of 12 trials. The experiment asks whether the melodic form of each type of scale constraint gives rise to melodies that are easier to learn and discriminate than their controls.

Some care was necessary in selecting the control scale. It is important to ensure that it violates the constraints of both systems (i.e., composed of notes which are not adjacent along the appropriate q dimensions). At the same time, it is important to maintain comparability of the controls by making the frequencies of its notes similar in both pitch systems. The scale we chose is based on the following intervals of a 19-fold octave: 2, 3, 1, 1, 2, 3, 2, 3, 1, 1. This gives a 9-note scale when the keynote is excluded. The (von Hoerner, 1976) q values of this scale are -8, -7, -5, -3, $+3$, $+4$, $+5$, $+6$, $+8$. In C20, the intervals of the control scale are 2, 3, 2, 1, 2, 3, 2, 3, 1, 1. This is again a 9-note scale when the keynote is excluded. The C20 q values of this scale are -9, -8, -5, -3, -2, $+2$, $+3$, $+5$, $+10$.

Two other constraints were implemented in synthesising these melodies, but they were not systematically varied. One constraint increased the probability of smaller intervals, whereas the other kept the change in q from note to note relatively small.

Findings

The results showed a clear superiority for the melodic melodies, based on von Hoerner's (1974, 1976) scale over the controls, but the melodic melodies derived from C20 gave no such superiority.

These findings seem to offer support for the simple-ratio type of system advocated by von Hoerner; however, there are other interpretations. The problem is that, with von Hoerner's system, the note frequencies that correspond to the diatonic scale of the 12-tone octave are also found in the 9-note scale of the new tuning system. This means that listeners may not be generalising their knowledge of 12-tone invariants but are simply interpreting these 19-tone melodies as 12-tone melodies with a few mistuned notes thrown in. For the time being, our findings offer only tentative support for the simple-ratio approach.

The possibility remains that Group Structure is important for the perception of scale, but because of the pervasiveness of 12-tone tonality, such invariants are not readily generalised. Once again, our attention is drawn to the inflexibility of perception in its dealings with complex events, and we are faced with the inadequacy of many theories in this respect. It is not sufficient to explain away this aspect under such rubrics as overlearning, while outlining inherently flexible structural descriptions. In many ways, the robustness of tonal structure is its most engaging property.

REFERENCES

Attneave, F. Some informational aspects of visual perception. *Psychological Review*, 1954, *61*, 183–193.

Attneave, F. *Applications of information theory to psychology.* New York: Holt, 1959.

Attneave, F. Three approaches to perceptual organisation. In M. Kubovy and J. R. Pomerantz (Eds.), *Perceptual organisation.* Hillsdale, NJ: Erlbaum, 1981.

Babbitt, M. Twelve-tone invariants as compositional determinants. *The Musical Quarterly*, 1960, *46*, 246–259.

Bailey, P. J., and Summerfield, Q. Information in speech: Observations on the perception of [s]-stop clusters. *Journal of Experimental Psychology: Human Perception and Performance*, 1980, *6*, 536–563.

Baker, M. A. and Loeb, M. Implications of measurements of eye fixations for a psychophysics of form perception. *Perception and Psychophysics*, 1973, *13*, 185–192.

Balch, W. R. The role of symmetry in the good continuation ratings of two-part tonal melodies. *Perception and Psychophysics*, 1981, *29*, 47–55.

Balzano, G. J. The group-theoretic description of 12-fold and microtonal pitch systems. *Computer Music Journal*, 1980, *4*, 66–84.

Balzano, G. J. Music perception as detection of pitch-time constraints. *Journal of the Acoustical Society of America*, 1982, *72*, S10. (a)

Balzano, G. J. The pitch set as a level of description for studying musical pitch perception. In M. Clynes (Ed.), *Music, mind and brain*. New York: Plenum, 1982. (b)

Bartlett, J. C., and Dowling, W. J. Recognition of transposed melodies: A key-distance effect in developmental perspective. *Journal of Experimental Psychology: Human Perception and Performance*, 1980, *6*, 501–516.

Bernstein, L. *The unanswered question*. Cambridge, MA: Harvard University Press, 1976.

Best, C. T., Morrongiello, B., and Robson, R. Perceptual equivalence of acoustic cues in speech and nonspeech perception. *Perception and Psychophysics*, 1981, *29*, 191–211.

Bolinger, D. L. A theory of pitch accent in English. *Word*, 1958, *14*, 109–149.

Bregman, A. S. Auditory streaming: Competition among alternative organisations. *Perception and Psychophysics*, 1978, *23*, 391–398.

Bregman, A. S. Asking the ''What for'' question in auditory perception. In M. Kubovy and J. R. Pomerantz (Eds.), *Perceptual organisation*. Hillsdale, NJ: Erlbaum, 1981.

Bregman, A. S., and Achim, A. Visual stream segregation. *Perception and Psychophysics*, 1973, *13*, 451–454.

Bregman, A. S. and Campbell, J. Primary auditory stream segregation and perception of order in rapid sequences of tones. *Journal of Experimental Psychology*, 1971, *89*, 244–249.

Burns, E. M. Circularity in relative pitch judgments for complex tones: The Shepard illusion revisited again. *Perception and Psychophysics*, 1982, *30*, 467–472.

Burns, E. M., and Ward, D. W. Intervals scales and tuning. In D. Deutsch (Ed.), *The psychology of music*. London: Academic Press, 1982.

Chalmers, J. A collection of scales with nineteen tones. *Xenharmonikon*, 1979, *7* and *8*.

Cohen, E. Fusion and consonance relations for tones with inharmonic partials. *Journal of the Acoustical Society of America*, 1979, *65*, S123.

Cohen, A. and t'Hart, J. On the anatomy of intonation. *Lingua*, 1967, *19*, 177–192.

Cooper, W. E., Soares, C., Ham, A., and Damon, K. The influence of inter- and intraspeaker tempo on fundamental frequency and palatalization. *Journal of the Acoustical Society of America*, 1983, *73*, 1723–1730.

Cooper, W. E. and Sorenson, J. M. Fundamental frequency contours at syntactic boundaries. *Journal of the Acoustical Society of America*, 1977, *62*, 683–692.

Cuddy, L. L., Cohen, A. J., and Miller, J. Melody recognition: The experimental application of musical rules. *Canadian Journal of Psychology*, 1979, *33*, 148–156.

Cutting, J. E. Four assumptions about invariance in perception. *Journal of Experimental Psychology: Human Perception and Performance*, 1983, *9*, 310–317.

d'Amato, M. R. *Experimental psychology*. London: McGraw-Hill, 1970.

Dannenbring, G. L. Perceived auditory continuity with alternately rising and falling frequency transitions. *Canadian Journal of Psychology*, 1976, *30*, 99–114.

Davies, J. B. *The psychology of music*. London: Hutchinson, 1978.

Davies, J. B. and Jennings, J. Reproduction of familiar melodies and the perception of tonal sequences. *Journal of the Acoustical Society of America*, 1977, *61*, 534–541.

deBoer, E. On the ''residue'' and auditory pitch perception. In W. D. Keidel and W. D. Neff (Eds.), *Handbook of sensory physiology* (Vol. V/3). Berlin: Springer-Verlag, 1976.

Deutsch, D. Tones and numbers: Specificity of interference in immediate memory. *Science*, 1970, *168*, 1604–1605.

Deutsch, D. Effect of repetition of standard and comparison tones on recognition memory for pitch. *Journal of Experimental Psychology*, 1972, *93*, 156–162.

Deutsch, D. Octave generalization of specific interference effects in memory for tonal pitch. *Perception and Psychophysics*, 1973, *13*, 271–275.

Deutsch, D. Delayed pitch comparisons and the principle of proximity. *Perception and Psychophysics,* 1978, *23,* 227–230. (a)

Deutsch, D. The Psychology of Music. In E. C. Carterette and M. P. Friedman (Eds.), *Handbook of Perception.* New York: Academic Press, 1978. (b)

Deutsch, D., and Feroe, J. The internal representation of pitch sequences in tonal music. *Psychological Review,* 1981, *88,* 503–522.

Divenyi, P. L. and Hirsh, I. J. Identification of temporal order in a 3 tone sequence. *Journal of the Acoustical Society of America,* 1974, *56,* 144–151.

Divenyi, P. L. and Hirsh, I. J. The effect of blanking on the identification of 3 tone sequences. *Perception and Psychophysics,* 1975, *17,* 246–252.

Divenyi, P. L. and Hirsh, I. J. Some figural properties of auditory patterns. *Journal of the Acoustical Society of America,* 1978, *64,* 1369–1386.

Dowling, W. J. The perception of interleaved melodies. *Cognitive Psychology,* 1973, *5,* 322–337.

Dowling, W. J. Scale and contour: Two components of a theory of memory for melodies. *Psychological Review,* 1978, *85,* 341–354.

Dowling, W. J. and Fujitani, D. S. Contour, interval and pitch recognition in memory for melodies. *Journal of the Acoustical Society of America,* 1971, *49,* 524–531.

Faure, G., Hirst, D. J. and Chafcouloff, M. Rhythm in English: Isochronism, pitch and perceived stress. In L. R. Waugh and C. H. van Schooneveld (Eds.), *The melody of language.* Baltimore: University Park Press, 1980.

Fourcin, A. J., Rosen, S. M., Moore, B. C. J., Douek, E. E., Clarke, G. P., Dodson, H., and Bannister, L. H. External electrical stimulation of the cochlea: Clinical, psychophysical, speech-perceptual and histological findings. *British Journal of Audiology,* 1979, *13,* 85–107.

Fry, D. B. Experiments in the perception of stress. *Language and Speech,* 1958, *1,* 126–152.

Glasier, E. Confessions of a microtonal convert. *Interval,* 1978, *1,* 2–3.

Goldstein, J. L. An optimum processor theory for the central formation of the pitch of complex tones. *Journal of the Acoustical Society of America,* 1973, *54,* 1496–1516.

Green, R. T. and Courtis, M. C. Information theory and figure perception: The metaphor that failed. *Acta Psychologica,* 1966, *25,* 12–36.

Grice, G. R., Canham, L., and Boroughs, J. M. Forest before trees? It depends where you look. *Perception and Psychophysics,* 1983, *33,* 121–128.

Hahn, J., and Jones, M. R. Invariants in auditory frequency relations. *Scandinavian Journal of Psychology,* 1981, *22,* 129–144.

Heise, G. A. and Miller, G. A. An experimental study of auditory patterns. *American Journal of Psychology,* 1951, *64,* 68–77.

Helmholtz, H. L. F. On the sensations of tone (A. J. Ellis, Trans.) New York: Dover, 1954. (Original work published 1885)

Hiller, L. Composing with computers: A progress report. *Computer Music Journal,* 1981, *5,* 7–21.

Hiller, L. and Isaacson, L. M. *Experimental music.* New York: McGraw-Hill Book Co., 1959.

Hochberg, J. Levels of perceptual organisation. In M. Kubovy and J. R. Pomerantz (Eds.), *Perceptual organisation.* Hillsdale, NJ: Erlbaum, 1981.

Hoffman, J. E. Interaction between global and local levels of a form. *Journal of Experimental Psychology: Human Perception and Performance,* 1980, *6,* 222–234.

House, K. S., Stevens, K. N., Sandel, T. T. and Arnold, B. On the learning of speechlike vocabularies. *Journal of Verbal Learning and Verbal Behavior,* 1962, *1,* 133–143.

Howard, J. H. and Ballas, J. A. Feature selection in auditory perception. In D. J. Getty and J. H. Howard (Eds.), *Auditory and visual pattern recognition.* Hillsdale, NJ: Erlbaum, 1981.

Idson, W. L., and Massaro, D. W. Cross octave masking of single tones and musical sequences: The effects of structure on auditory recognition. *Perception and Psychophysics,* 1976, *19,* 155–175.

Idson, W. L., and Massaro, D. W. A bidimensional model of pitch in the recognition of melodies. *Perception and Psychophysics*, 1978, *24*, 551–556.

Jackendoff, R. Review of Bernstein's "The unanswered question." *Language*, 1977, *53*, 883–894.

Jackendoff, R. and Lerdahl, F. A grammatical parallel between music and language. In M. Clynes (Ed.), *Music mind and brain*. New York: Plenum, 1982.

Jeans, J. H. *Science and music*. New York: Dover, 1968. (Original work published 1937)

Jones, K. Compositional applications of stochastic processes. *Computer Music Journal*, 1981, *5*, 45–61.

Jones, M. R. Levels of structure in the reconstruction of temporal and spatial serial patterns. *Journal of Experimental Psychology: Human Learning and Memory*, 1976, *2*, 475–488.

Jones, M. R. A tutorial on some issues and methods in serial pattern research. *Perception and Psychophysics*, 1981, *30*, 429–504.

Julesz, B., and Hirsh, I. J. Visual and auditory perception: An essay of comparison. In E. E. David and P. B. Denes (Eds.), *Human Communication: A Unified View*. New York: McGraw-Hill, 1972.

Kallman, H. J. Octave equivalence as measured by similarity ratings. *Perception and Psychophysics*, 1982, *32*, 37–49.

Kallman, H. J. and Massaro, D. W. Tone chroma is functional in melody recognition. *Perception and Psychophysics*, 1979, *26*, 32–36.

Kameoka, A., and Kuriyagawa, M. Consonance theory: Part II. Consonance of complex tones and its calculation method. *Journal of the Acoustical Society of America*, 1969, *45*, 1460–1469.

Kroll, J. F., and Hershenson, M. Two stages in visual matching. *Canadian Journal of Psychology*, 1980, *34*, 49–61.

Krumhansl, C. L. The psychological representation of musical pitch in a tonal context. *Cognitive Psychology*, 1979, *11*, 346–374.

Krumhansl, C. L. and Keil, F. C. Acquisition of the hierarchy of tonal functions in music. *Memory and Cognition*, 1982, *10*, 243–251.

Krumhansl, C. L. and Shepard, R. N. Quantification of the hierarchy of tonal functions within a diatonic context. *Journal of Experimental Psychology: Human Perception and Performance*, 1979, *5*, 579–594.

Kubovy, M., and Pomerantz, J. R. (Eds.). *Perceptual organisation*. Hillsdale, NJ: Erlbaum, 1981.

Lehiste, I. *Suprasegmentals*. Cambridge, MA: M.I.T. Press, 1970.

Lerdahl, F., and Jackendoff, R. Toward a formal theory of tonal music. *Journal of Music Theory*, 1977, *21*, 111–172.

Liberman, A. M. On the finding that speech is special. *American Psychologist*, 1982, *37*, 148–167.

Lieberman, P. Some acoustic correlates of word stress in American English. *Journal of the Acoustical Society of America*, 1960, *32*, 451–454.

Longuet-Higgins, H. C. Perception of melodies. *Nature*, 1976, *263*, 646–653.

Longuet-Higgins, H. C. The perception of music. *Interdisciplinary Science Reviews*, 1978, *3*, 148–156.

Lorrain, D. A panoply of stochastic "canons." *Computer Music Journal*, 1980, *4*, 53–81.

Massaro, D. W., Kallman, H. J. and Kelly, J. L. The role of tone height, melodic contour and tone chroma in melody recognition. *Journal of Experimental Psychology: Human Learning and Memory*, 1980, *6*, 77–90.

Mathews, M. V. and Pierce, J. R. Harmony and nonharmonic partials. *Journal of the Acoustical Society of America*, 1980, *68*, 1252–1257.

McAdams, S. Spectral fusion and the creation of auditory images. In M. Clynes (Ed.), *Music mind and brain*. New York: Plenum, 1982.

McNicol, D. *A primer of signal detection theory*. London: Allen and Unwin, 1972.

Meyer, L. B. *Explaining music: Essays and explorations*. Berkeley, CA: University of California Press, 1973.

Miller, G. A. The magical number seven, plus or minus two: Some limits on our capacity for processing information. *Psychological Review*, 1956, *63*, 81–96.

Miller, J. Global precedence in attention and decision. *Journal of Experimental Psychology: Human Perception and Performance*, 1981, *7*, 1161–1174.

Miller, G. A., and Heise, G. A. The trill threshold. *Journal of the Acoustical Society of America*, 1950, *22*, 637–638.

Moore, B. C. J. *Introduction to the psychology of hearing* (2nd ed.) London: Academic Press, 1982.

Moore, B. C. J. and Rosen, S. M. Tune recognition with reduced pitch and interval information. *Quarterly Journal of Experimental Psychology*, 1979, *31*, 229–240.

Morton, J., and Jassem, W. Acoustic correlates of stress. *Language and Speech*, 1965, *8*, 159–181.

Navon, D. Forest before trees: The precedence of global features in visual perception. *Cognitive Psychology*, 1977, *9*, 353–383.

Null, C. N., and Young, F. W. Auditory perception: Recommendations for a computer assisted experimental paradigm. In D. J. Getty and J. H. Howard (Eds.), *Auditory and visual pattern recognition*. Hillsdale, NJ: Erlbaum, 1981.

O'Connor, J. D., and Arnold, G. F. *Intonation of colloquial English*. London: Longmans, 1961.

Ortmann, O. On the melodic relativity of tones. *Psychological Monographs*, 1926, *35*, 1–47.

Partch, H. *Genesis of music* (2nd ed.). New York: Da Capo, 1974.

Plomp, R. *Aspects of tone sensation*. New York: Academic Press, 1976.

Repp, B. H. Phonetic trading relations and context effects: New experimental evidence for a speech mode of perception. *Psychological Bulletin*, 1982, *92*, 81–110.

Risset, J., and Wessel, D. L. Exploration of timbre by analysis and synthesis. In D. Duetsch (Ed.), *The psychology of music*. London: Academic Press, 1982.

Rock, I. *An introduction to perception*. New York: Macmillan, 1975.

Rosner, B. R., and Meyer, L. B. Melodic processes and the perception of music. In D. Deutsch (Ed.), *The psychology of music*. New York: Academic Press, 1982.

Rothenberg, D. A model for pattern perception with musical applications: Part I: Pitch structures as order preserving maps. *Mathematical Systems Theory*, 1978, *11*, 199–234. (a)

Rothenberg, D. A model for pattern perception with musical applications: Part II: The information content of pitch structures. *Mathematical Systems Theory*, 1978, *11*, 353–372. (b)

Schafer, T., and Piehl, W. Musical instruments in nineteen-tone equal temperament. *Journal of the Acoustical Society of America*, 1947, *19*, 730.

Schouten, J. F. The residue, a new concept in subjective sound analysis. In J. D. Harris (Ed.), *Forty germinal papers in human hearing*. Groton, CT: The Journal of Auditory Research Publishers, 1969. (Original work published 1940)

Schouten, J. F., Ritsma, R. J. and Cardozo, B. Pitch of the residue. *Journal of the Acoustical Society of America*, 1962, *34*, 1418–1424.

Schubert, E. D. *Hearing, its function and dysfunction*. New York: Springer-Verlag, 1980.

Seebeck, A. Beobachten über einige Bedingungen der Enstehung von Tonen. *Annalen der Physik und Chemie*, 1841, *53*, 417–436.

Shaw, R., and Turvey, M. T. Coalitions as models for ecosystems: A realist perspective on perceptual organisation. In M. Kubovy and J. R. Pomerantz (Eds.), *Perceptual organisation*. Hillsdale, NJ: Erlbaum, 1981.

Shepard, R. N. Circularity in judgments of relative pitch. *Journal of the Acoustical Society of America*, 1964, *36*, 2346–2353.

Shepard, R. N. Psychophysical complementarity. In M. Kubovy and J. R. Pomerantz (Eds.), *Perceptual organisation*. Hillsdale, NJ: Erlbaum, 1981.

Slaymaker, F. H. Chords from tones having stretched partials. *Journal of the Acoustical Society of America*, 1970, *47*, 1569–1571.

Stevens, S. S. On the theory of scales of measurement. *Science*, 1946, *103*, 677–680.

Terhardt, E. Pitch, consonance and harmony. *Journal of the Acoustical Society of America*, 1974, *55*, 1061–1069.

Terhardt, E. The two-component theory of musical consonance. In E. F. Evans and J. P. Wilson (Eds.), *Psychophysics and physiology of hearing*. New York: Academic Press, 1977.

Terhardt, E. Psychoacoustical evaluation of musical sounds. *Perception and Psychophysics*, 1978, *23*, 483–492.

Thomassen, J. M. Melodic accent: Experiments and a tentative model. *Journal of the Acoustical Society of America*, 1982, *71*, 1596–1605.

Turvey, M. T., Shaw, R. E., and Mace, W. Issues in the theory of action: Degrees of freedom, coordinative structures and coalitions. In J. Requin (Ed.), *Attention and performance VII*. Hillsdale, NJ: Erlbaum, 1978.

von Hoerner, S. Universal music? *Psychology of Music*, 1974, *2*, 18–28.

von Hoerner, S. The definition of major scales, for chromatic scales of 12, 19 and 31 divisions per octave. *Psychology of Music*, 1976, *4*, 12–23.

van Noorden, L. P. A. S. Temporal coherence in the perception of tone sequences. Unpublished Ph.D. thesis. Eindhoven, Holland: Technische Hogeschool, 1975.

van Noorden, L. P. A. S. Two-channel pitch perception. In M. Clynes (Ed.), *Music Mind and Brain*. New York: Plenum Press, 1982.

Ward, L. M., and Wexler, D. A. Levels of feature analysis in processing visual patterns. *Perception*, 1976, *5*, 407–418.

Warren, R. M., and Wrightson, J. M. Stimuli producing conflicting temporal and spectral cues to frequency. *Journal of the Acoustical Society of America*, 1981, *70*, 1020–1024.

Watson, C. S., and Kelly, W. J. The role of stimulus uncertainty in the discrimination of auditory patterns. In D. J. Getty and J. H. Howard (Eds.), *Auditory and visual pattern recognition*. Hillsdale, NJ: Erlbaum, 1981.

Watson, C. S., Kelly, W. J., and Wroton, H. W. Factors in the discrimination of tonal patterns: II. Selective attention and learning under various levels of stimulus uncertainty. *Journal of the Acoustical Society of America*, 1976, *60*, 1176–1186.

Watson, C. S., Wroton, H. W., Kelly, W. J., and Benbasset, C. A. Factors in the discrimination of tonal patterns: I. Component frequency, temporal position and silent intervals. *Journal of the Acoustical Society of America*, 1975, *57*, 1175–1181.

Werner, H. Musical "micro-scales" and "micro-melodies." *Journal of Psychology*, 1940, *10*, 149–159.

White, B. W. Recognition of distorted melodies. *American Journal of Psychology*, 1960, *73*, 100–107.

Wightman, F. L. The pattern transformation model of pitch. *Journal of the Acoustical Society of America*, 1973, *54*, 407–417.

Wightman, F. L. and Green, D. M. The perception of pitch. *American Scientist*, 1974, *62*, 208–215.

Wilson, J. P. Psychoacoustics of obstacle detection using ambient or self-generated noise. In R. G. Busnel (Ed.), *Animal Sonar Systems*. Jouy-en-Josas, France: Hautes-Alpes, 1967.

Winograd, T. Linguistics and the computer analysis of tonal harmony. *Journal of Music Theory*, 1968, *112*, 3–49.

Xenakis, I. *Formalised music*. Bloomington: Indiana University Press, 1971.

Young, R. W. Eleven articles related to musical acoustics. *Encyclopedia of Science and Technology*. New York: McGraw-Hill, 1960.

Yunik, M., and Swift, G. W. Tempered musical scales for sound synthesis. *Computer Music Journal*, 1980, *4*, 60–65.

5

Structural Relationships in the Perception of Musical Pitch

Ian Cross, Peter Howell, and Robert West

INTRODUCTION

Of the elements of music that can be regarded as outlining or imparting structure, pitch is the most discussed. Any attempt to study the cognitive representation of pitch must, sooner or later, confront the mass of music theory. In doing so, it must not simply accept the prescriptions of music theory; it must examine critically the claims about the nature of pitch that a theory—implicitly or explicitly—makes and assess the relevance and utility of those claims for the study of musical pitch cognition.

The most basic claim made concerning pitch by nearly all traditional Western music theorists is that pitch, or pitch organisation, in music is special; certain aspects of pitch usage in music are particular to music. To confront this claim is to raise the question of whether a general universal account of pitch perception and cognition would suffice to account for all aspects of musical pitch perception. Moreover, the question also arises of whether pitch may be legitimately regarded as a separable aspect of music. That is, can structure in music be articulated in one dimension such as pitch alone, or must the cognition of musical structure be regarded as necessitating the confluence of several dimensions (e.g., at the least, pitch, rhythm–metre, and timbre)? This chapter focuses on an attempt to confront the first question by experimental means—an attempt that almost inadvertently, requires consideration of the second.

An account is given of the experimental investigation of how the logical relationships between groups of pitches can affect the perception of pitch organisation. The possibility that these logical relationships play a significant role in the perception of real-world music is discussed.

PSYCHOACOUSTIC APPROACHES TO PITCH
PERCEPTION

The simplest way to study the perception of musical pitch seems to be within the confines of a psychoacoustic approach—to study how the physical quantity of frequency maps onto the subjective quality of pitch. Unfortunately, this approach is anything but simple. The different functions mapping frequency to pitch discovered by Stevens and Volkmann (1940) and by Attneave and Olson (1971) point up the difficulties involved. In Stevens and Volkmann's studies, differences in perceived pitch were elicited in response to differences between stimuli consisting of single, simple tones. In Attneave and Olson's study, a particular configuration of simple tones was shifted around in frequency, and the integrity of the corresponding configuration of pitches was tested. In Stevens and Volkmann's (1940) case, relationships between individual tones determined relationships perceived between individual pitches; in Attneave and Olson's (1971) study, relationships between groups of tones determined those perceived between groups of pitches.

Different psychophysical functions mapping frequency to pitch were observed to operate in each study. In Stevens and Volkmann's (1940) study, the mel scale (in which frequencies separated by the same ratio were perceived as closer in pitch at the low end of the frequency range than they appeared at the high end) was evoked. (This result is closely related to vibration pattern and neural distribution on the basilar membrane in the inner ear.) Attneave and Olson's (1971) study elicited a logarithmic scale; frequency ratio mapped consistently onto pitch proximity, so that the same frequency ratio was perceived as constituting the same pitch interval over a wide frequency range (up to about 5 kHz). The logarithmic scale equates far more closely to musical conceptions and usages of pitch than does the mel scale.

The type of function that maps frequency to pitch depends upon whether single tones or groups of tones are mapped to the pitch domain. The structural identity—or integrity—of a group of tones affects our judgment in ways that cannot be deduced from the study of perception of single tones. Indeed, as Costall (Chapter 8, this volume) points out, the fact that sets of tones possess a particular structure may influence ostensibly absolute judgments of identity of single tones. Intuitively, it would seem more reasonable to study musical pitch perception through studying the perception of groups of tones as—in Western music, at least—tones rarely occur in isolation. They occur as constituents of melodies, motifs, and chords; and the theoretical significance of a particular tone is held to depend on the context within which it occurs. Some writers deny that single, discrete tones form part of musical experience (Reti, 1951; see also Serafine, 1983). Be that as it may, examining the perception of groups of tones and relationships between groups of tones raises an immediate problem: that of characterising groups of tones and their interrelationships.

There are several alternative ways of describing such groups, each bearing different implications and resting on different assumptions. One such scheme (with a long and distinguished history behind it) is that groups of tones are best thought of in terms of perception of the frequency ratios between constituent tones. The problem with this is that groups of tones may appear to have some perceptual identity even if their constituent ratios are radically different (Dowling, 1978). Moreover, although we seem to be able to differentiate between frequency ratios to a very fine level of accuracy when tones are presented in single pairs, that level of accuracy diminishes rapidly when tones occur in a more extended context (Burns and Ward, 1982). It also appears that sensitivity to frequency ratios, although of potential significance in perception when tones are presented simultaneously (Terhardt, 1978; Terhardt et al., 1982), is of considerably less importance when tones are presented consecutively (Balzano, 1977). It is necessary to go beyond physical or psychophysical levels of description to account adequately for the perception of pitch in a musical context.

STRUCTURAL APPROACHES TO PITCH PERCEPTION

An alternative to physical or psychophysical modes of description is to seek out those structures and relationships to which musicians and music theorists have accorded importance and to use these to characterise groups of tones. Such structures might be musical scales, modes, chords, and so on, or, perhaps, more abstract entities (see Rosner and Meyer, 1982). This approach also has its problems, for music is not a fixed, static entity and the views of theorists are not particularly unanimous on what constitute important structural components of music. Music changes over time, and varies from culture to culture; thus, any attempt to describe structural invariants in music must take account of the difference between style, or culture-bound, and style-free elements of music and attempt to characterise style-free elements in terms that are (as far as possible) extrinsic to music theory. Of course, any such attempt will bear the imprint of the musical culture within which the research is carried out; the imprint can, perhaps, be removed only by a process of elegant attrition, such as the analysis–synthesis procedure described and used by Watkins and Dyson (Chapter 4, this volume).

In spite of this, the use of musically privileged relationships and structures (such as intervals, scales, keys, and chords) to provide a framework for the study of musical pitch perception is now widespread (e.g., Deutsch and Feroe, 1981;

Krumhansl, 1979; Dowling, 1978; and Cuddy, Cohen and Miller, 1979). The approach has been described by Śhepard (1982a, 1982b) as *cognitive-structural*, a term he also applies to his own highly developed model of pitch representation. Shepard's model of the cognitive representation of musical pitch is founded on the constraints and assumptions that underlie the multidimensional, spatial representation of structure; the constraints of positivity, symmetry, and triangle inequality. Pitches are depicted as points in a multidimensional space, and the distance between them serves as an index of their perceptual proximity. Each point represents one and only one pitch; to informally characterise the constraints referred to, any pitch is more proximate or similar to itself than to any other pitch (positivity or minimality); the proximity or similarity between any two pitches is the same measured in both directions (symmetry) and "the closer any two pitches are to any third tone, the closer those two pitches must be to each other" (Shepard, 1982b, p. 355; for a critique of these constraints, see Krantz and Tversky, 1975; Tversky, 1977). Shepard takes the dimensions within which pitches are related to be musically privileged structures, these dimensions comprising unilinear pitch height (analogous to Attneave and Olson's [1971] pitch scale), the chroma circle (a circle consisting of the 12 notes of the chromatic scale within which each note stands for all notes octave-related to it), and the circle of fifths (a reordering of the chroma circle within which adjacent notes are separated by the musical interval of a perfect fifth, or seven semitones). The circle of fifths is a compact way of illustrating the proximity of notes that fall within one key (see Cross, Chapter 1, this volume).

Shepard's (1982a, 1982b) model is an attempt to give a complete account of the ways in which Western musical pitch can be represented cognitively. However, its completeness is in itself a source of problems.

1. Shepard's resultant structure consists of a five-dimensional double helix; whereas the implications of this structure are precisely predictable and logical, a structure of such complexity is not particularly easy to represent, which seems to vitiate the advantages of constructing a multidimensional representation.

2. The structure is conceived of as absolutely fixed and static. (Shepard is aware of this and suggests that perceptions and intuitions that differ from those predicted by the model can be accommodated by considering them, literally, as constituting different views of the mode, a mode of accommodation he considers might also account for the changing perceptions of pitch relationships that can occur in the process of listening to a piece of music).

3. Despite its completeness, certain ways of apprehending pitch structure remain outside the confines of the model. For example, within Shepard's model, it is possible to construe distances or intervals between the successive tones of the diatonic scale as being equal, which does accord with some perceptions of those (physically unequal) intervals; it is not, however, possible, within the

model, to construe intervals between consecutive notes of the Western pentatonic scale as being equal without doing violence to the previous construct. This point may seem trivial, but bears examination; if the evidence for diatonic scale-step equality is (apart from Dowling, 1978; Balzano, 1982) largely derived from informal observation of musical usages and intuitions, at least some informal observations would bear out equality of pentatonic scale step. If the evidence is derived from structural considerations (Shepard, 1982b, p. 379), then, as Shepard points out, apart from cardinality (number of notes to the octave), the two scale forms—diatonic and pentatonic—share the same structural characteristics including coherence (see Rothenberg, 1975, 1978; also Cross, Chapter 1, this volume), so neither scale type may claim priority of scale-step equality representation in the model.

These three points, however, lead to more fundamental grounds for a critique. Shepard's model is intended to be a complete description of the cognitive representation of musical pitch; its near-completeness seems to render it empirically unfalsifiable. Its genesis in structures deriving from music theory seems to indicate that its ultimate appeal for validity must be to those music-theoretic structures rather than to more general cognitive principles, and its music-theoretic bases are those of the West. However, many other musical cultures possess systems of (mainly melodic) pitch organisation no less complex than those of Western music, so any account of the cognitive representation of musical pitch must be founded on principles sufficiently general to apply to any or all of the seemingly different musical systems of the world rather than specifically to one musical system, even if that one musical system is increasingly (and impoverishingly) coming to dominate the world's ears.

Rather than proceeding from a model that seeks to be a complete embodiment of privileged musical-pitch relationships, it might be better to examine the cognition of musical pitch by means of more limited, but apparently general, descriptions of pitch structure in music. Contour, or pattern of ups and downs in pitch height of a melody, is a way of describing musical pitch that can be applied to the musical usages of Western and non-Western cultures (Becker, 1982; Reti, 1951) as well as referred to general (Gestalt) perceptual principles (see Edworthy, Chapter 7, this volume; also Watkins and Dyson, Chapter 4, this volume). Contour, moreover, describes relationships within groups of pitches over time and, for that reason, seems particularly compatible with our experience of pitch.

Contour provides a more limited (and thus, perhaps, more intrinsically testable) framework for investigating musical-pitch perception than does a model such as Shepard (1982a, 1982b); the fact that it does operate in many types of judgments of pitch organisation has been demonstrated experimentally (see, e.g., Edworthy, Chapter 7, this volume; Dowling and Fujitani, 1971; Dowling and Bartlett, 1981). However, to use contour alone in examining and manipulating pitch sequences experimentally is to constrain severely the range of inferences about the nature of pitch representation that may be drawn from such experiments. To express a sequence of pitches in terms of its contour reduces the complexity and discriminability of the pitch sequence; as Davies (1979) points out, the contour of a pitch sequence cannot be manipulated independently of the relationships or musical intervals between discrete pitches, whereas discrete pitch relationships can be altered without necessarily altering contour. In addition, to use contour alone as the primary dimension of musical-pitch cognition is to be unable to account (other than fuzzily) for the explicit musical memories and productions of even musically untrained people (see Sloboda and Parker, Chapter 6, this volume). Therefore, although contour may be a useful domain of enquiry, some means of expressing pitch relationship more precisely is required.

As stated previously, a variety of studies have been conducted using musically privileged relationships and structures as a framework for the study of musical-pitch perception. These musically privileged relationships do provide a means of expressing pitch relationships more precisely than does contour, but their experimental usage involves the difficulty of differentiating between culturally or stylistically bound relationships and those that have a broader cultural or historical extension.

Most studies carried out by these means have not aimed to formalize their musical premises to the same degree as Shepard 1982a, 1982b, (though see Deutsch and Feroe, 1981; West, Howell, and Cross, Chapter 2, this volume); they have aimed to account for pitch perceptions through the use of partial rather than complete systems of musical-pitch organisation. This approach has both advantages and drawbacks; incomplete or limited systems of pitch organisations, such as scales or keys, can be rigorously tested more easily by experiment than can a complete formalization, but the use of music-theoretic premises in empirical enquiry into musical cognition can carry the risk of accounting for musical cognition in musical rather than cognitive terms. It would seem that a rigourous formalisation of some limited system(s) of pitch organisation is required in order to provide a means of empirical investigation of the perception of musical pitch. The questions remain: Which system or systems? and, How can it or they be formalised?

PITCH ORGANISATION AND THE CIRCLE OF FIFTHS

Systems of pitch organisation that have been used as a basis for experiments include musical interval (Burns and Ward, 1978, 1982; Deutsch, 1972, 1977), scale (Bartlett and Dowling, 1980; Dowling, 1978), and tonality or key (Cuddy, 1982; Cuddy, Cohen, and Miller, 1979; Krumhansl, 1979).

For these (and other) studies, it is apparent that musical intervals and scales play a part in our perceptions of melodic musical pitch; the evidence for tonality or key (as distinct from scale) is less compelling, largely because of the difficulty of clearly defining what is meant by tonality (see Cross, Chapter 1, this volume). This is not to deny that tonality or key may play a considerable (perhaps, dominant) role in our perception of musical pitch organisation. However, to invoke tonality as a causal factor in the experimental study of melodic-pitch cognition requires consideration of many factors (such as pitch centrality); these factors must first serve as the object of empirical study. These interrelated systems of pitch organisation (interval and scale) can, however, be expressed within a simple formalisation, already mentioned as constituting part of the Shepard (1982a) model—the circle of fifths.

Most studies of musical interval, scale, or key have either assumed or demonstrated some degree of octave equivalence (see Attneave and Olson, 1971, cf., however, Sargeant, 1983). If octave equivalence is taken as read and the number of pitches distinguished within the octave is taken as 12 (see Burns and Ward, 1982), then a simplified version of pitch organisation in Western music can be examined in terms of 12 elements arranged in a circle, or a cyclic group of Order 12 (C_{12}) as in Figure 1(a).

For convenience of manipulation, one can replace note-names with numbers as in Figure 1(b) (here 12 is written as 0 since 12 added to or subtracted from any number in the circle produces the original number again). There are only two ways of organising a circle of numbers 0–11 so that the difference between all adjacent numbers is the same; that difference can be either 1 mod 12 (as in Figure 1(b) or 7 mod 12 (as in Figure 1c). Figure 1(c) is the circle of fifths, so-called

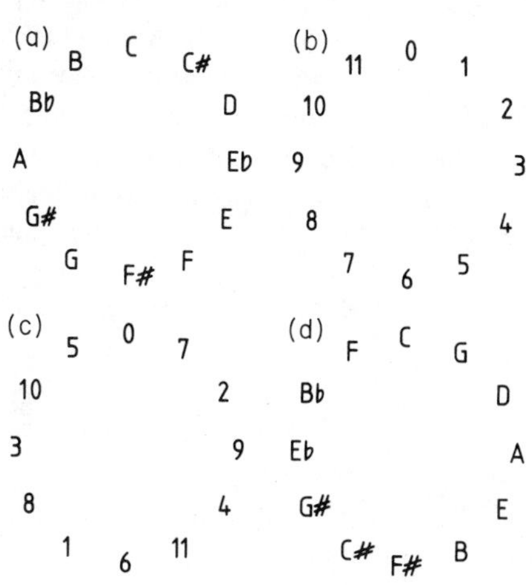

Figure 1. The chroma circle and the circle of fifths.

because any two adjacent elements (or pitch-classes, as they represent all octave-related pitches) is a musical interval of a perfect fifth, comprising seven semitones, as can be seen in Figure 1(d). The circle of fifths has a special property: Any group of seven adjacent notes on the circle constitute the notes of a major diatonic scale as shown in Figure 2 (Balzano, 1980). This property enables the circle of fifths to be used to depict relationships between scales, groups, and notes, and between groups of notes in formal rather than music-theoretic terms. It should be noted that any named note in Figure 1(d) can be represented as any number in Figure 1(c); mapping between the note-name and numerical representation preserves relationships or intervals between elements no matter which note in Figure 1(a) is taken as, say 0 in Figure 1(c). This conservation of interval structure enables us to use the circle of fifths to model the ways in which groups of pitches might interrelate. We use the circle of fifths here not as a structure showing the relative proximities of individual pitches, but as a structure within which logical relationships between groups of pitch-classes can be modelled and manipulated experimentally without recourse to music-theoretic assumptions other than octave equivalence and a fixed number of steps to the octave.

Within this formalisation, any set of pitch-classes can be said to be equivalent (in terms of the intervals its members can form with one another) to all other sets having the same number of pitch-class sets and the same layout on the circle of fifths. By differentiating between pitch-class sets in this way, it can be shown that the major diatonic scale set form (i.e., any seven adjacent notes) has particular qualities that distinguish it *structurally* from other types of pitch-class sets (Balzano, 1982, Browne, 1981; see also Cross, Chapter 1, this volume). The fact that diatonic scale structure is, in some way, privileged, does not mean that, ipso facto, it has special status in the cognition of musical pitch; it does mean, however, that if it can be shown that diatonic scale structure is, in fact, privileged in cognition, a rationale for such privilege can be advanced in terms of the simple logical model outlined (the cyclic group of Order 12) rather than solely in terms of musical usages or traditional music-theoretic formulations.

As mentioned, many studies of the perception of musical pitch have made use of the concepts of scale and tonality. Most studies have relied on music-theoretic

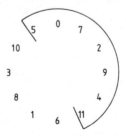

Figure 2. The diatonic scale as a connected region of the circle of fifths.

definitions of these terms, which are rarely sufficiently clear to provide testable premises. One particular study that does make explicit its bases, is that of Dowling (1978). Dowling (after Helmholtz) puts forward the view that the function of scale in perception is to divide the pitch continuum into discrete steps so that melodic movement might be more apparent to a listener, since it is between discrete steps rather than unanchored movements in a continuum). He indicates that the most concrete level of scale in music is that at which "pitch intervals get translated into notes [and] . . . a tonal focus . . . is selected" (p. 343). This tonal focus takes the form of the selection of a tonic note, regarded music-theoretically as being more stable than other notes in acting as a target for melodic movement and in starting and finishing melodies, together with other scale notes—the mediant and dominant—which are regarded as less stable than the tonic but more so than other scale notes. In the key of C, the tonic is C, the mediant E, and the dominant G. Dowling refers to this most concrete level of musical-scale usage as mode.

It is not clear that a differential set of degrees of stability or mode forms a necessary part of a listener's representation of musical scale. It is difficult to account for such differential degrees of stability in terms of the cyclic structure outlined previously (though see Cross, Chapter 1, this volume, for a possible basis). It can be argued that modal properties are not inherent in scale structure per se but that such properties arise as a concretisation of scale structure, coming about through the different probabilities of occurrence of notes and internote transitions in a specific melody or body of melodies as well as through the differing perceptual saliences of initial and terminal (as opposed to medial) notes of musical phrases (Divenyi and Hirsh, 1978). It is possible that perception of mode arises through perception of time-dependent relationships, rather than through perception of scale structure, which can be described independently of the time domain through the use of the circle-of-fifths formalisation.[1]

Thus, it becomes possible to test this proposition through the use of the formalisation; if scale structure—independent of time-dependent saliences of particular notes—can be shown to operate in musical-pitch perception, then the formal structure embodied in the circle of fifths can be shown to have perceptual significance.

---

[1]Although reasons for stability or prototypicality of particular scale members can be advanced on structural grounds (Cross, Chapter 1, this volume), it is difficult to accord prototypical value to one particular note on structural grounds alone. It would seem that some consideration must be taken of the influence of the prevalent system of organising pitch simultaneities or chords (see Erickson, 1982) on the perception of melodies, together with an evaluation of temporal determinants of pitch stability, to account for the particular form (key structure; see Zuckerkandl, 1971) that the use of differential degrees of pitch stability has taken in Western music. Despite the work of Shepard (1982b), Krumhansl et al. (1982), Terhardt et al. (1982), and Balzano (1980), a formal, testable approach to the perception of pitch simultaneities in music has not clearly been demonstrated.

PERCEPTION OF NOTE SEQUENCES RANGING
IN APPROXIMATION TO SCALAR CONFORMANCE

A series of experiments was conducted (Cross, Howell, and West, 1983) in which the contention that scalar structure—as distinct from modal structure—might form part of the developed competence of Western listeners was explored by testing listeners' preferences for sequences of notes that conformed to scalar structure in a range of degrees while avoiding conformance to any particular modal structure. Degree of conformance to scale structure was defined by how many consecutive notes of a melodic sequence could be assigned to a single diatonic major scale and thus, was bounded by interscale relationships as apparent in the circle of fifths. Neither one nor two notes can suffice to define a scale. Because a scale covers an area of seven proximate elements in the circle, any two notes, no matter how far apart (e.g., the notes 0 and 6; see Figure 2), must fall into at least two scales. To define a scale unambiguously requires at least three notes; hence, for a melodic sequence to conform as little as possible to scale structure, no three consecutive notes should be derived from one scale. Such a sequence was termed *first-order* scale conformant and was highly restricted in structure as only four types of three-note group can be formed that do not derive from a single scale (i.e., three-note groups of the type 0, 1, 2; 0, 4, 8; 0, 1, 4; and 0, 3, 4). The second least conformant type of sequence was constructed so that three and only three consecutive notes could come from one scale and was termed *second-order* scale conformant. Similarly, in *third-order* conformant sequences, four and only four consecutive notes come from one scale, and so on.

Within these constraints, sequences notes were produced at random (though pitch range and maximum interval size were controlled). Subjects were required to rate sequences for preference and musicality. We found that subjects with little or no musical training were indistinguishable in their pattern of judgments from musically trained subjects and that instead of preference and ajudged musicality increasing with increasing order of scalar approximation, a U-shaped function was obtained, with first-order sequences receiving an unexpectedly high rating (Cross et al., 1983).

Apparently, subjects were basing their judgments on some factor other than simple conformance to scale structure as we defined it. Three main factors were considered: the small interval sizes associated with first-order sequences, the relative structural parsimony of first-order sequences, and the possibility of subjects imposing their own subjective metre on the sequences (even though there were no explicit cues to such a metre). In first-order sequences (of the length used here), every fourth note has to fall within a single scale. Thus, if subjects were implicitly stressing every fourth note, the stressed notes (producing a three in the bar metre) form a fully scalar sequence that may have influenced sequence ratings. The structure of other orders of approximation require the imposition of unfamiliar or, possibly, overlong rhythmic groupings: second-, third- and fourth-orders requiring five-, six-, and seven-beat metres, respectively.

An experiment was carried out in which either every fourth or fifth beat of each sequence was stressed, producing either three- or four-beat metres. If the subjective metre hypothesis is correct, preferences for first-order four-beat sequences are depressed, whereas first-order three-beat sequence preferences would remain high. If any of the other factors (e.g., interval size) is operant, then imposing metres on the sequences should have no effect. Thus, if the first-order metre interaction occurred, it could be inferred that scale structure was operational in listeners' perceptions.

It was found that the four-beat metre did, indeed, lower first-order preferences (Figure 3). It would appear that listeners did discriminate between note sequences on the basis of scalar conformance per se and that this factor interacted with rhythmic grouping to produce the paradoxical U-shaped preference function (see Cross, et al., 1983). The additional peak at the second-order point with the imposed three in the bar metre would be expected on the basis that it made the six-beat grouping required in second-order sequences to extract scalarity more available to subjects' perceptions. As the other factors—structural parsimony and small interval size—which might have affected listeners' judgments of first-order sequences, remained the same in both metrical conditions, it would seem that listeners can use diatonic structure independently of extrinsic modal cues.

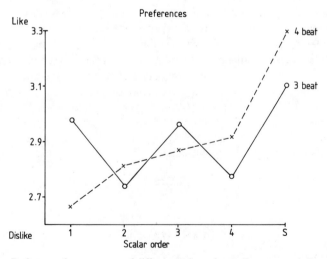

Figure 3.   Preferences for sequences of different scalar orders under two metrical conditions.

DERIVING A SENSE OF SCALAR CONFORMANCE

Following from this finding is the issue of what form a listener's representation of scale structure may take and how it might be derived in the course of a melodic sequence. Judging scalar conformance can be done only by reference to the pitches of the notes in the melody. Listeners may do it in one of two ways: They may match notes or intervals against those that are permissible within scales, or they may build up a representation of a specific scale or set of scales and match new notes against that representation. In the first case, each new note, together with its predecessors, would have to be matched against scale-conforming or non-scale-conforming combinations. For instance, the notes C, D♭, and D (or 0, 1, 2) cannot come from one major scale; such a sequence could be rejected by a listener without the need to consider exactly which scale or scales were being violated. This process would require that a listener retain in memory individual sequence notes or intervals up to the point where a judgment as to scalar conformance was required.

In the second case, a listener forms a representation of a scale or set of scales (scalar schema) in the course of a sequence; the listener would not need to remember all the sequence notes. As each new note occurs, it would be matched against an existing scalar schema. If it is scale conformant, it could strengthen the scalar schema; otherwise, it would be identified as out of scale.

There are two principal ways in which a listener might use sequence notes to build up a scalar schema. It could be constructed according to the number of within-scale notes presented; thus, the notes C, B, and F would produce a less stable structure than C, B, F, and D, which would necessarily produce a weaker schema than C, B, F, D, and A. Alternatively, a scalar schema could be set up by using structural scale-defining properties of sequence notes. As has been stated earlier, to define a scale requires the use of at least three notes: two opposite one another in the circle of fifths plus any other note. As can be seen in Figure 4, the use of notes 11 and 5 permits only two alternative scales; the addition of any other note unambiguously identifies one or other of those scales. This property of *scale specificity* requires the use of two such opposite notes separated by the musical interval of a tritone (diminished fifth or augmented fourth), together with one or more scale notes. Any other group of notes occurring within a scale cannot, uniquely, specify a single scale.

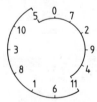

Figure 4.   Overlap between two maximally distinct diatonic scales in the circle of fifths.

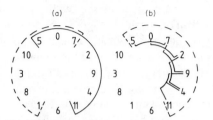

Figure 5. (a) Range of scales with which the set ⟨ 5, 0, 7 ⟩ occurs. (b) Frequency of occurrence within one scale of ⟨ 5, 0, 7 ⟩-type sets.

It should be noted that the more bunched a group of notes is within the circle of fifths, the more frequently that type of group occurs within a single scale and the greater the number of scales from which the group may be drawn. For instance, in Figure 5(a), the group of notes ⟨5, 0, 7⟩ can occur in any one of the five scales bounded by the two limiting scales shown; in Figure 5(b), all three-note groups within one scale that have a form analogous to ⟨5, 0, 7⟩ are indicated, a total of five groups in all. It may be that although the group itself can occur within several scales, the frequency of occurrence of the type of group within one scale could permit inferences about a scalar schema to be made in a listener's perceptions. So two potential usages of pitch structure are possible if listeners assign a scalar schema in the course of a sequence. Both usages are, in any case, dependent on a single structural variable, the spread of sequence notes within the circle of fifths.

As has been shown, sequences of notes that fall within one scale are differentiable in perception from those that do not come from a single scale (Cross et al., 1983). Requiring a subject to identify a non-scalar note as a wrong note in the course of an otherwise scalar sequence should indicate the degree to which a listener has formed a sense of scalar conformance from the notes preceding the non-scalar note. Properties of the group of notes preceding the wrong note may be varied independently to investigate how they affect the identification of the wrong note and the basis for judgments of scalar conformance. Consider the sequences in Figure 6. Both sequences conform to scalar structure up to the sixth note; there are five scale-conformant notes prior to the non-scalar note. In Figure

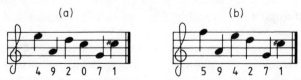

Figure 6. Note sequences conforming to scalar structure up to the sixth note. (a) First five notes are closely grouped in the circle of fifths. (b) First five notes have a greater spread in the circle of fifths.

6(a), the first five notes are grouped closely within the circle of fifths and thus can be found in more than one scale. In Figure 6(b), the first five notes can occur only within two scales and show a greater spread within the circle of fifths. In Figure 6(a), one has to trace back three notes from the non-scalar note before its non-scalarity becomes apparent. Thus, notes 1, 7, and 0 are scale conformant, whereas notes 1, 7, 0, and 2 are not. In that sense, note 2 is the *contradicted* note and the distance to the contradicted note is 3. In Figure 6(b), the distance to the contradicted note is 4 (i.e., one has to count back from 1 to 7, 2, 4, 9, where 9 is the contradicted note).

It can be seen that within certain limits, the following three factors can be varied: (1) the number of scalar notes prior to the non-scalar note; (2) the distance to contradicted note; and (3) the spread of notes prior to the non-scalar note within the circle of fifths. The effect that these factors have on detection of the non-scalar note throws light on how judgments of scalar conformance are made. If subjects simply match successive notes of intervals against those permissible within scale, they need to remember those notes or intervals individually. Therefore, performance should deteriorate with factors that increase the memory load. The factor most clearly fitting this bill is distance to the contradicted note. The further back the subject has to go to detect non-scalarity, the less able the subject should be to pick out the non-scale note. If subjects base judgments of scalar conformance on matching successive notes to a scalar schema that is developed on the basis of number of scalar notes presented, non-scale note detection should improve with number of notes prior to the non-scalar note. Finally, if subjects base their judgments on matching successive notes to a scalar schema whose strength is determined by scale generality or specificity, performance should differ with a difference in spread of note prior to the non-scalar note within the circle of fifths. If greater logical scale specificity is the crucial factor, then performance should improve with the greater spread of notes. If greater scale generality is important, then performance should improve with greater bunching of notes within the circle of fifths.

An experiment was carried out in which subjects were required to listen to a series of notes and indicate when they thought one of the notes did not fit in with its predecessors (Howell, West, and Cross, 1984). The sequences consisted of a scalar group of notes preceding a non-scalar note. The scalar group varied as described previously. In addition to this wrong note detection task (WNDT), subjects performed a note repetition detection task (NRDT) that was included to provide an analogous memory task. In the NRDT, the sequences were identical to those in the WNDT except that the wrong note was replaced by a repetition of the contradicted note. The subjects' task was to identify the note that had been heard before. Sequence parameters were manipulated in exactly the same way as for the WNDT. It was expected that subjects' performance in the NRDT would deteriorate with increasing distance between the two occurrences of the repeated note and with increasing number of notes prior to the note repetition (see Deutsch, 1972). If the WNDT failed to be affected by these two parameters in a similar way, this would lend support to the view that memory for individual notes or intervals was not the crucial factor in judgments of scalar conformance.

Eight subjects with no formal musical training participated in this experiment. Each sequence consisted of eight notes. The number of notes prior to the non-scalar repeated note varied between 3 and 5. Distance to the contradicted was either 2 or 3, and the number of scales permitted by the sequence notes prior to the non-scalar note was either 1 or 2. All factors were varied orthogonally and there were five sequences to each cell. The number of times subjects identified the non-scale note as the wrong note was counted for each cell (maximum was 5). It should be noted that subjects were not instructed specifically to look for non-scalar notes. They were asked simply to indicate when they thought a particular note did not fit in with its predecessors. It was of interest in its own right whether subjects used non-scalarity as a basis for their choice.

The results of the experiment indicate considerable difference in performance between the WNDT and the NRDT. The NRDT gave better performance generally ($p < .01$). With the NRDT performance deteriorated with increasing distance between occurrences of the repeated note ($p < .05$) while there was no such effect in the WNDT. Performance in the NRDT also decreased with increasing number of prior notes ($p < .025$), whereas, in the WNDT, there was no such monotonic trend. On the other hand, WNDT performance improved with greater bunching of notes prior to the non-scalar note within the circle of fifths ($p < .05$) with no similar effect in the NRDT.

These results indicate that subjects did indeed use scalar conformance as a basis for judging whether a given note fitted with its predecessors and that this judgment was made by matching successive notes against a scalar schema rather than by identification of scalar or non-scalar intervals per se. The strength of the scalar schema was influenced by the spread of notes within the circle of fifths— the schema being stronger with greater bunching of notes (and hence, less logical scale specificity). However, as only two levels of spread had been used (corresponding to scale specificity of 1 or 2), this interpretation was open to question. It could be that performance in the scale specificity condition was influenced simply by the possibility of occurrence of the tritone in sequences of scale specificity of 1 but not scale specificity of 2. (The tritone is the interval between notes opposite each other in the circle of fifths and is an "unfamiliar" interval.)

To test this possibility, two further experiments were performed. Subjects were required, as before, to identify the wrong note in a sequence. In one experiment, five scalar notes preceded the wrong note, whereas in the other four, scalar notes preceded the non-scalar note. In the first experiment, the distance to the contradicted note was varied between 2 and 4; in the second experiment, it varied between 2 and 3. In the first experiment, the logical scale specificity varied between 1 and 3; in the second experiment, it varied between 1 and 4. Sequences in the two experiments were mixed together and performed by the subjects as one task (to prevent subjects simply determining that the wrong note came in the same position in the sequence each time).

The results of both experiments give support for the earlier finding that logical scale specificity (or bunching of notes within the circle of fifths) influences the strength of the scalar schema so that less logical scale specificity or greater bunching of notes results in a better established schema. In both experiments, there were significant trends for better performance with less logical scale specificity of notes preceding the non-scalar note ($p < .05$ and $p < .0005$, respectively).

As previously noted, the higher the number of scales from which a set of notes can derive, the more frequently sets of notes having similar form can occur within one scale (Figure 5). Thus, the efficacy of narrow-spread sets of notes in enabling identification of wrong notes may derive from the commonality of occurrence of such types of sets within single scales and the consequent familiarity for subjects. However, a necessary corollary is that the spread of a set of notes defines the number of possible non-scalar notes. For example, in Figure 5, the note set $\langle 5, 0, 7 \rangle$ is shown together with the range of scales from which it can derive. As can be seen, only one note, 6, cannot fit together with the note set in any scale. Figure 5 shows that the addition of any other note to the set $\langle 5, 11 \rangle$ necessarily delimits a single scale; there remain, therefore, another five notes from the circle of fifths that cannot come from the scale. So the subjects' use of tightly grouped sets of notes within the circle of fifths could reflect either of two strategies: Sets such as $\langle 5, 0, 7 \rangle$ can serve to build strong scalar schemas either because the set type is familiar in scalar music or because they cut down the number of possible non-scalar notes which, because there are fewer of them, may be more cognitively salient.

A further set of experiments was conducted to investigate this problem, and to explore the operating limits of scale specificity in perception (West, Howell, and Cross, in preparation). This set of experiments focused solely on scale specificity and its efficacy as a cue to "wrongness" of note; subjects heard blocks of three-note sequences (controlled as to scale specificity) and were required to rate single notes occurring after each sequence for goodness of fit with preceding three notes.

In the first experiment, pitch-class sets of the type $\langle 5, 0, 7 \rangle$ occurring five times within one scale, were used. Any particular pitch-class set of this type occurs within five scales, leaving only one note together with which it cannot fit into some scale; that is, only one possible wrong note. Four-note sequences were constructed of which the first three notes constituted a pitch-class set of the type $\langle 5, 0, 7 \rangle$ (order of pitch-classes within the set are always randomised) and the fourth note either fell within some scale with, or was out of scale with, the preceding three notes. Subjects rated out-of-scale (wrong) notes as significantly worse fitting than in-scale notes. A further experiment, using a similar paradigm, showed that the order in which the notes of the three-note set occurred had no effect.

A third experiment showed that pitch-class sets of the $\langle 5, 0, 7 \rangle$ type were significantly stronger in inducing subjects to rate out-of-scale notes as badly fitting than were three-note sets of the type $\langle 5, n, 11 \rangle$, where n can be any number other than 5 or 11 within the circle of fifths. Sets of the type $\langle 5, 0, 7 \rangle$ occur most frequently (five times) within a major scale, occur in five scales, and permit only one possible out-of-scale (wrong) note; sets of the type $\langle 5, n, 11 \rangle$ occur least frequently in a scale (once), and any such set occurs in only one scale and allows five wrong notes (see Figure 5). The predicted effect of logical scale specificity (i.e., the lower the logical scale specificity, the stronger the scalar schema) can be seen to hold right to the limits of scale specificity.

Two experiments confirmed this relationship. In the first, $\langle 5, 0, 7 \rangle$-type sets enabled subjects to differentiate consistently between in-scale and out-of-scale notes in their ratings, whereas first-order type sets (e.g., $\langle 0, 1, 2 \rangle$ produced no consistent effect on subjects' ratings of subsequent notes. (It should be noted that any note following a three-note, first-order set will be in scale with at least two of the notes of the first-order set.) In the second experiment, $\langle 5, 0, 7 \rangle$-type sets produced significantly lower ratings for wrong notes than did major and minor triad sets (that is, sets of the type $\langle 0, 4, 7 \rangle$ and $\langle 0, 3, 7 \rangle$). This finding is somewhat surprising musically, as it is generally accepted that major or minor triads are the best cue to particular musical keys (see, e.g., Schenker, 1954; Deutsch and Feroe, 1981). It is less surprising if a differentiation is drawn between scale and key, such that scale identity is founded in structural or time-independent considerations, whereas key seems founded on time-dependent note relationships and also in some necessary consideration of pitch simultaneities or chords (see fn. 1). Thus, $\langle 5, 0, 7 \rangle$ sets seem a better cue to scale structure than do major and minor triads; they may not be a better cue to key identity.

This series of experiments indicates that scale specificity is a major factor in determining strength of scalar schema across the complete range of scale specificities. However, it seems that it is not possible to address the problem of set-type frequency of occurrence or number of scales within which a set may be found by this experimental means; indeed, it seems impossible to address the problem at all, as the frequency of occurrence and the number of scales appear as two sides of the same coin, one being simply the inverse of the other.

Nevertheless, the problem may become tractable if certain of the assumptions that have underlain our descriptions and treatment of equivalence between sets of pitch classes are reexamined. We have taken the basis for equivalence between pitch-class sets to be number of pitch-class sets and layout *in one direction* in the circle of fifths. This can be described as transpositional equivalence between sets; any pitch-class set can be transposed into an equivalent pitch-class set by the addition of the same number (mod 12) to each of its members. However, another basis for equivalence (more common in contemporary "atonal" theory) can be taken; this involves treating two pitch-class sets as equivalent if they have the same number of members and the same layout in either direction on the circle of fifths. This is illustrated in Figure 7, where the pitch-class set ⟨5, 0, 2⟩ is shown together with the pitch-class set ⟨5, 7, 2⟩; both sets have the same number of members, and the layout of one is the mirror image of the other. They can be said to be equivalent if a set's layout and its mirror image are considered as representative of the same underlying structure (see Rahn, 1980; see also Cross, Chapter 1, this volume). This form of equivalence can be described as transpositional–inversional.

On this basis, sets of the type ⟨5, 0, 2⟩ can be shown to occur more frequently within a major scale than do sets of the type ⟨5, 0, 7⟩; ⟨5, 0, 2⟩-type sets occur eight times within a scale (Figure 7). However, the number of scales within which ⟨5, 0, 7⟩-type sets can occur remains greater than the number of scales that ⟨5, 0, 2⟩-type sets may derive from, as the former are more tightly bunched on the circle of fifths than are the latter. Accordingly, if ⟨5, 0, 7⟩-type sets can be shown to be better cues to wrongness of note than ⟨5, 0 2⟩-type sets, then either the cognitive basis for equivalence between sets is, by and large, transpositional, or judgments of wrongness of note are founded on the number of scales from which a pitch-class set may derive (or number of permitted wrong notes, as number of scales and number of wrong notes are covariant). This outcome would tell us nothing we did not already know. On the other hand, if ⟨5, 0, 2⟩-type sets act as a better cue to wrong notes than do ⟨5, 0, 7⟩-type sets, then the basis of wrong-note judgments (and thus strength of scalar schema) is shown to be frequency of occurrence of set-type within scale, and cognitive equivalence between sets is shown to be founded on transpositional–inversional equivalence between the sets. The latter outcome would be considerably more informative than the former and somewhat more perplexing.

An experiment was conducted in which sets of types ⟨5, 0, 2⟩ and ⟨5, 0, 7⟩ were followed by wrong notes, and subjects were required to rate this wrong note for goodness of fit with the preceding set. Subjects consistently rated wrong notes significantly lower after ⟨5, 0, 2⟩-type sets than after ⟨5, 0, 7⟩-type sets; this result was replicated with a different group of subjects.

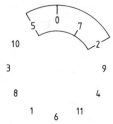

Figure 7.   Inversional equivalence between the sets ⟨ 5, 0, 2 ⟩ and ⟨ 5, 7, 2 ⟩.

It would seem that subjects' judgments of wrongness of note tend to be determined by frequency of occurrence within the major scale structure of the context set of notes, rather than by the number of scales or number of wrong notes that context set permits. Hence, subjects tend to act heuristically rather than logically. Moreover, subjects seemed to take transposition/inversional equivalence as their basis for equivalence between sets, rather than, as expected, to take transpositional equivalence as a perceptual basis. This is surprising in view of evidence (e.g., Dowling, 1972) that recognition of melodic fragments, when re-presented in an inverted (i.e., mirror-image) form, is considerably worse than when the melodic fragments are simply transposed. It could, however, be argued that the levels at which transposition and inversion are applied (together with task) are different in Dowling's and our study. In Dowling's study inversion was applied to temporal forms (melodic fragments); in ours, inversion was applied structurally, and equivalence between sets was time-independent.

CONCLUSIONS

From this investigation of scale structure and its cognitive representation, we conclude that scalar representation in perception is better thought of in terms of general scalarity than in terms of sharply defined scalar structure. Scale seems to be a category, of which the constituents are groups of notes and their interrelationships; the diagnostic features of the constituents are primarily the interval relations they permit and their frequency of occurrence within scale (Tversky, 1977). Here, musical pitch seems to operate as a cognitive domain within which relationships within and between patterns may be expressed and articulated. These relationships may be time-dependent or partially or wholly independent of temporal considerations, rather than perceptual correlates of simple or complex physical quantities and qualities.

These sets of experiments are not intended to give a complete account of musical-pitch perception or even musical-scale perception. The model (mod 12 arithmetic) within which relationships between pitch events are characterised is highly selective and restrictive; because of that, simple hypotheses can be formulated and rigorously tested. It has been shown that structural relationships between groups of notes are perceptually important; the description of these relationships and of groups of notes (properly, pitch-classes) are carried out at a highly abstract (i.e., time-independent) level. It seems from other evidence (e.g., Dowling, 1978; Cuddy, 1982; Brown and Butler, 1981; Edworthy, Chapter 7, this volume) that time-based structure of groups of pitches (not pitch-classes) or melodic fragments is also of considerable importance in musical-pitch cognition. It may be that melodic fragments form a fairly concrete level of musical-pitch representation; the integration of such fragments within a constrained framework such as the circle of fifths and the logic deriving from that integration could account for the abstract level of pitch cognition studied here (see Allport, 1980; see also Serafine, 1983).

In our study, only one method of formally representing pitch structure is tested although it would seem that others are possible. One method might be be to take the notes of a scale as constituting a cyclic group of Order 7 (see Cross, Chapter 1, this volume; see Rothenberg, 1975); another might be to take the notes of the scale as a network of major and minor thirds (Balzano, 1980). Given this range of possibilities, it seems plausible that multiple formal representations of the same pitch structure are available in cognition. As Hankiss (1981) speculates, semantic oscillation (i.e., oscillation between two or more sets of interpretive functions that map the same events into different structural contexts) may play a central role in aesthetic perception. It is perhaps this range of possible representations that accounts for the primacy in articulating structure that pitch has and has had in Western (and much non-Western) music.

Of course, the fact that certain types of logical relationships are determining factors in listeners' perceptions and judgments of pitch does not, in itself, imply that pitch is musically a separate and self-contained domain. Listeners may derive pitch information by imposing or assuming metrical structural for which no *physical* cues exist. Indeed, both Clarke (Chapter 9) and Sloboda and Parker (Chapter 6) indicate that interaction between different musical dimensions is more likely to be the rule rather than the exception. Nevertheless, it does imply that however pitch is construed in music (as a separate domain or as necessarily integrated in a more complex domain together with metre, and so on), those types of logical relationships may be accessible in some form and their presence or absence may be a factor in our ability to make sense of as music—or accept as music—what we hear.

REFERENCES

Allport, D. A. Patterns and actions: Cognitive mechanisms are content specific. In G. Claxton, (Ed.), *Cognitive psychology: New directions*. London: Routlage and Kegan Paul, 1980.

Attneave, F., and Olson, R. K. Pitch as a medium: A new approach to psychophysical scaling. *American Journal of Psychology*, 1971, *84*, 147–166.

Balzano, G. J. *Chronometric studies of the musical interval sense*. Unpublished doctoral dissertation, Palo Alto: Stanford University, 1977.

Balzano, G. J. The group-theoretic description of 12-fold and microtonal pitch systems. *Computer Music Journal*, 1980, *4*, 66–84.

Balzano, G. J. The pitch set as a level of description for studying musical pitch perception. In M. Clynes (Ed.), *Music, mind and brain*. New York: Plenum, 1982.

Bartlett, J. C., and Dowling, W. J. Recognition of transposed melodies: A key distance effect in developmental perspective. *Journal of Experimental Psychology: Human Perception and Performance*, 1980, *6*, 501–515.

Becker, J. *Traditional music in modern Java*. Honolulu: University of Hawaii Press, 1982.

Bent, I. Analysis. In *Grove's New Dictionary of Music*. London: Macmillan, 1980.

Brown, H., and Butler, D. Diatonic trichords as minimal tonal cue-cells. *In Theory Only*, 1981, *5*, 39–55.

Browne, R. Tonal implications of the diatonic set. *In Theory Only*, 1981, *5*, 3–21.

Burns, E. M. and Ward, W. D. Categorical perception—phenomenon or epiphenomenon: Evidence from experiments in the perception of melodic musical intervals. *Journal of the Acoustical Society of America*, 1978, *63*, 456–468.

Burns, E. M., and Ward, W. D. Intervals, scales and tuning. In D. Deutsch (Ed.), *The psychology of music*. London: Academic Press, 1982.

Cross, I., Howell, P. and West, R. Preferences for scale structure in melodic sequences. *Journal of Experimental Psychology: Human Perception and Performance*, 1983, *9*, 444–460.

Cuddy, L. L. On hearing pattern in melody. *Psychology of Music*, 1982, *10*, 3–10.

Cuddy, L. L., Cohen, A. J., and Miller, J. Melody recognition: The experimental application of musical rules. *Canadian Journal of Psychology*, 1979, *33*, 148–157.

Davies, J. B. Memory for melodies in tonal sequences: A theoretical note. *British Journal of Psychology*, 1979, *70*, 205–210.

Deutsch, D. Effect of repetition of standard and comparison tones on recognition memory for pitch. *Journal of Experimental Psychology*, 1972, *93*, 156–162.

Deutsch, D. Memory and attention in music. In M. Critchley & R. A. Henson (Eds.). *Music and the brain*. London: Heinemann, 1977.

Deutsch, D. and Feroe, J. The internal representation of pitch sequences in tonal music. *Psychological Review*, 1981, *88*, 503–522.

Divenyi, P. L., and Hirsh, I. J. Some figural properties of auditory patterns. *Journal of the Acoustical Society of America*, 1978, *64*, 1369–1385.

Dowling, W. J. Recognition of melodic transformations: Inversion, retrograde and retrograde inversion. *Perception and Psychophysics*, 1972, *12*, 417–421.

Dowling, W. J. Scale and contour: Two components of a theory of memory for melodies. *Psychological Review*, 1978, *85*, 314–354.

Dowling, W. J., and Bartlett, J. C. The importance of interval information in long-term memory for melodies. *Psychomusicology*, 1981, *1*, 30–49.

Dowling, W. J., and Fujitani, D. S. Contour, interval and pitch recognition in memory for melodies. *Journal of the Acoustical Society of America*, 1971, *49*, 524–531.

Erickson, R. New music and psychology. In D. Deutsch (Ed.), *The Psychology of Music*. London: Academic Press, 1982.

Hankiss, E. Semantic oscillation: A universal of artistic expression. In W. Steiner (Ed.), *The sign in music and literature*. Austin, Texas: University of Texas Press, 1981.

Howell, P., West, R., and Cross, I. *The detection of notes incompatible with scalar structure. Journal of the Acoustical Society of America*, 1984, *76*, 1682–1689.

Krantz, D. H., and Tversky, A. Similarity of rectangles: An analysis of subjective dimensions. *Journal of Mathematical Psychology*, 1975, *12*, 4–34.

Krumhansl, C. L. The psychological representation of pitch in a tonal context. *Cognitive Psychology*, 1979, *11*, 346–374.

Krumhansl, C. L., Bharucha, J. J., and Kessler, E. J. Perceived harmonic structure of chords in three musical keys. *Journal of Experimental Psychology: Human Perception and Performance*, 1982, *8*, 24–36.

Rahn, J. *Basic atonal theory*. New York: Longmans, Green, 1980.

Reti, R. *The thematic process in music*. New York: Macmillan, 1951.

Rosner, B., and Meyer, L. Melodic processes and the perception of music. In D. Deutsch (Ed.), *The psychology of music*. London: Academic Press, 1982.

Rothenberg, D. A mathematical model for perception applied to the perception of pitch. In *Lecture Notes in Computer Science* (Vol. 22). New York: Springer-Verlag, 1975.

Rothenberg, D. A model for pattern perception with musical applications: Part II: The information content of pitch structures. *Mathematical Systems Theory*, 1978, *11*, 353–372.

Sargeant, D. The octave—Percept or concept. *Psychology of Music*, 1983, *11*, 3–18.

Schenker, H. *Harmony* (O. Jones and E. M. Borgese, Trans.). Chicago: University of Chicago Press, 1954.

Serafine, M. L. Cognition in music. *Cognition*, 1983, *14*, 119–183.

Shepard, R. N. Geometrical approximations to the structure of musical pitch. *Psychological Review*, 1982, *89*, 305–333. (a)

Shepard, R. N. Structural representations of musical pitch. In D. Deutsch (Ed.), *The psychology of music*. London: Academic Press, 1982. (b)

Stevens, S. S., and Volkmann, J. The relation of pitch to frequency: A revised scale. *American Journal of Psychology*, 1940, *53*, 329–353.

Terhardt, E. Psychoacoustic evaluation of musical sounds. *Perception and Psychophysics*, 1978, *23*, 483–492.

Terhardt, E., Stoll, G., and Seewann, M. Algorithm for extraction of pitch and pitch salience from complex tonal signals. *Journal of the Acoustical Society of America*, 1982, *71*, 679–688.

Tversky, A. Features of similarity. *Psychological Review*, 1977, *84*, 327–352.

West, R., Howell, P., and Cross, I. *Circle of fifths relations and sense of scalar conformance*. In preparation.

Zuckerlandl, V. *The sense of music*. Princeton, NJ: Princeton University Press, 1971.

6

Immediate Recall of Melodies

John A. Sloboda and David H. H. Parker

INTRODUCTION

The primary purpose of this chapter is to present musical transcriptions of the attempts of eight adult subjects to recall part of a folk melody that was repeatedly presented to them. We also present the results of some analyses of these transcripts, which seem to point particularly clearly to the involvement of structural knowledge in musical memory.

Problems of Transcription

The study of free recall in music has not commended itself to many researchers. This is understandable: For one, there is no generally accepted criterion for what counts as a reliable transcription. The conventional notation of Western musical culture forces the transcriber to translate what may be a fluctuating and richly variable signal into a limited set of pitch and time categories prescribed by the notation. Much information is inevitably lost in the process. This is, of course, true of linguistic transcription, too, but the problems are less acute because it is often possible to assume that the speaker intends to address the categories the notation embodies (e.g., he or she intends to utter words contained within a shared natural language). In music, it is less clear to what extent a singer *intends* a performance to be interpreted within the categories of tonal music. The problem arises largely because the intentions of a musical performer are not bound by *practical* constraints in the way that they usually are in language. Linguistic communication is embedded in an extralinguistic context, and it is often easy enough to discover when a speaker's intentions have been misinterpreted. Music is not a communication system in the way that language is. It is relatively self-contained and has no major consequences for domains of cognition beyond music.

How, then, can we know when a singer intends his or her performance to be interpreted by a listener within the categories supplied by conventional notation?

We think there are at least three factors that should be taken into consideration:

1. If a Western listener *hears* the bulk of a performance as fitting the pitch/time categories of tonal music, then it is likely that the performer intends it to be heard this way. In other words, if a performance *makes sense* tonally, then it is probable, though not completely certain, that such sense was intended by the performer, especially if the performance is fairly long. There are so many degrees of freedom for a musical performance that it would be coincidence indeed it a sequence generated non-tonally had consistent and strong tonal implications. Successful transcription is in itself some indication that an intention exists to address the categories embodied in the notation.

2. There is evidence that children immersed in a musical culture (such as our own) internalize the structures that are implicit in the bulk of music they hear (e.g., Gardner, 1981; Zenatti, 1969). We therefore, feel that most adults, conceive of music in terms of these enculturated structures. This is as true of performance as it is of perception.

3. Given positive indications on the preceding two counts, a performance is most likely to address intentionally the normal categories of the culture when its context encourages this. One such context involves the presentation of an unambiguously well-formed musical sequence for recall. We may argue that if a singer *hears* the music as tonal, then he or she will attempt to reproduce it as tonal.

These criteria raise particular problems for the transcription of the performances of children or of people from cultures whose musical structures are different from those of the transcriber. It is especially difficult to interpret transcriptions of songs by very young children (e.g., Dowling, 1982; Moog, 1976) or of songs from specialised or isolated subcultures (e.g., the Serbo-Croatian folk songs transcribed by Bartók and Lord, 1951). We are not concerned with resolving these difficulties here. Rather, we argue that our own data do not fall foul of these difficulties and are, therefore, optimal for transcription into conventional notation.

The foregoing does not entirely dispose of the problems associated with making transcriptions. One very important and well-documented fact about performance is that, even when the intention is unambiguously directed towards the categories of pitch and time enshrined in our notation, performance deviates significantly and systematically from the notated ideal. Conventional notation is not up to the task of recording the expressive variation that is present in any musical performance. Furthermore, such variations are not reliably diagnosed as variations by listeners. This means that whereas variations may contribute to the sense of muscial life or articulation and may even help a listener to assign the intended tonal or metrical structure (Sloboda, 1985), they are unlikely to be capable of reliable transcription by ear, even if a notation were available to represent them. They are reliably captured only by mechanical transcription that records the exact timing and pitch parameters of successive notes (e.g., Seashore, 1938; Gabrielsson, 1974; Shaffer, 1981).

If the primary concern of an empirical study is with such expressive variation, then, clearly, conventional transcription is of little use. If, however, the primary concern is with the basic pitch and timing structures on which expressive variations operate, then there is some merit in a transcription process that necessarily discards much of these variations. Only when a variation is so large as to cause some uncertainty about which category a note should be assigned to (e.g., crotchet or quaver, G or G#) does it need to find its way into a transcription. If the performance is, indeed, one based on the structures inherent in our culture, then the proportion of variations causing uncertainty should not be large. If it is, we can hardly say that the performance strikes the ear as unambiguous. Such a performance does not fulfill the first of our criteria for transcription. In our own data, subjects produced a total of 1069 notes. We judged 62 (5.8%) of these to be ambiguous in the time domain and 33 (3.1%) in the pitch domain. Of this small proportion, many timing deviations were apparently due to the taking of a breath that distorted an established metre; and several pitch deviations were associated with large pitch leaps, suggesting response programming problems rather than intrinsic deviations from tonality as an explanatory cause.

We are satisfied that our transcriptions do not misrepresent the performance in any way that is germane to the issues under discussion. We do not rule out, however, the possibility that we—and other potential transcribers—are subject to systematic perceptual distortions. For instance, the effects of categorical pitch and time perception will almost inevitably be to render transcriptions more coherent than they might be.[1] One merit of transcription in conventional notation is, of course, that it is immediately comprehensible to literate musicians. More literal transcriptions, in terms of precise performance parameters, are invaluable for some purposes, but they must be interpreted into something approaching conventional notation before they can be understood as music. Formal procedures for translating between numerical performance parameters and conventional notation (e.g., Longuet-Higgins, 1976; Steedman, 1977) have not yet solved the full range of problems presented by real auditory signals. We believe that, for the type of research reported here, there is, at present, no viable alternative to aural transcription by musically trained listeners.

---

[1]Copies of the original tape recordings are available from the authors on request, and we would welcome independent transcriptions.

The Analysis of Recall Data

A different reason for the paucity of empirical work on musical recall is the lack of agreed upon and well-motivated methods of describing and analysing the content of a performance in relationship to an original model. It is clear that crude measures such as number of notes correct tell us little of interest about the nature of the recalls.

The recent study of recall processes in language provides some pointers to the type of analysis that might be appropriate (Bower, 1976; Kintsch, 1977). We know that verbal recall is rarely word-for-word correct, but it matches the original at a higher level of meaning and structure. We find substitution and inference, selective loss of information, and other distortions, but preservation of essential meaning and structure. We do not wish to be constrained by the details of recall analysis methods in language, but we are concerned to explore methods of musical analysis that provide information at an analogous level of abstraction. This makes certain conditions necessary. First, the music to be remembered must be long enough to contain within it a variety of the types of structural progressions and relationship that characterise the typical music of the culture; we have chosen the folk song or popular song melody as such a typical structure. Second, the music to be remembered must be short enough to allow for the possibility that subjects can encode it completely at some level of abstraction within a single hearing; pilot observations suggest that a melody containing about 30 notes fulfills these conditions. It is worth pointing out that most contemporary research on musical memory has used some form of recognition procedure (e.g., asking subjects to judge whether two melodies are the same or different) and has used sequences containing much fewer than 30 notes.

Recall versus Recognition

Recall and recognition testing both have a long and well-established history within the study of memory. Both have strengths and weaknesses, and to a large extent, complement one another. Recognition studies are particularly amenable to factorial hypothesis-testing designs in which a high degree of stimulus control is exercised. By restricting subjects' responses to a few preordained categories, it is possible to obtain precise answers to preformulated questions. Yet, as many, including Newell (1973) and Allport (1975) have noticed, such research strategy can be counterproductive. In many cases, the binary theoretical choices that this forces one to make are naïve and ill-conceived. Successive refinements and elaborations can lead one away from what was important about the original question, so that the research, although technically sound, sheds little light on the most salient aspects of the phenomenon under study.

There are other reasons for being cautious about the overextensive use of the recognition paradigm in music research. In many instances, subjects are required to do things that are not familiar to them and that find no parallel in their normal musical behaviour. Experiments which, for instance, use the probe technique of extracting a small segment from a longer one for recognition are of doubtful ecological validity, as are those requiring recognition of any short, decontextualized musical fragments. The most prevalent type of natural recognition behaviour involves the identification of the name of a piece of music or the feeling that "I have heard this before," where "this" can be as long as a whole movement or as short as a theme in context (Halpern, 1983; Pollard-Gott, 1983).

Recall studies provide more "messy" data, since subjects' responses are not confined to preordained categories. Although hypothesis testing is still possible, the amount of behaviour left unaccounted for is much larger. This is the price that many researchers are prepared to pay for data that bear on integrated sets of complex processes and that reflect more directly the exercise of preexisting skill. Recall data provide many more opportunities for abrasive contact between theoretical preconceptions and reality. They are also, perhaps, the most appropriate kind of data to gather when theory is relatively unrefined. One is less likely to overlook some vital aspect of the behaviour in question when faced by a rich data base than when restricting oneself to the impoverished behaviour that is the typical outcome of recognition experiments.

A particular difficulty with the recall method as applied to music is that many subjects have no well-practised response mode, have no instrumental skill, and may be totally inept at vocal techniques such as singing, humming, or whistling. Such ineptitude naturally predisposes the researcher toward recognition testing. We wonder, however, whether psychologists of music have sometimes made too pessimistic assumptions about the ability of untrained subjects to retain material and make coherent responses. With a methodological and theoretical predisposition toward recognition studies, such assumptions may not have been as critically examined as they should have been. We have been pleasantly surprised by the quantity, quality, and coherence of the data we have obtained from committed but relatively untrained subjects.

Our investigation was prompted by the wish to provide a data base of musical recalls. We began with no strong hypotheses about what we would find, other than the intuition that high-level structures would be implicated. Rather than present a rational reconstruction that embeds our data in theoretical preconceptions, we proceed roughly historically, describing first our method of data collection, then our results and some of the analyses performed, and finally, theoretical comments. This seems the most appropriate way to proceed in a study that has a strong component of natural history.

METHOD

Our subjects were eight students drawn from a volunteer pool in the Department of Psychology, City of Liverpool College of Higher Education. All were females between the ages of 19–22. Four of the subjects had not had any special musical training but enjoyed listening to music. These we will call the "non-musicians." The other four subjects were musically trained and were active performers of classical music.

We recorded piano performances of several sequences taken from folk-song melodies. Each subject was asked to listen to each sequence six times in a row, providing an attempt at sung recall after each hearing (to "la" or any other chosen syllable). Each recall was recorded for subsequent analysis. After preliminary examination of the recall data, it was decided to discard the results for all sequences other than the first one presented. This was because material from the first set intruded massively into subsequent recalls. Sometimes, the first recall of the second sequence was almost identical to the last recall of the first sequence, even though the presented melodies were quite different. It was surprising for us to obtain this high degree of intersong contamination, and the finding is intriguing in itself. It is also something that only a recall study could have shown. However, we decided to leave it aside in this context as an unnecessary complicating factor.

Accordingly, the data we present are from the six recalls of the first sequence given to the subjects alone. The sequence, given in Example 1, was played at a speed of about two crotchets per second. It comprises the first three phrases of the Russian folk song, "Sailor," contained in a collection of Russian songs (O'Toole, 1974). This song was not known to any of our subjects. The sequence contains 29 notes, subdivided into three phrases (11 + 9 + 9). There are multiple cues to this phrase subdivision: (1) the rests after Notes 11 and 20, (2) the fact that each phrase occupies an identical metrical slot of two bars, and (3) the fact that Note 13 begins a repetition of the melodic and rhythmic pattern that starts the sequence (Note 12 is an added upbeat). In terms of traditional analysis, the sequence shows an A_1A_2B form, where A_1 and A_2 are variants of the same material and B introduces new material. In fact, the B phrase shares features with A as well as differs from it. Notes 25–28 repeat the rhythmic pattern of notes 6–9 at an equivalent point in the metrical structure (third half-bar). Harmonically, the A phrase implies a I–I–V–I movement in D minor, and the B phrase is best interpreted as V–I–V–I in F major. In the full song, B is followed by a repetition of A_2 to bring the verse to a close in D minor.

Example 1. The stimulus sequence used in the study.

We believe that the melody is highly unambiguous in that most listeners within the Western tonal culture hear the structural groupings we have informally assigned, in strong preference to other possible groupings. We base this belief on our own musical intuitions, but also on the formalisations provided by Lerdahl and Jackendoff (1983), Longuet-Higgins (1976), and Steedman (1977). These formalisations embody heuristics for assigning metrical and harmonic structure to note sequences in a way that appears to match the intuitions of experienced listeners. As we understand them, such heuristics provide unanimous support for our parsing.

The appendix to this chapter provides complete transcriptions of the six recall attempts by each of the eight subjects. Subjects 1–4 are the non-musicians, subjects 5–8 are the musicians. The recalls are numbered in sequence so that, for instance, 3.4 denotes the fourth recall of Subject 3. The transcriptions use conventional notation, but with certain differences and additions:

1. All recalls are transcribed in D minor/F major even when, as in a few cases, subjects transposed their response to a new key (usually a semitone up or down). We may take such transpositions to be unintentional and of little interest in the present context, except to show that subjects are coding in terms of pitch relationships rather than absolute pitches.

2. We have not given metrical interpretations above the level of the crotchet beat. Thus, bar lines are omitted.

3. The symbols, *x* and *o,* denote approximations to notated duration and pitch, respectively. When we were in doubt about which pitch or time category was nearest to the note sung, we assigned the note to the category that best preserved a consistent metrical and harmonic interpretation. Although this does make the transcriptions look more coherent than arguably they ought to be, the proportion of notes involved is small enough to make us feel that this is not a serious problem.

4. The curved slur mark encloses notes sung within a single breath.

5. The symbol *v* denotes a slight but discernible pause that bends rather than disrupts an established metre. It is usually associated with the taking of a breath.

RESULTS OF DATA ANALYSES

Melodic Contour Analysis

The first analysis is a fairly low-level one. It measures the degree to which the melodic patterns of the original are retained in the recalls. For this purpose, we derived a melodic contour for Example 1 that shows the pitch movements within the three phrases without regard for duration or contiguous repetition. This is shown in Example 2.

Example 2. The melodic contour Example 1.

We then obtained the melodic contour of each recall by the same method. For instance, the melodic contour of 1.1 is given in Example 3, and that of 1.6 in Example 4. When the subject sang one phrase or less, we looked across the entire contour in Example 2 for the best-fitting phrase. Thus, 1.4 was evaluated against the contour for the second phrase of Example 2, on account of the D–A movement at the beginning. When a subject provided two or more phrases, as in most cases, then the first phrase sung was matched against the first phrase of the original, and so on.

Within each phrase, a recall scored 1 for each of its notes that formed part of a melodic pattern (of two or more notes) found in the original. For example, Example 3 scores 6, because the first six notes match the first six notes of Example 2. Recall 1.2 provides a more difficult example. Its contour is given in Example 5. To score this recall, one has, in effect, to slide the original contour along the recall contour. Thus, the first six notes of the original are found at Notes 1–6 in Example 5. Notes 7–10 do not match anything in the original, but then Notes 11–12 match Notes 7–8 of the original. Therefore, this recall scores 8 on 14 for this measure.

A final example of our scoring procedure is given for Recall 8.4. The melodic contour of its first phrase is given in Example 6. In this case, we find no match to the beginning of the original, so we move through the original contour until we find a match. Notes 7–9 of the recall match notes 7–9 of the original, so this phrase scores 3 on 9.

Table 1 presents summary data from this analysis. Column 1 gives, for each subject, the melodic contour score summed over the six recalls; Column 2 gives the total number of melody notes in the recall contours; and Column 3 expresses 1 as a percentage of 2. These percentage data show wide individual differences ranging from 0% for Subject 6 to 88% for Subject 5. Is there any particular reason for the exceptionally low scores of Subjects 4 and 6? Our view is that

Example 3. The melodic contour of Recall 1.1.

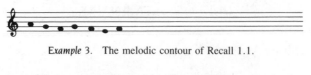

Example 4. The melodic contour of Recall 1.6.

Example 5. The melodic contour of Recall 1.2.

Example 6. The melodic contour of Recall 8.4.

these two cases can be explained, but differently. Let us take Subject 6 first. If we examine a recall such as 6.5, we experience a strong intuition that, despite its low melody score, it is *very* similar to Phrases 1 and 2 of the original. We argue later that its perceptual similarity is based on a shared underlying metrical and harmonic structure; that this subject has constructed a new melody which, in effect, *means* the same thing as the original. Subject 4's recalls demand a different explanation. Visual and aural inspection make it fairly clear that the first two phrases of these recalls are based, not on Phrases 1 and 2 of the original, but on Phrase *3;* and that Phrase 3 of the recall is variable, sometimes resembling the original Phrase 3 (e.g., 4.6), sometimes Phrase 1 (e.g., 4.1), and sometimes neither (e.g., 4.5).

A new structure has been composed by rearranging the phrases of the original, possibly encouraged by a recency effect that favoured memory for Phrase 3 at input. If we rescore this subject, allowing for her phrases to be matched to the original phrase that they most resemble, then her score rises to 67 on 118 (57%). What is particularly striking about these data is the extreme resilience of the new recall schema, once established. There is no move towards a more faithful

Table 1

MELODIC CONTOUR ANALYSIS, BY SUBJECT

Subject	Contour score	Total pitch movements	Contour score as percentage of pitch movements
1	32	62	52
2	45	158	28
3	66	145	46
4	2	116	2
5	84	96	88
6	0	60	0
7	72	140	51
8	86	120	72
	387	897	43

Table 2
MELODIC CONTOUR ANALYSIS, BY TRIAL

Trial	Total produced	Score	Percentage
1	109	54	50
2	144	74	51
3	135	56	41
4	162	77	48
5	162	91	56
6	181	98	54

reproduction of the original over its six repetitions. This persistence of an initial erroneous schema is evident in the recalls of other subjects, although on a smaller scale. It is most evident in the discarded data for subsequent melodies.

We may ask a different question of the data provided by this scoring. To what extent do subjects improve in melodic recall over trials? Table 2 presents melody scores summed over subjects for each of the six trials. Although the number of notes matching the original melodic contour rises from 54 to 98 over the six trials, the total number of melody notes produced increases too, so that the *proportion* of accurate melodic recall stays fairly constant at around 50%. Thus, the failure of this scoring method to account for much of what subjects do is not simply a matter of poor performance in early trials. Later trials show the same freedom from exact imitation as do the earlier trials. A two-way (ANOVA) on the percentage score of each subject for each trial confirms this picture. Although there are highly significant differences between subjects ($F(7, 35) = 18.34, p < 0.0001$), the trials factor is not significant ($F(5, 35) = 0.39$).

Metrical Analysis

The freedom suggested by the melody scores contradicts our intuitions that these recalls are often highly constrained by the original. Our second analysis is aimed at capturing one portion of those intuitions. This is a score of metrical consistency. We assigned a score of 1 to each crotchet beat of a recall over which an unsyncopated and uninterrupted quadruple metre was maintained. This was done by attempting to assign bar lines, either by counting from the first beat in fours or, if appropriate, from the second beat with the first beat as an upbeat. We noted the points at which such a process yielded a barring at odds with our perceptions of metrical stress. We believe our intuitions match those formalised by Steedman (1977), although we have not subjected the recalls to a computer program based on Steedman's rules.

Example 7 shows the results of one of our analyses (on Recall 1.2). The first eight beats of this can be unambiguously interpreted in a quadruple metre with

Example 7. Metrical analysis of Recall 1.2.

Example 8. Alternative metrical analysis of Recall 5.5.

primary stresses on Beats 1 and 5. However, the events on Beats 9 and 10 do not fit such a metrical interpretation; therefore, this recall scores 8 on 110.

Another case is shown in Example 8 (Recall 5.5). The first 16 beats, encompassing the first two phrases, are straightforward. If, however, we take Beat 17 as the first beat of the next bar, we obtain a pattern of double quavers on strong beats and crotchets on weak beats. It is, in fact, almost impossible to hear Beat 22 as weak. The barring that matches the metrical feel of this sequence most exactly is given in Example 9. This makes Beat 17 into an additional upbeat, enlarging Bar 4 to contain five beats. This beat is, therefore, scored as anomalous, as is Beat 20, which is noticeably longer than the consistent metre would predict. This recall scores 23 on 25.

Table 3 presents summary data from this analysis for each subject. Not only is the total percentage of metrical consistency very high, it is also high for each

Table 3

METRICAL ANALYSIS

Subject	Total beats played	Metre score (beats)	Score as percentage of total
1	45	43	95
2	135	108	80
3	146	137	94
4	140	120	86
5	102	92	90
6	54	46	85
7	145	112	77
8	122	115	94
	889	773	88

Example 9.   Alternative metrical analysis of Recall 5.5.

individual subject. Whatever subjects are doing with the details of the melody, they are, on the whole, ensuring that their recalls use the metre of the original.

Rhythmic Analysis

One possible reason for the high scores on the metrical analysis is that subjects have accurate memories for the rhythmic patterns of the original. If they correctly reproduce most of the rhythms, then it automatically follows that they will reproduce the metre. Accordingly, we assessed the degree of rhythmic reproduction by awarding each half-bar of a recall 1 point if it matched the rhythm at the same position in the original. Summary results of this analysis are shown in Table 4. Fewer than 50% of rhythms are exact copies of the original rhythmic sequence. It seems, therefore, that metrical consistency cannot be explained in terms of rhythmic reproduction. Rather, subjects are creating new rhythmic combinations within an underlying quadruple metre.

Table 5 presents the rhythmic reproduction analysis summed across subjects for each trial. Like the melodic reproduction scores, these scores do not seem to increase across trials. A two-way ANOVA on the percentage data factored by subject and trial shows a significant effect of subject ($F(7, 35) = 3.09, p < 0.02$) but not of trial ($F(5, 35 = 2.27, p > 0.05$). If subjects do improve across trials, their improvement is not due to more.accurate rhythmic recall.

Table 4

RHYTHM ANALYSIS, BY SUBJECT

Subject	Total produced	Score	Percentage
1	27	10	37
2	62	14	23
3	66	36	55
4	66	29	44
5	47	31	66
6	24	10	42
7	64	33	52
8	56	25	45
	412	188	46

Table 5

RHYTHM ANALYSIS, BY TRIAL

Trial	Total produced	Score	Percentage
1	55	21	38
2	66	31	47
3	62	26	42
4	75	40	53
5	77	35	45
6	77	35	45

Breath Analysis

We now turn to some scoring measures that try to take direct account of the phrase structure of the recalls. We first examine the way that subjects group notes by breathing. In this analysis, a score of 1 is given for each audible breath between notes or groups of notes. We partitioned the recalls into two unequally sized segments: (1) the last notes in Phrases 1 and 2, and (2) all other notes. Those in the first group were determined by examining the barring assigned to recalls in the metrical analysis. The last note of Phrase 1 was defined as the last note in Bar 2 whose duration (including any subsequent rest) was a crotchet or longer. The last note in Phrase 2 was similarly defined for Bar 4. The only recall where this gave a result at odds with our intuitions was 7.5. Our procedure places the phrase boundary after the crotchet F (Note 10), whereas we would view it as occurring after the D quaver (Note 11). This uncertainty presents no problems in the present analysis since neither note is associated with a breath.

Table 6 presents summary data from this analysis, showing the percentage of

Table 6

BREATH ANALYSIS

Subject	Percentage of Breaths	
	At phrase endings	At other places
1	100	0
2	91	10
3	92	1
4	100	7
5	100	0
6	100	6
7	92	10
8	90	5

breaths following notes in Categories (1) and (2) for each subject. Almost all phrase endings were followed by breaths, but less than 10% of other notes were followed by breaths. This is overwhelming evidence that subjects are choosing to breathe at phrase ends rather than at other places.

Phrase Structure Analysis

Our next analysis attempts to quantify the degree to which subjects construct their phrases using the patterns of melodic and rhythmic imitation present in the original. That is, do they preserve the A_1A_2B phrase structure? To answer this question, we need a measure of the degree to which Phrases 2 and 3 imitate Phrase 1. If subjects are reproducing this aspect of the original, then we predict that the similarity of Phrase 3 to Phrase 1 is significantly less than the similarity of Phrase 2 to Phrase 1. Accordingly, we compared each beat in one phrase with the corresponding beat in the other phrase, awarding a score of 1 if the pitch(es) in the two beats were identical and a score of 1 if the timing pattern was the same. These scores, represented as a percentage of total possible score, are given in Table 7. The missing data occur because Subjects 1 and 6 did not provide a third phrase in any of their recalls.

All six subjects for whom comparison is possible show a greater match between phrases 1 and 2 than between Phrases 1 and 3. Nonetheless, most still show a considerable degree of similarity between Phrases 1 and 3. Applying our scoring technique to the original melody yields the percentage values given at the bottom of Table 7. It is apparent that most subjects make Phrases 1 and 3 more similar than in the original. This suggests two things: (1) Subjects do reproduce the A_1A_2B schema of the original, and (2) there is a tendency to make the recall

Table 7

PERCENTAGE MATCH OF PHRASE ANALYSIS

Subject	Phrase 1 to phrase 2	Phrase 1 to phrase 3
1	79	—
2	71	70
3	69	41
4	73	44
5	78	22
6	88	—
7	70	11
8	58	44
Mean	71	41
Original	63	13

more consistent than the original. Memory tends towards structural simplification.

Harmonic Analysis

Our next analysis concerns the harmonic structure of the recalls and the degree to which they match the harmonic structure of the original. The original has a simple and unambiguous harmonic structure that is primarily conveyed by harmonic notes falling on the strong beats in each bar (Beats 1 and 3) with passing notes falling on weak beats (2 and 4). The harmonic implication of each two-beat segment is determined by its strong beat and is shown as follows:

$$// I\ I\ /\ V\ I\ //\ I\ I\ /\ V\ I\ //\ V\ I\ /\ V^7\ I\ //$$
(D minor)   (F major)

We scored the recalls by counting the number of half-bars that began with a note drawn from the chord of the harmonic sequence prescribed at that point for the original. For example, the first note of Bar 1 had to be D, F, or A for it to be scored positively. This scoring matched our intuitions about the harmonic structure of the recalls in all cases except the recalls of Subject 2, where it seemed to us that the E that began the fourth half-bar functioned as an appoggiatura to the following D and thus fulfilled a tonic function. This was therefore allowed as a correct harmony.

Table 8 shows the percentage of harmonic replication for each subject, broken down over phrases. We observe a great difference among subjects on this measure, ranging from 8% to 97%. The distribution of scores across phrases is, however, also highly variable, with Subjects 4 and 7 representing the two extremes of a distribution. The only previous analysis that showed such intersubject variability was the melodic contour score previously discussed. The possibility

Table 8

PERCENTAGE OF REPLICATION OF HARMONY ANALYSIS

Subject	Phrase 1	Phrase 2	Phrase 3	Total
1	63	100	—	70
2	38	39	36	38
3	83	100	13	66
4	0	0	25	8
5	92	75	82	84
6	91	100	—	93
7	79	83	0	56
8	100	100	90	97
	68	67	37	

exists that the harmonic score might represent simple differences in melodic contour recall. One may argue that high melodic contour recall will necessarily lead to an improved harmonic score. If this is so, we might expect a high positive correlation between the two measures. Accordingly, we computed Spearman's rho and found a non-significant positive correlation of .429. Inspection of Tables 1 and 8 show striking dissimilarities. For instance, Subject 6 scores lowest on melodic contour recall (zero) but scores highest on harmonic recall (93%). Her recalls show that she has constructed a new melody on the harmonic and rhythmic structure of the original. Although this subject demonstrates the most wholesale use of this strategy, it crops up in the other subjects, too. Good examples are found in Recalls 1.6, 3.1, and 8.4. Even subjects who show poor harmonic retention overall display isolated pockets of retention. Recall 2.3, for instance, shows a good harmonic match in Phrase 3, even though the previous two phrases show an odd amalgam of Phrases 1 and 3. Likewise, Subject 4 seems to have been totally dominated by Phrase 3 of the original (as remarked upon previously). If we allow her data to be matched against the harmonic structure of Phrase 3 in all cases, then her score rises to 82%.

Between-Subjects Analyses

Our final analysis constitutes a sweep over all the previous analyses to ask whether any shows a clear difference between musicians and non-musicians. Table 9 presents the mean percentage score for non-musicians and musicians on each measure, and the result of two-way ANOVA carried out on the percentage scores factored by subject group and trial. The only analysis yielding any significant differences is that on the harmonic retention scores. Musicians as a group do significantly better on this measure than non-musicians.

Table 9

COMPARISON BETWEEN MUSICIANS AND NON-MUSICIANS

Analysis	Non-musicians	Musicians	F-ratio	p
Melodic contour	32	52	.935	NS
Metre	89	87	.441	NS
Rhythm	39	51	1.342	NS
Breaths[a]	94	94	.175	NS
Phrase match[b]	14	43	1.131	NS
Harmony	45	82	18.718	.0001

[a]Proportion of phrase endings followed by a breath (omitting Subjects 1 and 6 for missing data).

[b]Percentage match of Phrases 1 and 2 minus percentage match of Phrases 1 & 3. Trials 5 and 6 only. Subjects 1 and 6 omitted for missing data. See Table 7.

Example 10. The carol, "We Three Kings," compared to Recall 3.1.

There are doubtless many other analyses that these results could afford. For instance, it is possible to examine the degree to which crude contour (up–down movement) is retained even when precise melodic imitation is lost (e.g., the start of Recall 6.5 has the same contour as the start of the original—two downward steps). One may assess the degree to which general stylistic features of the original (such as characteristic pitch or timing intervals) are reproduced in the recalls. Some of these features may be perceived as particularly salient by some subjects and overdone in the recalls. For instance, Subject 2 overuses the octave leap from the beginning of Phrase 3 of the original. One might also try to ask whether themes and motives from a subject's wider musical knowledge are incorporated into the recalls. For instance, Recalls 3.1–3.4 suggest a contribution from this subject's knowledge of another tune that resembles the original. This is the Christmas carol, "We Three Kings of Orient Are." Example 10 gives the first three phrases of this carol above Recall 3.1. The recall resembles the carol's melodic structure more than that of the experimental sequence, particularly at Bars 2 and 5. Other analyses will no doubt suggest themselves. Our data present a small but rich base of material against which to test future hypotheses, and we make no claim to have provided an exhaustive account of the data here. Nonetheless, we feel that the analyses performed so far allow us to draw some quite definite conclusions.

CONCLUSIONS

Let us summarise our main findings:

1. Recall of this simple melody is never note-for-note perfect, even in the best case.

2. The inexact recalls provided by these subjects are highly related to the original in many respects.

3. The most fundamental feature that is preserved in this melody is the metrical structure. Almost all the recalls are interpretable as maintaining a quadruple metre. This suggests that metre is a primary structural frame for melodic comprehension and recall.

4. Most subjects articulate the metrical frame at a level higher than the bar. The stimulus sequence is coded into two-bar phrases, and the recalls show overwhelming evidence of being governed by this phrase subdivision. Subjects breathe more often between phrases than in other places and reproduce the melodic and rhythmic imitations between phrases that preserve an A_1A_2B structure.

5. Within the metrical phrase structure, subjects do not reproduce the exact rhythms of the original. Rather, they substitute metrical equivalents in about half of the cases.

6. Subjects vary significantly in the degree to which their recalls match the harmony and melodic pattern of the original. This suggests that listeners can attain a metrical representation independently of attaining a harmonic representation. Memory for harmonic structure seems to be related to musical expertise.

7. There is evidence that harmonic structure may be coded even when exact melodic structure is lost. On some occasions, this leads to a radically new melody, although, more commonly, subjects make small variations on the original melody that are harmonically and metrically consistent.

8. Musicians and non-musicians differ significantly on only one of our measures. This is the ability to retain the harmonic structure of the original.

9. Subjects do not show an improvement in performance over the six trials on any of our measures. Some recalls get longer, but they do not get any better.

What do these results tell us about memory for music? They point toward the notion that memorising simple, well-formed tonal melodies involves building a mental model of the underlying structure in which not all of the surface detail is necessarily retained. Recall involves processes akin to improvisation, which fill in structurally marked slots according to general constraints about what is appropriate to the piece or genre. We have evidence that different levels of structure are available to people with differing amounts of musical expertise. Musicians code harmonic relationships that seem less accessible to non-musicians. In both groups, however, there is evidence of a great amount of common processing. Subjects seem to share the pool of basic melodic and rhythmic building blocks. Contiguous movements up and down scales and chords of the key account for much of the melodic content; and simple dactylic or equal interval rhythms for almost all of the timing content.

It is not our intention to make detailed theoretical proposals for the nature of the representational system implied by these results. However, we notice that our results fit quite well with the system proposed by Sundberg and Lindblom (1976) for generating Swedish nursery tunes (whose structures are similar to our own material). In their system, a hierarchical metrical tree is generated, which specifies binary subdivisions of a piece into phrases, bars, and beats. Harmonies and rhythms are assigned to terminal elements on the basis of their status within the tree structure, and pitches are chosen to satisfy the harmonies and rhythms specified. To account more precisely for our results, we need to modify the system to allow for the possibility of only *part* of a tree being generated, and we also need to construct a melodic generation process that samples some lexicon of possible melodic patterns. Some individual differences could be accounted for by a weighting system that makes it more likely that a frequently encountered pattern will be chosen for any particular role. It would also be necessary to build in some real-time constraints. The speed at which a melody is presented clearly has an important bearing on the detail of representation achieved, although we are not in a position to make detailed predictions.

We see the development of theory in this area as working towards a formal system, embodied in a computer program, which takes melodies like ours as its input, and models the type of recall obtained as its output. Sundberg and Lindblom's (1976) system provides the most detailed sketch of a possible output generation system. Several theoretical approaches are relevant to the input procedures. At the level of the individual note, the notions of tonal space developed by, for instance, Sheperd (1982) and Krumhansl (1983) might be used to predict the kind of individual pitch error most likely to find its way into recalls. Our intuition is, however, that such simple relationships will often be overridden in extended melodic representation by factors relevant to melodic shape and imitation and to the preservation of metrical and harmonic structure. We look, therefore, to theories of music perception that generate temporally extended hierarchic structures by means of parsing procedures (in particular, Lerdahl and Jackedoff, 1983; Longuet-Higgins, 1976; and Steedman, 1977).

It may be argued that musical recall data cannot directly disconfirm these theories, because a particular unpredicted recall can always be accounted for by some additional factor ignored by the theory (e.g., the freedom exercised by an individual to preserve some linear or statistical feature of the music at the expense of harmony, metre, and hierarchical structure). It would, however, be disconcerting for such theories if a significant proportion of recall distortions could not be accounted for under their assumptions. Nonetheless, we may wish to see recall data not so much as detailed testing grounds for existing theories, but rather as pointers to aspects of memory and representation for which, as yet, no well-developed theory exists. There is no psychological theory of melodic or thematic identity; neither is there any detailed theoretical framework in terms of which we could articulate the nature of the intrusion errors that we noted.

Whatever view one takes about the relationship between recall data and theory testing, we believe our data to be a more concrete and appropriate explanandum for the development of theory than the oft-appealed-to "intuitions of experienced listeners," concerning which there can be legitimate and unresolvable dispute.

APPENDIX

This appendix contains transcriptions of six recall attempts by each of eight subjects aurally presented with Figure 1. The following are the special symbols used; details of interpretation are given in the text.

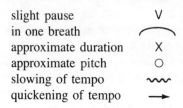

slight pause	V
in one breath	⌒
approximate duration	X
approximate pitch	O
slowing of tempo	∿
quickening of tempo	→

Subject I

Subject 8

REFERENCES

Allport, D. A. The state of cognitive psychology. *Quarterly Journal of Experimental Psychology,* 1975, *27,* 141–152.

Bartók, B., and Lord, A. B. *Serbo-Croatian folk songs.* New York: Columbia University Press, 1951.

Bower, G. H. Experiments in story understanding and recall. *Quarterly Journal of Experimental Psychology,* 1976, *28,* 511–534.

Dowling, W. J. Melodic information processing and its development. In D. Deutsch (Ed.), *The psychology of music.* New York: Academic Press, 1982.

Gabrielsson, A. Performance of rhythm patterns. *Scandinavian Journal of Psychology,* 1974, *15,* 63–72.

Gardner, H. Do babies sing a universal song? *Psychology Today,* 1981, *14*(4), 18–27.

Halpern, A. Organization in memory for music. *Bulletin of the British Psychological Society,* 1983, *36,* A124.

Kintsch, W. On comprehending stories. In M. A. Just and P. A. Carpenter (Eds.), *Cognitive processes in comprehension.* Hillsdale, NJ: Erlbaum, 1977.

Krumhansl, C. L. Perceptual structures for tonal music. *Music Perception,* 1983, *1,* 24–58.

Lerdahl, F., and Jackendoff, R. *A generative theory of tonal music.* Cambridge, MA: MIT Press, 1983.

Longuet-Higgins, H. C. Perception of melodies. *Nature,* 1976, *263,* 646–653.

Moog, H. *The musical experience of the pre-school child* (C. Clarke, Trans.). London: Schott, 1976.

Newell, A. You can't play 20 questions with nature and win. In W. G. Chase (Ed.), *Visual information processing.* London: Academic Press, 1973.

O'Toole, L. M. *The Gateway Russian song book.* London: Collets, 1974.

Pollard-Gott, L. Emergence of thematic concepts in repeated listening to music. *Cognitive Psychology*, 1983, *15*, 66–94.

Seashore, C. E. *The psychology of music. New York: McGraw-Hill, 1938.*

Shaffer, L. H. *Performance of Chopin, Bach, and Bartok: Studies in motor programming. Cognitive Psychology*, 1981, *13*, 326–376.

Shepard, R. N. Structural representation of pitch. In D. Deutsch (Ed.), *The psychology of music.* New York: Academic Press, 1982.

Sloboda, J. A. *The musical mind: The cognitive psychology of music.* London: Oxford University Press, 1985.

Steedman, M. J. The perception of musical rhythm and metre. *Perception,* 1977, *6,* 555–570.

Sundberg, J., and Lindblom, B. Generative theories in language and music descriptions. *Cognition,* 1976, *4,* 99–122.

Zenatti, A. Le développement génétique de la perception musicale. *Monographs Français de Psychologie.* No. 17.

7

Melodic Contour and Musical Structure*

Judy Edworthy

INTRODUCTION

A melody or theme is not merely a series of intervals. That is, one can often change a note in a melody without causing others to feel it is a new melody. Contour is a musical concept that may be closer to the concept of melody or theme. It is logically a generalised form of interval information; that is, it can be derived from the sequence of intervals, whereas the reverse is not the case. This chapter aims to demonstrate that contour may be more than simply generalised interval information and, in particular, that it can be distinguished experimentally from interval information. The experiments reported in this chapter show that contour information can be encoded accurately independently of key, whereas interval information becomes increasingly precise as key is established. This suggests that a representation of a contour might sometimes be more useful than a representation of a precise sequence of intervals in music.

In the film *Casablanca,* there is a scene in the hotel bar where Ingrid Bergman says, "Play it, Sam," referring to the song "As Time Goes By." She sings the melody of the song without any identifying words and Sam then plays it. In point of fact, he does not play the same set of intervals that Bergman sings. Neither Sam, Bergman, nor the filmgoers are concerned about the differences, because the two sets of intervals both represent the same melody. The two versions do, however, share the same contour.

A musical theme is even less restricted to a specific set of intervals than is a melody, as illustrated by the opening of Beethoven's Fifth Symphony. The opening theme is shown in Figure 1. This theme undergoes a number of transformations over the course of the piece. Two of the earliest transformations are shown in Figures 2 and 3. The contour is preserved in both of these variations, but the interval between the last two notes changes each time. This suggests that the contour may be functional in maintaining thematic unity. Contour is a con-

*This chapter reports on work carried out at the Department of Psychology, University of Warwick, Coventry CV4 7AL.

Figure 1.   Opening theme of Beethoven's Fifth Symphony.

Figure 2.   Second phrase of Beethoven's Fifth Symphony.

Figure 3.   Middle section of third phrase of Beethoven's Fifth Symphony.

cept that seems somewhat closer to the concept of a theme than does a specific series of intervals.

CONTOUR

Contour has been interpreted in a number of ways by psychologists and musicologists. On the one hand, we find that themes and melodies can be described in terms of their predominant configuration, using terms such as *archlike* (Hood, 1971). These global concepts of contour have been used in musical compositions such as "La Cathedrale Engloutie" by Debussy, in which the arches of the cathedral are conveyed through the slowly rising and then falling contour of the opening theme. This use of contour as a designative aspect of music is widespread. On the other hand, we find a much more specific, quantifiable view of contour such as that described by Herndon (1974), in which contour is almost a graphical representation of the interval sequence and both the direction of movement and the size of the interval are taken into account. This type of contour representation appears to be very similar to the way one might represent a specific sequence of intervals. Between these two extremes, a more common view exists whereby contour is defined by the changes in direction in a sequence of notes independent of precise interval size.

In musicological studies, contour is often the identifying feature of a melody or theme that undergoes change over time. Coker (1964) shows that contour is a useful concept in jazz improvisation where themes are repeated in different keys as a piece progresses. Studies of the song "Barbara Allen" (Kolinski, 1968; Seeger, 1966) show that contour is a unifying element between melodies that occur in different cultures at the same time. Over a longer time span, these same studies show that contour often unifies melodies that recur in the same culture over generations.

Figure 4. Example of a simple melody.

In psychological studies, contour is often considered to be a generalised version of the interval information (Davies and Yelland, 1977; Dowling, 1982; Dowling and Bartlett, 1981; Sloboda, 1977). Dowling (1978) presents a two-component theory of memory for melodies, with scale and contour as two separate entities. His definition of contour is the sequence of ups and downs in a melody independent of the precise interval sizes (the definition to be used in this chapter). The direction of movement of each successive note of a melody or theme is taken into account. Figure 4 shows a simple melody and Figure 5 shows the contour associated with this melody in these terms.

A number of experiments (Dowling, 1978; Dowling and Fujitani, 1971) suggest that the roles of precise interval and contour information in melody recognition vary, depending on whether or not transposition occurs. Even when melodies were tonal (Dowling, 1978), subjects found it very difficult to distinguish between comparison melodies that were exact transpositions and those that were contour-preserving but were not exact transpositions. This was not as difficult when melodies were untransposed. Subjects were better able to distinguish between melodies that were exactly the same and those that shared the same contour (i.e., not the same intervals or pitches). Furthermore, the ability of subjects to tell whether or not the contour was preserved was not affected by transposition. These results suggest that contour information might be available regardless of whether a melody is transposed or not; precise interval information appeared to be more available when melodies were not transposed. Contour is thus a useful concept in the analysis of data from music experiments.

Because it is not clear whether, or how, people actually use it, a set of six experiments were designed to determine how contour is used. In each of the experiments, the ease with which one can establish the key of a melody is manipulated by making the melodies novel or familiar and by transposing or not transposing them. The first experiment tested the viability of the experimental technique used throughout. In the second and third experiments, the melodies were both novel and transposed: They were heard once in C major and then transposed to F-sharp major, one of the most distantly related keys. Establishing the key should be particularly difficult under these conditions. In the fourth experiment, the melodies were novel but untransposed: They were heard twice in

Figure 5. The contour associated with the melody shown in Figure 4.

C major. Under these conditions, establishing the key should be a great deal easier. In the fifth experiment, the melodies were familiar but were transposed from C major to F-sharp major. Establishing a key is still necessary, even for familiar melodies.

The experiments show that contour information is immediately available to the listener regardless of novelty, familiarity, transposition, or nontransposition, but that it is easily lost with increasing melody length and serial position. They also show that interval information is imprecise immediately after transposition and that the ability of the listener to detect a small change in an interval actually improves as a melody progresses. Interval information is resistant to forgetting once key is established. This contrast between interval and contour information is demonstrated in the sixth experiment, which shows that the encoding of interval information is affected by key-distance but that the encoding of contour information is performed equally well regardless of the relationship between the two keys in which melodies are heard.

METHODOLOGY

The experiments were all carried out within the same experimental paradigm. In each experiment, subjects—all musicians—performed at least one interval-judgement task and one contour-judgement task.

In an interval task, subjects were asked to attend to the sequence of intervals in a melody. After a short pause, a second melody was heard, which was either transposed or not, depending upon the experiment. This melody possessed one altered note, which was always a member of the new scale. Figure 6 shows an initial melody, and Figure 7 shows a transposed comparison. The subjects' task was to detect this alteration, the dependent variable being reaction time in all but one of the experiments reported here.

In a contour task, subjects were asked to attend to the contour of a melody. After a pause, a second melody was heard, again either transposed or not, depending on the experiment. This melody had the same contour as the first melody, but, for some sequences, there was a contour alteration such that a note went either down if it had gone up in the first melody or up if it had gone down in the first. Figure 8 shows an initial melody and Figure 9 a transposed comparison. The task was to detect this contour alteration.

Figure 6.   Example of an initial melody for an interval task.

Figure 7. Example of a comparison melody for an interval task.

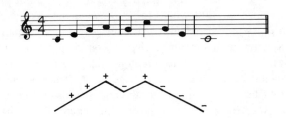

Figure 8. Example of an initial melody (and contour) for a contour task.

Figure 9. Example of a comparison melody (and contour) for a contour task.

Melodies

A trial consisted of two melodies, an initial melody followed by a comparison melody. The comparison was either transposed or untransposed, depending on the experiment. Subjects were asked to perform either an interval-judgement or a contour–judgement task on these melody pairs. The nature of the comparison melody varied depending upon the task (Figures 6–9).

Several constraints were placed on the initial melodies in order to make them realistic. They were exclusively tonal, that is, the notes were chosen from the diatonic scale, and the melodies often began with notes of the tonic triad. Larger intervals were less frequent than smaller ones as (there is some evidence to suggest that) larger intervals occur less often in music (Deutsch, 1978; Dowling, 1967). All notes were 500 msec in length.

For half of the melodies, interval-judgement comparison sequences were generated (Figures 6 and 7); for the other half, contour-judgement comparison sequences were generated (Figures 8 and 9). Interval-judgement comparison sequences were either exact pitch replications or transpositions. At one point in the comparison melody, there was an alteration that was never smaller than a semitone and never larger than a major third.

For the contour-judgement comparison sequences, the constraints were somewhat different. The comparisons were always different from the initial melodies, as can be seen from Figures 8 and 9. They had the same contour as the initial melodies except at one point where the contour deviated from its equivalent serial position in the initial melody. The intervals of the comparison melodies were never more than a major third different from their equivalent notes in the initial melodies. At the point where a contour change was intended, a note went up where it should have gone down or vice versa. The contour of the initial melody was reinstated as soon as the alteration occurred; the melodies were constrained in order to make this happen. The nature of the melody and the altered contour never necessitated the following contour to be altered.

In all sets of melodies, the alterations were distributed evenly throughout the serial positions with the exclusion of the first note, which was never altered. The number of trials per condition—and the number of conditions—varied with the experiment.

Apparatus

The experiments were run using an LSI–11 minicomputer. The order of the melody pairs for any condition for each subject was randomised before the experiment began, and the computer was set to call up each melody pair in turn. Each trial was initiated by the subject pressing a foot pedal; then the computer played the first melody. The melody was played through a sine-tone generator attached to the computer and was heard binaurally through headphones. After completing the first melody, the program waited five seconds. It then played through the comparison melody, monitoring reaction-time apparatus throughout. If the subject pressed a button during the second melody, the serial position of the note and the time in milliseconds from the start of that note to the point of reaction were recorded and stored for subsequent analysis.

Procedure

In some of the experiments, subjects were required to learn either the interval sequence or the contour of a melody before each set of experimental trials began. On these occasions, subjects heard the melody several times in quick succession, always in the key of C major. In all six experiments, the subject participated in a number of practice trials before the experimental trials began. The procedure for these practice trials was the same as for the experimental trials.

In each experiment, subjects participated in at least one and usually more, interval-judgement and contour-judgement tasks. The procedure for one trial within an interval task follows.

In each experimental trial, subjects heard a melody in the key of C major and were required to attend to the interval sequence (Figure 6). After a 5-second pause, a comparison melody was heard, which was either in the same key or transposed, depending upon the experiment. The subject was required to monitor the second melody and to detect an altered note (Figure 7). On detecting the alteration, the subject was required to press a button as quickly as possible. At the end of each trial, the subject pressed a foot pedal to start the next trial. There were approximately 25% catch trials (exact transpositions possessing no altered notes) in each of the conditions.

The procedure for the contour task was the same except that subjects were required to attend to the contour of the initial melody (Figure 8). After a 5-second pause, a comparison melody was heard that was either transposed or not, depending upon the experiment (Figure 9). The subject was required to monitor the contour of the comparison melody and to press a button as quickly as possible on detecting a change in direction. Again there were 25% catch trials, in which the comparison melody shared the same contour as the initial melody throughout. The intervals of the comparison melodies were constrained as described under "Melodies."

EXPERIMENTAL RESULTS

A preliminary experiment was carried out to test the viability of the technique described (Edworthy, 1983a). Subjects learned both the interval sequence and the contour of a 13-note melody, which was heard in C major. Subjects then performed contour- and interval-judgement tasks. In both conditions, the initial and comparison melodies were heard in C major.

No significant effect for task was obtained, although the figure approached significance ($F = 4.2$, $df = 1, 15$, $p = .052$). The total error rate, including responses to the wrong note, false positives, and failures to respond, was 9.7% for the interval task and 16.4% for the contour task. This is much lower for both tasks than would be predicted by chance alone.

A Task × Serial Position interaction was obtained ($F = 6.5$, $df = 10, 150$, $p < .001$), suggesting that serial position has a differential effect on the availability of interval and contour information, even when both types of information are presented in the same melody. This interaction was investigated in subsequent experiments.

Contour and Interval in Novel, Transposed Melodies

Establishing a key is likely to be difficult when melodies are heard only once and are then transposed to a distantly related key. Dowling (1978) found that listeners easily became confused between "exact same" and "same contour" comparison melodies when these melodies were heard only once and then transposed. That is, they found it difficult to distinguish between exact transpositions of melodies and comparisons that shared the same sequence of ups and downs but not exactly the same intervals. This suggests that precise interval information may be difficult to obtain under these circumstances, which may, in turn, relate to the difficulty of establishing the key of a melody.

The following experiment (Edworthy, 1983a, Experiment 2; 1983b) investigated the relationship between interval information, contour information, melody length, and serial position in novel, transposed melodies. Subjects performed one interval and one contour task, hearing 48 melody pairs in each condition. Within each condition, half of the melodies were five notes and half were 15 notes in length. In each trial, the initial melody was heard in C major. After a short pause, the comparison melody was heard in F-sharp major, one of the most tonally distant keys possible according to musical theory. Key is likely to be difficult to establish under these conditions. Krumhansl and Kessler (1982) found that listeners became aware of a new key more quickly when modulation was effected to a closely, rather than distantly, related key.

Instead of the reaction-time paradigm used in all the other experiments reported here, subjects were given a score sheet on which, for each trial, the numbers $1-n$ indicated the serial positions of notes for a melody of length n. Subjects were required to mark the serial position of the note they thought had been altered in the comparison melody in much the same way as in a test of melodic memory (e.g., Seashore, 1960). The major difference was that subjects were asked to make judgements about the contour of the comparison melodies as well as of the interval sequence.

A significant effect for task was obtained ($F = 7.63$, $df = 1$, 29, p < .01). Performance was better overall in the contour than in the interval task (average scores were 42.6% for contour, 34.9% for interval). Under the conditions described, contour was more available than precise interval information. Furthermore, subjects were better able to compare melodies on the basis of contour alone (as the initial and the comparison melodies shared only the same contour) than on the basis of intervals alone.

An indication of the effect that the establishment of key has on the encoding of interval and contour information comes from the presence of a significant Task × Length interaction ($F = 93.06$, $df = 1$, 29, $p < 0.001$). Performance was better in the contour task than in the interval task for the five-note melodies (average scores were 75.8% for contour, 46.7% for interval), whereas performance was better in the interval task than in the contour task for the 15-note melodies (average scores were 23.2% for interval, 9.5% for contour). Both differences were significant (Tukey's HSDs = 17.8 and 8.6, respectively, $p < 0.01$).

These performance levels suggest that contour information is immediately available when melodies are transposed but is lost when melodies are long. Interval information, although initially not as available as contour information, is more resistant to loss in the longer melodies. However, performance was worse in both tasks for the 15-note melodies, which may have been due to task difficulty. The serial-position effects within the 15-note melodies shed further light on the relationship between the encoding of interval and contour information and the progressive establishment of key.

The 15-note melodies were divided into three serial-position groups; Notes 1–5 (Group 1), Notes 6–10 (Group 2), and Notes 11–15 (Group 3). Performance fell off very quickly in the contour task, being significantly better in Group 1 than in either of the other groups. Thus, although contour information was available at the beginning of the 15-note melodies, it decayed rapidly with increasing serial position. In contrast, performance on the interval task actually improved from Group 1 to Group 2 (average scores were 34.1% in Group 1, 48.5% in Group 2; Tukey's HSD = 3.9, $df = 2, 58, p < .005$). The comparison between Groups 1 and 2 shows interval encoding to be more precise after a few notes were heard. This might suggest that interval information becomes more precise once a key is established. However, performance fell off in Group 3, a finding that does not agree with this hypothesis. The overall accuracy scores do suggest, however, that interval information is more resistant to forgetting than contour information. An experiment reported later in this chapter deals with this anomaly.

The results of this experiment suggest that when melodies are both novel and transposed, contour information is immediately salient but is rapidly lost with increasing melody length and serial position. In contrast, the encoding of interval information becomes more precise once a few notes have been heard and is more resistant to forgetting. The function of the first few notes may be to establish the key of the transposed melody; the encoding of contour and interval information thus appears to be differentially dependent upon the listener's sense of key.

The interaction between task, length, and serial position was investigated further in an experiment conducted within the reaction-time paradigm described previously (Edworthy, 1983a, Experiment 3). In this experiment, subjects participated in seven interval and seven contour tasks, one each for melodies of 3, 5, 7, 9, 11, 13, and 15 notes. In each trial, the initial melody was heard in C major followed by a comparison in the key of F-sharp major. Different novel melodies were heard in each trial. Subjects were required to detect contour and interval alterations in these comparisons, depending on the task currently set.

An interaction between task and length was again obtained ($F = 8.0, df = 6, 54, p < .001$), showing that performance was better in the contour than in the interval task for melodies of up to nine notes in length. There were no significant differences between tasks for the 11- and 13-note melodies, but for the 15-note melodies, performance was better in the interval than in the contour task. These results again suggest that when melodies are novel and transposed, contour information is initially precise but is easily lost with increasing melody length. In contrast, interval information is initially imprecise but is more resistant to loss with increasing melody length.

The serial-position effects further demonstrate the relationship of contour and interval encoding to the progressive establishment of key. Melodies were divided into serial-position groups of three notes. These were Group 1 (Notes 1–3), Group 2 (Notes 4–6), Group 3 (Notes 7–9), Group 4 (Notes 10–12), and Group 5 (Notes 13–15). If a melody did not divide exactly by three—as many groups of three were formed as was possible—the last serial-position group was made up of the remainder of notes. Performance in the tasks began to fall off at 11 notes (more rapidly in the contour than in the interval task), so the results for melodies of up to nine notes are considered here. The results for each of these lengths (excluding the three-note melodies) can be seen in Table 1.

For all three melody lengths, performance was better in the contour task than in the interval task, again showing contour information to be available before interval information. There is also a significant effect of serial position for each of the three melody lengths; however, the interactions are of most interest.

There are two trends within these interactions. The first is that, between tasks, the mean reaction times were significantly faster for contour than interval for the earlier serial-position groups but not for the later groups. This shows that contour information unlike interval information, is available as soon as a transposed melody begins. The second trend is within each of the tasks. For the contour task, there were no significant effects of serial position. Contour information was thus immediately available, and performance was maintained throughout the

Table 1

SUMMARY OF RESULTS OF TASK × SERIAL POSITION ANOVAS FOR 5-, 7-, AND 9-NOTE MELODIES[a]

Length in notes	Task (p)	Position (p)	Interaction (p)	Significant differences within tasks	Significant differences between tasks	Critical value at 0.01 level (Tukey's a)
5	.01	.01	.01	$I2 < I1$	$C1 < I1$	292 msec
7	.01	.01	.01	$I2 < I1$	$C1 < I1$	245 msec
				$I3 < I1$	$C2 < I2$	
				$I3 < I2$		
9	.01	.01	.01	$I2 < I1$	$C1 < I1$	249 msec
				$I3 < I1$	$C2 < I2$	
				$I3 < I2$		

[a] I = interval; C = contour. $X < Y$, RT in condition X significantly faster than RT in condition Y.

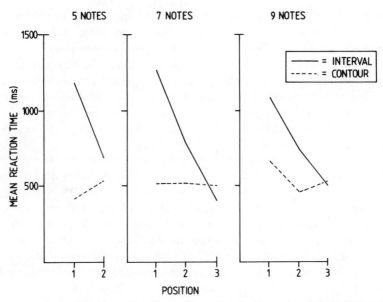

Figure 10. Three graphs of mean reaction time versus position for 5-, 7-, and 9-note melodies.

melodies. Performance fell off rapidly after this length. For the interval tasks, the mean reaction times were significantly faster for each successive serial position; there was thus a progressive improvement in performance as the melodies progressed, suggesting that interval information was becoming more precise. The effects can be seen in the three graphs shown in Figure 10.

The interactions again suggest that contour information is immediately available and remains available for melodies of moderate length. When melodies are long, contour information is rapidly lost. Interval information is initially imprecise, becoming more precise as more notes are heard. It is also more resistant to decay with increasing melody length.

In the two experiments described in this section, the melodies were both novel and transposed. Establishing a key under these conditions is likely to be particularly difficult. However, in the following section, conditions less difficult for establishing a key are discussed.

Contour and Interval in Novel, Untransposed Melodies and Familiar, Transposed Melodies

Establishing the key of a comparison melody should be much easier when both initial and comparison melodies are played in the same key. Furthermore, when a melody has been heard a number of times, retaining the interval information should be easier than when a melody is novel. In this section, two experiments are described that investigate the factors of non-transposition and familiarity and their effects on the encoding of interval and contour information.

If the interactions between task and length were due to the transposition of the comparison melody and its effect on the availability of the interval information, then when the key of the comparison melody is certain from the outset—that is, it is untransposed from a previous hearing and the listener knows it to be un-transposed—this interaction should disappear. A further experiment (Edworthy, 1983a, Experiment 6) investigated this hypothesis.

Subjects again performed one interval and one contour task. In both tasks, melodies were either 5 or 15 notes in length. The same melodies were used as in the experiment described in the previous section (Edworthy, 1983a, Experiment 2), although this time, the reaction time task was used and the comparison melodies were untransposed. Subjects heard twenty-four 5-note melodies and twenty-four 15-note melodies in each of the conditions. The initial melody was heard in the key of C major. After a 5-second pause, a comparison melody, also in the key of C major, was heard. Subjects were required to make interval or contour judgements about the comparison melodies in the same way as before.

An overall significant effect for task was obtained ($F = 6.9$, $df = 1$, 19, $p < .05$). In contrast to when the same comparison melodies were transposed, performance was better in the interval than in the contour task (the mean reaction times were 538 msec for the interval task and 608 msec for the contour task; Tukey's $a = 64$ msec $p < .05$). No interaction was obtained between task and length. For the 5-note melodies, there was no significant difference between performance on the two tasks (the mean reaction times were 433 msec for the interval task and 454 msec for the contour task). For the 15-note melodies, there was a significant difference between the tasks (the mean reaction times were 642 msec for the interval task and 761 msec for the contour task). Again, perfor-mance fell off more rapidly in the contour than in the interval task. Under the new set of conditions, interval information is immediately available to the lis-tener. The effect for the 5-note melodies shows the greater immediate availability of interval information when melodies are not transposed. The ease with which a key can be established thus affects the availability of interval information. Con-tour information is also available, but is more easily lost in the longer melodies.

In summary, when the problem of establishing the key of a melody is mini-mised by playing both initial and comparison melodies in the same key, then the interaction between task and length disappears. Interval information is immedi-ately available and can be encoded precisely. Contour information is also imme-diately available but decays more rapidly in longer melodies and is less resistant to forgetting than interval information.

Greater familiarity with a melody also appears to make interval information more available to the listener. Deutsch (1979) found that when a melody was repeated in the same key several times, subjects subsequently were more able to discriminate between exact transpositions of that melody and transposed melodies sharing the same contour but not the same intervals, than when melodies heard only once were immediately transposed. This was so even when melodies were transposed to keys previously unused. Thus, repeated exposure to a melody seems to consolidate interval information, regardless of the keys in which it is heard. The next experiment investigates whether or not this is also true of contour information.

Even when melodies are familiar, the listener needs to determine the key of a comparison melody if it is transposed. So, even if interval information becomes consolidated with increasing familiarity, it may become more precise once the current key is clearly established.

In this experiment, subjects heard a 13-note melody 10 times in quick succession, always in the key of C major. They then performed an interval task with the initial melodies in C major and the comparison melodies in F-sharp major. In a second session, subjects heard a different 13-note melody, also in C major, 10 times. They then performed an equivalent contour task.

In an earlier experiment (Edworthy, 1983a, Experiment 2) a serial-position effect was found wherein performance in the interval task improved from Group 1 (Notes 1–5) to Group 2 (Notes 6–10); this improvement was not maintained into Group 3 (Notes 11–15), rather it tailed off. This effect for Group 3 was not necessarily linked to the listener's sense of key but of the difficulty of retaining 15 notes in short-term memory after only one hearing. When subjects are more familiar with a melody, this effect might disappear.

In order to compare the effects for this and the current experiment, the melodies were divided into three serial-position groups: Group 1 (Notes 2–5), Group 2 (Notes 6–9), and Group 3 (Notes 10–13). There was an overall effect for task ($F = 60.07$, $df = 1,19$, $p < .001$). Performance was significantly better in the interval task than in the contour task (the mean reaction times were 409 msec for the interval task and 532 msec for the contour task; Tukey's $a = 61$ msec, $p < 0.01$). Thus, increased familiarity with a melody conferred a greater availability on the interval information relative to the contour information. Repeating a melody several times consolidates the interval information but not the contour information. A significant interaction between task and serial position was obtained ($F = 6.32$, $df = 2,38$, $p < .05$). From Group 1 to Group 2, performance in the interval task significantly improved and stayed at that higher level into Group 3 (the mean reaction times were 449 msec for Group 1, 396 msec for Group 2, and 387 msec for Group 3). However, performance on the contour task was best in Group 1 and Group 2, falling off in Group 3; performance was better in the interval task than the contour task for all three groups.

Thus, when familiar melodies are transposed, the listener still needs to hear a few notes in order to establish the key. Interval information becomes more precise once this is done. Once key is established, performance on the interval task is resistant to forgetting. The serial-position effect found in an earlier experiment can be seen as a memory-span problem rather than one specifically relating to the listener's sense of key in the interval task. In contrast, it was again found that, although contour information was initially salient, it became lost with increasing serial position. Repeated exposure to a melody did not make contour more resistant to forgetting.

Contour and Interval Information Separated

In the five experiments previously described, the initial melodies were always heard in the key of C major. The comparison melodies, when transposed, were always in F-sharp major. In the final experiment, the comparison melodies were heard in three different keys: G major, E major, and F-sharp major.

There is some research that suggests that the relationship between the two keys in which a melody is heard affects the ability of the listener to encode the interval information (Cohen, 1975; Cuddy, 1982; Cuddy and Cohen, 1976; Cuddy, Cohen, and Miller, 1979; Cuddy and Lyons, 1981). It has been found that when melodies are transposed to keys that are closely related rather than to keys that are distantly related (in the circle of fifths), they are more easily recognisable. This, in turn, may suggest something about the dependence of interval encoding on the ease with which the listener can determine the new key. As the experiments reported in this chapter show, interval information is encoded more precisely when a key can be established, which may be easier for closely related keys (Krumhansl and Kessler, 1982).

In this final experiment (Edworthy, 1983a, Experiment 8) subjects performed one interval and one contour task. In each trial, the initial melody was heard in the key of C major. The comparison melody was heard in one of three keys: G major (a key closely related to C major), E major (a key less closely related to C major; although see Longuet-Higgins, 1962), and F-sharp major (one of the two most distant keys possible in the circle of fifths and the key to which melodies were transposed in all the previous experiments reported here when a transposition actually occurred). Subjects never knew which transposition would occur from trial to trial. The melodies were nine notes long.

There was an overall significant effect for task, with performance being better in the contour task than in the interval task ($F = 4.23$, $df = 1, 15$, $p < 0.05$). Thus, when the listener cannot predict in which key a melody is to be heard, the contour information is more available than the interval information. A Task $\times$ Key Relationship interaction was also obtained ($F = 3.91$, $df = 2, 30$, $p < 0.05$). Key had a significant overall effect for the interval task but not for the contour task (the mean reaction times were 843 msec, 725 msec, and 633 msec for the interval task, but 606 msec, 636 msec, and 692 msec for the contour task;

Tukey's $a = 200$ ms, $p < .01$). Thus, interval performance was significantly better when melodies were transposed to the distantly related key than when transposed to the closely related key. This effect, in itself, is surprising and will be a topic for future research. For the present, it is enough to note that key had a significant effect for the interval task but not for the contour task. Contour is equally available regardless of the nature of the transposition, whereas interval information becomes more or less available depending on the precise nature of the transposition.

This result shows contour and interval information to be differentiated experimentally, and the findings support the hypothesis set out at the beginning: that contour can perform a function as a meaningful psychological entity in music perception.

CONTOUR IN MUSIC PERCEPTION

The experiments described in this chapter show that the relationships of contour information to key and interval information to key are strikingly different. Contour information is immediately available regardless of novelty, familiarity, transposition, or non-transposition. Equally, regardless of these factors, it is easily lost with increasing melody length and serial position. When the inherent difficulty of establishing a key is great, when melodies are both novel and transposed, interval information is initially imprecise. It becomes more precise only as a key becomes established. When key is immediately available, interval information is encoded immediately and precisely. As long as the listener is not asked to retain too much information in short-term memory, then interval information remains precise, once key is established. Increased familiarity with melodies makes interval information much more resistant to decay than contour information.

Dowling (1982) summarises the conditions under which contour appears to be important in music perception. He suggests that contour is important when tonal context is weak or confusing and not to be aided by meaningful musical context. In addition, contour is easier to extract from melodies than interval information but is no easier to retain. It appears to be less important in familiar melodies and melodies retained over a period of time. The experiments reported in this chapter systematically verify these suggestions.

Dowling is concerned with melody recognition rather than encoding. Thus, melodies are recognised on the basis of contour information rather than interval information under some conditions because, within the available tonal context, interval information is rendered imprecise. When tonal context is weak or confusing, establishing a key is necessarily difficult. This renders interval information relatively unavailable—or imprecise—but it does not affect the availability of contour information. Contour is easy to extract from a melody because it does not depend on the establishment of key in the same way as interval information. Thus, contour is more important, relative to interval information, under those circumstances that make the establishment of a key difficult. Repeated exposure to a melody seems to consolidate interval information but has little effect on the availability of contour information; the same may be true of melodies heard over longer periods of time.

In general, the conditions under which contour appears to be important in melody recognition are unified by the observation that the inherent difficulty of establishing a key under the existing musical context is usually great. The experiments reported here show that as this difficulty of establishing a key is reduced, so interval information becomes more readily available. Contour information is not affected by the inherent difficulty of establishing a key.

The opening of the chapter suggests that the concept of a contour is closer to the concept of theme, or melody, than the concept of a precise sequence of intervals. Because themes are often repeated both at different pitch levels and in different keys, the independence of contour of the current key of the music might be extremely helpful in the recognition of themes that reappear during the course of a piece.

How then, does the listener determine the key of the opening theme of Beethoven's Fifth Symphony? There is a small body of research dealing with the nature of the establishment of keys in music (Brown and Butler, 1981; Butler, 1983; Steedman, 1972). Butler's and Brown and Butler's studies show that, if a tritone occurred along with a third note to provide a context, the key would be unambiguous in only three notes. In Beethoven's Fifth, the only interval that the listener hears is a major third; this is not enough to determine a single, unambiguous key. Steedman describes computer algorithms that determine the key of all of Bach's 48 preludes and fugues. This takes anywhere from 3 to 18 notes, depending upon the precise sequence of notes, but most commonly takes between 3 and 8 notes. The data reported in this chapter and the interpretation placed upon them are consistent with Steedman's results.

Let us return to the opening of Beethoven's Fifth Symphony. Bissell (1921) shows that the vast majority of classical pieces begin with notes of the tonic triad; thus, if the listener were to infer that the first few notes were indicative of the key, instead of actually misleading the listener, they would normally be correct. In Beethoven's Fifth Symphony, the first notes come from the tonic triad of C minor, the key of the movement. They also come from the tonic triad of E♭ major, which is not the key of the opening. The listener is not misled and might infer that the key is either E♭ major or C minor; however, the composer does not, in the initial theme, give the listener enough information to determine which of the two keys is correct. The listener's sense of key does not concern his or her ability to name the absolute key of the piece but to "fix" the music in some area of tonal space through the relationships between notes and to arrive at a decision as to which notes are fundamental to that key—particularly the tonic triad—and which are less important. E♭ and C are simply the names of the possible keys involved in this example. The problem would, in principle, be exactly the same if the whole symphony were transposed in pitch.

The key of the opening of Beethoven's Fifth Symphony is thus ambiguous. The contour, because it can be encoded independently of the listener's sense of key, unifies the opening of the symphony. The sequence is short; therefore, the listener is, on average, less likely to be able to determine an unambiguous key. In addition, the listener's capacity to encode contour is not overloaded. Thus, contour may be seen here as a meaningful psychological entity, functioning in a different way to interval information.

At this point, it is important to note that the rhythm also conveys important, perhaps even more specific, information about the theme than the contour. However, rhythm is obviously independent of a sense of key in a much clearer way than contour. The aim of the chapter is to demonstrate that contour, a much closer concept to interval than to rhythm, also functions independently of key.

A contour alone is often a conveyor of thematic unity; in the *Concorde* sonata by the American composer, Charles Ives, the opening of Beethoven's Fifth Symphony is quoted at various points, being heard only once in any quotation. Even appearing in this disembodied form, immersed in other music, the theme remains recognisable. This unity is largely conveyed through the contour.

Key is ambiguous from the outset in a theme that plays a central part in the exposition and development of Beethoven's Third Symphony (Figure 11). The key becomes clearer the second time the theme is heard (Figure 12).

This theme, which is very short and whose essence is conveyed through the contour and rhythm rather than through the precise sequence of intervals, ties together many of the modulations that take place in the first movement of this symphony. Uncertain key, which is a necessary outcome of a modulatory passage, renders the interval information temporarily imprecise. Tonally ambiguous passages thus are linked by an invariant contour, which remains salient regardless of current tonal context.

A further example of a case where short contour-preserving themes link tonally ambiguous music is at the beginning of Wagner's *Tristan und Isolde*. After the initial opening section, the theme in Figure 13 is heard. The next time the theme is heard, the interval between the two last notes is a sixth different from

Figure 11. Linking theme from the first movement of Beethoven's Third Symphony.

Figure 12.   Second phrase of linking theme from the first movement of Beethoven's Third Symphony.

Figure 13.   First phrase of theme from Wagner's *Tristan und Isolde*.

Figure 14.   Second phrase of theme from Wagner's *Tristan und Isolde*.

Figure 15.   First phrase of the opening of Schubert's Fifth Symphony.

the first hearing (Figure 14). Thus, even a large change in interval size does not necessarily affect the unity of the theme. Notice that the rhythm is also slightly altered. In the first instance, the last two notes are ♩♪; on the first reiteration, these notes are ♪♩. The identity of the theme remains unchanged. Contour is thus seen as a strong, unifying element in this opening.

A theme may be stated so that the key is almost completely clear; for example, in the first theme of Schubert's Fifth Symphony, where all three notes of the tonic triad are heard (Figure 15). Because the first theme is heard in a clear tonal context, it need not necessarily always be heard under these same conditions; later in the movement, the key becomes more ambiguous. The contour remains invariant when the theme reappears, enabling the listener to note that the theme has recurred.

In conclusion, the experiments show that interval information is well-defined and precise only when the listener is able to establish a key and to be resistant to forgetting once it has been established. Contour information is immediately precise but decays rapidly as a melody progresses and its length increases. However, accurate encoding of contour does not depend upon the listener's ability to establish a key. Thus, a representation of a contour can be useful to the listener in the recognition of thematic unity and thematic identity, as it will be available to the listener regardless of whether or not a key can be established in the current tonal context.

ACKNOWLEDGEMENTS

I thank John Pickering, June Fotheringhame, and Mark Steedman for their guidance in conducting the research reported in this chapter. My thanks also to Roy Patterson and Brian Moore for comments on earlier drafts of the chapter.

REFERENCES

Bissell, A. D. The role of expectation in music. Unpublished Ph.D. thesis. New Haven: Yale University, 1921.

Brown, H. and Butler, D. Diatonic trichords as minimal tonal cue-cells. *In Theory Only*, 1981, *5*, 39–54.

Butler, D. The initial identification of tonal centres in music. In D. R. Rogers and J. A. Sloboda (Eds.). *Acquisition of Symbolic Skills*. New York: Plenum Press, 1983, 251–261.

Cohen, A. J. Perception of tone sequences from the Western European chromatic scale: Tonality, transposition and the pitch set. Unpublished Ph.D. thesis, Kingston, Canada: Queen's University, 1975.

Coker, J. *Improvising Jazz*. Englewood Cliffs, New Jersey: Prentice-Hall, 1964.

Cuddy, L. L. On hearing pattern in melody. *Psychology of Music*, 1982, *10*(1), 3–10.

Cuddy, L. L. and Cohen, A. J. Recognition of transposed melodic sequences. *Quarterly Journal of Experimental Psychology*, 1976, *28*, 255–270.

Cuddy, L. L., Cohen, A. J., and Miller, J. Melody recognition: The experimental application of musical rules. *Canadian Journal of Psychology*, 1979, *33*, 148–157.

Cuddy, L. L. and Lyons, H. I. Musical pattern recognition: A comparison of listening to and studying tonal structures and tonal ambiguities. *Psychomusicology*, 1981, *1*(2), 15–33.

Davies, J. B. and Yelland, A. Effects of training on the production of melodic contour in memory for tonal sequences. *Psychology of Music*, 1977, *5*(2), 3–9.

Deutsch, D. The psychology of music. In E. C. Carterette and M. P. Friedman (Eds.). *Handbook of Perception* (Volume 10). New York: Academic Press, 1978, 191–218.

Deutsch, D. Octave generalisation and the consolidation of melodic information. *Canadian Journal of Psychology*, 1979, *33*, 201–204.

Dowling, W. J. Rhythmic fission and the perceptual organisation of tone sequences. Unpublished Ph.D. thesis. Cambridge: Harvard University, 1967.

Dowling, W. J. Scale and contour: Two components of memory for melodies. *Psychological Review*, 1978, *85*(4), 341–354.

Dowling, W. J. Melodic information processing and its development. In D. Deutsch (Ed.). *The Psychology of Music*. New York: Academic Press, 1982, 413–429.

Dowling, W. J. and Bartlett, J. C. The importance of interval information in long-term memory for melodies. *Psychomusicology*, 1981, *1*(1), 30–49.

Dowling, W. J., and Fujitani, D. S. Contour, interval and pitch recognition in memory for melodies. *Journal of the Acoustical Society of America*, 1971, *49*, 524–531.

Edworthy, J. An experimental investigation into the relationship between pitch-interval and contour in melody processing. Unpublished Ph.D. thesis. Coventry, England: Warwick University, 1983a.

Edworthy, J. Towards a contour-pitch continuum theory of memory for melodies. In D. R. Rogers and J. A. Sloboda (Eds.). *Acquisition of Symbolic Skills*, New York: Plenum Press, 1983b, 263–271.

Herndon, M. Analysis: The herding of sacred cows? *Ethnomusicology*, 1974, *18*, 219–262.

Hood, M. *The Ethnomusicologist*. New York: McGraw-Hill Book Co., 1971.

Kolinski, M. Barbara Allen: Tonal vs melodic structure, Part I. *Ethnomusicology*, 1968, *12*(2), 208–218.

Krumhansl, C. L., and Kessler, E. J. Tracing the dynamic changes in perceived tonal organisation in a spatial representation of musical keys. *Psychological Review*, 1982, *89*, 334–368.

Longuet-Higgins, H. C. Letter to a musical friend. *Musical Review*, 1962, *23* (August), 244–248.

Seashore, C. E. *Seashore Measures of Musical Talents*. New York: The Psychological Corporation, 1960.

Seeger, C. Versions and variants of the tune "Barbara Allen." Selected Reports, Los Angeles Institute of Ethnomusicology. Los Angeles: University of California, 1966, *1*(1), 120–167.

Sloboda, J. A. Perception of contour in music reading. *Perception*, 1977, *7*, 323–331.

Steedman, M. J. The formal description of musical perception. Unpublished Ph.D. thesis. Edinburgh, Scotland: University of Edinburgh, 1972.

8

The Relativity of Absolute Pitch

Alan Costall

INTRODUCTION

Father had "absolute pitch," as men say. But it seemed to disturb him; he seemed half ashamed of it. "Everything is relative," he said, "Nothing but fools and taxes are absolute."

Charles Ives, 1969, p. 111)

Some years ago, in a well-known paper, "The Magical Number Seven, Plus or Minus Two", George Miller (1956) drew attention to the remarkable difficulty we have in identifying stimuli that vary along only one sensory dimension, be it loudness, brightness, length, or pitch itself. Thus, when listeners are asked to identify tones of different pitch in the absence of any reference tone, they make errors when there are even as few as five different alternatives to be identified. In his review, Miller did confess that this low limit was not universal—that there are just a few strange characters around who can easily identify many different levels of pitch—but, as he disarmingly explained, he fortunately had no time to discuss these remarkable exceptions.

I encountered the problem of absolute or perfect pitch in a manner very similar to George Miller's: from the direction of rather straitlaced psychophysical research on pitch identification and an initial interest in the mathematical modelling of such performance. However, in contrast to Miller, I will try to address the question of absolute pitch in the light of the very limited pitch-identification performance shown by most listeners.

It is not my intention to present a thorough review of the fascinating research on perfect pitch (for comprehensive reviews see Ward and Burns, 1982; Wynn, 1973; Siegel, 1972; Ward, 1963a, 1963b). Nor is the question of development my immediate concern. Unfortunately, the controversy over the innate basis of perfect pitch has given rise to rather extreme positions (Ward, 1963a). As an early reviewer (Wallace, 1914) wrote, those who possess absolute pitch "are disposed to connect it with a hypersensitivity of the auditory apparatus, and to regard it as a rare and mysterious endowment" (p. 105). Non-possessors, however, seem suspiciously keen to explain it away in terms of "mere" past experience. The developmental question is important and can be approached with greater sensitivity (e.g., Jeffress, 1962; Sergeant, 1969a, 1969b; Sergeant and Roche, 1973; Wynn, 1973). But my specific concern is to examine whether the identification performance of those who possess perfect pitch differs *in principle* from that of the rest of us (see Neu, 1948). How far can the pitch identification strategies used by us lesser mortals help to explain the puzzle of perfect pitch?

THE RELATIVITY OF MUSICAL PITCH

There are two broad approaches to the study of pitch perception: an analytical approach, which treats tones in isolation as the building blocks of more complex musical structures; and a holistic approach, which treats such structures as essentially irreducible.

Within traditional psychophysics, pitch is considered—rather unremarkably—as a single continuum relating more or less directly to the frequency of the tone and extending from very low to very high. Attempts have been made to isolate the sensory qualities of isolated tones and to derive psychophysical scales of these qualities (cf. Poulton, 1968; Warren, 1981; Attneave and Olson, 1971).

Pitch, in the context of music, proves to be a good deal more interesting. Although the Gestaltists' use of visual demonstrations is now most familiar, their pioneering writings dwell upon the question of musical structure (von Ehrenfels, 1890/1937; Wertheimer, 1924/1938). The absolute pitch levels of individual tones, they insisted, do not provide a useful basis for understanding the perception of intervals and melody. As von Ehrenfels explained in 1890:

> The theory of Gestalt-qualities began with the attempt to answer the question: What is melody? First and most obvious answer: the sum of the individual notes which make up the melody. But opposed to this is the fact that the same melody may be made up of quite different groups of notes, as happens when the self-same melody is transposed into different keys. If the melody were nothing else than the sum of the notes, different melodies would have to be produced, because different notes are involved. (von Ehrenfels, 1890/1937, p. 521)

A better way to cope with this property of transposability of musical forms, according to the Gestaltists, is to consider the relationships or intervals between successive tones, rather than their pitch levels as such. The Gestaltists' insight concerning the primacy of relational structures in perception is central to recent theories of musical tonality. The power of the holistic approach has been demonstrated most effectively and developed most radically by Balzano (1980; 1982) at the level of the *total set of pitches* employed in the musical system. It is not simply the relationships among tones, but *the relationships among their relationships* that provide the "key" to tonality.

This principle of relativity promises more than just a ready explanation of why manufacturers bother to provide many more notes on musical instruments than the requisite seven (or so) suggested by Miller (1956). As I will try to show, the relativity of musical pitch may well excuse the embarrassingly poor efforts of most of us at the absolute identification of pitch and begin to explain how non-possessors of absolute pitch—and, perhaps, even possessors—cope with this task at all.

RELATIONAL STRATEGIES
IN PITCH IDENTIFICATION

In the pitch-identification task, the experimenter selects a set of different tones and assigns numbers to them in order of their ascending pitch. The tones are then presented one at a time in random order, and the listener is required to identify each tone by means of its appropriate label. Usually, and certainly in all of my experiments, the listener is provided with feedback about the correct value of the tone, if only to make life bearable for all concerned. Nevertheless, listeners usually start to confuse one tone with another when a ridiculously small number of alternatives are used—as few as six or even five different tones, even though the tones are so widely spaced that they would be impossible to confuse in a discrimination experiment. The fact that the tones can be so widely spaced and yet identification performance can remain so poor indicates that the limitation is not one of *sensory* resolution as such.

Miller (1956) was keen to invoke the might of the mathematical theory of information to provide an explanation in terms of a more central constraint on the processing of information. Although the explanation of absolute identification performance in terms of information theory was soon discredited on both logical and empirical grounds (Laming, 1968; MacRae, 1970), the temptation has remained to find an alternative tidy and unitary theoretical explanation. For the belief persists that performance in such a simple task *must* be subject to simple explanation, as if this task has uncovered an important and general constraint upon human performance (cf. Corcoran, 1971).

Over 50 years ago, Bartlett (1932) stressed the need for caution in inferring the simplicity of performance from the simplicity of the situation in which it occurs. Discussing the research on memory for nonsense syllables, Bartlett (1932) offered the following warning to experimental psychologists:

> The psychologist, of all people, must not stand in awe of the stimulus. Uniformity and simplicity of structure of stimuli are no guarantee whatever of uniformity and structure in organic response. . . . [Isolation of response] is not to be secured by simplifying situations or stimuli and leaving as complex an organism as ever to make the response. What we do then is simply to force this organism to mobilise all its resources and make up, or discover, a new complex reaction on the spot. (pp. 3–6)

Bartlett's suggestion may well apply to the absolute identification experiment. The attempt by the experimenter to prevent the listener from utilizing relational tonal structure may not, after all, serve to uncover a unitary, underlying constraint upon performance. Pitch identification may not only be difficult, but complex. Perhaps the pitch-identification task constitutes not a theoretically simple situation at all, but rather a kind of psychological lesion study. The task may serve to disrupt normal performance, and hence, force listeners to "mobilise" (and reveal) all their remarkable resources.

In my research, I have tried to understand absolute identification performance in terms of the rather old idea in psychophysics of *anchoring*—the idea that we try to relate what we encounter to a broader framework or context. It makes little sense for the listener to treat pitch as an entity in itself since, typically, pitch constitutes merely the *medium* of meaningful structures, be they musical or otherwise. To attend to pitch as such would be to mistake the medium for the message. I have therefore examined pitch identification guided by the assumption that, even in so-called *absolute* identification, the listener is trying to transform the task into one of *relative* pitch, seeking to "anchor" the presented tone to an available context.

Evidence for such an anchoring strategy comes from a study by W. Siegel (1972) of sequential effects in identification performance. In a series of experiments on pitch identification with feedback, he found that accuracy was very high on those trials in which the presented tone had also occurred on the immediately preceding trial (i.e., repetition trials) and deteriorated as a function of the number of trials that had elapsed since the previous occurrence of the presented tone. Siegel suggests that the listener copes with the task by trying to match the presented tone to the remembered pitch levels of the tones that had occurred on the preceding trials.

In an unpublished study, I essentially replicated Siegel's main experiment. The set of tones consisted of seven frequency levels (pure tones). Following his procedure, the lowest tone was 700 Hz, and the ratio between successive frequencies was 1.064, that is, a frequency interval of just over a semitone. (He does not explain why he chose this particular spacing of the tones. The aim may have been to avoid a musical ratio, but it is difficult to prevent listeners from assimilating unfamiliar intervals of pitch to familiar musical categories; see, for example, Dowling, 1978.) Each tone was presented for 2 secs, and there was a minimum interstimulus interval of 2 secs. I went on to compare musically trained listeners with non-musicians. Although the performance of the musicians was clearly superior, the pattern of the sequential effects was similar for both groups, and closely resembled Siegel's original finding (see Figure 1a). However, I further analysed the results to check for a possible artifact arising from a sequential response bias. People might just seem to be doing better when the same tone occurred shortly before, if they were more likely to use this response category

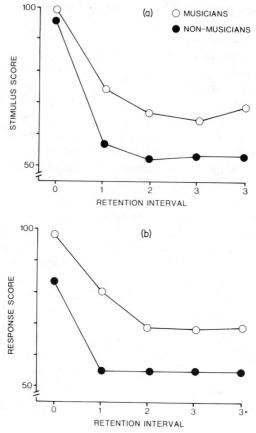

Figure 1. Accuracy of identification as a function of number of trials intervening since the previous occurrence of the presented tone, based on (a) stimulus score, and (b) response score.

again in the immediately following trials. To take an extreme case, performance on repetition trials would obviously seem impressive if the listener were to guess the value of the presented tone by simply echoing whatever category occurred just before. Analyzing performance so as to compensate for this sequential response bias did not change the pattern dramatically but did reveal that only the musicians were able to use the matching strategy effectively on other than repetition trials (see Figure 1b).

The non-musicians (i.e., those who neither played a musical instrument nor sang in a choir) were equally poor on all non-repetition trials. Only towards the end of the experiment (i.e., after some hundreds of trials) did they begin to show some success at matching farther back in the sequence of trials.

However, even for the musicians, the strategy of matching back seems to have

been effective over only a very limited number of intervening trials. Yet performance was well above chance level (i.e., 14.3%) even when several trials had
elapsed. Clearly, the matching strategy suggested by Siegel cannot provide the
sole explanation of performance.

Listeners may shift to an alternative strategy when it is clear that the presented
tone has not occurred for some time. One alternative strategy the listeners claim-
ed to have adopted was the use of the preceding tone as an anchor even on non-
repetition trails. In this strategy, the listener would respond, in effect, to the
difference or *interval* between the presented tone and the preceding one. The
results, which, in this case, are very similar for both the musicians and the non-
musicians, are consistent with this extrapolation strategy. Figure 2 (filled circles)
shows the improvement in identification for each of the seven alternative tones
(relative to overall performance level on that tone) as a function of the value of
the preceding tone. Again, because response preferences may have been influenced by the preceding feedback, identification is measured in terms of the
percentage of correct response assignments. For both the musicians and the non-
musicians, identification not only improved on repetition trials, but also on trials
where the presented tone was preceded by its close neighbours (cf. Pollack,
1953). The results, as they stand, are not necessarily inconsistent with the matching strategy proposed by Siegel, who considered the possibility that tones close
in value to the presented tone might cause less "retroactive interference" to the
"trace" from the previous occurrence of the presented tone (Siegel, 1972; p.
130; but see Deutsch, 1977). However, further analysis of extrapolation interval
effects for those trials on which the presented tone had not occurred within the
six preceding trials (and on which the trace would presumably be highly de-
graded) reveals a remarkably similar pattern (Figure 2, open circles). It appears,
therefore, that the preceding tone serves as a useful basis for identification not
only on repetition trials, but also on trials in which its neighbours were presented.

The matching and extrapolation strategies involve rather short-term anchoring
to a relatively immediate framework. Yet, even at this level, the possibilities are
not exhausted. For example, even if no feedback is provided, the end stimuli
(i.e., the highest and lowest tones) serve as a useful basis for identification.
Thus, if a tone has been mistakenly identified as an end stimulus, then the
subsequent presentation of a more extreme tone serves to correct future performance (John, 1973). A further strategy, which I have not formally investigated
but which was evident from the strange noises made by some listeners in my
experiments, is the use of oneself, as it were, as an anchor, by relating the
presented tone to one's own vocal range. When piano tones are used as the test
stimuli, variations in quality of the sound with increasing pitch can also prove a
helpful basis for identification (Cuddy, 1968; Ward, 1963a; see also Terhardt
and Seewann, 1983). The use of more exotic strategies, such as the reliance upon

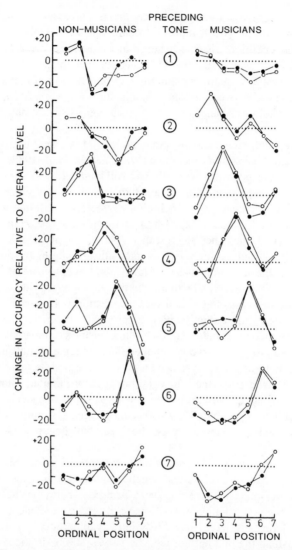

Figure 2. Change in identification accuracy of presented tone as a function of the value of the preceding tone. Accuracy is measured in terms of percentage of correct response assignments.

synaesthetic "colour hearing" (e.g., Block, 1983; Critchley, 1977) or upon tinnitus (Ward, 1963a; cf. Stanaway, Morley and Anstis, 1970), cannot be discounted and deserves investigation.

As a further corrective to unitary accounts of identification performance, it is worth noting that the strategies available in pitch identification are not always possible in the case of other sensory continua. For example, in a study of loudness identification with feedback, I could find no evidence for improved recognition on repetition trials once allowance had been made for sequential response bias (cf. Luce et al., 1982). I suspect that this is because intervals among pitch levels are usually meaningful to listeners with any musical experience, whereas those between loudness levels are not obviously so, except, for example, to audiologists used to decibel measures (Rowley and Studebaker, 1969).

Most of the pitch-identification strategies considered so far would be prevented in any careful test of perfect pitch (Ward, 1963a; Hall, 1982). My aim has been to show that listeners are evidently up to all kinds of tricks in their efforts to transform the absolute identification task into one of relative judgement.

The possibility of longer-term anchoring strategies in absolute identification tasks was recognised some time ago by Eriksen and Hake (1957) in their subjective-standard hypothesis. They suggest that a person might attempt to retain just one or two of the stimulus alternatives as standards for judging the remainder and again transform the task into one of relative pitch identification. Eriksen and Hake suggest that the two "end stimuli" in the set might provide very appropriate anchors for such a strategy, and their suggestion is consistent with a very marked effect observed in identification experiments. When accuracy of performance is represented as a function of the ordinal position of the items in the set, a very obvious bow-shaped curve is obtained: The extreme stimuli in the set are usually much more easily identified than those in the middle.

Eriksen and Hake performed an experiment on a circular colour series to determine what stimuli, if any, might be chosen as subjective standards when no such end stimuli are available. They suspected that those stimuli assigned to the ends of the response continuum might be used, but their results were inconclusive.

A similar experiment for pitch identification is possible since Shepard (1964) has devised a "circular" pitch series, which seems to have no ends, analogous to the never-ending staircases that appear in Escher's engravings. The tones are specially generated on a computer and consist of octave components only. When a series of such tones is played repeatedly in ascending order of pitch, each tone sounds higher than the one before; yet, the very first tone in the sequence also sounds higher than the last. Either six or eight tones from around this pitch circle, equally spaced in terms of log frequency, were selected for use in an absolute identification experiment with feedback (Costall, Platt and MacRae, 1981). The task proved difficult but entertaining. In this experiment, there was no evidence at all of any long-term anchoring, not even to the ends of the response set (Figure 3). In this strange task, the listeners were forced to rely very heavily upon the short-term anchoring strategies of matching and especially extrapolation from the value of the preceding tone (Figure 4).

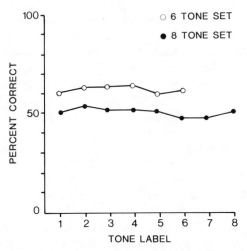

Figure 3. Identification performance as a function of tone label. The measure of performance is the percentage of responses correctly assigned.

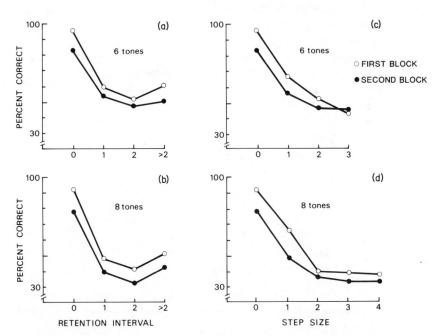

Figure 4. Identification accuracy as a function of retention interval (a and b) and extrapolation interval (c and d). The measure is the percentage of responses correctly assigned.

In a subsequent study, we investigated the effect of musical structure. As it happens, the spacing of the tones in the set of six alternatives corresponded to equal-temperament tuning, the tones being a whole tone apart. The whole-tone scale is notorious for its diffuse character, that is, its lack of a definite tonal focus. The successive tones of the whole-tone scale are equally spaced; therefore, each of its members is not individuated in terms of any unique set of intervals that it forms with other notes of the scale. However, the major scale does possess this property of *uniqueness* as a result of the uneven spacing of its members (the scale steps are whole tones except for those between the third and fourth degrees of the scale, and the seventh degree and the tonic). Each of its elements has, as Balzano (1982) has noted, "a unique set of relations with the others and therefore has the potentiality for a unique musical 'role' " (p. 326). Interestingly, despite its uneven spacing, the major scale shares with the whole-tone scale the property of *coherence;* that is, although a step along the scale can correspond to a semitone or a whole tone, a particular interval between two elements (with the single exception of the tritone interval) unambiguously specifies the number of steps along the scale (for further details, see Balzano, 1980, 1982; Chapter 1, this volume).

In the follow-up experiment, therefore, we repeated the study, using circular tones spaced according to a major scale, and compared the performance of musicians and non-musicians (Costall, Platt, and MacRae, 1983). The tonic of a

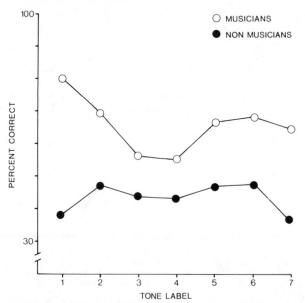

Figure 5.   Ordinal position effects for identification of "circular" pitch tones spaced according to a major scale (with Tone 1 as tonic). Performance is measured as percentage of correct response assignments.

major scale has a special quality as the *home note* even though it is not necessarily the highest or lowest tone heard in the melody. The overall results (Figure
5) show that the musicians, but only the musicians, were sensitive to the musical
structure of the set. (These findings complement those obtained in an earlier
study by Cuddy, 1971, of absolute judgements of musically related tones. She
used pure tones, spaced according to a major triad and spanning several octaves,
and similarly found that musicians, but not non-musicians, benefited from the
available musical structure.)

The overall performance for the musicians resembles the classical pattern for
anchoring to a particular item. Their enhanced identification of the tonic and of
the neighbouring tones appears to be consistent with the possibility that the tonic
served as a *self-contained* reference tone for the identification of all of the other
tones in the set. But to interpret the results in this way would be to disregard the
principle of relativity. After all, the tonic is not the tonic in its own right, but
only by virtue of its own relationships to all of the tones in the set. The musicians
may not, therefore, have latched onto the tonic as an isolated anchor, but rather
utilized the overall structure of the entire set of tones.

THE TRAINING OF PITCH IDENTIFICATION

The existence of a diversity of anchoring strategies in pitch identification must
surely raise the question of whether possessors of absolute pitch are not up to the
same game: the transformation of the task of the absolute pitch identification into
one of relative pitch. But there is a further line of research that promises to forge
a much closer link between the psychophysical studies of pitch identification and
the topic of perfect pitch. These studies do not investigate the strategies people
happen to use in pitch identification; instead, they attempt to train listeners in the
use of a particular strategy in order to improve their identification performance.

Cuddy (1968) investigated a technique of *reference training* which, although
in accord with Eriksen and Hake's (1957) idea of subjective standards, was based
more directly on what turned out to be good advice given by Hindemith (1946)
and Seashore (1919). The training involved the attempt to retain just one tone as
a reference standard among the set of alternatives as a basis for identifying the
others. The tone set used in one of Cuddy's original experiments (Experiment 3)
consisted of tones ranging from F_4 (349 Hz) to D_5 (587 Hz), and spaced in
semitone steps. In training, the listener was required to focus upon A_4 (440 Hz),
and, initially, this tone was presented much more frequently than the others. As
training progressed, it became gradually less frequent until, finally, all the tones
were equally probable. Feedback was provided but was given only for Note A.
Over the course of a relatively short training period, performance with reference
training was much improved. This result is remarkable in that the usual finding in
the research on pitch identification is that not only is performance remarkably

poor, but it shows little change over a large number of trials (e.g., Hartman, 1954; cf. Fulgosi and Zaja, 1975). In fact, Cuddy included a control group, which was given a standard training in which the tones were presented equally often, with feedback given after each tone was identified; no obvious improvement was shown. A subsequent study by Cuddy (1971) indicates that only trained musicians benefited to any degree from the special training schedule. The non-musicians were presumably handicapped by their poor sense of relative pitch, an ability crucial to reference training (Cuddy, 1971, 1972; Heller and Auerbach, 1972).

Brady (1970), a keen musician with good relative pitch, was sufficiently impressed by Cuddy's results to subject himself to very intensive training with a version of her technique. However, the reference note used by Brady occurred in three successive octaves, and complete feedback was provided. He prepared a set of pure tones spaced by semitones and spanning three octaves from A♯ (117 Hz) to A (880 Hz). Brady chose to focus on C—in fact the C above middle C—and so, in his training tapes, the C's initially appeared much more frequently than the other tones in the set. The idea was to relate each presented tone to C, rather than the preceding tone. After 2 months of daily training on a half-hour tape, Brady found he could easily identify the tones without feedback, so he moved on to the test phase. For the next 57 days, his wife would begin their day by playing just one note on the piano for him to identify (he describes this as her "one-note-a-day" piano recital). The results of his efforts are really quite impressive. Of the 57 test tones, Brady managed to get 37 completely correct, and the incorrect responses were very close: 18 semitone errors and just 2 whole-tone errors.

It is evident that Brady managed to achieve quite precise pitch identification through this training technique; and his performance, as he pointed out, would seem to satisfy the accuracy criterion adopted in some of the definitions of absolute pitch (e.g., Ward, 1963a). The question remains, however, of whether Brady was achieving this level of performance in *the same way* as those with absolute pitch. Overall measures of accuracy and even latency do not necessarily distinguish different modes of performance. For example, an especially enthusiastic one-finger typist might well match the speed and accuracy of a touch typist. It is necessary, therefore, to consider further bases of comparison.

First, the effect of Brady's training has proved far from ephemeral (cf. Meyer, 1899, 1956; Ward, 1963b). As he reports in his original paper, some 6 months after all training ceased, his identification ability showed no obvious deterioration (Brady, 1970). Thirteen years later, he reports that he still finds that he can recall C to within a semitone without any deliberate attempt to nurture this skill (Brady, personal communication, 1983).

Those with an interest in protecting the prestige of perfect pitch might wish to stress that Brady fails to qualify as a true possessor, simply because his skill was acquired. Possessors of absolute pitch are aware of having made no unusual efforts to achieve their eminence and report simply having noticed their unusual

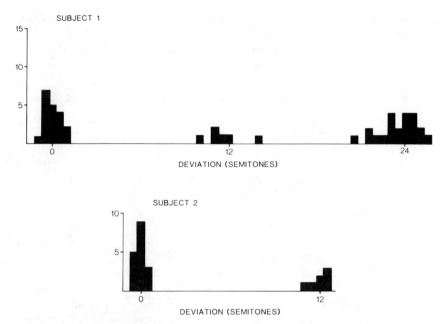

Figure 6. Histograms of pitch reproductions of musical notes by two possessors of absolute pitch. The axis represents deviations (in steps of half a semitone) from the correct setting. Responses were produced with a variable pure-tone oscillator. Note the clustering of responses at intervals of an octave. (Hayward and Costall, 1982.)

ability, usually at a very early age. But experience is evidently important in the development of this ability (Sergeant 1969a, 1969b; Sergeant and Roche, 1973); indeed, if it were not, it would be impossible to explain its close calibration to a very particular musical system—a system, moreover, in which pitch levels were tied to internationally standardized frequencies only as late as 1939 (Wood, 1944).

If one compares the pattern of errors made by those with absolute pitch and those without, there is a striking difference. Possessors of absolute pitch are not absolutely precise. Their sense of pitch is not only subject to constant errors (Ward, 1963a) and drift (Vernon, 1977; Wynn, 1973), but their judgements also show some scatter. However, as Figure 6 shows, their errors are not simply clustered around the correct value, as are those of non-possessors, but occur at intervals of an octave (see also Bachem, 1937; Revesz, 1953; Carroll, 1975; Lockhead and Byrd, 1981) and perhaps also of a fifth or a fourth (Baggeley, 1974).

Ward (1963b) and Meyer (1956) dismissed these octave errors as incidental. Ward suggested that they simply arise from confusions in dealing with complex tones and should be easily eliminated (cf. Ward, 1970; Ward and Burns, 1982). But they occur even for the identification of pure tones and do appear to reflect an important aspect of absolute pitch. Possessors of true absolute pitch insist they are not responding to the pitch height at all, but to the "chroma" of the tone, that is, whether it is a C, a D, and so on. Even if octave errors were trained out, therefore, the placing of the tone in a particular octave would still seem to require a separate decision (see Shepard, 1982; see also Bachem, 1937, 1955).

In his own experiment, Brady (1970) did not attempt to identify the octave in which the note fell, but only its chroma, that is, whether it was an A, a B, and so forth. However, he subsequently took part, as a subject, in a study by Carroll (1975), which also included a number of true possessors of absolute pitch. Brady's performance was indistinguishable from theirs, not only in terms of accuracy, but also, as closer inspection of the data reveals (Carroll, 1975), in terms of the existence of octave errors.

Brady points to one aspect of his performance that he believes does distinguish him from 'true' possessors of absolute pitch. He reports that the identification of keys other than C was only achieved with great difficulty, and hearing melodies in such keys was very disruptive to his sense of pitch (Brady, 1970). On hearing music in an alien key, his framework of reference immediately shifted to conform to the new tonic. He suggests also that those with absolute pitch have a much more immediate and secure sense of key: "Possessors of AP have told me that their easiest task is musical key identification; random tones are much harder. . . . Whereas the major scale sounds the same to me regardless of starting note, it sounds like 12 different melodies to the AP possessor" (p. 886).

However, this contrast is not as clear as Brady seems to suggest. Certainly, Vernon (1977, p. 486) reports that, in his own case, each musical key has a "distinctive quality" (see also Bachem, 1955), but there is evidence to suggest that the immediate sense of key among possessors of absolute pitch is far from universal. Corliss (1973), a possessor of absolute pitch, notes that she does not recognize key or harmonic relationships as a primary characteristic but, like Brady, responds first to the chroma of the individual tonal elements. A thorough investigation by Terhardt and Seewann (1983) of key identification and its relationship to absolute pitch came to essentially the same conclusion (see also Terhardt & Ward, 1982). Their absolute-pitch subjects located the key of a melody, not by an immediate experience of a distinctive quality, but by a process of inference, after having first identified the individual notes.

It is Brady's fixation upon one particular reference tone that seems to distinguish him most obviously from possessors of absolute pitch. Of course, Brady's training method involved relating each presented tone to the note C, but he reports that even at the end of his course of training, he continued to use C as his reference standard, and, as his subsequent comments reveal, he continues to identify other tones by their relationship to this standard (Brady, personal communication, 1983). In this respect, Brady's performance clearly conforms with Bachem's (1937) category of "quasi-absolute pitch" where "pitch determination is based upon an aural standard and upon the interval sense, which allows pitch determination over several octaves" (p. 148). Those with spontaneous perfect pitch claim that they can immediately recognise any tone in its own right. Each tone, for them, has its own individual character. For example, Corliss (1973) reports that "in my experience, the identity of tones heard is perceived as part of a continuous gamut, some characteristics of which repeat in every octave. The position of a tone with respect to its place in the gamut is recognized immediately as it is heard, without sensible delay. . . . It is not tied to a specific tonal relation" (p. 1737).

It appears therefore that my analogy with one-finger typing may not have been far-fetched. Brady can relate the pitch presented to only one tonal focus, whereas possessors of absolute pitch seem to have available a whole gamut of categories. They claim that they have a spontaneous and immediate recognition of every note category—and I have no reason to doubt their word—but as far as I know, the relevant test has yet to be done: that is, to show that both the accuracy and speed of identification is fairly even over the whole chromatic scale, as is the pattern of their errors.

If people with absolute pitch do indeed possess more than Brady's (1970) single internal standard, some studies suggest that it is not the case that they possess a standard for every discriminable level of pitch. Both delayed comparison and delayed pitch-reproduction tasks show that possessors of absolute pitch are superior to controls only when dealing with pitch differences that make a musical difference, that is, differences that span a note category (Rakowski, 1972; J. A. Siegel, 1974; see also Bachem, 1954; Baggeley, 1974; Eaton & Siegel, 1976).

A more recent study by Siegel and Siegel (1977a) on magnitude estimation and absolute identification of sets of tones spaced by only one-fifth of a semitone reveal some striking evidence of categorical effects. In terms of their categorization performance, possessors of absolute pitch show very clear resolution between note categories but not within them. It is as though possessors of absolute pitch cannot readily tell sharp from flat notes. (The topic of categorical perception has been the subject of much interest and, more recently, of much dispute. The standard definition is based not only on categorization performance, but on the complete failure to discriminate items from within the same category. In practice, this definition has proved much too restrictive; the perception of no stimulus continuum conforms to the requirements without important qualifications. By categorical perception, I mean that in certain experimental paradigms discrimination is much higher across category boundaries than within them.)

J. A. Siegel (1972) proposes that those with absolute pitch possess a set of pitch templates or subjective standards corresponding to each note category, tones that are mistuned being assimilated to the nearest note category. The idea is attractive, but it does leave some conspicuous loose ends. First, Siegel fails to explain how these standards were derived; she refers the reader to Brady's and Cuddy's work on pitch training, but the whole point of that work was to show that striking results occur only if the listener tries to retain just one tone (or a limited set of tones) as a reference standard. Second, it is evidently the case that at least some of those with absolute pitch show a precision in their reproduction of pitch much greater than that implied by categorical perception. Wynn (1971), for example, who presents a detailed account of his wife's remarkable pitch-identification ability, reports that she not only could identify a randomly present-ed pure tone without error, but could also tell whether it was sharp or flat by as little as 1 Hz (Wynn, 1971). A difference of 1 Hz in frequency is much smaller than a semitone: For example, at middle A, a semitone step corresponds to almost 24 Hz. My third qualification is more of a logical quibble, but it worries me nevertheless. It is tempting to say that absolute pitch is just a case of relating a rather labile impression of pitch to a relatively stable verbal code based upon the note names of music and then to feel that nothing more needs to be added (J. Siegel, 1974; Spender, 1980). But I am not convinced that this will do. I cannot help recalling the non-explanation offered to the astonished child watching the tightrope walker high above: Of course the tightrope walker doesn't fall, the child is told, the performer is hanging onto a pole. The unanswered question, of course, is, What keeps the pole up in the air? The verbal code available to the possessor of perfect pitch, like the pole for the tightrope walker, must figure as part of the story, but it provides only the beginnings of an explanation.

The apparent importance of verbal labelling in absolute pitch might well reflect, in large part, a serious bias in the methods of testing. Usually, absolute pitch is assessed by asking the listener either to identify isolated tones in terms of their musical note names or to reproduce the pitch corresponding to a particular note name using a tone generator. Such procedures are obviously convenient, yet disqualify listeners unfamiliar with musical notation at the very outset. Sporadic and tantalizingly brief reports in the literature indicate that possessors of absolute pitch might be included among such people yet seldom come to the attention of theorists. For example, some people spontaneously discover, in the course of psychoacoustic research, an ability to calibrate frequency oscillators without reference to a standard (e.g., Corliss, 1973). These cases are clearly of great relevance to the questions of labelling and of the role of musical structure. Research in this direction is long overdue.

The studies of categorical effects have been premised upon the assumption that possessors of absolute pitch have at their disposal a whole gamut of internal standards, and an attempt is made to determine their nature. But the research has run ahead of itself. The initial premise is by no means proven. As Siegel and Siegel (1977a, 1977b) demonstrate, categorical responding also occurs for *inter-val* judgements, at least by musicians (see also Burns and Ward, 1978). There-fore, a listener, such as Brady (1970), who attempts to identify tones relative to a *single* reference tone would also produce categorical effects in what is, ostensi-bly, an absolute identification task. Of course, even listeners who rely heavily upon relative pitch to identify tones successfully must ultimately anchor their judgements to a relatively stable framework, but the question of whether possessors of real absolute pitch rely upon one, a few, or a whole gamut of reference standards has yet to be settled.

Absolute pitch was initially defined simply in terms of the accuracy of identifying tones in the absence of any objectively present anchor. To deal with seemingly dubious cases, the definition was eventually restricted to exclude the possibility of any use of relative pitch. Absolute pitch, it was insisted, is not relative. But now the burden of proof has surely shifted. In the past, we were so concerned not to credit such people as Brady with perfect pitch that we neglected the crucial question of whether *anyone* conforms to the restricted definition with all of its exclusion clauses. And to answer that question, it is clearly not enough to measure overall accuracy, nor even relative accuracy, across a range of musical notes, for even Brady, when on form, could identify tones "immediately" and with great accuracy (Brady, 1970; 885; Carroll, 1975). Only intensive and sensitive investigations of individual cases, with a greater emphasis upon the temporal aspects of performance, will resolve the question of the relativity of absolute pitch.

CONCLUSION

The current conception of absolute pitch assumes that some people can immediately identify tones as entities in their own right. In this chapter, I have examined the problem of absolute pitch in the light of the growing emphasis upon the importance of relational structures in perception. I have argued that the existence of many strategies that transform the identification task into one of relative judgements can begin to explain the performance of those of us who do not possess absolute pitch and can provide the basis for very effective training procedures. I have also argued that the present evidence for the absoluteness of absolute pitch does not bear close examination. But the question of the relativity of absolute pitch remains to be solved, and given the concern of this book with the relational structure of music, it is a question of great interest. For *if* absolute pitch is truly absolute, then it would seem that there are a number of people in our midst who are exempt from the full force of the principle of musical relativity.

ACKNOWLEDGEMENTS

I am very grateful to Drs. J. B. Carroll and P. Brady for their helpful comments.

REFERENCES

Attneave, F., and Olson, R. K. Pitch as a medium. *American Journal of Psychology*, 1971, *84*, 147–166.

Bachem, A. Various types of absolute pitch. *Journal of the Acoustical Society of America*, 1937, *9*, 146–151.

Bachem, A. Genesis of absolute pitch. *Journal of the Acoustical Society of America*, 1940, *11*, 434–439.

Bachem, A. Chroma fixation at the ends of the musical frequency scale. *Journal of the Acoustical Society of America*, 1948, *20*, 704–705. (a)

Bachem, A. A note on Neu's review of the literature on absolute pitch. *Psychological Bulletin*, 1948, *45*, 161–162. (b)

Bachem, A. Tone height and tone chroma as two different pitch qualities. *Acta Psychologica*, 1950, *7*, 80–88.

Bachem, A. Time factors and absolute pitch determination. *Journal of the Acoustical Society of America*, 1954, *26*, 751–753.

Bachem, A. Absolute pitch. *Journal of the Acoustical Society of America*, 1955, 27, 1180–1185.

Baggeley, J. Measurement of absolute pitch: A confused field. *Psychology of Music*, 1974, 2(2), 11–17.

Balzano, G. J. The group-theoretic description of 12-fold and microtonal pitch systems. *Computer Music Journal*, 1980, *4*(4), 66–84.

Balzano, G. J. The pitch set as a level of description for studying musical pitch perception. In M. Clynes (Ed.), *Music, mind and brain*. New York: Plenum, 1982.

Bartlett, F. *Remembering*. Cambridge: Cambridge University Press, 1932.

Block, L. Comparative tone-colour responses of college majors with absolute pitch and good relative pitch. *Psychology of Music*, 1983, *11*, 59–66.

Brady, P. A fixed scale mechanism of absolute pitch. *Journal of the Acoustical Society of America*, 1970, *48*, 883–887.

Burns, E. K., and Ward, W. D. Categorical perception—Phenomenon or epiphenomenon: Evidence from experiments in the perception of melodic musical intervals. *Journal of the Acoustical Society of America*, 1978, *63*, 456–468.

Carpenter, A. A case of absolute pitch. *Quarterly Journal of Experimental Psychology*, 1951, *3*, 92–93.

Carroll, J. B. Speed and accuracy of absolute pitch judgments: Some latter-day results. *Educational Testing Service Bulletin*, 1975, RB-75-35.

Corcoran, D. W. J. *Pattern recognition*. Harmondsworth, England: Penguin, 1971.

Corliss, E. L. R. Remark on "fixed-scale mechanism of absolute pitch." *Journal of the Acoustical Society of America*, 1973, *53*, 1737–1739.

Corso, J. F. Absolute judgments of musical tonality. *Journal of the Acoustical Society of America*, 1957, *29*, 138–144.

Costall, A. P., Platt, S., and MacRae, A. Memory strategies in absolute identification of 'circular' pitch. *Perception and Psychophysics*, 1981, *29*, 589–593.

Costall, A. P., Platt, S., and MacRae, A. Absolute identification of the tones of a "circular" pitch scale by musicians and non-musicians. Unpublished manuscript, 1983.

Critchley, M. Ecstatic and synaesthetic experiences during music perception. In M. Critchley and R. A. Henson (Eds.), *Music and the brain*. London: Heinemann, 1977.

Cuddy, L. L. Practice effects in the absolute judgement of pitch. *Journal of the Acoustical Society of America*, 1968, *43*, 1069–76.

Cuddy, L. L. Training the absolute identification of absolute pitch. *Perception and Psychophysics*, 1970, *8*, 265–269.

Cuddy, L. L. Absolute judgement of musically related pure tones. *Canadian Journal of Psychology*, 1971, *25*, 42–55.

Cuddy, L. L. Comment on "Practice effects in the absolute judgment of frequency" by M. A. Heller and C. Auerbach. *Psychonomic Science*, 1972, *28*, 68.

Deutsch, D. Memory and attention in music. In M. Critchley and R. A. Henson (Eds.), *Music and the brain*. London: Heineman, 1977.

Dowling, W. J. Scale and contour: Two components of a theory of memory for melodies. *Psychological Review*, 1978, *85*, 341–354.

Eaton, K. E., and Siegel, M. H. Strategies of absolute pitch possessors in the learning of an unfamiliar scale. *Bulletin of the Psychonomic Society*, 1976, *8*, 289–291.

Eriksen, C. W., and Hake, H. W. Anchor effects in absolute judgments. *Journal of Experimental Psychology*, 1957, *53*, 132–138.

Fulgosi, A., and Zaja, B. Information transmission of 3.16 bits in absolute identification of auditory pitch. *Bulletin of the Psychonomic Society*, 1975, *6*, 379–380.

Hall, D. E. "Practically perfect pitch": Some comments. *Journal of the Acoustical Society of America*, 1982, *70*, 754–755.

Hartman, E. B. The influence of practice and pitch-distance between tones on the absolute judgment of pitch. *American Journal of Psychology*, 1954, *67*, 1–14.

Hayward, R., and Costall, A. [Pitch reproductions of possessors of absolute pitch]. Unpublished raw data, 1982.

Heller, M. A., and Auerbach, C. Practice effects in the absolute judgment of frequency. *Psychonomic Science*, 1972, *26*, 222–224.

Hindemith, P. *Elementary training for musicians*. New York: Associated Music Publishing, 1946.

Ives, C. *Essays before a sonata* (H. Boatwright, Ed.). London: Calder and Boyars, 1969.

Jeffress, L. A. Absolute pitch. *Journal of the Acoustical Society of America*, 1962, *34*, 987.

John, I. D. Sequential effects in absolute judgments of loudness with feedback. In S. Kornblum (Ed.), *Attention and performance IV*. New York: Academic Press, 1973.

Laming, D. R. J. *Information theory of choice-reaction times*. London: Academic Press, 1968.

Lockhead, G. R., and Byrd, R. Practically perfect pitch. *Journal of the Acoustical Society of America*, 1981, *70*, 387–389.

Lockhead, G. R. Practically perfect performance. *Journal of the Acoustical Society of America*, 1982, *71*, 755–756.

Luce, R. D., Mosofsky, R. M., Green, D. M., and Smith, A. F. The bow and sequential effects in absolute identification. *Perception and Psychophysics*, 1982, *32*, 397–408.

MacRae, A. W. Channel capacity in absolute judgment tasks: An artifact of information bias? *Psychological Bulletin*, 1970, *73*, 112–121.

Meyer, M. Is the memory of absolute pitch capable of development by training? *Psychological Review*, 1899, *6*, 514–516.

Meyer, M. F. On memorizing absolute pitch. *Journal of the Acoustical Society of America*, 1956, *28*, 718–719.

Miller, G. A. The magical number seven, plus or minus two: Some limits on our capacity for processing information. *Psychological Review*, 1956, *63*, 81–97.

Neu, D. M. A critical review of the literature on "absolute pitch." *Psychological Bulletin*, 1947, *44*, 249–266.

Neu, D. M. Absolute pitch: A reply to Bachem. *Psychological Bulletin*, 1948, *45*, 534–535.

Pollack, I. The information of elementary auditory displays. II. *Journal of the Acoustical Society of America*, 1953, *25*, 765–769.

Poulton, E. C. The new psychophysics: Six models for magnitude estimation. *Psychological Bulletin*, 1968, *69*, 1–19.

Rakowski, A. Direct comparison of absolute and relative pitch. *Symposium on Hearing Theory*. Eindhoven, Holland: Institute for Perception Research, 1972.

Revesz, G. *Introduction to the psychology of music*. London: Longmans, 1953.

Rowley, R. R., and Studebaker, G. A. Monaural loudness-intensity relations for a 1000-Hz tone. *Journal of the Acoustical Society of America*, 1969, *45*, 1186–1192.

Seashore, C. *The psychology of musical talent*. New York: Silver Burdett, 1919.

Sergeant, D. Experimental investigation of absolute pitch. *Journal of Research in Music Education*, 1969, *17*, 135–143. (a)

Sergeant, D. Pitch perception and absolute pitch: Some aspects of musical development. Unpublished doctoral dissertation, University of Reading, 1969. (b)

Sergeant, D., and Roche, S. Perceptual shifts in the auditory information processing of young children. *Psychology of Music*, 1973, *1*(2), 39–48.

Shepard, R. N. Circularity in judgments of relative pitch. *Journal of the Acoustical Society of America*, 1964, *36*, 2346–2353.

Shepard, R. N. Geometrical approximations to the structure of musical pitch. *Psychological Review*, 1982, *89*, 305–333.

Siegel, J. A. The nature of absolute pitch. In I. E. Gordon (Ed.), *Studies in the Psychology of Music* (Vol. 8). Iowa City: University of Iowa Press, 1972.

Siegel, J. A. Sensory and verbal coding strategies in subjects with absolute pitch. *Journal of Experimental Psychology*, 1974, *103*, 37–44.

Siegel, J. A., and Siegel, W. Absolute identification of notes and intervals by musicians. *Perception and Psychophysics*, 1977, *21*, 143–152. (a)

Siegel, J. A., and Siegel, W. Categorical perception of tonal intervals: Musicians cannot tell sharp from flat. *Perception and Psychophysics*, 1977, *21*, 399–407. (b)

Siegel, W. Memory effects in the method of absolute judgement. *Journal of Experimental Psychology*, 1972, *94*, 121–131.

Spender, N. Absolute pitch. In *The New Grove Dictionary of Music and Musicians* (Vol. 1). London: Macmillan, 1980.

Stanaway, R. G., Morley, T., and Anstis, S. M. Tinnitus not a reference signal in judgements of absolute pitch. *Quarterly Journal of Experimental Psychology*, 1970, *22*, 230–238.

Terhardt, E., and Seewann, M. Aural key identification and its relationship to absolute pitch. *Music Perception*, 1983, *1*, 63–83.

Terhardt, E., and Ward, W. D. Recognition of musical key: Exploratory study. *Journal of the Acoustical Society of America*, 1982, *72*, 26–33.

Terman, M. Improvement of absolute pitch naming. *Psychonomic Science*, 1965, *3*, 243–244.

Vernon, P. E. Absolute pitch: A case study. *British Journal of Psychology*, 1977, *68*, 485–489.

von Ehrenfels, C. On gestalt-qualities. *Psychological Review*, 1937, *44*, 521–524. (Original work published 1890)

Wallace, W. *The musical faculty*. London: Macmillan, 1914.

Ward, W. D. Absolute pitch: Part 1. *Sound*, 1963, *2*, 14–21. (a)

Ward, W. D. Absolute pitch. Part 2. *Sound*, 1963, *2*, 33–41. (b)

Ward, W. D. Musical perception. In J. V. Tobias (Ed.), *Foundations of modern auditory theory* (Vol. I). New York: Academic Press, 1970.

Ward, W. D., and Burns, E. M. Absolute pitch. In D. Deutsch (Ed.), *The psychology of music*. New York: Academic Press, 1982.

Warren, R. M. Measurement of sensory intensity. *Behavioral and Brain Sciences*, 1981, *4*, 175–224.

Wertheimer, M. Gestalt psychology. In W. D. Ellis (Ed.), *A source book in Gestalt psychology*. London: Routledge and Kegan Paul, 1938.

Wood, A. *The physics of music*. London: Methuen, 1944.

Wynn, V. T. "Absolute pitch": A bimensual rhythm. *Nature*, 1971, *230*, 337.

Wynn, V. T. Absolute pitch in humans: Its variation and possible connections with other known rhythmic phenomena. In G. A. Kerkut and J. W. Phillis (Eds.), *Progress in Neurobiology* (Vol. I). Oxford: Pergamon, 1973.

9

Structure and Expression
in Rhythmic Performance

Eric F. Clarke

INTRODUCTION

The study of musical cognition, in common with a good deal of other cognitive research, has been bedevilled by the problem of finding an appropriate experimental paradigm within which to pursue its aims. The considerable differences in people's executive and receptive musical skills and the difficulty of assessing the extent and nature of a person's musical education have led experimenters to adopt comparatively passive experimental designs. A high proportion of research in the area involves subjects listening to experimental material and making comparisons, expressing preferences, or giving rating scores. A limited amount of research has involved a more active participation by the subject who, for instance, may tap in synchrony with presented material (e.g., Handel and Oshinsky, 1981), but, in general, the tasks studied are rather far removed from normal musical practice. It would seem desirable to study musical cognition by means of some more intrinsically musical activity, not only for the sake of ecological validity, but also because the more interesting features of musical understanding may be expressible only in a musical medium.

The attempt to find a sensitive experimental paradigm for music research is by no means without precedent. In the 1930s Seashore (1938/1967), using an ingenious recording technique, undertook detailed analysis of a variety of musical performances, focusing on the accuracy, consistency, and construction of single performances and series of performances. This line of research was not continued, perhaps because the manner of recording and representing the performances was extraordinarily laborious. The development of new technology has, to some extent, overcome these problems, and recently, there have been a number of studies that have tackled various aspects of musical performances (Clarke, 1982; Gabrielsson, 1974; Gabrielsson, 1983; Michon, 1974; Povel, 1977; Shaffer, 1981; Sloboda, 1983). These studies have, to differing degrees, attempted to relate features of the performance to structural features of the music being performed, on the basis that the variable features of a performance are co-determined by the musical notation and a structural interpretation supplied by the performer.

The material in this chapter is taken from research undertaken at the Exeter University Psychology Department, which has concentrated on the relationship between detailed features of timing in piano performances and the musical structure of what is performed. The approach adopted has been to get skilled pianists to play music—usually under naturalistic conditions and from a notated score—and to examine the timing of events in the performance in the light of the music's notated source. With accurate measurement, discrepancies are always found between the temporal properties of the performance and those indicated by the score. It is a fundamental hypothesis of this research that those discrepancies are related to structural properties of the music and to the ways in which performers organise those properties.

Human performances, however, are not controlled by a deterministic timing system and, as a consequence, always contain a random element in their temporal structure. The separation of this random element from that of timing fluctuation that is the result of an intentional[1] cognitive operation presents something of a problem, as Seashore realised. Depending on the particular data being analysed, we have sometimes attempted to eliminate random variance by statistical means where sufficient replications are available and have sometimes distinguished between real effects and random variance by more informal means that are, nonetheless, based on principles of distinctness and consistency.

The difficulty in making this separation stems from the uncertainty with which the concept of replication must be viewed in skilled musical contexts. It is an explicit aspect of musical performance that successive performances do not attempt to replicate or converge towards a target performance which acts as a reference, and around which other performances are regularly distributed. Rather, the aim of highly skilled performers is continually to explore the possibilities for new interpretative configurations at all levels of musical structure. A performer may decide to play a whole piece at a different tempo, to alter the dynamic balance of a phrase, or to change the length of a single note; but whatever the scale of the transformation, one can be sure that processes of this kind are continually operating. Consequently, requiring a performer to play the same piece a number of times, even within a short period, may not help to distinguish between intended and uncontrolled features of the performances, since variation between performances will be of both types.

The extent to which such continual reinterpretation goes on varies with both

---

[1]The term ''intention' is used here in the same sense as in Shaffer (1976): An intention is considered to be the information input to an executive system and carries no associations of consciousness, will, or deliberation.

the sophistication of the performer and the material performed. The closer one gets to the conditions of a laboratory experiment, the less interpretive flexibility is observed—although the influence of boredom as a motivation for varied response should not be underestimated. In an attempt to isolate some of the basic processes involved, the research described in this chapter contains studies conducted under the more impoverished but controlled conditions associated with laboratory experiments as well as those undertaken in a freer context.

A further factor contributing to the analysis of performance effects—and one that lies closer to the core of this research—is the part played by musical structure. Referring back to the premise that the features of a performance are co-determined by structural properties of the music and the organising processes of the performer, it should be possible to identify real effects on the basis of structural plausibility. Two considerations jeopardise the success of such a project: (1) the indeterminacy that exists between a structural description and the way the structure is treated in performance (a further consequence of interpretative flexibility), and (2) the absence of any generally accepted system of musical analysis and structural description. Both are points to which I return at the end of this chapter.

The preceding paragraphs suggest that musical structures may be thought of as possessing a double aspect: a relatively fixed canonical representation equivalent to the notations in a score and a more flexible and indeterminate representation that is evident in expressive performance. This chapter concentrates on these two aspects of the cognition of rhythmic structures, which are referred to here as *structural* and *expressive* representations, respectively, focusing on timing as the primary performance variable. The next section presents some features of the structural representation of rhythm, and the section following that deals with the manner in which those representations are expressively transformed.

RHYTHMIC STRUCTURES

Used broadly, the term *rhythm* often applies both to the regular, periodic features of the temporal structure of music, and to aperiodic features. The former category concerns *metrical* properties, whereas the latter is the true domain of rhythm. This confusion is due to a complex interaction between these two parameters, which blurs the distinction between them, as well as to the absence of any consensus among music theorists as to how the two should be defined. I adopt a definition close to that of Lerdahl and Jackendoff (1983), using the term *metre* to refer to the regular alternation of accents with one or more weak beats and the term *rhythm* to refer to the grouped organisation of relative durations without regard to periodicity. The close interaction of these two parameters is the object of the first of the studies reported here.

The data for this study and all others in this chapter, originate from a piano interfaced with a PDP-12 computer, a setup designed by Shaffer (1981). Briefly, an array of photocells within the piano monitors the movement of the piano hammers, and the information is stored on magnetic tape. The program separates the information into the onset and offset times of each note, the hammer velocity (which is proportional to the dynamic of the note), and the times at which the pedals are depressed and released. From onset and offset information, the program constructs a measure of the articulation type and its degree—staccato when successive notes are separated by a short, silent gap, and legato when successive notes follow one another exactly or with varying amounts of overlap. In this way, the three performance variables under the control of a pianist (timing, dynamics, and articulation) can be studied.

In analysing the performances obtained, the most generally studied property is the time from the onset of one note to the onset of the next note—the inter onset interval (IHI). This is the most significant measure as far as the rhythmic function of the note is concerned since the other possible measures (onset to offset or offset to onset) refer mainly to the articulation properties of the note.

Rhythm and Metre

If rhythm and metre interact, then one way to illustrate and examine this interaction is to study the changes that take place when a fixed rhythmic structure is set in a variety of metrical contexts. For this purpose, a monody with the rhythmic structure given in Figure 1 was constructed and notated in 10 different metrical contexts: 6 different orientations within a $\frac{6}{8}$ time signature (i.e., beginning on each of the six available quaver positions within the bar), and four within a $\frac{2}{4}$ time signature (the four different quaver starting positions). The melodic outline of the tune (which was a simple tonal melody) was altered slightly from context to context in order to support the metrical orientation suggested by the notation, with as little alteration of the overall melodic and implied harmonic shape as possible. Three skilled pianists were given time to practise each of the 10 different sequences and then gave five note-perfect performances of each sequence, in random order.

In order to assess the effect of metrical context on the rhythmic sequence, the IHI data for all the pianists (normalised so as to eliminate differences in tempo between performances) were put into a two-way analysis of variance with metrical context and note position as the independent variables and IHI as the depen-

NOTE NUMBER: 1   2 3   4   5   6 7 8   9 10 11   12   13   14   15   16   17

Figure 1.   Duration string used in all melodic sequences for the experiments on rhythmic–metric interaction.

dent variable. All three pianists showed significant interactions between metrical context and note position, indicating that the relative timing of notes is affected by metrical orientation.

More detailed analysis shows that this interaction depends upon the operation of at least three principles. The single principle that accounts for the largest number of peaks and troughs in the timing profile relates note length to metrical strength. The stronger the metrical position occupied by a note, the greater the amount of positive deviation in the note's IHI; conversely, the weaker the note's metrical position, the greater the amount of negative deviation in its IHI.

The neat, closed cycle of changes in note length coupled to a pattern of metrical reorientations that such a principle would predict does not, however, emerge. This is due to the operation of at least two other principles, the more prominent of which is that notes that complete musical groups or phrases (at a number of levels of structure) are lengthened—a principle also identified by Gabrielsson (1983). This principle often operates in direct opposition to the first, since the final note of a musical group is frequently in a metrically weak position. The third, an infrequently operative principle, appears to lengthen notes that are positioned immediately *prior* to a note that is structurally prominent for metrical, melodic, or other reasons. The aim of this principle seems to be to delay the onset of the immediately following note so as to heighten the impact of its arrival. It is therefore a miniature version of that compositional principle found in much nineteenth-century music whereby an important structural event, such as a tonic cadence, is repeatedly avoided or put off so as to intensify its eventual arrival.

The effect of these three principles is to produce a set of timing profiles in which changes in note length have a rather complex relationship to metrical orientation. This relationship is, in part, direct (the agogic accentuation of metrically strong notes) and in part, indirect, being mediated by the grouping structure of the tunes (the lengthening of notes that complete musical groups) and a variety of other structural features in those cases where a note serves to delay a significant structural event, since metre is only one of a number structural factors contributing to structural significance. As a consequence, changes in performance timing, although precipitated by a metrical change, may bear little direct relationship to the details of that metrical reorientation.

In preparing the melodies for this study, a rather significant difficulty was encountered. In order to make the sequence plausible in a given metrical orientation, small changes had to be made to the melodic structure relative to the original tune. At the outset, such changes seemed unimportant, but in the course of the data analysis, it became clear that, in some cases, these small changes interact with the associated metrical changes so as to affect the structure of the tune quite markedly. It was consequently difficult to dissociate timing changes caused by metrical alterations from those caused by changes in melodic structure. A second study was therefore undertaken using the same duration sequence and the same set of metrical orientations but using non-tonal pitch material. Since non-tonal pitch organisation has a far less decisive relationship to metre, this allowed the same pitches to be used in each of the 10 metrical variants.

The results of this study are no different from those with tonal melodies. A significant interaction between metrical orientation and note position is found (with IHI as the dependent variable); again, there is no significant concordance between note length and metrical accent pattern due to the interaction of the three principles discussed previously. Any effects arising out of melodic changes in the tonal melodies are therefore marginal in comparison to those produced by the metrical change itself.

The results of these two studies demonstrate a number of significant attributes of the relationship between rhythm and metre. First, the changes in relative timing that accompany metrical reorientation indicate that the internal representation of a tune's rhythmic structure is considerably more abstract than the notated representation. Relative note durations, which are notationally constant throughout the experimental material, are modified by the performers in response to changes in metre that have no direct bearing on relative duration. This demonstrates that the relative duration of a note is a property that emerges from the interaction of a number of features that include its symbolic representation, its metrical position and position within a group, and its melodic and harmonic significance. The explicitness with which these features are represented in the score varies considerably: from the highly explicit durational symbol to the possibly very inexplicit grouping or harmonic characteristics. The performer's task, therefore—far from being a simple translation between a series of discrete, explicit symbols and some internalised analog—is to integrate a variety of types of information over a number of symbols and to incorporate this information into a rather abstract matrix of determining structural forces.

The consequences of this multiple determination are seen in the second attribute of the rhythm–metre interaction revealed by this study. This is an effect (which might be called the chameleon effect) whereby notes adapt their rhythmic functions to the metrical context in a way that goes beyond a simple distinction between strong and weak accents. It is easiest to illustrate this effect by way of example. Let us take the timing profile for the first 8 notes of the 17-note sequence in two different metrical orientations. Figure 2 shows the musical notation for the two 8-note sequences, and Figure 3 shows their relative timing profiles.

The profiles demonstrate three differences in the timing of Tune B relative to Tune A: The emphasis of the long–short relationship between N1 and N2 is eliminated; the lengthening of N4 in relationship to N3 and N5 is eliminated; and the pronounced lengthening of N8 in relationship to N7 is reduced. Figure 2 shows that the change in N1–N2 is explained by the movement of the note pair

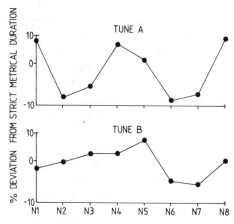

Figure 2. Notated metrical orientations of two tunes from study of rhythm–metre interactions.

away from metrical strength to a position where they span a beat boundary and that the changes in N4 and N8 are due to their movement away from group-final positions. What such an analysis misses, however, is the way in which the rhythmic function of virtually every note in the eight-note passage has been modified and how the durational characteristics of each note influence the type of function it adopts.

Those durational characteristics dictate that long notes function primarily as group endings, due to the extended IHI that they initiate, and possibly as group beginnings, due to the accentual value that long notes tend to acquire. Short notes, however, tend not to function as group endings, since they project forward onto subsequent notes. This means that, in the present example, N7 cannot function as a group ending in Tune B but must become part of the upbeat to N8. Conversely, N5, in the same tune, has a tendency to function as a group ending, despite its position in the middle of the bar. This, in turn, means that N3, which could function as an ending to the first two-bar group, is undermined by its proximity to N5 and pushes forward through N4 onto N5. The same type of

Figure 3. Comparison of relative timing deviations in two tunes.

analysis applies to Tune A, showing that N8 functions as a group ending due to the brevity of the two notes that precede it and that the intermediate duration of N4 gives it an ambiguous function as either a group ending or as an upbeat to the longer N5 that follows.

Such analysis demonstrates that each note is tied into a complex network of dependencies such that if the function of one note changes as a result of its metrical realignment and durational properties, a series of related changes may take place in adjacent notes. Whereas each note demonstrates something of the nature of a chameleon in its ability to assume a variety of functions, that adaptability is limited by the functional resistance, or inertia, that a note's duration imposes on it. For this reason, the pattern of timing changes brought about by a regular cycle of metrical reorientations is less clear than might be anticipated.

A full discussion of the roles of dynamic and articulation in shaping the boundaries and directional forces of the changing rhythmic groups in this study is outside the scope of this chapter. It is nonetheless worth noting that a highly significant interaction between metrical orientation and note position is found with both parameters as dependent variables. Dynamic intensity shows the highest degree of concordance with metrical accent of all three parameters, suggesting that metrical information may be most unambiguously conveyed by means of dynamic differences (see also Sloboda, 1983). For present purposes, however, it is important to recognise that both dynamic and articulation are also extremely effective in altering the position of group boundaries and the sense of directed motion within rhythmic groups. A detailed analysis of both the tonal and the non-tonal tunes used in this study shows that the pattern of subtle functional adaptations discussed in relationship to durational characteristics is further enriched by the influence of the other two performance parameters. Thus, whereas dynamic and articulation lie outside the narrow definition of rhythm adopted in this chapter, it is acknowledged that they both play a vital role in generating and modifying that sense of directed motion that has been recognised as an essential component of rhythm in the broad sense (Schachter, 1980; Yeston, 1976).

In analysing the material in these two studies, it became evident that a fundamental ambiguity accompanies the task of interpretation. The expressive effects observed in a performance can either be considered a *response* to structural features of the material being performed or an attempt to *impose* a particular structure on structurally indeterminate material. In the case of the tonal melodies, it seems more plausible that the expressive effects be regarded as responses, since, as we have seen, changes in the pitch structure of the melodies were made in order to project the appropriate metrical structure. With the non-tonal melodies, the very fact that the material remains unaltered through all metrical reorientations suggests that the expressive effects are primarily impositions of structure, since the material itself is metrically highly malleable. Nonetheless, in the specific detail of analysis, a clear separation is not usually possible, since musical structures are themselves frequently functionally indeterminate. The problem, which initially appears simply methodological, is revealed to lie at the heart of the complex relationship between musical structure and performance expression. This is an issue to which I return at the end of this chapter.

Rhythm and Tempo

Tempo, understood simply as the absolute rate at which music is performed, has not, in general, been considered to contribute to structural characteristics of musical rhythm. The belief, until recently, has been that rhythm remains unaffected structurally by transpositions in tempo, just as melodic contour has been thought to remain unaffected by pitch transposition. This neat parallelism was put in doubt by Michon's (1974) finding that in a prolonged performance of Erik Satie's piano piece "Vexations," the pattern of relative note durations varied with tempo. A replication and more detailed analysis of this effect (Clarke, 1982) demonstrated that the changes are due to modifications of the grouping structure of the piece concomitant with fluctuations in tempo. The general trend was for the music to be segmented into fewer units at faster tempi, with additional group boundaries at slower tempo appearing at locations in the music that coincide with structural boundaries. These structural boundaries are identifiable as discontinuities of pitch and duration, structural parallelisms, and other considerations similar to those outlined in Lerdahl and Jackendoff (1983). In performance, group boundaries are evident as peaks of positive deviation in the timing pattern, the peaks being both more numerous and more sharply defined at slower tempo.

The explanation offered is that at slower tempi, the upper limit of the perceptual present puts a constraint on overall group size and requires a performer to subdivide large groups and to establish the boundaries of smaller groups more convincingly. Additional subdivisions are located by the performer at positions in the music where they are facilitated by structural considerations. Since grouping structure is an aspect of rhythm that is accepted by most current definitions, the finding shows how the rhythmic structure of a piece is modified by its performance tempo, and it shows that those modifications are closely related to a variety of structural characteristics.

"Vexations" is a rather unconventional piece of music, both at low levels (having no bar lines and consisting only of augmented and diminished harmony) and at higher levels (an open-ended fragment that is repeated 840 times). Its repetitive and ambiguous structure encourages reinterpretations and changes of grouping structure of the sort found in the study. In order to determine whether the same sort of effect is found more generally, the study was repeated with a highly conventional piece of music (Clementi's Sonatina, op. 36, no. 3, second movement). The first 16 bars of this piece (Figure 4) constitute a relatively closed section that can be performed at a variety of tempi.

Figure 4.   First 16 bars of second movement of Clementi's Sonatina op. 36, no. 3.

One of the most obvious features of the piece, and a primary reason for selecting it, is the contrast between the dotted rhythms of the right-hand part and the even rhythms of the left. The comparative lack of rhythmic differentiation in the left hand makes it the more appropriate part to compare with "Vexations," since changes in grouping structure can be shown more clearly. Analysis of the relative timing of notes in the left hand reveals an interaction between tempo and note position in the same way as was found in "Vexations"; and in at least one of the performers' data, the interaction is due to a decrease in group size from fast to slow tempo. The breakup of larger groups into subdivisions is again in accordance with structural properties of the music, so that we may conclude that the interaction of rhythm and tempo—and the explanation offered—have some general validity.

The dotted rhythms of the right-hand part also show a sensitivity to tempo, but in a manner that points towards rather different issues. Using the ratio between the two notes of the dotted rhythm as the dependent variable, both the short and the long (Example 1a and 1b, respectively) dotted rhythms show significant effects of tempo—but in opposite directions.

(1)   a. ♩. ♪   b. ♩. ♪

Whereas the ratio between the long and the short notes becomes smaller with faster tempo for the short rhythm, this ratio becomes larger for the long rhythm. The possibility that the decreasing ratio for the short rhythm is due to purely technical limitations can be eliminated on two counts: (1) the trend starts from even the slowest tempi, at which it is inconceivable that technical limitations might apply, and (2) the short note, which would presumably be the technical limiter, shows little sign of flattening out at some minimum duration at even the fastest tempo. This effect, and that observed in the long rhythm, is therefore cognitive.

The explanation for this feature of the interaction between rhythmic performance and tempo is rather different from that offered in connection with the "Vexations" study. Since the result is based on duration ratios averaged across all locations in the music, it clearly does not depend on any characteristics of the local structural context. It is, by contrast, the consequence of a more general feature of the cognition of rhythmic structures. As the tempo increases, the durational values of the short note in each of the rhythms (the semiquaver in Example 1a and the quaver in Example 1b) converge in absolute terms. If we consider the two rhythms at a tempo at which a crotchet has a duration of 800 msec, the short notes of the two dotted rhythms have values of 200 and 400 msec, respectively—a difference of 200 msec. At double the tempo, the two notes in question are now 100 and 200 msec, respectively—a difference of only 100 msec. Although the two dotted (3:1) ratios remain ideally unaffected by changes in tempo, the performer is nonetheless faced by a progressively more difficult cognitive task; namely, to keep separate two *categories* of note value whose absolute durations are converging. The present result indicates that beyond a certain speed, this becomes impossible in practice, the two categories being assimilated into a single intermediate value that is longer than a semiquaver but shorter than a quaver. Hence the *increase* in the value of the long dotted ratio (Example 1b) and the *decrease* in the value of the short ratio (Example 1a).

This explanation is borne out by examination of the absolute value of both the semiquaver and quaver at fast tempi. In three of the four performers' data, there is no significant difference between the mean quaver and semiquaver values, although the two longer notes (the dotted crotchet and the dotted quaver) are still distinct. The four rhythmic categories, shown in Example (2),

$$\quad \text{♩.}, \quad \text{♪.}, \quad \text{♪}, \quad \text{♪} \qquad (2)$$

that the score prescribes, and which are maintained at slower tempi, have been reduced to three (Example 3)

$$\quad \text{♩.}, \quad \text{♪.}, \quad \text{♪/♪} \qquad (3)$$

with a single short category combining with two categories of long note in two different rhythmic relationships. The strong implication is that rhythmic structures are internally represented in a categorical, rather than a continuous, fashion.

Rhythm and Categories

If rhythmic structures are internally represented in a categorical fashion, then it seems almost certain that such categories will be revealed perceptually as well as in performance. The only perceptual study discussed within this chapter demonstrates this to be the case. Subjects listened to rhythms varying by eight equal steps between an even division of the beat and a 2:1 division (Example 4a and 4b, respectively), in two different metrical contexts.

(4)   a. ♫   b. ♩ ♪
                                           3

One metrical context was binary ($\frac{2}{4}$), and the other ternary ($\frac{3}{8}$); the former context rendered the even beat division metrically conformant, and the latter context rendered the 2:1 division conformant. In both metrical contexts, subjects performed an identification task and a discrimination task of the type commonly employed in categorical perception studies (see Costall, Chapter 8, this volume). In both contexts, the results showed the typical midway cross-over of identification, coupled with an increase in discrimination success, that is associated with the functioning of perceptual categories (see Figure 5). Interestingly, there was also a clear effect of metrical context, the metrically conformant rhythm in each context being favoured by a shift in both the discrimination and the identification functions.

This is strong evidence for the idea that categorical distinctions are involved in the perceptual representation of rhythmic structures and that the categories are sensitive to metrical context. This sensitivity is expressed as a boundary shift between rhythmic interpretations so as to increase the range of presented rhythms that fall within the metrically conformant category. In a more realistic musical setting, this would have the effect of assimilating as wide a range of physically different rhythms to the same metrically conformant category as possible without serious distortion, thereby minimising the need to accommodate metrically disruptive structures or, more seriously, revise the prevailing metrical interpretation. As Longuet-Higgins (1976) and Steedman (1977) have pointed out, there is considerable resistance to a perceptual reinterpretation of metrical structure, and the flexible categorisation of rhythmic structures may be one way in which that resistance is achieved. It is also a further feature of the strong interaction between rhythm and metre discussed previously.

The generality of the categorical effect reported here should, in one respect, be treated with a certain amount of caution. The range of rhythms presented and the

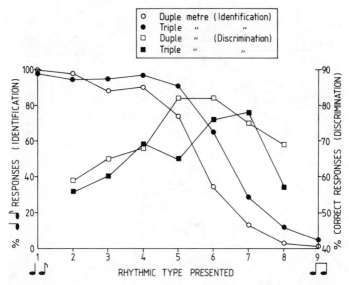

Figure 5.   Identification and discrimination functions for experiment on categorical perception of rhythm.

two categories into which they are subsumed (Example 4) correspond to a qualitative distinction (even and uneven beat division) that is not represented between other pairs of rhythms. It may be that categorical effects are found only between rhythmic types that exemplify this qualitative distinction and that, for instance, the rhythms in Example (5), being only quantitatively distinguished in durational terms, would fail to show categorical effects.

a. ♩ ♪ and ♩. ♩   and   b. ♩. ♩ and ♩.. ♩   (5)
    3

This is an empirical question which, though simple to investigate, awaits demonstration.

As a follow-up to the perceptual finding, the existence of categorical effects in performance was investigated by asking pianists to paly back, on the piano, short tunes that they heard over loudspeakers. These four-bar tunes (Figure 6a and b) were very similar to the sequences used in the perceptual part, the first two bars serving to establish a metrical context ($\frac{6}{8}$ or $\frac{2}{4}$), the third bar consisting of a variety of carefully constructed three-note rhythms, and the final bar consisting of a single concluding note. The third bar was the primary focus of interest and could contain one of seven possible rhythmic structures (Figure 6c). These were four rhythms (1, 3, 5, and 7) that are simple to represent with conventional notation and the three rhythms (2, 4, and 6) lying between each pair of adjacent rhythms, none of which can be easily notated. Pianists heard each tune as many

Figure 6.   Pitches and durations (msec) for tunes in (a) § and (b) ⅔ metre; (c) durations (msec) and equivalent musical notations for the three variable notes in Bar 3.

times as desired (in practice, this was never more than twice) before attempting to reproduce the tune on the piano as accurately as possible. The order of the tunes within each metrical context was randomised, and the pitch content of all tunes was identical.

The results from seven pianists (each of whom played each rhythm 10 times) demonstrate two principal effects: (1) the notatable rhythms are reproduced generally more accurately than those that are unnotatable, and (2) rhythms that conform to each metrical context (1 and 5 in §, and 3 and 7 in ⅔) are facilitated in reproduction. The data were scored by first expressing both the performed and presented rhythms as duration ratios and then assigning each performance to the nearest of the seven rhythmic types presented by the method of least squares. If the reproduction of a rhythm is scored as the same rhythmic type as was presented, it is considered a "hit." If it is scored as a different rhythmic type, it is a "miss" (or "confusion").

The first of the two effects is evident as higher hit rates for the reproduction of notatable rhythms than for the others. In attempting to reproduce rhythms that cannot be notated in any simple fashion, performers tend to produce rhythms that lie within one or other of the adjacent response categories, each of which corresponds to a straightforward notation. There is consequently a migration of responses toward simplicity of duration ratios, an effect demonstrated by Fraisse (1956) and Povel (1981) under more limited conditions. The second effect (facilitation of metrically conformant responses) appears as a tendency for incorrect reproductions to migrate towards metrically conformant—rather than metrically conflicting—responses and for rhythms to be reproduced with an increased hit rate when they are presented within a conformant metre. Both these performance results support the findings of the perceptual study and extend the range of rhythms to which categorical effects apply.

A more detailed analysis of the performances of the three best pianists draws a clearer picture of the representation of rhythmic structures. This analysis is oriented primarily toward discovering whether the timing of individual notes is organised around a structure of beats, whether the beat is a timed interval or simply an abstract marker, and what strategy a performer uses when the beat structure is disrupted. The analysis makes use of variance and covariance properties of the timing data, using the predictions that Vorberg and Hambuch (1978) derive to distinguish between alternative models of timing control. These predictions can be used to demonstrate that when individual events are subject to superordinate timing constraint, such as a directly timed beat within which they lie, negative covariance is found between the timing of those individual events. When no such constraint exists, covariance will be zero or positive, positive covariance reflecting an attempt to reduce durational inequalities between adjacent time intervals without regard for the overall duration of the combined intervals.

The picture that emerges from variance and covariance analysis is as follows. When a time span, such as the beat or a whole bar, is subdivided by two or more unequal durations, negative covariance predominates, indicating the existence of superordinate timing constraint. When the subdivision is into equal durations, covariance tends to be positive, indicating that superordinate timing constraint is relaxed and that an attempt to minimise accidental inequalities is made. This applies to the equal ternary division in Rhythm 1, to the equal binary division of the bar into two beats, to the equal binary division of the first beat into two quavers in Rhythm 3, and also to the ambiguous structure of Rhythm 2. This unnotatable rhythm divides the bar into two slightly unequal parts (840 and 600 msec) and the first part into two equal parts (420 and 420 msec). Some performers show overall positive covariance in the bar and positive covariance between the two components of the divided first part, indicating that their primary concern is to get the individual note relationships correct. Others show positive covariance between the first two components but negative covariance in the bar as a whole, indicating an attempt to equalise the first two durations coupled with the preservation of overall bar duration, presumably at the expense of the relative durational accuracy of the final note.

Of all seven rhythms, the greatest total variance (i.e., the sum of the variances of the three individual notes) is found in two of the unnotatable rhythms—Rhythms 2 and 4. These behave far more unstably than the third unnotatable rhythm (Rhythm 6), explanation for which is offered below. Furthermore, the variance of the ratio of the third bar's duration to that of the previous bar, although varying among the performers, is greatest in Tune 2. This, combined with the note variances, suggests that Tune 2 and, to a lesser extent, Tune 4 are the most unstable in reproduction and that this instability is expressed as an inability to control accurately both the relative durations of the constituent notes and the total duration of the bar. It is significant that the performer whose data show the least elevated variance for the overall bar duration in Rhythm 2 is also the most inaccurate in reproducing the relative durations of that rhythm. The implication is that there is a trade-off between the accuracy of relative note durations and preservation of overall bar length.

From evidence presented here and from other supporting data (Clarke, 1985, Shaffer, Clarke, and Todd, in press), the following outline is suggested as a model of rhythm representation. It must first be recognised that a model in which every individual duration is directly timed, although a theoretical possibility, would be unduly laborious and might lead to a rather unmusical lack of fluency. The inability of the pianists in this study to reproduce accurately rhythms that are not commonly encountered also suggests that a more abstract representation is appropriate. It is therefore suggested that rhythms are internally represented as a set of durations organised around a series of temporal markers, or beats. In performance, it is these beats that are directly timed (as the majority of data in this study demonstrate) although, on occasion, a performer may time individual notes directly, particularly if they are relatively long. Subdivisions of the beat are represented by means of procedures, which differ from beats in that they do not receive direct clock timing. Rather, they are essentially abstract movement specifications (e.g., three equal notes or a long and a short note) that result in a definite timing commitment. They are not timed as such but are parts of a motor program that, when realised by a muscle system, result in a temporal pattern of movements. The most significant difference between beats and procedures is that, whereas beats are a concatenated series of centrally timed events, procedures are hierarchically subordinate in terms of timing specification.

In the perception of rhythm, it has for some time been recognised that it is vital for a metrical framework (i.e., a framework of beats) to be established early on in a sequence. A listener is therefore engaged in a process that is the reverse of a performer—extracting beat intervals from a sequence (see Longuet-Higgins and Lee, 1982; Steedman, 1977) and organising individual notes around markers. Rather than specifying abstract movement patterns (since not all listeners are performers), these perceptual procedures specify a set of directed durational inequalities oriented toward, or away from, proximate beat markers.

It is possible to be more specific about the nature of these procedures and their relationship to the metrical framework within which they lie. A feature of the data reported here is the apparent unconcern with which performers treat precise duration ratios. Rhythms 5, 6, and 7 all involve an uneven division of the first beat of Bar 3, Rhythm 5 being a 2:1 ratio; Rhythm 7 being a 3:1 ratio; and Rhythm 6 lying in between (see Figure 6). In reproduction, the data for these three rhythms are fairly broadly spread across all three response categories, showing no evidence for a categorical distinction between the two notatable rhythms and very little evidence to suggest that the unnotatable rhythm is treated differently from the two notatable rhythms. In addition, when the metrical context is changed from $\frac{6}{8}$ to $\frac{2}{4}$, the effect on the data is to shift the broad response peak away from Rhythm 5 toward Rhythm 7, increasing the number of reproductions that fall within Response Category 6 (unnotatable) as well as in Response Category 7. This suggests that the performers treat all three rhythms in essentially the same way, as simply an unequal (long plus short) division of the first beat of Bar 3, with the long–short distinction more emphasised in Rhythm 7 than Rhythm 5 and with Rhythm 6 occupying an intermediate position. This would also account for the failure of Rhythm 6 to behave like the other unnotatable rhythms in terms of variance properties, as noted previously. This appears to confirm the proposition that categorical distinctions apply only when qualitative changes occur, as is the case between Rhythms 1 and 3, when a ternary bar division changes to a binary division and between Rhythms 3 and 5, where an even division of the first beat changes to an uneven division.

Since the precise ratio of durations within a rhythm appears not to be accurately preserved, it would seem enough for procedures simply to specify into how many subdivisions a beat interval is subdivided and whether these subdivisions are equal or not. If they are not equal, a simple distinction between long and short units of subdivision is all that appears necessary, a more precise duration specification being retrievable from metrical information. For instance, in $\frac{2}{4}$ metre, a long-plus-short beat subdivision is interpreted by the system as the (metrically conformant) rhythm in Example 7, with an ideal ratio of 3:1, whereas in $\frac{6}{8}$, the same specification results in the rhythm in Example 6, with an ideal ratio of 2:1. Unless a rather definite specification is made in the procedural representation, performers will produce metrically conformant rhythms, which is precisely what the data in this study demonstrate. Interestingly, there is support for this conception of rhythmic representation from music-historical evidence. In the baroque period, the value of a dotted note was variable, being determined by the metrical context. In a triple time signature, a dotted rhythm was played with a ratio of approximately 2:1, and in a duple time signature, with a ratio of 3:1. This makes the rhythm metrically conformant in either metrical context. Similarly, it was the practice when playing dotted rhythms against triplets (in, for instance, the two hands of a keyboard piece) to "underdot" the rhythm to allow it to synchronise with the triplets.

To summarise this model, it is proposed that rather than internally representing

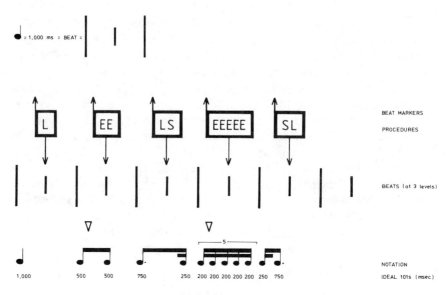

Figure 7. Diagrammatic illustration of the ideal representation of rhythmic structures.

rhythms by means of complex ratio information, a combination of two simple components is used. One is a system of metrical markers that are directly timed at one level but exist as abstract relationships at both higher and lower levels. (We may time crotchet beats only in $\frac{2}{4}$, but we "know" that pairs of crotchets form measures, pairs of measures form hypermeasures, and so on and that crotchets are divided into pairs of quavers, quavers into pairs of semiquavers, and so on. By contrast, we know that in $\frac{6}{8}$, the dotted crotchet beats are divided into three quavers). The second component is a system of untimed procedures, organised around these markers, specifying subdivisions in terms of equal and unequal time spans, the unequal subdivisions using a simple distinction between long and short. In order to cope with the distinction between dotted and double-dotted (Example 5b) rhythms, it may be necessary to add emphasising modifiers to the system (i.e., very long and very short; see Clarke, 1985), but this is essentially a difference of degree within the system, the only difference in *kind* remaining that between unequal and equal. Using this simple two-component system, which has similarities to the model of scale and contour developed by Dowling (1978) in connection with melody, it is possible to represent apparently complex rhythms in an entirely unambiguous way. Figure 7 illustrates the model.

The development of rhythmic skills in both listeners and performers is under-stood, within the model outlined here, as being largely a question of acquiring a wide variety of procedural representations to cope with the rhythmic structures commonly—and less commonly—found in music. When an unfamiliar rhythm is encountered, a performer must either cobble together a new procedure on the spot or modify an existing one, the result being initially unstable performances. This is reflected either in loss of accuracy in the timing of the beat interval or loss of accuracy in the subdivision of the beat interval. Performers appear to differ in their assessment of the relative importance of preserving the beat interval or the durational proportions between rhythmic components. Eventually, a new procedure will be properly developed, and the stability and accuracy of both beat intervals and their subdivisions restored.

In developing this account of the representation of rhythmic structures, I have attempted to avoid unduly abstract formulations. In one sense at least, however, the model is abstract, since it does not take account of the modifications that accompany the transformation of a representation into a performance. The purpose of the next section is to give some account of those processes: their nature, function, origin, and control.

EXPRESSIVE TRANSFORMATIONS OF RHYTHMIC STRUCTURES

It should be understood at the outset that rhythmic performances by human beings are never inexpressive. Such a possibility is as psychologically implausible as it is to imagine that a person might hear the ticks of a metronome as isolated, independent events. Nonetheless, the theoretical distinction between a level of representation that is inexpressive, or canonic, and one that is expressive, or interpreted, is not redundant. It reconciles the intuition that simple rhythms involve small whole-number ratios with the abundant evidence that stable rhythmic performances consist of durations related to one another by complex non-integral ratios. The level of representation consisting of integral relationships (the structural representation) is always transformed by a modifying expressive representation, but is distinct from it.

Although the primary focus of interest in this chapter is on the expressive transformation of inter onset intervals, this is, of course, only one of a number of expressive options available to a performer. In piano performance, changes in articulation (legato–staccato), dynamics, and pedalling perform expressive functions that are equally significant. It was pointed out in connection with the interaction of rhythm and metre that metrical reorientations result in significant changes in the pattern of dynamics and articulation and that these contribute powerfully to the sense of directed motion that is associated with a rhythmic structure. With other instruments, additional expressive possibilities are available: vibrato, intentional mistunings, variations in timbre, a variety of articulatory possibilities, portamenti, and many others. These effects may be combined in a large number of ways, resulting in a complex system of interactions and dependencies with an expressive richness that defies description. The more circumscribed range of expressive parameters available to a pianist makes the situation more amenable to detailed study, although the subtlety of variation within each parameter is considerable.

The most general function of these expressive devices is to point the significance of musical structures in specific directions. Virtually any musical structure is multiply interpretable, and the primary role of expression is to limit the extent of this ambiguity by emphasising certain structural interpretations at the expense of others. This does not mean, however, that expression always operates in the service of clarity. A performer may choose to emphasise either those structural characteristics that are most obvious or to extract more hidden and disruptive tendencies from the material. Similarly, although a performance must strive to be expressively coherent, that aim does not entail the resolution of all structural ambiguity, since a performance may attempt to manipulate the contradictory tendencies of what is performed quite intentionally.

At a detailed level, however, each expressive act operates to impose a particular functional meaning on a particular musical structure. This is achieved in a variety of ways, the most general underlying principle being the intensification of gestalt properties of the musical structure already evident or the establishment of gestalt features when the musical structure is interpretively neutral. Examples of this procedure are the establishment of boundaries in the grouping structure of the music by means of changes in dynamics, articulation, or rubato; the imposition or emphasis of a pattern of direction towards a structural focal point by means of dynamic, articulatory, and timing gradients; or the modification of the accentual status of events (i.e., changes in figure–ground relationships) by means of dynamic or agogic elements.

In a majority of these examples, the relationship between the expressive aim and the expressive means is direct: Boundaries are indicated by relatively large parametric changes, forward directed motion is indicated by graduated parametric increase, and accentual strength is indicated by relative parametric intensity. Within at least two of these parameters (timing and articulation), however, the directness of this expressive function is threatened by ambiguity. The lengthening of a note can, as we have already seen, indicate that it is accented, that it finishes a structural unit at some level, or that the following (delayed) note is of structural significance. Similarly, although an underlying correlation between structural significance and increased legato articulation appears to prevail, it is not uncommon to find structural significance indicated by means of emphatically staccato articulation.

This uncertainty appears to stem from the combination of a variety of strongly iconic with more arbitrary or conventional semiotic functions in one systematic framework. Both agogic and dynamic accentuation and the establishment of boundaries by contrasts in length, dynamic, or articulatory type, are iconic functions, since in the former, parametric intensification and in the latter parametric discontinuity are directly related to accentuation and structural division. Expressive delay and phrase-final lengthening are similarly iconic in their semiotic function. By contrast, the relationship between the structural significance of an event and its style of articulation is more arbitrary, perhaps because the perceptual salience of note length with legato articulation is balanced by the perceptual salience of attack-point emphasis with staccato articulation. As a result, articulation receives a purely oppositional value to which no necessary structural significance can be attributed.

The systematic uncertainty that follows from this mixture of iconic and arbitrary functions is largely clarified in practice by the structural context in which expressive gestures appear. It is unlikely that the expressive characteristics of an event would leave a listener confused about its intended structural significance, since in the majority of contexts, structural information makes that clear in broad outline. The function of expression is predominantly to refine the significance of those immanent properties, rather than to generate structural meaning from scratch. This subtle interaction between structural and expressive properties is an issue to which I return after discussing the control and origin of expressive transformations.

The Control of Expressive Timing

The control of all the expressive parameters of piano performance is a subject too broad and still unresearched to be discussed here. Shaffer (1981) gives an account of some features of both timing and dynamic control in piano performance, and Sloboda (1983) considers the communicative function of timing, dynamic, and articulation. This discussion is limited to timing alone, since it is only with this parameter that adequate information concerning internal representation exists for a consideration of control mechanisms to be possible. A striking feature of skilled piano performance is the way in which flexibility and accuracy of timing control are combined. Data from Clynes and Walker (1982), Shaffer (1980), and Clarke (1985) demonstrate that musicians couple the ability to reproduce timing profiles with vanishingly small standard deviations with the ability to restructure parts of the timing profile in a distinct and spontaneous manner. The control system that generates such performances must therefore integrate information at a number of levels so as to preserve both the musical sense and the precision of the result. In order to understand how this might be achieved, we must return to the internal representation of rhythmic sequences.

The model outlined earlier represented rhythmic structures by means of two components: metrical time spans (beats) and time-span subdivisions (procedures). The former are directly timed, in a clocklike fashion, in a concatenated series (see Vorberg and Hambuch, 1978), whereas the latter are subordinate to the former, have the quality of abstract movement patterns, and receive a definite timing profile when realised by a specific muscle system. Just as the canonic representation of rhythmic structures makes use of two kinds of information, so, too, does the expressive transformation of these structures operate at two levels and by means of two types of mechanism.

Shaffer (1981) shows by means of hierarchic analysis of variance that there exists in a musical performance a level of regularly repeating time spans (beats) for which random variance is minimised. This suggests strongly that these time spans are timed in a direct fashion. However, beats at this level also vary in duration according to context in a consistent and highly reproducible manner. This suggests that the clocklike mechanism that times these beat intervals is modifiable, or programmable, so as to vary its momentary rate. It has also been demonstrated that these fluctuations in beat timing are related to structural characteristics of the music being performed (Clarke, 1982, Gabrielsson, Bengtsson, and Gabrielsson, 1983, Shaffer, 1981; Sloboda, 1983), indicating that the programming of clock rate has access to information concerning musical structure.

At a more detailed level, the individual notes within these beats also demonstrate precise and consistent timing profiles related to structural properties of the music. Because the timing specification for these notes is relational rather than metrical, their expressive transformation must be represented by means of continuously variable modifications of those relational specifications. Once again, musical structural information is the basis for the transforming operation.

Drawing the two components together, the pattern of rubato observed in performance is seen to be the product of two distinct types of transformation, both of which have continuous reference to a large body of abstract musical knowledge. That knowledge, when coupled with the notational symbols of a performance score, generates a motor program containing timing information at two levels. The higher level consists of a concatenated series of time spans that are notionally equivalent in duration, are timed by an internal clock mechanism, and are modified in actual duration by programmed modifications of the clock rate. Whereas the time spans are concatenated in terms of clock mechanism, the modifications, being responsive to hierarchical features of musical structure, are organised according to a hierarchical system of rate specifications. The result is a continual fluctuation in tempo that reflects musical structure. At the same time, individual notes within these varying beat intervals are specified according to collections of durational equalities and inequalities, which are themselves relationally modifiable on the basis of structural information available to the motor program. The two levels are analogous to the fluctuations in beat rate of a conductor on the one hand and the durational shaping of individual notes by each of a group of performers on the other. Figure 8, an expressively modified version of Figure 7, illustrates this.

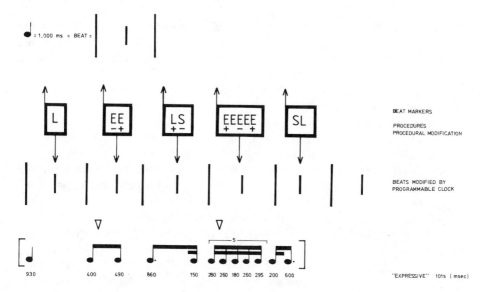

Figure 8. Diagrammatic illustration of the expressive representation of rhythmic structures.

Having considered the mechanisms by which expressive timing patterns may be controlled, it remains to consider how an expressive strategy for a given performance is developed. Since timing is only one of a range of expressive parameters available to a performer and since there is evidence, presented here and elsewhere (Shaffer, 1981; Sloboda, 1983), that performers construct expressive performances even when the music is unfamiliar, the aim of this discussion is to outline the diverse factors that contribute to the selection and structuring of expressive options. There are the resources of the chosen instrument, which, as already noted, vary considerably in restrictiveness. Since the same piece of music may be played on different instruments, a performer who switches from one to another may have to make a considerable adjustment to the resources of the instrument. Quite apart from the timbral differences, piano and harpsichord performances of Bach's keyboard music, for instance, differ markedly in their use of expressive timing. Such differences are even evident in performances of Mozart's or Haydn's keyboard music on an eighteenth-century fortepiano as compared with a modern grand. Performers who play a variety of keyboard instruments confirm that they must make a conscious stylistic adjustment to suit a particular instrument.

Such features of instrument design ultimately merge into a second factor influencing expressive choice, namely, performance convention—a subject too complex to treat in any depth here. Just as instrument design and construction shows historical and geographical development (see Chapter 10, this volume), so also do the conventions of performance demonstrate significant historical and geographical variation. These are often linked to instrument technology but are

by no means simply the consequence of such changes. Writings and pronounce-
ments on performance practice vary from simple prescriptive statements to more
considered and closely argued discussions of particular problems; but whether
informed or not, and whether consciously adopted or not, they undoubtedly
influence the manner in which performers adapt their expressive usage to a
particular composition.

Considerations of stylistic convention can be viewed broadly as part of the
performance context—in this case, historical context. The details of expression
are, however, also sensitive to contextual features of a far more local and immediate kind. These constitute the third of the factors operating on the structuring of
expressive options. As Sloboda (1983) points out, it is implausible to assume that
expressive features of a performance are triggered by individual notational symbols, an argument supported by the spontaneous interpretative changes between
successive performances of the same material that are found in the data discussed
earlier in this chapter. This means that structural information must be integrated
from a collection of notational symbols before it can form the basis for an
expressive strategy. It must also be supplemented by information about the
current expressive context and any logistical constraints that might apply: For
example, notes lying outside the hand's span cannot be played legato without
using the sustaining pedal.

The organisation of expressive features is thus closely bound up with the
structure of the musical material. We may pose the question, however, whether
this system of expressive features possesses a logic of its own that is independent
of musical structure—whether there is, in other words, a syntax of expression.
The evidence is against such a proposal. There appear to be no intrinsic constraints on the sequencing of expressive gestures within any expressive parameter, the combination of expressive parameters, or the sequential relationships
between compound expressive events. Certain expressive transitions seem unlikely, but this appears to be for the reason that they suggest implausible musical
contexts rather than for reasons associated with the expressive system itself.
Although a partial separation of structure and expression may occur in mannered
or ironic performances, the conclusion must be that the logic of expression is
almost entirely dependent upon the logic of formal structure. It would be surprising if this were not the case, since a situation might then arise in which the
demands of structure and expression were incompatible, leaving a performer
with an impossible choice between a distortion of structure or expression. Such a
conflict is not something that performers are aware of, and it is not demonstrated
in any performance data yet obtained.

The fourth factor affecting expressive choice is the manner in which a performer chooses to perform. Seashore (1938/1967) demonstrates that a performer
can play the same piece of music with an expressive profile that differs according
to whether he or she is instructed to play artistically or metronomically. The

differences are principally in the degree, rather than the pattern, of rubato, but there is every indication that a performer can choose to alter the pattern as well. Sloboda (1983) shows that a professional performer experienced in playing for aural examinations conveys the metre of a short tune to listeners more effectively than does a performer of similar calibre who does not undertake such duties. This suggests that the former player adopts a more didactic approach in the relationship between metrical and expressive features than the latter.

The choice of performance manner ("careful" or "expressive") is a product of the audience and occasion, as well as properties of the piece itself. A performer must ensure that listeners do not find a performance trite and obvious, and, at the same time, he or she must avoid introducing so much expressive sophistication that the structure becomes incomprehensible. For this reason, a performer's style in a concert recital is likely to be different from the same performer's style at a children's concert or during a melodic dictation exercise. The properties of the piece further complicate this situation, since a piece with an unambiguous and readily comprehensible structure may encourage a performer to experiment with contradictory expressive elements more than a piece with a complex or ambiguous structure, in which the structural forces may not be sufficiently strong to support conflicting expressive tendencies.

It is evident from this discussion that the expressive system must take a large number of varied factors into account when constructing an appropriate performance strategy. The system is undoubtedly generative, in the sense that an expressive profile is generated at the time of performance from stored information about stylistic conventions and particular expressive devices developed during rehearsal (if the performance is not sight-read), as well as from information processed during the performance itself. The non-random variability of performances testifies to the unmemorised nature of expressive strategies. But the expressive system does not itself consist of a set of generative rules that are different from the demands of musical structure. The idea of an independent generative grammar of expression appears to be unjustified.

CONCLUDING REMARKS:
STRUCTURE AND EXPRESSION

In discussing the expressive transformation of rhythmic structures, the way in which they fit into a wider expressive system, and the manner in which that system operates, we have moved some distance from the narrow definition of rhythm proposed at the beginning of this chapter. It has proved necessary to do so in order to account for the way in which rhythmic structures are implicated in a system of expressive transformations of which temporal transformation is a part. That whole system is, in turn, inextricably bound up with the system of representational structures called musical knowledge.

The close relationship between structure and expression is a matter of which Seashore (1938/67), in his pioneering work on expression in performance, was aware. Finding a surprising absence of overt expressive marking of the metre of a performed piece, he inquires:

> How shall we account for this relative absence of physical intensity and accent? It is a fair guess that it is due to the fact that the compositional structure suggests the beat unit, and subjective rhythms, for both the player and the listener, carry out the scheme. This presents a most interesting problem in the psychology of music, namely, what features attributed to the performer are really due to the subjective contribution of the listener?''
> (p. 243)

Seashore's proposal that explicit expressive features and implicit structural features combine to form the internal representation of a piece of music for both performer and listener seems certain to be correct. The observation suggests further that a similar relationship between structure and expression may enable a listener selectively to ignore inadvertent mistakes or inaccuracies in a performance by making use of structural information.

Let us consider the case of a piece of music with a strongly marked, unambiguous structure. If some feature of the performance conflicts radically with the music's structural implications, the structural stability is likely to force a listener to conclude that the expressive feature is, in fact, a mistake. If the performance feature itself is less prominent, it may not even be noticed by a listener. In the performance of a piece with a weak or ambiguous structure, however, a listener is left with no choice, in the absence of structural guidance, but to pay more attention to expressive features of the performance and to take more or less at face value any gesture that is noticed. In this circumstance, a performer is under particular pressure to pay the most acute attention to details of expression, since any unintended deviation is disproportionately disruptive. It may be for this reason that the performance of contemporary music puts such great expressive demands on performers, since both listeners and performers are generally less well equipped to extract and comprehend the structural implications of such music.

Considerable problems for the analysis of performances are raised by this state of affairs. If a performer is hearing into a performance features that are not measurably present, an analysis of the performance features must, at the very least, fall short of a complete description of the cognitive intentions of the performer. At worst, it may seriously distort those intentions and representations that are the basis for constructing a performance. At a low level, the need to make structural changes when metrically reorienting tonal melodies demonstrates that intrinsic structural properties may be far more strongly determining than expressive properties. At higher levels of structure, where it is extremely difficult for practical reasons for a performer to project expressive connections between widely separated events, structural features of the music are almost certainly the primary means by which the continuity and unity of a performance are achieved.

There is no simple solution to this interpenetration of structure and expression. What the issue highlights is the importance of paying careful attention to a structural analysis of the music when analysing performance data. This is not easy since the following two levels of indeterminacy exist between a musical structure and its interpretation in performance: (1) Having identified a structural feature, there is a large number of ways in which that feature could be successfully projected in performance, a particular choice being determined by a performer's personal stylistic idiosyncracies among other things; and (2) indeterminacy arises from the absence of any generally accepted analytical method for describing and understanding musical structures. The distinction between an approach based on, for instance, Schenker's (1979) ideas and one based on Meyer's (1973) not only attributes structural significance to different types of structure, but may analyse the properties of one and the same structure in fundamentally opposed ways. The most recent general analytical method to appear (Lerdahl and Jackendoff, 1983) leaves the relative importance of possibly conflicting analytical interpretations of a given structure unresolved, in the belief that this accurately represents the ambiguous nature of musical structures.

As far as the analysis of performance data is concerned, this situation makes for considerable difficulties. Lerdahl and Jackendoff's position on analytical indeterminacy may have the advantage of cognitive honesty and ecological validity, but it is more helpful to have analytical systems that adopt a stronger position and generate more restrictive interpretations. Rather than narrowing the gap between cognitive theories and formal theories, it may actually be more productive to maintain that clear separation and to develop each within its own sphere. Performance analysis, and the interaction between structure and expression in particular, offers an arena in which the clash between the two domains may be fruitfully investigated.

REFERENCES

Clarke, E. F. Timing in the performance of Erik Satie's "Vexations." *Acta Psychologica*, 1982, *50*, 1–19.

Clarke, E. F. Some aspects of rhythm and expression in performances of Erik Satie's "Gnossienne No. 5." *Music Perception*, 1985, 2(3).

Clynes, M., and Walker, J. Neurobiologic functions of rhythm, time, and pulse in music. In M. Clynes (Ed.), *Music, mind and brain*. New York: Plenum Press, 1982.

Dowling, W. J. Scale and contour: Two components of a theory of memory for melodies. *Psychological Review*, 1978, *85*, 342–354.

Fraisse, P. *Les structures rhythmiques*. Louvain, France: Publications universitaires de Louvain, 1956.

Gabrielsson, A. Performance of rhythm patterns. *Scandinavian Journal of Psychology*, 1974, *15*, 63–72.

Gabrielsson, A., Bengtsson, I., and Gabrielsson, B. Performance of musical rhythm in 3/4 and 6/8 meter. *Scandinavian Journal of Psychology,* 1983, *24,* 193–213.

Handel, S., and Oshinsky, J. The meter of syncopated auditory polyrhythms. *Perception and Psychophysics,* 1981, *30*(1), 1–9.

Lerdahl, F., and Jackendoff, R. *A generative theory of tonal music.* Cambridge: MIT Press, 1983.

Longuet-Higgins, H. Perception of melodies. *Nature,* 1976, *263,* No. 5579, 646–653.

Longuet-Higgins, H., and Lee, C. S. Perception of musical rhythms. *Perception,* 1982, *11,* 115–128.

Meyer, L. B. *Explaining music.* Berkeley: University of California Press, 1973.

Michon, J. Programs and "programs" for sequential patterns in motor behaviour. *Brain Research,* 1974, *71,* 413–424.

Povel, D. J. Temporal structure of performed music: Some preliminary observations. *Acta Psychologica,* 1977, *41,* 309–320.

Povel, D. J. Internal representation of simple temporal patterns. *Journal of Experimental Psychology: Human Perception and Performance,* 1981, *7*(1), 3–18.

Seashore, C. E. *Psychology of music.* New York: Dover, 1967. (Reprinted from McGraw-Hill, 1938).

Schachter, C. Rhythm and linear analysis: A preliminary study. In F. Salzer and C. Schachter (Eds.), *The music forum* (Vol. 4), New York: Columbia University Press, 1980.

Schenker, H. *Free composition* (E. Oster, Trans.) New York: Longman, 1979.

Shaffer, L. H. Intention and performance. *Psychological Review,* 1976, *83*(5), 375–393.

Shaffer, L. H. Analysing piano performance. In G. Stelmach and J. Requin (Eds.), *Tutorials in motor behaviour.* Amsterdam: North Holland Press, 1980.

Shaffer, L. H. Performances of Chopin, Bach, and Bartok: Studies in motor programming. *Cognitive Psychology,* 1981, *13,* 326–376.

Shaffer, L. H., Clarke, E. F., and Todd, N. P. Rhythm and metre in piano performance. *Cognition,* in press.

Sloboda, J. A. The communication of musical metre in piano performance. *Quarterly Journal of Experimental Psychology,* 1983, *35*(A), 377–390.

Steedman, M. J. The perception of musical rhythm and metre. *Perception,* 1977, *6,* 555–569.

Vorberg, D., and Hambuch, R. On the temporal control of rhythmic performance. In J. Requin (Ed.), *Attention and performance VII.* Hillsdale, NJ: Erlbaum, 1978.

Yeston, M. *The stratification of musical rhythm.* New Haven: Yale University Press, 1976.

10

Music Structure and Human Movement*

John Baily

INTRODUCTION

The study of music and cognition usually treats music as though it were a purely acoustical or sonic phenomenon: The central issues are seen to be the perception of music and the cognitive representations of the parameters of music structure through which perception is mediated. But the auditory perception of music is only one aspect of musical cognition; of equal interest and importance is the cognition of performance. Leaving aside the special cases of singing and vocal music, mechanical music, and the possibilities now available for the generation of synthesised music, the activity of music making involves patterned movement in relationship to the active surface of a musical instrument, regardless of whether the instrument is blown, bowed, plucked, concussed, percussed, or made to sound in some other way. Human movement is the process through which musical patterns are produced: Music is the sonic product of action. Looking at things in this way opens up two possible lines of inquiry. First, there is a need to study the way that musical patterns may be represented cognitively by the performer as patterns of movement rather than as patterns of sound. Second, since the motor apparatus and its control mechanisms (including those of conscious control), which together constitute the sensorimotor system, have certain intrinsic modes of operation, we need to consider the extent to which the creation of musical structures is shaped by sensorimotor factors.

It is, perhaps, hardly surprising that matters of performance have been neglected in the study of the psychology of music, which is, after all, a highly ethnocentric intellectual endeavour. In Deutsch (1982), for example, only one of 18 chapters is on the performance of music, that by Sloboda. And it is also not

* This research was supported by a research grant from the Social Science Research Council to John Blacking and the author, at the Department of Social Anthropology, The Queen's University of Belfast. The present paper was written while the author was a Visiting Research Fellow at the Laboratory of Experimental Psychology, University of Sussex, in 1983–1984. I wish to thank John Blacking and Paul Berliner for their comments on an early draft of this paper.

237

without significance that a new journal addressed to the study of musical phenomena is called *Music Perception*. Practitioners of the psychology of music
have not only tended to use for their researches those kinds of music that are most
highly valued in Western society but have also implicitly adopted certain views
about the nature of music put forward by western musicians, musicologists, and
teachers of music, for it must be said that research on music and cognition cannot
proceed in the absence of some set of assumptions about the nature of music
itself. A common Western view regards music as primarily a sonic phenomenon;
study of the motor control of musical performance may be interesting but is
ultimately irrelevant to the central issue, which is the perception of musical
sounds—from single sine waves to extended musical structures.

It is to ethnomusicology that the task of inquiry into the nature of music has
fallen, for only ethnomusicology has access to the necessary cross-cultural data
needed to distinguish between the culture-specific and the universal. Ethnomusicologists who have pursued this line of inquiry have realised that the
closer they come to specifying universals in music, the more they are dealing
with phenomena that are rooted in the psychophysiological nature of the human
being (Harwood, 1976; Kolinski, 1967; Meyer, 1960). The goals of ethnomusicology and the psychology of music are different, but this is one of
several areas where their interests overlap. The importance of ethnomusicology
for the study of music and cognition is not simply that it brings into the research
arena a wealth of seemingly exotic data from musical systems organized on
principles unknown or unused in Western music, but also that it emphasises the
study of music-making as a process instead of just music as a product. As one of
the architects of the anthropological approach in ethnomusicology has put it: "At
some level of analysis, all musical behaviour is structured, whether in relation to
biological, psychological, sociological, cultural, or purely musical processes;
and it is the task of the ethnomusicologist to identify all processes that are
relevant to an explanation of musical sound" (Blacking, 1973, p. 17).

Given this emphasis on the *processes* of music making, it is to be expected that
ethnomusicologists should have had some interesting insights into the relationship between movement and music. Some of this work is reviewed in the
next section of this chapter. The section following that discusses the results of
field research that involved a comparison of two types of plucked lute found in
Afghanistan. In the final section, certain relationships between sonic and motor
aspects of musical cognition are briefly discussed.

MOVEMENT PATTERNS IN AFRICAN MUSIC

The insights that ethnomusicologists have had about the relationship between
sonic patterns of music and human movement have come about mainly through

research on African music. There can be little doubt that overt body movement is a prominent feature in the performance of many kinds of music in Africa, and the conceptual link between music and dance is very close. According to Kubik (1979), there is an old view that "African music is not sound alone" (p. 227) because the element of dancelike movement in performance is so strong. In some African languages, the same word is used for both music and dance; for example, in the Igbo language the term "egwu" embraces music, song, dance and drama, which are thought of as inseparable components of a performance of "music."

In 1928, von Hornbostel[1] published a seminal paper on African music in which he discussed what were to become major issues in the later literature, such as the relationship between speech tone and melodic contour in tonal languages, the nature of African vocal polyphony, and the organization of polyrhythm. Von Hornbostel never visited Africa and, as far as we know, had no opportunity to observe directly the performance of African music. The source of his information was the phonogram, usually recorded in the field by anthropologists, missionaries, or explorers. Despite these limitations, von Hornbostel had some inspired insights, and one of them concerned the music-movement issue. In discussing a recording of xylophone music, he suggests that parallel motion of the hands with the beaters is controlled by spatial relationships rather than by musical considerations, and concludes: "[The player] realizes melody above all as an act of motility, regarding its audible quality rather as a side-issue, although a desirable one" (p. 49).

One of the first analyses of a piece of African music in terms of the movements made in its performance was carried out by Blacking (1955). In this pioneering work, Blacking made what he called musical and physical analyses of eight recorded tunes played on the Butembo flute (from the Congo). Through experimentation with a four-holed flute similar to that used for the recordings, Blacking (1955) was able to reconstruct the fingerings and blowing techniques used in playing the music. He found that the music was constructed from repeated patterns of fingering which, coupled with varying degrees of overblowing on the instrument to obtain upper partials, seemed to generate the melodic sequences of the tunes, and he suggested that the shape of the music was influenced by the spatial properties of the instrument.

Blacking (1961) produced a fuller analysis and discussion of the music-movement issue with reference to the Nsenga *kalimba,* a form of lamellaphone, a common type of African instrument consisting of a set of flexible keys (usually

---

[1]Erich von Hornbostel was one of the major figures in comparative musicology, as ethnomusicology was known up to the 1950s. It is interesting for psychologists to reflect that comparative musicology was first established at the Institute for Psychology in Berlin, then under the directorship of Carl Stumpf. Research on music was based on the analysis of field recordings placed in the Phonogram Archive, established at the institute in 1902. Von Hornbostel and a group of distinguished colleagues worked there until the 1930s.

of metal, although other materials are sometimes employed) that are plucked with the thumbs and, less often, the fingers. Such instruments are often called *mbira* (see Berliner, 1978, for a detailed study of the Shona mbira). A special feature of many kinds of lamella, including the Nsenga kalimba, is that the keyboard is divided, being symmetrically disposed for the two hands, with low tones in the centre, moving outwards on both sides to higher tones. Blacking (1961) analysed a number of kalimba tunes in terms of their music and the movements behind the music, and found the following:

> An analysis (of the tunes) reveals no patterns common to different melodies. But as soon as patterns of 'fingering' and of rhythm are compared, we see that several tunes differ only in so far as rhythmic variations are applied to certain nuclear, or total, patterns of 'fingering'. . . . The most significant common factors of the kalimba tunes are not their melodic structures, but the recurring patterns of 'fingering' which, combined with different patterns of polyrhythms between the two thumbs, produce a variety of melodies. (p. 6)

Blacking did not discuss in any detail what those nuclear movement patterns were but pointed out that "the tunes . . . are variations on a theme, but the theme is physical and not purely musical" (p. 7). The Nsenga, in fact, use several different mbira layouts for different kinds of melody.

A third ethnomusicologist who has taken an interest in these matters for many years is Kubik (1979). He makes much of the distinction between what he sometimes calls the motional pattern and the sonic pattern in musical performance, and he points out how these can be different. Kubik (1962) described in some detail what he called inherent rhythms (later he adopted the more neutral term, "inherent pattern"):

> I stumbled across this strange phenomenon for the first time when I was learning to play the xylophone music of Buganda. There I discovered one day that in the tape recordings everything sounded curiously different from what I had just performed together with the two other Baganda musicians. Our playing when recorded sounded much more complicated than it actually was, and I heard a number of rhythm patterns which I was sure that none of us had played, while on the other hand the rhythms which we had actually played were inaudible on the tape. (p. 34)

Kubik (1962) considers a variety of instances of inherent patterns and discusses the conditions necessary for their formation and perception. The phenomenon is closely connected with the melodic fission effect (originally described by Miller and Heise, 1950; Heise and Miller, 1951) and has been discussed more recently by other ethnomusicologists (e.g., Berliner, 1978). The discovery of inherent rhythms led Kubik to explore the distinguishing characteristics of motional and sonic patterns:

> The difference between *rhythm pattern* and *movement pattern* is that the former term implies something which sounds whilst the latter also includes musical phenomena which

are completely without sound . . . behind the so-called rhythm patterns of African music there are movement patterns which have both a sonic and a nonsonic dimension. (Kubik, 1979, p. 227)

> The organization of African music is motionally rigorous, right down to the tiniest areas. Whereas in Western music the movements of a musician playing his instrument generally have meaning only in terms of the sonic result, in African music patterns of movement are in themselves a source of pleasure, regardless of whether they come to life in sound in their entirety, partly, or not at all. In Western music movement is a means for producing auditive complexes, whereas in African music it can be self-sufficient. In such music auditory complexes may even only be an, albeit important, by-product of motional process. (p. 228)

This last statement is closely reminiscent of von Hornbostel (1928). Kubik (1979) goes so far as to claim that, "One can define African music in one of its fundamental structural aspects as a *system of movement patterns,* and argues that, "The same movement patterns are to be found both in the dance and in the musical aspects of the phenomenon which is African music" (p. 227). This may help to explain why African languages often categorize together what we in English distinguish as "music" and "dance."

Although he argues for the separation of motional and sonic patterns, Kubik (1979) also explains that non-sonic elements of the motional pattern may still be important determinants of the sonic pattern:

> The nature of the patterns of movement has a direct influence on the audible "music." . . . Although certain melodically sonic complexes can be produced in many different ways with a practically identical result, complete accuracy is dependent upon the correct pattern of movement. The imitation of African music by adherents to other musical cultures on the basis of gramophone records is frequently doomed to failure because the movement patterns on which the audible result is based are not included. (p. 228–229)

> The change in the motional pictures brings about a change, even if only slight, in the exact "spacing" of the notes to be struck. This leads to delays, anticipations, slight fluctuations in tempo, and a sense of lack of *drive.* The changing of the motional picture also destroys the original accentuation and the change in the mode of striking the individual notes also exerts an influence on their sound spectrum. (p. 229)

Kubik's comments are in line with the experience of many ethnomusicologists who have included learning to perform as part of their research methodology. Learning to play an instrument from a different music culture requires correct reproduction, insofar as this is possible, of the body postures and movements that are usually used in its performance. On instruments where the fingers are used to manipulate a keyboard then the question of reproducing the proper fingering may be of crucial importance. In other words, one has to learn to move in the right way on the instrument.

The observations, insights, and intuitions of these three workers on African music may be summarised as follows:

1. There is a recognition of the importance of studying the movement patterns used for playing an instrument. A musical instrument is a transducer, converting movement patterns into sound patterns. The exact nature of the sound pattern (its microstructure) depends on the characteristics of the movement pattern.
2. When a corpus of instrumental pieces is analysed, unity may emerge at the level of movement, suggesting that performance is in some sense based on a motor grammar.
3. The physical characteristics of an instrument influence, to a varying extent, the structure of the music played on it in such a way that those aspects of the music may be said to be generated from the instrument. Or an instrument may be constructed to suit particular motor patterns in order to fulfil certain musical requirements.
4. In musical performance, the cognitive representation in terms of which the performer operates may be a movement representation rather than an auditory one.

A point that merits clarification is that the importance of motional patterns in the performance of music is not unique to African music. Thus, although Kubik (1979) states that in Western music the movements only have a meaning in relation to the sonic result (Kubik 1979, p. 228), Blacking (1955) is confident that the movements of performance are an issue in Western music too:

> A pianist who plays the *Etudes* of Chopin or many pieces by Liszt cannot help being conscious of the sheer physical pleasure of numerous passages, and noticing how the music grows out of the physical movement. . . . We find numerous examples of Western classical music, where the musical form is much influenced by the properties of the instrument for which it was written. (p. 52)

Elsewhere, Blacking gives an example of this process in Western music. "When we analyze the music of Hector Berlioz it is useful to know that he often worked out harmonic procedures on a guitar, and that the structure of the instrument influenced many of his chord sequences" (p. 21).

Although it does seem to be the case that music in Africa is more movement-orientated than music in many other parts of the world, it would be quite wrong to conclude that African music is in any sense "primitive."

If motional patterns can be shown to be of significance in the most sonic of musics—the Western classical tradition—then it seems probable that all musics can be usefully studied in these terms.

A STUDY OF THE HERATI DUTĀR
AND THE AFGHAN RUBĀB

One of the most interesting lines of thought to emerge from the work reviewed is the notion that the spatial properties of an instrument may influence the shape of the music played on it. It is to this problem that we now address ourselves. The relationship between an instrument and its music has to be examined in terms of a third factor, the human sensorimotor system, which has its own intrinsic structure and modes of operation. In particular, it is necessary to look at the interaction between the structures of the human body and the structure of the instrument.

The research, carried out in 1973–1974, investigated the development of a new musical instrument, the 14-stringed Herati *dutār,* a type of long-necked lute found in Afghanistan. The music culture of Afghanistan is very different from that of Africa, with traits in common with other musics of the Middle East, Central, Asia and the Indian subcontinent. The music is modal and monophonic, with no harmonic framework and no chord sequences. Thus, the instrumental music we are considering consists of a single melodic line. The development of the new instrument was investigated from several angles in order to establish how the invention actually occurred and to explore the more general social and cultural factors that made this possible. For the purposes of the present discussion, the relationship of central interest is the interplay among three sets of factors: the morphology of the instrument, the movement patterns used in playing it, and the structural characteristics of the music produced. The question under consideration is this: If we disregard the sonic aspects of the music and look at the movements in relationship to the instrument, do we find any patterning in them that can be related to the inherent organisation of the human sensorimotor system? Can we identify any sensorimotor factors that help to explain why a particular kind of music is played on an instrument that has certain spatial characteristics?

The results of this research have been published in a different form elsewhere (Baily, 1976; 1977). My data derive, in part, from recordings and analytical films made to show movement patterns from a sample of 10 *dutār* players and from my own experiences and resultant introspections from learning to play (with native teachers) the *dutār* and *rubāb.* No experiments as such were carried out, although my analysis does suggest certain testable hypotheses. Comparison of the present essay with Baily (1977) reveals certain changes in the presentation of the argument; I have selected a better sample of tunes to represent the rubāb repertory, and certain changes in the conventions of the musical transcription have been adopted.[2]

The 14-stringed Herati *dutār* developed in the period from 1950 to 1965 from a much smaller two-stringed, long-necked lute of the same name (it means, literally, "two strings"). At an intermediate stage in this transformation, a three-

---

[2]The inappropriateness of Western staff notation for non-Western music is a much-discussed problem in ethnomusicology, and various solutions have been offered, each usually appropriate for the particular characteristics of the music to be represented. In order to deal with the variety of scale types in Afghan urban music, I adopt the convention of writing in the key of C with the use of various sharps and flats. This is also the convention for writing Indian music.

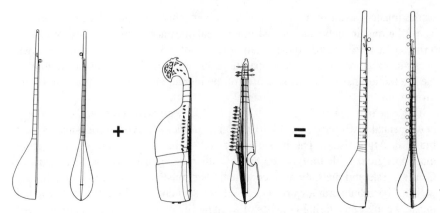

Figure 1. The three instruments under discussion: From left to right, two-stringed *dutār*, *rubāb*, and 14-stringed dutār.

stringed *dutār* was common but is disregarded in the following discussion. In becoming the 14-stringed instrument, the *dutār* was given certain features borrowed from another kind of lute, the Afghan *rubāb*, and in this way, the *dutār* was intentionally modified in order to enable it to be used to perform *rubāb* music. In a sense, the 14-stringed *dutār* can be regarded as a fusion of the two-stringed *dutār* and the *rubāb*, for it combines the general shape of the dutār with a new system of fretting to give the musical scale of the *rubāb* (12 semitones to the octave), the addition of sympathetic strings tuned to the scale-type of the mode being played, and a protuberance on the bridge to raise the shortest sympathetic strong for a special right-hand technique called *simkāri* (metal string-work) (see Figure 1).

An important difference between the 14-stringed *dutār* (hereafter referred to as *dutār*) and the *rubāb* is that the former has only one melody string, so that the note positions are arranged in a single row (a linear array), whereas the rubāb has three melody strings, with the note positions mapped across them (a tiered array) (see Figure 2). This fact has implications both for stopping the strings with the left hand and for plucking them with the right hand.

The methodology for this kind of study requires one to isolate a repertory of tunes that can, in some sense, be regarded as the traditional repertory of the musical instrument under investigation; one with which it is habitually associated. In the case of the rubāb and dutār, such repertories can be identified, although they are certainly not tightly bounded. Thus, the *rubāb*, which is regarded as the national instrument of Afghanistan, is used to play a variety of types of Afghan music, including folk, popular, and art music. For purposes of comparison with the *dutār,* I have selected a genre of instrumental music called *naghme-ye kashāl* (stretched-out instrumental piece) a type of Afghan art music, almost certainly composed on the rubāb, which combines elements of Afghan

Rubāb

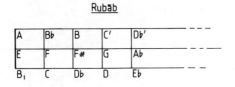

14-stringed Dutār

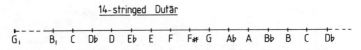

Figure 2. Spatial layout of notes on *rubāb* and 14-stringed dutār.

folk music with certain ideas borrowed from Hindustani (North Indian classical) music. This genre provides a better sample of *rubāb* music than the pieces discussed in Baily (1977).[3]

The *naghme-ye-kashāl* follows a set form: First, there is an extemporisation in free rhythm on the scale and melodic characteristics of the mode, played without rhythmic accompaniment. Then follows a series of fixed compositions in strict rhythm with drum accompaniment. The first composition in the sequence, called the *āstāi*, is played many times over, with a variety of rhythmic variations. The later compositions, variously called *antara, bhog,* and *sanchāri,* are shorter and played at a faster tempo. A good example of a *naghme-ye kashāl* composition is shown in Figure 3, in the mode called Yemen (cf. the Lydian of the Western Church modes). The sample of music for the *rubāb* consists of 12 such *āstāi* compositions in 12 different modes (see Baily, 1981).

Defining a repertory for the *dutār* is a little more difficult; although it is a new instrument, it has not generated a new repertory but is used to play a variety of preexisting types of music, including *naghme-ye kashāl.* Although the two-stringed dutār was formerly used in the villages to play instrumental music, there seem to have been very few purely instrumental compositions for the old *dutār.* When the two-stringed *dutār* was played as a solo instrument, its repertory consisted mainly of the melodies of Herati folk songs. Most of these songs are in a single melodic mode, today usually called *Bairami,* and the two-stringed dutār was fretted in such a way that only this mode could be played.[4] Because these are

[3]For example, *Ahir Bhairav* and *Bhupāli* (Baily, 1977) are really Indian compositions of the *Rezakhāni gat* type, used in Afghanistan for the genre *naghme-ye klāsik,* whereas the example in *Madhubanti* is an instrumental piece for radio orchestra composed by Ustad Mohammad Omar. The example in Bairami is, on the other hand, an āstāi for a naghme-ye kashāl.

[4]The fretting of the two-stringed dutār, which yields various neutral seconds (Baily, 1976), limits the instrument to a single scale type, although, within this scale, several modes can be derived through the selection of different tones as the finalis (cf. Western Church modes). But for the purposes of the present comparison with the rubāb, the two-stringed dutār may be regarded as limited to a single mode, which, in terms of the modes of Afghan urban music, is identified as Bairami, equivalent to the Indian Rāg Bhairavi.

Figure 3. *Naghme-ye kashāl* in Yemen mode.

song melodies, they were not necessarily composed with reference to the *dutār* at all, although they may have been. In a sense, this does not matter, for it is clear that they became habitually associated with the dutār. The sample of music for the dutār consists of 13 such song melodies, all in the Bairami mode. Many of these melodies are in two parts: The antara is the melody for the verse, and the *āstāi* for the refrain. Three *dutār* melodies are shown in Figure 4, notated for the transposition Bairami Rekap (with D rather than C as the finalis).

The Comparison of Rubāb and Dutār Music

Ambitus. In general, *rubāb* compositions have a considerably wider ambitus than *dutār* tunes. They are usually framed within the range of the octave, but certain sections ascend to the fifth of the higher octave, played in the unfretted range of the first string of the *rubāb*. *Dutār* tunes are rarely more than a minor seventh in ambitus and often fall within the range of a fifth.

Figure 4.   Three Herati tunes.

Size of Melodic Intervals.   An interval frequency count for the two samples is shown in Table 1. In both *rubāb* and *dutār* music, melodic movement is mainly stepwise, proceeding between adjacent tones of the scale.

Variety of Scale Types.   The tunes in the *dutār* repertory are all in one mode, Bairami, which relates to the way in which the two-stringed dutār was fretted. In contrast, the *naghme-ye kashāl* exists in a variety of modes, most of which have distinct scale types. The number of melodic modes that can be played on the

Table 1
FREQUENCY OF ASCENDING AND DESCENDING INTERVALS IN SAMPLES
OF TRADITIONAL REPERTORY OF *RUBĀB* AND *DUTĀR*

	Size of intervals in half-tone steps												
	1	2	3	4	5	6	7	8	9	10	11	12	Total
Rubāb													
Ascending	38	51	13	8	6	—	3	—	—	2	2	1	124
Descending	42	53	16	18	6	—	—	1	—	1	—	—	137
													261
Dutār													
Ascending	34	128	16	21	14	—	8	—	—	—	—	—	221
Descending	68	199	4	16	—	1	—	—	—	—	—	—	288
													509

Āsā

Kumāj

Pilu

Figure 5. Examples of three *āstāi* compositions for rubāb.

Bairami Rekap

Figure 6. Cluster patterns for "Mullah Mahmad Jan."

rubāb is large, but analysis shows that about eight modes are in common use (Baily, 1981).

Shape of Melodic Movement. The melodic patterns of *rubāb* music tend to be scalar, that is, running sequentially up and down the notes of the scale of the mode. This feature is not especially prominent in the example of *naghme-ye kashāl* shown in Figure 3 but is clearly evident in much of this music, as shown in Figure 5.

Dutār tunes, in contrast, exhibit a very different kind of organization, consisting of descending series of cluster patterns. Many such tunes start with a leap up to the fourth or fifth above the finalis, followed by a gradual, convoluted descending movement back to the finalis. This kind of structure is shown particularly well by the antara (verse) section of "Mullah Mahmad Jān." Analytically, this tune can readily be broken up into three overlapping clusters (see Figure 6). The third cluster returns the melodic line to the finalis (D). An even more elementary and geometrical manifestation of this structure is shown by an instrumental section often played between the song sections of Herati folk melodies (see Figure 7).

"Mullah Mahmad Jan" as a song melody is unusual in showing a tertiary structure so clearly, but binary structures are quite common. The tune "Eh Zamān" can be analysed in terms of the cluster sequence of Figure 8. Figure 9 shows the clusters of in *Moghol Dokhtar*.

Bairami Rekap

Figure 7. Cluster patterns for a typical instrumental section.

Figure 8.   Cluster patterns for "Ei Zaman."

Figure 9.   Cluster patterns for "Moghul Dokhtar."

Rhythmic Organization.   Both the *rubāb* and the 14-stringed *dutār* are played *punteado* (single-string style) with a plectrum. A highly sophisticated right-hand technique has been devised for the rubāb, based on an imbalance between the down (∨) and (∧) strokes. The former is stronger and heavier, is aimed towards the skin belly of the instrument, and has the added percussion of the right hand impacting on the belly. A stroke pattern such as Example (1)

(1)

v = downstroke
∧ = upstroke

has a somewhat different sonic result to Example (2)

(2)

This is an obvious example of how the exact structure of the motional pattern affects the microstructure of the music. A further refinement of *rubāb* technique: using the plectrum to strike the shortest sympathetic string to produce patterns such as Example (3).

(3)

= stroke on main string
= stroke on shortest sympathetic string

In playing the *āstāi* section of the *naghme-ye kashāl*, the *rubāb* player tends to run through a variety of these right-hand stroke patterns, usually maintaining a pattern for one round of the composition, then changing to a new pattern. These patterns are used to build up larger structures; typically, in a sequence of such patterns, there is an increase in the density of strokes per time unit and an acceleration of the tempo, together building up a rhythmic tension that is released through a rhythmic cadence. A common sequence of right-hand patterns in triple time (called Dadre) is shown in Figure 10.

The right-hand techniques for the 14-stringed *dutār* have been borrowed from the rubāb, but for playing *dutār* tunes, a simpler technique is normally used, which relates to the traditional manner of strumming the two-stringed *dutār,* for which the usual practice was to maintain a constant stroke pattern. Examples of

Figure 10. Common sequence of rhythmic patterns in Dadre.

these are shown in Figure 11. While this strum is maintained, the melody is fingered with the left hand. *Dutār* tunes may be played in this way on the 14-stringed *dutār* (as in Figure 4), but it is also common to articulate the metric structure of the song being played.

A Spatiomotor Analysis

The comparison of *rubāb* and *dutār* tunes shows that they are based on different principles of organization, although they share certain features. Can these differences in the music be correlated with the spatial characteristics of linear and tiered arrays? Do the differing spatial properties of the two kinds of array encourage the use of some kinds of movement patterns and tend to inhibit others in performance?

The fit between the two instruments and their respective repertoires is revealed when we look at the transfer of a repertory from one instrument to the other. In this analysis, it is the left hand that is of particular interest, especially the relationship between the movements of the left hand and the melodic contour of the music played. This relationship is illuminated by the difficulties of transferring *rubāb* music to the *dutār*. The right hand, although of interest, is less revealing.

Figure 11. Three strum patterns for two-stringed *dutār*.

Figure 12.   Layout of notes for Bairami mode on *rubāb* and *dutār*.

Left Hand

Spatial Mapping of Note Positions.   In playing the *dutār* or *rubāb*, the performer operates, in part, in terms of movements made within a spatial framework determined by the layout of the instrument. For the left hand, the frets on the instrument that have to be stopped (and the open positions of the strings on the *rubāb*) constitute a set of target positions. These might be located visually, kinesthetically, or tactually; the specific modality does not matter; movement patterns are planned and experienced in relationship to this internal representation of the fretboard's spatial properties. Hence I refer to this as a spatiomotor representation. Figure 12 shows the layout of the main tones for playing the mode Bairami on the two instruments.

As a spatial configuration, the *rubāb* presents the positions for Bairami in a way that is less confusing than does the *dutār*, because the positions are mapped in two dimensions rather than in one. It is easier both to apprehend this spatial pattern and to keep track of where you are within a sequence of positions around which the motor pattern is organised. Mistakes in locating the positions of target notes come through as errors in performance. This difference is compounded by the fact that the *rubāb* repertory is composed in a variety of modes, each with its own scale type, which gives rise to a distinct configuration of target positions. Figure 13 shows the note positions for three more modes on the two instruments. The variety of spatial patterns is more easily remembered and apprehended on the tiered array than on the linear array; this helps to explain why, from the point of view of the left hand, the *rubāb* is the easier instrument on which to play the *naghme-ye kashāl* repertory.[5]

Cluster and Scalar Patterns.   As already explained, *rubāb* music is characterised, in some degree, by scalar passages (see Figures 3 and 5). As patterns of

---

[5]This argument is a simplification, for seven of the eight common modes for the rubāb share a common underlying tonal framework which corresponds approximately to the Western major scale but with both minor and major sevenths. Bairami is one mode that does not fit neatly onto the rubāb; it is often played in the transposition Bairami Rekap on both dutār and rubāb, but this does not invalidate the present line of argument (see Baily, 1981).

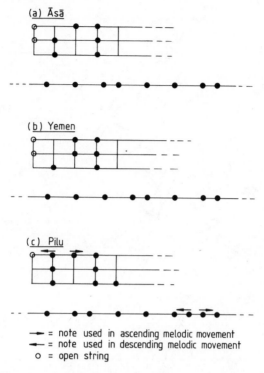

— = note used in ascending melodic movement
— = note used in descending melodic movement
o = open string

Figure 13. Layout of three more modes on *rubāb* and *dutār*.

movement, these are more easily rendered on the *rubāb* than on the *dutār*. On the *rubāb*, the notes of the main octave can be covered from one or, at the most, two adjacent hand positions, using finger movements. Here the notes "fall under the fingers" (see Baily, 1981, p. 30). In general, it seems that finger movements are faster and more accurate than hand movements and require less attentional control. When *rubāb* tunes are played on the *dutār*, the situation is very different. Scalar patterns now require ascending and descending sequences of hand movements. On the *rubāb*, the left hand can operate within a tactuokinesthetic field, whereas, on the *dutār*, visual information is more likely to be required to plan and control accurate movements of the left hand. Thus, scalar motional patterns fit less well on the *dutār* than on the *rubāb*.

It can be seen that *dutār* music is structured in such a way that this particular constraint of the linear array is minimised. I have already referred to the fact that *dutār* tunes can be analysed in terms of cluster patterns. At the level of action, the cluster pattern consists of a series of finger operations from a single hand position or from two adjacent hand positions. The most efficient way to perform a cluster pattern is to use the first, second, and third fingers as independent

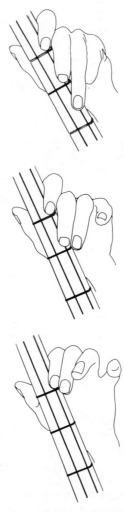

Figure 14.   Three-finger, three-component operation on the two-stringed *dutār*.

components, employing the first finger to hold the basic position and the second and third fingers used to stop notes above that position (see Figure 14).

The two-stringed *dutār* was perhaps played in this way, a point that is hard to establish because few players of the old kind of *dutār* were to be found in the mid-1970s. But there is an anatomical linkage between the ligaments of the second and third fingers that makes it difficult to achieve complete independence of the third finger and hence, to use the three fingers as independent components. On the 14-stringed *dutār*, the massive neck and the wide separation between the frets exacerbates the problems of stretch. Only one player of the 14-stringed *dutār* consistently uses the three-finger, three-component technique, and he is the acknowledged master of the instrument and its inventor. Some *dutār* players use a three-finger, two-component mode of operation where the second or third finger is used to stop frets above that held by the first finger, but the third is not used against the second. Many *dutār* players use only the first and second fingers of the left hand in a two-finger, two-component mode of operation. This obviously necessitates the use of more hand movements than would be required with the three-finger, three-component mode of operation. Here, one can speculate, there is a trade-off between two opposing constraints: independence of the third finger and the frequency ratio of hand–finger movements.

Right Hand

One problem of technique for the *rubāb* player is adjusting the position of the right hand when the melodic line moves from one string to another. Changing string is more readily achieved when the change precedes a downstroke, that is, when the hand's starting position is above the strings and all that is required is a small change in the angle of the downstroke to strike the appropriate string. Problems arise when the change of string precedes an upstroke, which, according to the principles by which stroke patterns are organized, will occur only after a downstroke. Now the plectrum has to be moved from below one string to below the next string to reach the starting position for the upstroke; a change of hand posture has now been inserted between $\vee$ and $\wedge$. Most *rubāb* stroke patterns for playing *āstāi* of *naghme-ye kashāl* fit the composition so that changes of string on the upstroke do not occur. These patterns fit the metre of the composition by starting each time unit with a downstroke and ending with an upstroke as in Example (4)

(4)

There are certain virtuoso stroke patterns that do start with the upstroke and in which changes of string before the upstroke become common. This kind of playing is called *chape*, related to ideas of left as opposed to right, of deviousness as opposed to straightforwardness, of being "back to front." It is clear enough why it is so termed.

The right-hand technique used to play *naghme-ye kashāl* on the *dutār* is modelled on the *rubāb*, employing a heavy downstroke towards the belly of the instrument, with added hand percussion. But because the player has to deal with only one melody string, problems of changing from one string to another do not arise, and the technique is therefore easier to use on the *dutār* than on the *rubāb*. These elaborate techniques are not used when playing *dutār* tunes on the *dutār*; here, the players may maintain a steady strum or play the metre of the song.

Some *dutār* tunes require changes of string on the upstroke when played on the *rubāb* and, for this reason, do not fit well onto that instrument.

In the previous sections, I suggest certain ways in which the layout of a musical instrument imposes constraints on musical performance. The relationship that emerges from this particular work is primarily between the spatial layout of a keyboard and the melodic contour of the music produced from it, a relationship that can be readily explained in terms of inherent sensorimotor structures that mediate between them. The two instruments selected for this research seem to demonstrate the shaping influence of the spatial layout clearly, for *dutār* and *rubāb* tunes seem to fit well onto their respective instruments. Whether the music can be said to have been generated from the instrument or the instrument to have been adopted or designed so that certain preexisting musical structures can be readily produced by patterns of movement, is perhaps immaterial, for both possibilities assume the presence of human factors that interact with the spatial layout of the instrument. But it is important to stress that the constraints imposed by a particular layout are only tendencies; they do not necessarily present insurmountable difficulties. This much is clear from the Afghan data: Playing *naghme-ye kashāl* on the *dutār* may be more difficult than playing *dutār* tunes, but the 14-stringed *dutār* was invented precisely so that this and other genres of *rubāb* music could be performed. The spatiomotor analysis helps to clarify what is involved and reveals the achievement of the *dutār* players in learning to play a technically difficult genre for their instrument.

SPATIAL REPRESENTATIONS
OF MUSIC STRUCTURE

In this section, I address a different problem, encapsulated in von Hornbostel's (1928) idea that "melody is realized as an act of motility" (p. 49), and consider the relative roles of auditory and spatiomotor representations of music structure. In the preceding section, I argued that an understanding of how the human sensorimotor system operates and how it interacts with particular kinds of spatial array is important for understanding some of the melodic characteristics of *dutār* and *rubāb* music. The analysis assumes that the performer operates within a spatial framework and, at some level, represents the task as a spatial one. The question now is whether this representation is a low-level cognitive process or whether it is, or can be, a high-level process at which the conscious planning of performance takes place.

In discussing the nature of performance plans, Sloboda (1982) states:

> We could take the performer's plan to be a list of items in which the pitch, duration and intensity of each note is specified relative to other notes. Before such a plan could result in action, absolute values of these dimensions would need to be assigned to the plan, and the

appropriate motor actions would then be determined by reference to knowledge about the specific performance mode being used (voice, instrument, etc). (p. 480)

Although couched in terms that avoid the question of subjective experience and the conscious control of performance, it is clear that Sloboda implicitly adopts a hierarchical model of performance that gives preeminence to the auditory representation. According to this idea, musical patterns are, or should be, manipulated as auditory images at the cognitive level, and the spatiomotor representation is clearly subordinate.

In fact, Sloboda gives a number of examples where "the existence of a highly abstract performance plan" (i.e., a plan conceived in auditory terms) does not explain the facts, and where a "knowledge of specific motor actions" has also to be taken into account (p. 482).

What they suggest is a hierarchy of levels of abstraction such that, according to circumstances or accomplishment, performance plans can exist at a higher or lower level in the hierarchy. In general, what we would call "musicianship" seems to entail the ability to mobilize the higher, more abstract levels in a wide variety of circumstances. (p. 482)

In other words, reliance on the spatiomotor representation is symptomatic of imperfect mastery (lack of musicianship). The development of performance skill on an instrument could be interpreted as leading to the development of a kind of auromotor coordination (by analogy with visuomotor coordination) that allows the musician to reproduce immediately musical patterns that he or she either hears or experiences as auditory images. Perhaps most skilled at the ability to articulate imagined sounds is the Western composer, who ideally treats composition as a purely mental operation, translating the streams of imagined music into symbols written on paper.

The issue is complex and one needs to take into account many factors, such as the transfer of musical skill from one instrument to another and different levels of performance encountered in the acquisition of an instrumental skill. But it is clear that what is remarkable about musical performance is the integration of auditory and spatiomotor representations of music structure; the same pattern can be attended to by the performer both as a pattern of movement and as a pattern of sound. Auditory, kinesthetic, and visual information may all be involved in the planning and feedback control of the pattern. Instead of viewing the spatiomotor component in musical cognition as a lower-level process through which auditory images are translated into sound patterns called music, it may be better to treat auditory and spatiomotor modes of musical cognition as of potentially equal importance. The spatiomotor mode can then be regarded as a legitimate and commonly used mode of musical thought, used to instigate and to control musical performance, and just as creative as the auditory mode, for creativity in music may often consist of deliberately finding new ways to move on the instrument, which are then be assessed, and further creative acts, guided by the aesthetic evaluation of the resultant novel sonic patterns.

This approach introduces the human body, as well as the human auditory system, into the debate about the nature of musical cognition. That step has important ramifications, for it raises the possibility, previously mentioned, that motor grammars may control certain aspects of the patterning of music. The comparison of the linear and tiered array reveals certain constraints that are parts of the motor grammars that are utilised for playing the *dutār* and the *rubāb*.

The psychology of music as we know it in the Western world is overly ethnocentric because it is founded on data drawn from our own literate music culture. Only a tiny proportion of musicians in the world use written notation in performance. If the study of music and cognition is to proceed from the culture specific to the universal, then a wider approach must be adopted, one that includes recognition of the possibility that music may be as much a motor event as a sonic event, as well as, of course, a social fact.

REFERENCES

Baily, J. Recent changes in the *dutar* of Herat. *Asian Music*, 1976, *8*(1), 29–64.

Baily, J. Movement patterns in playing the Herati *dutar*. in J. Blacking (Ed.), *The anthropology of the body*. New York: Academic Press, 1977.

Baily, J. A system of modes used in the urban music of Afghanistan. *Ethnomusicology*, 1981, *25*(1), 1–39.

Berliner, P. F. *The soul of Mbira*. Berkeley: University of California Press, 1978.

Blacking, J. Eight flute tunes from Butembo, East Belgian Congo. *African Music*, 1955, *1*(2), 24–52.

Blacking, J. Patterns of Nsenga *kalimba* music. *African Music*, 1961, *2*(4), 3–20.

Blacking, J. *How musical Is man?* Seattle: University of Washington Press, 1973.

Deutsch, D. *The psychology of music*, London: Academic Press, 1982.

Harwood, D. L. Universals in music: A perspective from cognitive psychology. *Ethnomusicology*, 1976, *20*(3), 521–534.

Heise, G. A., and Miller, G. A. An experimental study of auditory patterns. *American Journal of Psychology*, 1951, *64*, 68–77.

Kolinski, M. Recent trends in ethnomusicology. *Ethnomusicology*, 1967, *11*(1), 1–24.

Kubik, G. The phenomenon of inherent rhythms in East and Central African instrumental music. *African Music*, 1962, *3*(1), 33–42.

Kubik, G. Pattern perception and recognition in African music. In Blacking and J. W. Kealiinohomoku (Eds.), *The performing arts*. The Hague: Mouton Publishers, 1979.

Meyer, L. B. Universalism and relativism in the study of ethnic music. *Ethnomusicology*, 1960, *4*(2), 49–54.

Miller, G. A., and Heise, G. A. The trill threshold. *Journal of the Acoustical Society of America*, 1950, *22*, 637–638.

Sloboda, J. A. Music performance. In D. Deutsch (Ed.), *The psychology of music*. London: Academic Press, 1982.

von Hornbostel, E. M. African Negro music. *Africa*, 1928, *1*, 30–61.

11

Auditory Feedback of the Voice in Singing*

Peter Howell

INTRODUCTION

It is important for a singer to understand the process of speech production. Song and speech are intimately related, and the techniques developed to understand speech apply to singing as well. It is necessary for a singer to understand how people perceive song in order to appreciate the differences between what singers themselves hear and what the audience hears. Finally, understanding vocalisation and the perception of sound (including the voice) are necessary to assess whether the singer makes alterations intended to improve control of the voice on the basis of what is heard.

The aim of the present chapter is to describe the processes of vocalisation and auditory perception and discuss their implications for singing. First, the properties of vocal sound and how listeners perceive such sound are considered. The significance of these studies for extending vocal technique are outlined. Factors that make singers' perception of their voices different from listeners' are then described. These factors are then discussed to assess whether auditory feedback that a singer receives can be used as a basis for controlling performance.

PROPERTIES OF AIRBORNE VOCALISATION AND TRANSDUCTION OF SOUND BY THE PERIPHERAL AUDITORY SYSTEM

All vocalisation (including singing) can be modelled as a source and filter. The source arises from alterations made to the air flowing into the vocal tract. One example of a source of energy used in singing is voiced excitation, which arises

*This research was supported by grants from the Medical Research Council of the United Kingdom and the Central Research Fund of London University.

from the action of the vocal cords. The filtering derives from the shape of the vocal tract. Different vocal-tract shapes (or filters) produce the identifiably different sounds of a language. If an articulatory shape is used outside the native language or if a means of excitation not normally used is employed, a sound that is novel to the singer will result. The reasons for this are considered in this section.

Acoustic Properties of Vocal Sounds

To show how the source–filter theory applies to vocalisation, I illustrate it by considering monophthongal (i.e., single) vowels and show how the theory applies to the production of other vocal sounds.

The main way by which a speaker determines what vowel is produced is by locating the tongue at different positions in the vocal tract. (The palate, lips, or larynx may be positioned differently, too, but are not considered here.) Two factors are important in describing tongue position in vowel production: (1) the point where the tongue and roof of the mouth come closest together (e.g., near the lip end or further back), and (2) how close the tongue is to the roof of the mouth. In articulatory phonetics, these are called front–back position and tongue height, respectively. Schematic cross sections of the vocal tract indicating tongue position and height for a number of vowels are shown in Figure 1 and labelled with the phonetic symbol used to indicate the vowel produced. The symbol /i/ indicates that the vowel produced is like that in the word *beet*, /u/ like that in *boot*, /ɛ/ like that in *head*, and /ɔ/ like that in *hawed*. The vocal tract operates as an acoustic filter on sound that enters it and the shaping of the vocal tract to produce a vowel alters the filtering properties.

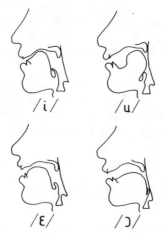

Figure 1.   Cross-section of the vocal tract indicating tongue position for four vowels.

Sound is not emitted from the vocal tract simply by holding the tongue in the position appropriate for the production of a vowel. For the vowel to "sound," energy has to be introduced into the vocal tract. Vocal sounds differ in the properties of the source of energy that enters the vocal tract, the most important way (and the one used in the production of English vowel sounds) being by the periodic opening and closing of the vocal cords. A pulse of air is released from the lungs every time they are open, and the airflow is stopped when the cords are closed. This action causes air flowing from the lungs into the vocal tract to be interrupted intermittently, which causes the airflow to sound buzzlike. All vocal sounds that involve periodic opening and closing of the vocal cords are referred to as "voiced." The properties of the buzz are altered as it passes through the vocal tract, and the different shapes of the vocal tract alter the properties of the buzz in different ways. The buzz is, therefore, the source of the sound and, together with the filter, makes a vowel.

The variation in the pressure of the air entering the vocal tract (caused by the action of the vocal cords) on each open-to-close cycle approximates a sawtooth-shaped pulse. The opening-and-closing cycle can repeat, taking virtually the same time for each cycle, and so, the pulse repeats regularly. When it does so and the repetition continues indefinitely, the signal is termed periodic. (Real signals never continue indefinitely but are quasi-periodic.) The air pressure caused by cord movement over time looks like the waveform in Figure 2a. This signal is the buzz that enters the vocal tract, and if the timing is constant, the pitch of the perceived vowel is constant. When a sound is sung on different pitches, the period of the pulse entering the vocal tract is altered. Thus, different pitches are produced by differences in the period of the buzz entering the vocal tract.

The easiest way to appreciate how the properties of the buzz are altered as the source signal is passed through the vocal tract is to represent the source signal and the vocal tract filter in the frequency domain, that is, represent them spectrally. (Throughout this chapter, speech production and hearing are treated as if the mechanisms involved constitute a linear system. This is true to a first approximation). To represent the source of voiced sounds spectrally, the frequency content of a periodic sawtooth waveform (which represents the airflow above the vocal cords in this case) has to be obtained. All periodic signals are composed of

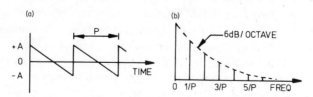

Figure 2. A sawtooth signal, and (b) its amplitude spectrum.

a set of sinusoids. The amplitude of the sinusoids that make up a periodic signal (such as the sawtooth waveform) can be represented by an amplitude spectrum, which is a graph of frequency (abscissa) versus amplitude (ordinate) showing the amplitude of the constituent sinusoids. When the signal contains a sinusoid at some frequency, a line whose amplitude is given by the ordinate is drawn. The amplitude spectrum of a sawtooth waveform is shown is Figure 2b.

The amplitude spectrum of the sawtooth indicates that the amplitude of the component frequencies drops off as frequency increases and contains energy at discrete frequencies that are spaced apart in equal-frequency steps. The contributory sinusoids of a complex waveform are referred to as "partials." When they are spaced apart regularly in frequency, they are harmonically related to one another. The partials of all periodic signals are harmonically related to the period of the waveform. It is also possible to obtain a phase spectrum of such a signal, but phase is considered unimportant in speech perception and is not treated here.

Next, the transmission of sinusoids by the vocal tract has to be ascertained. Any particular vocal-tract shape transmits some frequencies better than others. As stated, the process by which sinusoids are transmitted with different efficiency is called filtering. Some commonly encountered filters are low pass and high pass. An ideal low-pass filter lets all frequencies below some set frequency through a system and prevents all frequencies above it from being passed. Conversely, a high-pass filter passes high frequencies and stops low frequencies. The vocal tract is somewhat more complex. The filtering that occurs depends on the vocal-tract shape so that there are some bands of frequency in which transmission is good and others in which it is not. Those areas where frequencies are transmitted well are usually broad and may extend over several spectral components of the source. The regions in which good transmission occurs are called the formants (resonant frequencies of the cavities of the vocal tract). The position in frequency of formants differs depending on the shape of the vocal tract. The formants determine the shape of the spectrum of a vowel and are important in determining the identity of the vowel.

One way of ascertaining how well sinusoids are transmitted by a vocal tract held in the position to produce a particular vowel is to measure its response to sinusoidal stimulation (i.e., to measure certain of its filter properties). This measurement can be made by applying sinusoidal vibration at the bottom of the vocal tract (i.e., near the vocal cords) and measuring the amplitude of the output at the lips. The output amplitude relative to the input represents how well a sinusoid at that frequency is transmitted through the vocal tract. Similar measurements can be made at different frequencies with the input sinusoid at the same reference amplitude as that of the original. The results can then be plotted on a graph with amplitude of the output as the ordinate and frequency as the abscissa. This is called an amplitude response. The amplitude response of the vocal tract for the vowels /i/ and /u/ (as in *beet* and *boot*) obtained by applying this

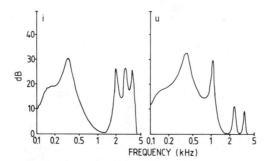

Figure 3.   Transfer functions for the vowels /i/ and /u/.

technique are shown in Figure 3 (Fujimura and Lindqvist, 1970). Peaks can be seen where transmission of frequency is good (the formants) and the points in frequency where the peaks occur differs for the various vowels (articulatory shapes). (This treatment is simplified somewhat as other corrections have to be made; e.g., the tissue of the neck causes some frequencies to be transmitted better than others.)

Since the source spectrum can be represented in terms of its frequency content, the effect on the spectrum of passing this through the vocal tract can be ascertained from the amplitude response. The amplitude response of the vocal tract is the vocal tract's response to sinusoids at constant amplitude. Therefore, to obtain the output for a sawtooth source, the component sinusoids of the source have to be selected and allowance must be made for the variation in their amplitude (because of the level of that component in the source and the filtering caused by the vocal tract). This is done by multiplying the amplitude response of the vocal tract by the spectrum of the source.

When the multiplication is performed, only those frequencies that are present in the input occur in the output because the source signal is zero at all but these frequencies. This operation, then, selects the frequencies that occur in the source. Multiplying the amplitude spectrum of the source by the amplitude response of the system also takes account of any variation in the amplitude of the components of the source signal. For example, if the spectrum tilts down (as with a voiced source signal), the level of the components that are multiplied drops successively lower in amplitude as frequency increases. The peaks in the amplitude responses of the vocal tract still occur in the output spectrum because a bigger quantity is being multiplied at a peak and a smaller quantity at a trough.

To summarise the effects: Passing a sawtooth source through the vocal tract tilts the output spectrum relative to the frequency response (because of the tilt on the spectrum of the source). Peaks in the output spectrum still occur at about the same frequencies as in the amplitude response. The steps taken to derive the spectrum of the vocal output are summarised diagrammatically in Figure 4.

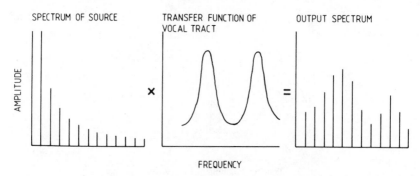

SPECTRUM OF SOURCE   TRANSFER FUNCTION OF   OUTPUT SPECTRUM
                           VOCAL TRACT

AMPLITUDE

×   =

FREQUENCY

Figure 4.   Summary of the steps involved in determining the output spectrum of a signal transmitted through the vocal tract.

The signal arising from the opening and closing of the vocal cords is only one type of signal that can be produced to excite the vocal tract. Another important type of excitatory signal is voiceless excitation. The same procedure used to derive the spectra of voiced sounds can be applied to ascertain the spectral output of voiceless sounds (such as the fricatives /ʃ/ as the first sound in *ship*, /f/ as in *fit*, /θ/ as in *thing*, and /s/ *as in sip*). The main difference between voiced and voiceless sounds is in the acoustic properties of the source. For voiceless sounds, the vocal cords do not vibrate; rather their source of energy is turbulent airflow caused by forcing air through a constriction in the vocal tract. This source of energy is a "hissy" sound (rather than the "buzzy" sound produced by the vibrating vocal cords). The source excitation of voiceless sounds is not periodic. However, an amplitude spectrum can still be obtained, but, because the signal is not periodic, there are no separate partials. Another feature of the source spectrum of voiceless sounds is that it rises in amplitude as frequency increases. The spectral output for voiceless sounds is obtained, as with voiceless sounds, by multiplying the source spectrum by the amplitude response of the vocal tract. (The amplitude response of the vocal tract for voiceless sounds can be measured in the same way as for voiced sounds). When the source spectrum of voiceless sounds is multiplied by the amplitude response of the vocal tract, energy occurs across the frequency range since the energy in the source spectrum occurs at all frequencies (not just at the frequencies of the partials). Also, the spectrum of the output tilts upwards relative to the amplitude response of the vocal tract because of the upward tilt on the source spectrum. The procedure of multiplying the source spectrum by the amplitude response of the vocal tract to obtain the spectral output applies to all vocal sounds, not just to voiced and voiceless excitation.

The general principles described indicate some ways in which vocal techniques can be extended.

1. There are possibilities suggested by considering the sources of excitation: When describing source excitation, the two most important excitatory signals (voiced and voiceless sources) are outlined. If sources of excitation different to these enter the vocal tract, different sound occurs as output. Thus, other ways of exciting the vocal tract, which, in fact, occur in non-Western languages, can be employed to extend the vocal range. For example, air flowing into (rather than out of) the vocal tract is used as a source of excitation for sounds in some languages; in other languages certain sounds are excited by a click produced in the vocal tract.

2. When the vocal-tract filter, rather than the means of excitation, is considered, more ways of extending vocal technique are implied. All languages make use of only certain articulatory positions to produce the distinctive sounds. Other positions are possible, however. If the vocal tract is positioned in articulatory positions outside those usually used, the singer can increase the range of vocal sounds.

3. No language uses all the combinations of sources and filters that are possible. Thus, the range of sounds can be extended farther by employing combinations of sources and filters that do not usually occur in the singer's native language.

Although this treatment has relied upon a comparison of singing and speaking, it is possible that there are some differences between the production of song and speech. For example, mandible positions during singing are different from those used in speaking. To date, no assessment of the difference this would cause between speech and song have been made.

Transduction of Sound by the Peripheral Auditory System

A brief description of how pressure variation at the eardrum ultimately causes activity to be transmitted up the auditory nerve is provided in this section. This description is not exhaustive; the basic process of hearing is outlined so that a comparison can be made between transduction of air-conducted and bone-conducted sound (see section beginning p. 274).

Three parts of the peripheral auditory system are usually distinguished—the outer, middle, and inner ears. These are shown schematically in Figure 5.

The outer ear consists of the pinna and auditory meatus. The pinna collects sound from the surrounding medium (usually air) and conducts it down the auditory meatus. At the bottom of the auditory meatus lies the tympanic membrane, which moves in response to pressure that reaches it.

At the other side of the tympanic membrane lies the middle ear, which is an air-filled, bony cavity containing three ossicles (the malleus, incus, and stapes). The malleus is embedded in the tympanic membrane; and as the tympanic mem-

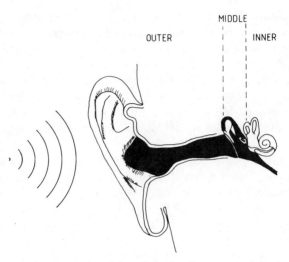

Figure 5.   Schematic cross section of the peripheral auditory system indicating the outer-, middle-, and inner-ear divisions.

brane moves in response to sound transmitted down the auditory meatus, the malleus also moves. The movement of the malleus is conducted to the stapes through the incus.

Besides the three ossicles, the middle ear contains two muscles: the tensor tympani, which attaches to the malleus, and the stapedius, which attaches to the stapes. These attachments are shown diagrammatically in the expanded schematic figure of the middle ear (Figure 6).

When either of these muscles contracts, the ossicle-linkage system of the

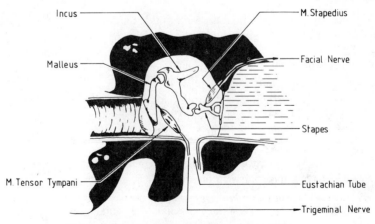

Figure 6.   Expanded schematic figure of the middle ear.

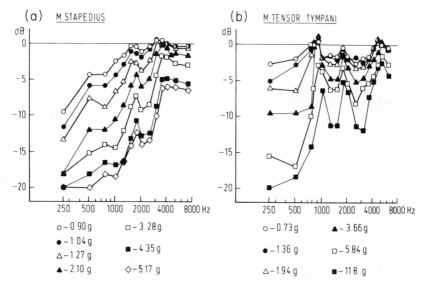

Figure 7. Teig's (1973) data on the effect of middle-ear muscle contraction on sound transmission. Reproduced with permission of the author and *Acta Physiologica Scandinavica.*

middle ear stiffens and the ease of sound transmission through the middle ear is reduced. The data presented in Figure 7 demonstrate this, showing the amount of attenuation caused by different amounts of contraction of the stapedius and tensor tympani. Force of contraction was measured in grammes. It can be seen that both muscles attenuate sound in the low-frequency region (i.e., both show a high-pass characteristic), that the amount of attenuation increases as the contraction of the muscles increases, and that the stapedius attenuates sound more than the tensor tympani.

Since muscle contraction affects sound transmission, events that cause them to contract must be considered. Acoustic stimulation causes the stapedius to contract (Metz, 1951). Inhalation of ammonia (Gersdorff and Vogeeler, 1973), swallowing, yawning (Ingelstedt and Johnson, 1966), or directing a jet of air to the eyes (Greisen and Neergaard, 1975) elicits contraction in the tensor tympani. Acoustic stimulation does not cause contraction in the tensor tympani of humans except at very high sound-pressure levels (120 dB and over), and then the reason is probably that the stimulation elicits a startle response (Djupesland, 1965; Klockhoff, 1961). Middle-ear muscle activity also occurs prior to vocalisation since electromyographic (EMG) activity has been recorded in both muscles (Salomon and Starr, 1963).

The parts of the peripheral auditory system outlined so far are concerned with transmission of sound to the inner ear. The most important property that these structures exhibit is that sound-pressure variation is transmitted from the external medium to the inner ear without new frequencies being introduced into the signal. The output of these structures is stapes movement. The movement of the stapes in and out of the inner ear causes fluids in it to move and, eventually, causes sound to be perceived.

The inner ear consists of a spiral-shaped structure called the cochlea, which is encased in bone and filled with fluid. If a cross-section is taken through one of the turns of the cochlea, three divisions can be seen: the scala vestibuli, scala tympani, and scala media (Figure 8). The scala media is separated from the two other scalae, whereas the scala tympani and scala vestibuli connect at the apical end of the cochlea.

The scala media is divided from the other two scalae by two membranes—the basilar membrane at the bottom and Reissner's membrane at the top. These membranes run nearly the whole length of the cochlea. The organ of Corti sits on the basilar membrane and rows of hair cells project from it. There are three rows of hair cells on the outside edge and one on the inner. Another membrane (the tectorial) sits above the hair cells. When the basilar membrane moves, the hair cells brush against the tectorial membrane causing neural discharge. The hair cells are synaptically connected to the auditory nerve fibres and the discharge at different points along the basilar membrane is collected and transmitted via the auditory nerve to the auditory cortex. A section through the scala media showing these structures is presented in Figure 9.

The basilar membrane is caused to move by hydrodynamic forces set up by the stapes that enters the cochlea by the oval window. The fluid set into motion by the stapes displacement causes a travelling wave on the basilar membrane to be sent down the cochlea, and the excess pressure is released at the other end of the cochlea through the round window. The travelling wave caused by sinusoidal stimulation at one point in time is shown diagrammatically by the dashed line in Figure 8.

Though vocal sounds are of interest here, it is easiest to understand what

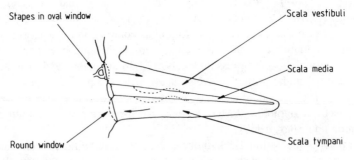

Figure 8.   Schematic diagram of an uncoiled coclea indicating the scalae and a wave travelling down the cochlea.

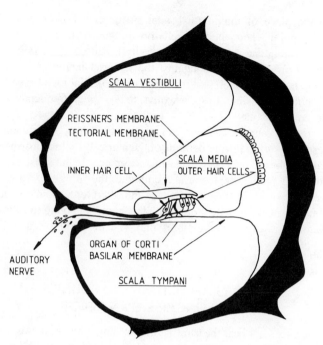

Figure 9. Cross-section through a turn of the cochlea indicating the principal structures described in the text.

happens by considering sinusoidal stimulation. This does not mean that the significance for vocal sounds cannot be ascertained, because, as shown previously, vocal signals can be considered to be composed of a sum of sinusoids. How, then, does the peripheral auditory system respond to sounds of different frequency? The travelling wave has the same periodicity as that of the stapes, so any point on the basilar membrane goes through an up–down cycle of displacement at the same rate as the in–out movement of the stapes. Besides this, the place at which the basilar membrane shows most displacement depends on the stimulating frequency. (The basilar membrane is most flaccid at the apical end and stiffest at its base near the round window.) This variation in the mechanical properties means that the basilar membrane is able to perform some frequency analysis, with different points on the basilar membrane causing biggest displacements for different frequencies. Low frequencies cause most movement at the round window end and high frequencies near the oval window (because of the difference in the mechanical properties along the length of the basilar membrane).

There are two ways in which basilar membrane movement can cause the frequency of sound to be perceived.

1. Since the place of maximum basilar membrane movement differs with frequency, the point where the hair cells brush against the tectorial membrane also varies with frequency. Most neural activity is caused at the point where the hair cells brush most vigorously against the tectorial membrane. Thus, if the auditory nerve monitors which part (or parts) of the basilar membrane have most activity, it would be possible, to some extent, to code what frequency or frequencies are present in a sound.

2. The peripheral auditory system can respond to sounds of different frequency in the periodicity of the firing patterns of the hair cells, which brush up against the tectorial membrane once per cycle of movement. If they discharged every time they brushed against the tectorial membrane, the firing pattern would have the same periodicity as the travelling wave (and, therefore, the movement of the stapes). Although nerve firing cannot take place rapidly enough to follow signals of high frequency, several nerve fibres may fire in "volley" to follow such signals.

FACTORS AFFECTING THE SOUND OF THE SINGER'S OWN VOICE

An audience does not hear the same sound the singer hears. In this section, the factors causing this are discussed: bone-conducted feedback, middle-ear muscle contraction before and during vocalisation, and effects due to the direction of sound at the mouth relative to the ears. These factors are integral to the singer although the environment also affects the sound of the voice. The implications of all this for the possibility of using auditory feedback for vocal control are assessed.

Bone-conducted Sound

Bone-conducted sound will be considered first and in most detail as it is the most important of the effects unique to the singer. Then, the generation of bone-conducted sound during vocalisation will be described, followed by its transduction; and finally, some measurements of bone vibration during vocalisation will be presented.

Sound-conduction Through Bone during Vocalisation

When referring to sound, bone-conduction means that a signal is transmitted to the auditory system via bone rather than through the air-conducted pathways described previously. In order for sound associated with the voice to be transmitted through bone, some structure that vibrates in the process of vocalisation has to pass its vibration on to the bone. It is theoretically possible for the air-pressure variation of the voice to cause the bone to vibrate. However, sound in air has to be 60 dB greater than vibration applied directly to bone to cause the same amount of movement of the bone (von Bekesy, 1948). A 60-dB difference indicates that vibration caused by airborne sound is $\frac{1}{1000}$ of that applied directly to the bone. Thus, if the main way of causing bone to vibrate during vocalisation is by airborne sound, bone-conducted feedback would never be very loud compared with the airborne part of the speaker's speech.

However, certain observations indicate that bone-conducted feedback is louder than $\frac{1}{1000}$ of that of air. For example, von Bekesy (1949) estimated the loudness of bone-conducted feedback relative to air-conducted feedback by eliminating the air-conducted route during vocalisation. He found a 6-dB drop in the sound-pressure level of feedback when this was done.[1] A 6-dB drop in level is equivalent to a halving of amplitude; therefore, when only bone-conducted feedback is transmitted, the level drops to half of when feedback is received through bone and air. From this, it follows that bone-conducted feedback must be about as loud as airborne feedback. Because of the marked discrepancies between the estimate of vibration caused by air and vibration that occurs during vocalisation, it would seem that there are significant contributions to bone-conducted feedback apart from vibration of bone caused by airflow associated with vocalisation itself.

In order to outline other sources of bone vibration, it is necessary to distinguish two ways in which vibration occurs during vocalisation: First, movements of structures going on in association with vocalisation force the bones to vibrate. Vibration related to the vocal tract filter and voice pitch could occur by this means. Second, the bones, muscles, and ligaments involved in articulation constitute a vibratory structure that has its own resonances, which refers to stimulations at or near the natural frequency of an object causing large amplitude responses (e.g., formants are the resonance frequencies of the vocal tract, which result in energy at that frequency being transmitted more efficiently than energy at other frequencies). The resonances of the articulators arise from the mechanical properties of the structures, not because of the movements they are forced to make during vocalisation. Thus, the vibration is not related to the resonant frequencies of the air contained in the vocal tract: Something has to excite these resonances (just as the resonances of the vocal tract have to be excited by a source of excitation). The excitation of the bone resonances is probably produced by one or both of the types of forced vibration. Thus, the two sorts of vibration (forced or resonance) that could occur during vocalisation are not exclusive. Forced vibration can occur in association with either the laryngeal vibration or the air in the vocal tract, and these are considered in turn.

---

[1]The occlusion effect would not affect the results of von Bekesy's (1949) experiment in which he eliminated the airborne route.

Forced Vibration Associated with Movement of the Vocal Cords.   It was noted when considering airborne vocalisation that the vocal cords move and this causes the airflow from the lungs to be interrupted. The interest was then in the effect of this interruption on the airflow signal. When considering bone-conducted feedback of the voice, the movement of the cords themselves is of interest. The cord movement is first passed to the laryngeal cartilages and then, via their suspensions, to bone. In fact, this vibration is the only one that occurs in the audio-frequency range that is directly associated with articulation. Although the airflow and vibration are related, it does not follow that the signal is identical in form in the two cases. (This does not, of course, mean that the air and bone signals differ in all respects.) The period of the vibratory signal in bone and that in the airflow above the vocal cords is likely to be the same. However, it is extremely unlikely that the shape of each period is the same in these two situations. The reason for this is as follows: The principal determinant of airflow is the area of the opening between the vocal cords. There are many ways in which the vocal cords can vibrate so that they give rise to a slit that would cause a sawtooth waveform in the airborne signal. Certain of these possibilities arise from the fact that the cords move in sagittal (i.e., up–down) and lateral (i.e., sideways) planes (Sonesson, 1960). If one assumes that the most important movement in relationship to bone-conducted sound is in the sagittal plane (as does von Bekesy, 1949), it is unlikely to be sawtooth in form.

Forced Vibration Caused by Movement of the Air in the Vocal Cavities.[2]
The spectrum of the source is altered by the shape of the vocal tract even when movement of the air within the vocal cavities (i.e., before it emerges at the lips) is considered. Thus, this signal contains information about the resonances of the vocal cavities. The air in the vocal tract cannot cause appreciable bone vibration directly because of the high level of sound in air needed to cause bone to vibrate. However, there is an indirect route by which vibration of the air in the vocal cavities could arise in bone; the moving air in the vocal cavities could cause the cheeks to flap at the same rate. This flapping is passed on to the mandible and then to the cartilage around the auditory meatus (von Bekesy, 1941). The position of the mandible relative to the meatal cartilage and bones of the skull is shown in Figure 10.

The movement of the cartilage in the auditory meatus caused by movement of the mandible sets the air close to the cartilage into motion and this is conducted down the auditory meatus. Although vibration of the mandible is always described as emerging into the auditory system at the auditory meatus via the cartilage that surrounds it, vibration through the mandible can also be passed on

---

[2]This route is really indirect since the vocal tract does not cause the bone to vibrate directly but does so via the cheeks and mandible.

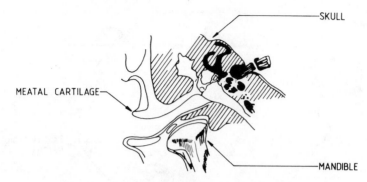

Figure 10. The position of the mandible relative to the peripheral auditory system.

to bone; the head of the mandible fits in to the mandibular fossa of the temporal bone (Zemlin, 1968), so the temporal bone (and, in fact, the other bones of the skull since they all abut each other) vibrates in response to vibration that gets to the mandible.

The Resonances of the Vibratory Structures Actually Involved in Vocalisation. It has already been noted that the vibration of the vocal cords is passed on to the cartilages of the larynx. These, are, in turn, connected to other bony structures by muscles; some of the bony structures close to the larynx are shown schematically in Figure 11 (Howell and Powell, 1984). These bones are set into vibration by movements originating in the larynx; and once the bones start vibrating, they set up vibration that interacts with the original vibration. Other vibration that occurs in the bones could excite such resonances as well. For example, if the mandible vibrates, as described, it could produce energy at or near the resonant frequencies of other bones that would be transmitted well. This complex vibratory structure is made more complex because of three other factors: (1) The efficiency with which vibration is passed to and from the bone structures is determined by the state of contraction of the muscles around them. The more the muscles are contracted, the less the bony structures are able to vibrate. (2) The vibration of the bony structures is limited by the number (and state of contraction) of the muscles connected to them. (3) the distribution of flesh around these structures serves to bring vibration to a halt (i.e., damps out the vibration). Since the amount of flesh around these structures differs, differences would be expected in their damping.

In summary, there are three potential contributions to bone-conducted vibration during vocalisation—two forced and one resonant. The two sources of forced vibration are associated with vibration of the vocal cords and air in the vocal tract. The resonant component is that of the bone-vibratory system.

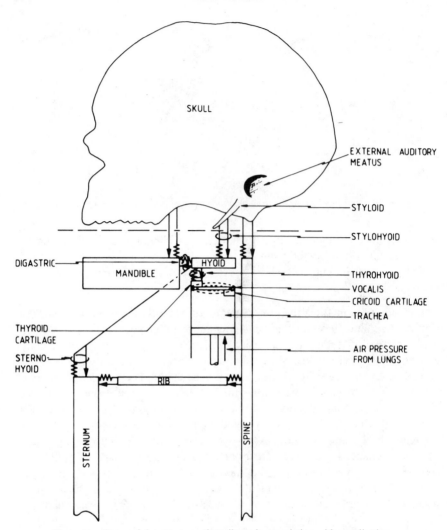

Figure 11.   Some of the structures that vibrate in association with vocalisation.

Transduction of Bone-conducted Sound by the Peripheral Auditory System

The vibration in bone that arises during vocalisation emerges at some point into the auditory system and causes sound to be heard. Again, the response of the auditory system to sinusoidal stimulation is considered (as with air) rather than the response to complex signals.

In early studies, it was thought that bone-conducted vibration could stimulate the auditory nerve directly and cause sound to be heard. Von Bekesy (1932) showed that this was probably not so. He demonstrated that it is possible to cancel a sinusoid transmitted to the auditory system through bone by varying the amplitude and phase of an air-conducted tone of the same frequency. Cancellation of two waves that are at the same amplitude and frequency but out of phase by 180° would occur since the two waves would sum to zero at all points along each cycle. Thus, no sound would be heard. There is no obvious way that cancellation could occur in the auditory nerve; and so, most likely, this finding demonstrates that bone-conducted sound is transduced at some point in the peripheral auditory system (not at the level of the auditory nerve or higher). Lowy (1942) proved conclusively that transduction of bone-conducted sound occurs in the peripheral auditory system by showing that after such cancellation, the entire cochlear partition comes to rest. (Note that the fact that the cochlear partition comes to rest does not mean that all bone-conducted sound goes directly to the inner ear.)

Though bone-conducted vibration is transduced by the peripheral auditory system, the way this happens differs somewhat from transduction of air-conducted sound and is more complex, since there are more ways that vibration conducted through bone could cause sound to be perceived. Tonndorf (1972) identified eight ways that bone-conducted sound is transduced by the peripheral auditory system. These are described by the division of the peripheral auditory system at which they first occur. (When sound is conducted through air and bone, they do not interact, because of the principle of superposition).

The pinna and auditory meatus consist of cartilage that is suspended on the bones of the skull. The cartilage is able to vibrate with and, to some extent, independently of the skull. The vibration of the cartilage causes the air close to the surface of the meatus to move; this air is transduced in the same way as air-conducted sound (described previously). If sinusoidal vibration is applied to the skull, the mandible vibrates at the same frequency but out of phase. The out-of-phase movement of the skull and mandible and the different amplitude of movement of these structures causes the cartilage of the auditory meatus to some move some air in the ear canal at this same frequency.

However, the evidence about the route from the mandible to the cartilage in the auditory meatus is somewhat mixed. If this route is important, the vibration of the mandible should be different from that of the skull when vibratory stimulation is applied. As stated previously, if sinusoidal stimulation is applied from an audiometer, the mandible and skull should vibrate at the same frequency but at a different amplitude and out of phase. Franke, von Gierke, Grossman, and von Wittern (1952) confirmed that the skull and jaw move out of phase in response to externally applied vibratory stimulation by direct measurement of skull and jaw movement. This result seems to indicate that an important route for bone-conducted vibration is to the auditory meatus.

Allen and Fernandez (1960) examined this in a different way and came to the conclusion that this route is of little importance; they measured the sound level in the enclosed ear canal of two subjects with the mandible missing on one side. Whereas it would be expected that the sound level would be greater in the ear canal on the side where the mandible is present, no marked difference was found in such measurements of the two ears of these subjects.

The reason for the discrepancy between Franke et al., (1952) and Allen and Fernandez (1960) may be that there is out-of-phase movement between the skull and jaw (as Franke et al., found) but the main point of emergence is at the temporal bone rather than the cartilage around the auditory meatus (Figure 10). This would explain why Allen and Fernandez found no difference in level measured in the ear canal because, although vibration is transmitted down the mandible, the major point of emergence is not in the ear canal via the cartilage but into the bones of the skull. If this explanation is correct, mandible vibration might be an important source of bone-conducted feedback of the voice, but the vibration would be passed on mainly to the bone rather than the meatal cartilage and would be transduced in the same way as air conducted down the meatus.

There are two components to the bone-conducted response of the middle ear. It was noted that with air-conducted sound, the movement of the stapes in and out of the oval window causes sound to be perceived. A movement of the stapes also occurs relative to the skull when the bones of the skull vibrate. The cochlea moves with the skull as it is embedded in its bones. The middle-ear ossicles are suspended loosely in the skull. Because of their inertia, they tend to remain stationary when the skull moves. Thus, there is movement of the stapes relative to the cochlea, and sound is caused as described with air-conducted sound.

The second middle-ear effect arises because the air in the middle ear is compressed by the bone that surrounds it. Groen (1962) has shown that this adds an elastic term to the ossicular inertia contribution. The movement of the stapes relative to the cochlea represents the combined effect of these two factors. A finding that is relevant to the contribution of the middle-ear components to bone-conducted feedback comes from Bárány (1938), who demonstrated that vibration applied to the temple causes least ossicular movement. The placement of the vibrator on the temple is at roughly the same orientation as that of the larynx. Lateral movement of the cords in the same direction as vibration applied to the temple is passed poorly to the ossicles. However, the movements at other orientations, whose occurrence has been noted, passes better.

The remaining five components occur in the cochlea. The cochlear aqueduct and the two windows of the inner ear (round and oval) have more "give" than the bone that surrounds the cochlea. The cochlea aqueduct is located near the round window in the scala tympani. It connects the scalae to spaces filled with cerebrospinal fluid. The cochlear aqueduct is referred to as the third window because it responds in a similar way to the round and oval windows when bone vibration is applied. Because of the way the windows are distributed around the

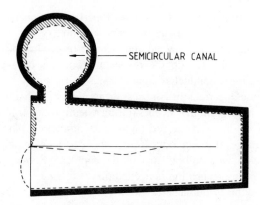

Figure 12. The effect of compressional waves on the cochlea.

cochlea and the differences between the compliances of the windows and bone, there are unequal volume changes in the scala vestibuli and scala tympani. This, in turn, causes the cochlea partition to move; and as it moves, the hair cells are sheared, causing neural activity, which is ultimately heard as sound. The effects of compressing the cochlea and the influence of the two windows plus the contribution from the cochlea aqueduct are shown diagrammatically in Figure 12.

It has been shown experimentally that the windows contribute to the bone-conducted response. When any of them are sealed off with cement, the bone-conducted response decreases. The reason the response is less is that the cement reduces the differential in compressibility between the windows and the bone that surrounds the cochlea.

The fluid in the inner ear has an inertia much like that described in connection with the ossicles of the middle ear. When the bone surrounding the cochlea is compressed, the fluids tend to remain stationary; this stimulates the hair cells of the inner ear. The final inner-ear component is due to distortional waves in the cochlea that occur because the cochlea shell changes shape in synchrony with the applied signal (i.e., shape changes but not necessarily volume changes).

In summary, studies on bone-conducted sound by sinusoidal stimulation show that such sound can be perceived in at least eight different ways. Thus, bone-conduction, both in the signal that is conducted and in the manner of its transduction, is a complex process. The question of how to get some measure of bone-conducted sound during vocalisation is addressed in the following section.

Comparison of Air-Conducted and Bone-conducted Feedback of the Voice

The acoustic properties of airborne vocal sound are well understood—there are components attributable to the source of excitation and the filter action of the vocal tract. Less is known about bone-conducted sound. The following questions are considered in this section: (1) What properties of vocal sound within the vocal tract (i.e., with some of the resonant structure of the filter) get into the bone-conducted signal and how do they do so (e.g., by the mandible route already described)? and (2) do the resonant properties of the bone-vibratory system affect the bone-conducted signal?

To address these questions, it is necessary to measure vibration in parts of the peripheral auditory system that occurs during vocalisation. It has been seen that bone-conducted feedback is caused because a number of things vibrate when sound is transmitted through bone (e.g., the cartilage in the ear canal, the middle-ear ossicles, and the bone around the cochlea). Some way of measuring the vibration during vocalisation is needed that is related to some or all of these and that can be done in humans.

Skull vibration is related to all the bone-conducted components although it does not represent exactly any single component of bone-conducted sound. The cartilage of the auditory meatus vibrates in response to vibration of the skull (and, to some extent, independently of it). The two middle-ear effects are represented by the movement of the ossicles relative to the skull. Thus, the vibration of the skull has to be measured to determine what the movement of the ossicles relative to it is. In fact, if the ossicles did not partake in movement of the skull at all, vibration of the skull in the plane of stapes movement would be the same as stapes movement caused by the inertia of the middle-ear ossicles. The five inner-ear components occur in direct response to vibration of the skull (i.e., oval, round, third window bulges, distortional effects, and fluid inertia).

Measurements of skull vibration have been made previously by Mullendore (1949). He reported that resonances occur in the vibratory signal at the same frequencies as the formants. He did not detect any resonances that arose from the bone-vibration structure itself. If these occur, they should be roughly constant, whatever vocal sound is produced. Also, their resonant frequencies should be independent of the formants in airborne recordings of the sound made simultaneous with the bone-vibration recordings. They should be constant because they are mainly determined by the mass of the bones and the properties of the flesh and muscles. They should bear no relationships to the resonances of the vocal signal, because they arise from the properties of a vibratory system unrelated to resonances in the vocal signal.

Recordings were made of bone vibration and speech output for one male speaker speaking the vowels /i/, /ʊ/, /ɑ/ and /ɛ/ (Howell and Powell, 1984). (Although speech was used, the findings should apply to song, too.) The vowels were sustained for about 5 sec. (The accelerometer recordings are referred to throughout as "bone," but this is only approximately true). The measurements of bone vibration were made with an accelerometer, which was secured on the mastoid bone. Long-term, averaged spectra were made of the air- and bone-conducted signals (Figure 13). The spectra of the air-conducted signals are given

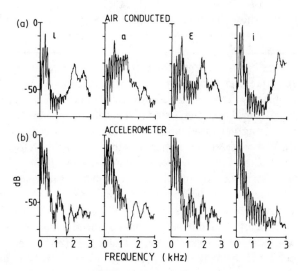

Figure 13. (a) Spectra of vowels from airborne records; and (b) spectra of vowels from an accelerometer placed on the skull, which represents (approximately) the bone-conducted component of feedback.

in (a); the bone-conducted signals are presented similarly in (b). If the air and bone signals are compared, it can be seen that the bone-conducted signal has peaks at about the same frequency as the peaks in the airborne signal (i.e., the formants). These peaks may get into the bone through the mandible route described previously.

There is some indication of resonances at frequencies between 1 and 2 kHz, which occur independently of the vowel being spoken, and these are not correlated with the formants. They may be resonances of the skull, as von Bekesy and Rosenblith (1951) report skull resonances at 800 and 1600 Hz. One notable fact is that the air and bone signals are not that similar.

The implications of these spectra are summarised with respect to the three aspects introduced in the preceding section (i.e., forced resonance attributable to factors associated with laryngeal and vocal-tract characteristics and resonance of the articulatory structures themselves). The jagged peaks in the bone-conducted spectra in Figure 13 are partials of some periodic signal in the vibratory signal. This signal has some similarities to the (airborne) excitatory signal (i.e., the periodicity of the two signals is about the same since the interharmonic spacing is similar). However, as discussed, it cannot be assumed that the shape of the period of air-pressure variation and the vibratory signal are the same. The question about the shape of each period of the bone-vibration signal is left open since the form of the vibratory signal in each period in bone cannot be obtained without making assumptions.

These data also show that forced vibration related to the resonant frequencies of the vocal tract occurs for voiced speech. The evidence for this is the coincidence of the peaks corresponding to the formants in the air and bone signals. Resonances of the bone-vibratory structures occur in the recordings made on the male adult at frequencies between 1 and 2 kHz. A general characteristic of the recordings is that low frequencies are overrepresented in the bone-conducted signal compared with the airborne signal. This fits with subjective impressions that the voice, during vocalisation, sounds boomier than when recorded.

It is necessary to consider the implications these results have for using auditory feedback to control the voice. The bone-conducted signal has both similarities to and differences from the air-conducted signal. The formants do occur in the bone-conducted signal, but they are reduced in amplitude. Since the formants contain information about which sound was articulated, the reduction in amplitude makes it difficult to identify the sound produced from these signals alone. The presence of the resonances between 1 and 2 kHz (for this subject) also affects the intelligibility of the sound since these might be confused with the formants. The effects of these resonances are not marked, however, since they are at a low level.

The Effects of Middle-ear Muscle Activity on the Sound of the Voice Prior to and during Vocalisation

The data of Teig (1973), shown in Figure 7, show that contraction of the middle-ear muscles affects the properties of sound transmitted through the middle-ear system. This may be important for the question of auditory-feedback regulation of the voice since contraction of the middle-ear muscles during vocalisation could alter auditory feedback of the voice. Any sound transmitted through the middle-ear system would be affected; that is, all air-conducted sound and bone-conducted components save those travelling directly to the cochlea through bone.

To understand the effect the middle-ear muscles have on vocal feedback, many questions need answering: What causes of contraction are there for each of the muscles? How much does each of the muscles contract and does the amount of contraction vary with the events that elicit their activity? When do the muscles contract relative to vocalisation: before, simultaneously with, or after its onset? Does the activity of the muscles vary throughout an utterance or is contraction sustained throughout? A question that cuts across many of the preceding is whether one or both of the muscles can be contracted voluntarily during vocalisation (so as to maintain a constant alteration to vocal feedback) or whether contraction is involuntarily related to vocalisation.

A complete understanding of the influence of the middle-ear muscles on vocal feedback requires answers to all these questions for each of the middle-ear muscles, but the data that are presently available do not permit definite conclusions. However, although the effect of middle-ear muscle contraction on vocal feedback has been given some importance (e.g., by Webster and Dorman, 1970, who suggest that it may have a causative role in stuttering), it is unlikely to be of substantial importance. Thus, the data of Teig (1973) in Figure 7 show that the attenuation caused by middle-ear muscle contraction has an effect of attenuating sound by only 20 dB at maximum.

Air-Conducted Feedback to the Speaker's Ears

Before the treatment of vocal-feedback effects internal to the singer is completed, it is necessary to describe the properties of air-conducted feedback at the singer's ears, as this differs from that at other peoples ears. Measurements on speech (rather than singing) were made by von Bekesy (1949). (There is no reason that the findings on speech would not generalize to singing, however.) Von Bekesy measured the speech level at the speaker's lips and at various points of the speaker's body during vocalisation. A 20–25 dB drop from the lips to the auditory meatus (averaged across all frequencies) was reported. The attenuation also varied somewhat with frequency. This was shown by band-pass filtering speech with the band set at different centre frequencies (each band was an octave wide). The attenuation of a band centred on 75 Hz was 12 dB and the attenuation increased up to 30 dB or more for a band centred on about 9 kHz. If, as assumed, this applies to singing, the effect to singers is that airborne song that reaches them would be low-pass filtered. As with bone, the airborne part of song has an overrepresentation of the low frequencies at the singer's ear compared with a listener who receives sound at normal incidence. The directional properties of air-conducted sound detracts from the intelligibility of a person's auditory feedback.

Effects of Auditoria on Vocal Feedback

There are many factors in the external environment that affect the singer's vocal feedback. For example, if the singer is a member of a choir, the sound made by the surrounding singers would affect what is heard of the voice (Ternstrom and Sundberg, 1982). There are many aspects of the auditorium that would affect auditory feedback, too: the acoustics of the room; whether or not an amplification system is used, and if so, what amplification system; and whether an audience is present or not. All of these alter the properties of the sound and its time of arrival at the performer's ears. (See Harvey, Chapter 12, this volume, for further discussion of some of these environmental factors).

Summary and Assessment

The data reviewed so far in this chapter show that bone-conducted sound is not identical to air-conducted sound. Middle-ear muscle contraction and the direction the voice emerges at the lips relative to the ear also exert some effect on sound of the voice. These factors make auditory feedback different from what a member of the audience receives. Although singing teachers have advocated that singers use auditory feedback to control the voice (e.g., Coffin, 1980), the findings reviewed here bring this into question. Auditory feedback cannot be used directly to control all aspects of the voice require many compensations on the part of the singer to get any idea of what a member of the audience would hear. Voice pitch is one aspect of the voice that may be controllable by listening to auditory feedback. This is determined mainly by the rate of vocal-fold vibration. The signal in bone has the same periodicity as that in air and so has roughly the same pitch. When environmental factors are taken into account, the problem of using auditory feedback becomes more severe; all auditoria differ in the effect they have on the sound of the voice. these idiosyncracies argue strongly against auditory feedback being used for vocal control.

ALTERED AUDITORY FEEDBACK
AND VOCAL CONTROL

In the preceding part of this chapter, it is shown that auditory feedback that a singer receives is different from an audience's experience of the singer; it has been argued that this makes the signal of minimal use for the purpose of vocal control. However, it has been shown on many occasions that when vocal feedback is altered in certain ways, vocal control suffers. The most extensively studied ways of altering the voice are to change its level or to introduce a delay between when the sound is produced and when it is heard. These effects have been studied in detail by researchers interested in speech control. As with many of the findings discussed previously, the findings with speech should apply to singing, too. Contrary to this argument, these studies have been interpreted as support for the view that speech is under feedback control.

In this section, studies of altered feedback are reviewed critically. The review is not exhaustive; only the main findings and alternative explanations of the effects of altering level and time of arrival of feedback are presented.

Level

If the level of the voice is amplified before speakers hear it, they reduce their voice level (Siegel and Pick, 1974). Conversely, if the level of their voice is attenuated, they increase their voice level (Lane and Tranel, 1971). A number of authors have suggested that these effects provide evidence that speakers use auditory feedback for voice control. Common to the explanations offered is that the level of the voice is controlled so that feedback is loud enough for the performer to hear what is necessary in order to be able to control the voice.

Lane and Tranel (1971) discuss several problems for the hypothesis that speakers alter their voice level to keep feedback loud enough for the purpose of feedback control. For example, such an account only explains the effect of attenuating the voice, since there is nothing about feedback that is at too high a level that prohibits it being useful for the purpose of vocal control. Also, speakers increase voice level when feedback is altered on one ear only, yet a speaker should be able to use feedback on the ear that is unaltered to control speech. If alteration to feedback is kept up for some time, speakers adapt to it, and their voice level tends to return to normal but, if the feedback account is correct, they should continue with the change in level of their voice the whole time that the alteration to feedback is maintained.

The explanation offered by Lane and Tranel (1971) of why voice level changes when the level of feedback is altered is based on the correspondence between speaking in noise and speaking under conditions of altered feedback. Speakers speak louder when the noise level goes up, and speak softer when noise level drops (data on this are summarized in Lane and Tranel, 1971). This is the converse of what happens when the level of the speech signal is altered. Lane and Tranel show that in both situations, speakers attempt to keep the signal-to-noise ratio constant (i.e., raising the level of the noise or reducing the level of the speech signal alters the signal-to-noise ratio unfavourably to the signal, and speakers adjust their voice levels up to compensate for these effects). It can be seen that alterations to voice level that are difficult to account for in the feedback-regulation account can be readily explained on the basis of this hypothesis. Increasing voice level by amplification alters the signal-to-noise ratio and speakers compensate for it by reducing voice level. These alterations are effected to maintain a satisfactory level for other listeners, not to keep the level of feedback up for oneself.

Delayed Auditory Feedback

Speech is usually heard at about the same time as it is spoken. If airborne speech is delayed, the speech sound that is produced is altered in that voice level and pitch increase as the delay is increased up to 200 ms and then level off. Time to read a list (reaction time) and error rate show most disruption at this delay, that is, the function over delays is peaked (Fairbanks, 1955).

It has been assumed that auditory feedback is normally used for vocal control, and speakers continue to try to use the signal they hear when it has been artificially delayed. The sorts of disturbance observed on time and errors described previously have been interpreted as supporting this explanation. If speech units of about 200-ms length are issued and the speech is delayed by 200 ms, the speaker may believe the unit he/she is currently hearing is from the one that is currently being produced; however, it would be from the previous one. Since syllables are about 200 ms long, they may be the unit issued.

Effects similar to those observed when speech is delayed have been observed in a variety of other tasks. An example that may be relevant to a music readership is Gates, Bradshaw, and Nettleton's (1974) report that keyboard musicians show effects similar to those observed in delayed feedback of speech.

However, studies in which speech is delayed may not provide support for a process of auditory-feedback regulation of vocalisation since the disruption observed can be explained in other ways. For example, Howell, Powell, and Khan (1983) explain the effects of delayed auditory feedback (DAF) as arising from interference in performing a serially organised behavior when an intruding rhythmic event is going on. The rhythm in speech is created by the rise and fall in the amplitude contour associated with the syllables. When speech is delayed by 200 ms, this signal starts as a syllable has just finished. Howell et al. hypothesize that events that start as performance of an activity is completed are particularly disruptive on performance. In the case of speech under delayed auditory feedback, the delayed speech starts after each syllable, and this causes the disruption. There are many examples drawn from music that illustrate disruption in performing an activity when a second rhythmic event starts concurrently with the offset of the piece being performed; for example, the difficulty in ringing a handbell so that its onset coincides with the offset of a ring by another player. Also, in this view, DAF is similar to many musical-performance situations in which a note has to be played in some (non-synchronous) relationship to that of another player. Thus, there is the difficulty experienced in playing notes so that they are synchronized with the offset of those produced by a second player (as, for example, in hockets; see Reese, 1941). The sound that another musician produces cannot be used as feedback, yet musicians experience similar difficulties to those that occur in DAF tasks. The common factor in the two situations is that some intruding event starts after a speaker or musician has produced a syllable or note, so vocalisation may not be controlled by feedback either.

Support for this hypothesis is reported by Howell and Archer (1984). They calculated the amplitude contour of speech, delayed it, and used the delayed-amplitude contour to gate on a square wave. Similar effects occurred with this feedback (which could not be used for any aspect of vocal control) as with delayed-speech feedback. This signal causes the same amount of rhythmic disruption; therefore, it seems that this is what causes disruption under DAF. It is also of note, apropos the preceding discussion of the differences between air- and bone-conducted sound, that a delayed version of the vocal tract output at the lips would be unlikely to be used for vocal control; the technique only delays the air-conducted sound, but under normal vocal control, bone-conducted sound is present, too.

In summary, studies of altered feedback do not provide incontrovertible evidence for auditory-feedback control of the voice.

CONCLUSIONS

The aim of this chapter is to present background information that is necessary to evaluate the influences that auditory feedback have in the production and control of song. On the positive side, this review should indicate to a singer the physical basis of methods that might be employed to understand and extend vocal techniques. On a somewhat negative note, the evidence suggests that auditory feedback is not likely to be used for vocal control. There is no doubt that the possibility of using auditory feedback for vocal control will be a topic that continues to attract attention; however, the implication of the present review is that it would be more profitable to examine alternative sources of information, such as kinesthetic or proprioceptive feedback, for vocal control.

REFERENCES

Allen, G. W., and Fernandez, C. The mechanism of bone conduction. *Annals of Otology, Rhinology and Laryngology*, 1960, *69*, 5–28.

Bárány, E. A contribution to the physiology of bone conduction. *Acta Oto-Laryngologica*, 1938, Suppl. 26.

Coffin, B. *Overtones of bel canto: Phonetic basis of artistic singing.* Metuchen, NJ: Scarecrow Press, 1980.

Djupesland, G., Electromyography of the tympanic muscles in man. *International Audiology*, 1965, *4*, 34–41.

Fairbanks, G. Selected vocal effects of delayed auditory feedback. *Journal of Speech and Hearing Disorders*, 1955, 20, 333–345.

Franke, E. K., von Gierke, H. E., Grossman, F. M., and von Wittern, W. W. The jaw motions relative to the skull and their influence on hearing by bone conduction. *Journal of the Acoustical Society of America*, 1952, *24,* 142–146.

Fujimura, O., and Lindqvist, J. Sweep-tone measurements of vocal-tract characteristics, *Journal of the Acoustical Society of America*, 1970, *49,* 541–558.

Gates, A., Bradshaw, J. L., and Nettleton, N. C. Effect of different delayed auditory feedback intervals on a musical peformance task. *Perception and Psychophysics*, 1974, *15,* 21–25.

Gersdorff, M., and Vogeeler, M. L'impédancemetrie clinque. *Cahiers d'oto-rhino-laryngologie et de chirurgie cervico-faciale*, 1973, *8,* 16–54.

Greisen, O., and Neergaard, B. Middle ear reflex activity in the startle reaction. *Archives of Otolaryngology*, 1975, *101*, 348–353.

Groen, J. J. The value of the Weber test. In H. F. Schuknecht (Ed.), *International symposium on otosclerosis, Detroit.* Boston: Little Brown, 1962, 165–174.

Howell, P., and Archer, A. Susceptibility to the effects of delayed auditory feedback. *Perception and Psychophysics*, 1984, *36,* 296–302.

Howell, P., and Powell, D. J. Hearing your voice through bone and air; Implications for explanations of stuttering behaviour from studies of normal speakers. *Journal of Fluency Disorders,* 1984, *9,* 247–264.

Howell, P., Powell, D. J., and Khan, I. Amplitude contour of the delayed signal and interference in delayed auditary feedback tasks. *Journal of Experimental Psychology: Human Perception and Performance,* 1983, *9,* 772–784.

Ingelstedt, S., and Jonson, B. Mechanisms of the gas exchange in the normal human middle ear *Acta Oto-Laryngologica,* 1966, Suppl. 224, 452–461.

Klockhoff, J. Middle ear reflexes in man., *Acta Oto-Laryngologica,* 1961, Suppl. 164.

Lane, H., and Tranel, B. The Lombard sign and the role of hearing in speech. *Journal of Speech and Hearing Research,* 1971, *14,* 677–709.

Lowy, K. Cancellation of the electrical cochlear response with air- and bone-conducted sound. *Journal of the Acoustical Society of America,* 1942, *13,* 156–158.

Metz, O. Studies on the contraction of the tympanic muscles as indicated by changes in the impedance of the ear. *Acta Oto-Laryngologica,* 1951, *39,* 309–314.

Mullendore, J. M. An experimental study of the vibration of the head and chest during sustained vowel sounds. *Speech Monographs,* 1949, *16,* 163–176.

Reese, G. *Music in the middle ages.* London: Dent, 1941.

Salomon, G., and Starr, A. Electromyography of middle ear muscles during motor activities. *Acta Neurologica Scandinavica,* 1963, *39,* 161–168.

Siegel, G. M., and Pick, H. L. Auditory feedback in the regulation of the voice. *Journal of the Acoustical Society of America,* 1974, *56,* 1618–1624.

Sonesson, B. On the anatomy and vibratory pattern of the human vocal cords. *Acta Oto-Laryngologica,* 1960, Suppl. 156.

Teig, E. Differential effect of graded contraction of middle ear muscles on the sound transmission of the ear. *Acta Physiologica Scandinavica,* 1973, *88,* 387–391.

Ternstrom, S., and Sundberg, Acoustical factors related to pitch precision in choir singing. *STL–QPSR,* 1982, *2–3,* 76–90.

Tonndorf, J. Bone conduction. In J. V. Tobias (Ed.) *Foundations of modern auditory theory* (Vol. 2). New York: Academic Press, 1972.

von Bekesy, G. Zur Theorie des Horens bei der Schallaufnahme durch Knochen leitung *Poggendorff's Annln. Physical Chemistry,* 1932, *13,* 111–136.

von Bekesy, G. Ueber die schallausbreitung bei knochenleitung. *Zeitschrift Hals-Nasen-U Ohren heilk,* 1941, *47,* 430–442.

von Bekesy, G. Vibrations of the head in a sound field, and its role in hearing by bone conduction. *Journal of the Acoustical Society of America,* 1948, *20,* 749–760.

von Bekesy, G. The structure of the middle ear and the hearing of one's own voice by bone conduction. *Journal of the Acoustical Society of America,* 1949, *21,* 217–232.

von Bekesy, G., and Rosenblith, W. A. The mechanical properties of the ear. In S. S. Stevens (Ed.), *Handbook of Experimental Psychology.* New York: Wiley, 1951.

Webster, R. L., and Dorman, M. F. Decreases in stuttering frequency as a function of continuous and contingent forms of auditory masking. *Journal of Speech and Hearing Research,* 1970, *13,* 82–86.

Zemlin, W. R. *Speech and hearing science: Anatomy and physiology.* Englewood Cliffs, NJ: Prentice Hall, 1968.

12

Vocal Control in Singing: A Cognitive Approach*

Nigel Harvey

INTRODUCTION

Like golf, knitting, and driving a Sherman tank, singing is a motor skill. Via practice, the singer has learnt to coordinate contractions in various different sets of muscles so that their changing pattern over time produces desired effects. Like all skills, singing is flexible. The actions used to reach a particular set of goals are tailored to suit the precise circumstances encountered on each occasion. Here I concentrate on experimental studies of singing performance (i.e., the production of singing). The reader who is particularly interested in the perception of singing is referred to in an important review of the subject by Sundberg (1982b).

Various reviewers (e.g., Harvey and Greer, 1980) have suggested that one of the common intellectual threads running through much of cognitive psychology is the notion that behaviour depends on learning, using, and modifying rules or schemata. Instead of acquiring many separate associations linking particular stimuli to particular responses, people internalize a rule relating a set of stimuli to a set of responses. The advantages of adopting the rule-learning approach of cognitive psychology over the earlier associational approach of behaviourism are generally recognised to be twofold: (1) A single rule takes up less storage space in long-term memory than a set of many separate associations, and (2) a rule allows a response to be made to a new stimulus—a stimulus that is drawn from the set subject to the rule but which the person has never previously experienced. In other words, it allows people to be flexible enough to deal appropriately with novel situations—something that is especially important in exercising skills. It is this rule-oriented approach of cognitive psychology that I adopt here.

*This work was supported by Grant G 979/647/N from the Medical Research Council.

287

Although the notion of a behavioural rule or schema may be traced back at least to the work of Head (1926), Bartlett (1932) is recognised to be one of the most important early exponents of the idea. He was concerned to account for his observation that, when making a tennis stroke, he did not produce something absolutely new and never merely repeated something old. However, it was not until the 1960s, when psycholinguists inquired into the psychological reality of rules pertaining to linguistic structures (Chomsky, 1965), that the notion of rule-governed behaviour became prevalent among cognitive psychologists. It is only with the recent revival of interest in motor control within cognitive psychology that schema theories have been developed to account for skilled behaviour. The work of Schmidt (1975, 1976, 1982a, 1982b) is especially important in this respect. He argues that two types of rule are internalized when skills are learned. The first specifies how muscle contraction parameters relate to movement outcome under various conditions of movement. The second specifies how the individual's own sensation of movement relates to the outcome under these same conditions of movement.

Schmidt's theory provides a parsimonious account of how people learn and perform the type of skill involved in various types of military, industrial, and sport performance, in which goals, movements, and outcomes can be easily characterized in terms of external events. For instance, in golf, the hole is the goal, the swing is an easily recordable movement made in an attempt to reach it, and the position of the ball after the swing is an outcome that is easily established. Highly skilled golfers are recognised as those who reach holes with few movements, and the movement characteristics they share may be taken to define highly skilled golf performances. The difference between their performance and that of naïve players represents what it is that is learned during golf training.

Singing is different in at least two important ways. First, and in a rather practical vein, most movements involved in singing are well hidden inside the body. Any special techniques used to reveal them must not interfere with performance. Second—and in common with all communicative and artistic skills—the goals of singing and how closely they are reached cannot be defined in terms of solely objective criteria in the manner that a golf hole and the proximity of the ball to it can be. This is because the goals are to produce certain perceptions in an audience. Although these depend, in part, on the acoustic signals the singer produces, they also depend on conditions affecting the audience's perception and evaluation of those signals.

The recent developments in the cognitive psychology of motor control can be brought to bear on the problems involved in singing. Someone acquiring and exercising singing skill may be regarded as someone learning, using, and subsequently modifying rules or schemata. Together, these internalized rules must be able to reflect the musical structure specified by a composer in the same way that psychological rules for generating language must reflect the linguistic structures specified as acceptable by a native speaker. Because singing is an artistic skill, I argue that the singer needs to learn not only the two types of schema suggested by Schmidt but also one relating the singer's sensation of what has been produced to listeners' reports of the sensations they experience.

THE PROCESSES INVOLVED IN SINGING

Singing involves exhalation, phonation, and articulation (Figure 1). The essential features of the production of a sung vowel are described by Howell (Chapter 11, this volume) and can be summarized as follows. Chest contraction results in a reduction in lung volume. The air pressure in the lungs therefore increases relative to that in the vocal tract. With the vocal folds well apart, air then flows noiselessly through the glottis to remove the pressure difference. With the vocal folds tightly closed, it would be preserved. However, vocal folds together but not tightly closed can provide a periodic sound source. Pockets of air burst through them at regular intervals to produce audible pressure waves. This occurs because the air pressure is initially sufficient to open the folds. Once open, their natural elasticity and the Bernoulli effect (lowering in pressure as air velocity increases), caused by the rush of air through the glottis, act to close them again. Once closed, the Bernoulli effect disappears, and subglottal pressure is again sufficient to force them open. This cycle continues for as long as the vocal folds remain in the same phonating position and a sufficient transglottal pressure difference is present to force them open.

The periodic wave produced by this phonatory process is complex. Its fundamental frequency is given by the number of times the vocal folds open and close each second. Its higher harmonics are multiples of this fundamental frequency. The intensity of these harmonics usually falls off at approximately 12 dB per octave. This complex periodic wave is modified (filtered) by the resonant characteristics of the vocal tract, which depend on the positions of the articulators (e.g., tongue and velum). When the positions of the articulators and, hence, vocal-tract resonances (formants) are fixed, certain harmonics in the wave produced by the vocal folds are emphasized more than others and the resulting sound is perceived as some particular vowel. When the articulators and formants are changed to new positions, the relative emphasis given to the harmonics in the glottal waveform also changes and a new vowel is heard.

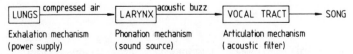

Figure 1. Block diagram of the main processes involved in singing.

APPLICATION OF SCHEMA THEORY TO SINGING

Scientists can express a relationship they have discovered between two or more variables by means of a regression equation. Such an equation serves to summarize data they have obtained and to predict data they expect to obtain. It is not a model of the processes that produced the data. However, schema theorists argue that the observed relationship between particular movement variables occurs because the performer has derived and stored an internal regression equation between these variables. This internal equation is used in the production of movement. In this case, therefore, the statistical procedures and considerations involved in extracting and using regression equations are taken to model the processes underlying the acquisition and performance of a skill.

What is the alternative to schema theory? How else could the performer produce the observed relationship between the muscle variables? The only direct way would be by remembering a large set of associations between particular values of those variables. As an example, suppose that electromyographic

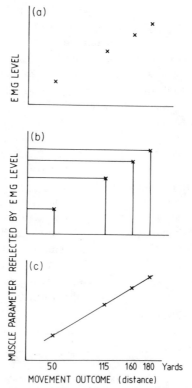

Figure 2. (a) Hypothetical data from experiment on golf swings; (b) associational account of data; and (c) schema theory account of data.

(EMG) recordings are taken from some muscle involved in producing a golf swing when the ball is hit over various distances. The hypothetical data are shown in Figure 2a. Assuming that EMG reflects a muscle-contraction parameter controlled by the performer, we must ask how these data are produced. How does the performer go about choosing the value of the parameter to be applied to the muscle when the ball has to be hit some particular distance? Separate associations between particular values of the parameter applied to the muscle and the particular distances achieved could have been learnt. The appropriate one would then be retrieved for use whenever one of those distances was required as a movement outcome. The separate associations that would produce the data given in Figure 2a are shown in Figure 2b. Alternatively, the performer could use internalized procedures analogous to a regression analysis to extract a schema or rule that relates the value of the muscle parameter to distance over the whole range of each variable. The regression line in Figure 2c represents the outcome of such a process. It is important that the schema can be used to derive muscle parameters appropriate for some movement outcome never before produced (e.g., between 50 and 115 yards).

Schema theory has some important implications for people who are learning to sing. In particular, highly varied practice should be more beneficial than relatively restricted practice. For instance, training the voice with many combinations of loudness, pitch, and vowel should be more effective than the same amount of training with fewer such combinations. This is because higher variability in practice allows strong schemata to be developed (Schmidt, 1982b). The importance of highly variable training extends to the environmental conditions in which practice is carried out. Thus, experience at singing in a large variety of different venues should enhance the internalization of rules that allow the performer to compensate for variations in the reverberation time of different rooms.

In the next three sections, I discuss exhalation, phonation, and articulation separately. In each case, I outline the essential features of what is known about the movements subserving the process. Then, I argue that these movements are unlikely to be produced by a system that depends on the acquisition and retrieval of a large set of separate associations between particular values of the variables involved in the movement (see Figure 2b). I outline, instead, a schema account of them. After these separate analyses of exhalation, phonation, and articulation, I suggest how they may be coordinated during performance. The last two sections deal with the implications of schema theory for voice training and with the limitations of the approach.

EXHALATION

The lungs and the thoracic walls surrounding them are elastic. Because they are also linked together by adhesion of their respective pleural membranes, the elastic forces tending to expand the thoracic walls are counterbalanced by the elastic forces simultaneously tending to contract the lungs. The volume of this coupled system when its equilibrium is not disturbed by activity of the inspiratory or expiratory muscles is the resting level. Vital capacity is the sum of the maximum volume of air that can be inhaled above the resting level (inspiratory capacity) and the maximum volume that can be exhaled below it. Total lung volume is the sum of the vital capacity and the residual volume of air in the lungs that cannot be exhaled. Tidal volume is the total volume of air inhaled or exhaled during some respiratory activity.

The Movements Subserving Exhalation

During quiet breathing, tidal volume is about 15% of vital capacity. The individual typically inhales from resting level of about 40% of vital capacity up to a maximum inspiration level of about 55% of vital capacity and then exhales. The inhalation phase depends on active use of inspiratory muscles, but exhalation relies solely on elastic recoil. As these movements vary little from breath to breath, a simple motor program is adequate to produce them. Such a program is usually regarded as an internal representation of the procedures required to produce a movement sequence or cycle. It specifies the muscles that are to contract, the temporal phasing of the various contractions, and their relative strengths. Most authors (e.g., Keele and Summers, 1976) feel that movement under the control of a simple motor program cannot be modified on the basis of sensory input.

The greater the displacement of lung volume from resting level, the greater the elastic recoil forces. The subglottal pressure developed by these forces alone is known as the relaxation pressure and is related to lung volume as shown in Figure 3, so that, for example, if the lungs are first inflated to 80% of vital capacity, relaxation of all respiratory muscles then produces a subglottal pressure of about 40 cm H_2O. A curve of subglottal pressures developed at different lung volumes by elastic recoil forces supplemented by expiratory muscle forces would appear to the right of the one in Figure 3, and a curve of subglottal pressures developed by elastic recoil forces supplemented by inspiratory muscle forces would appear to its left.

One of the most important determinants of the loudness of speech or song is subglottal pressure. For conversation, this must be maintained between +6 cm H_2O and +10 cm H_2O. However, when speaking, an individual initially inhales to about 60% of vital capacity—a lung volume that would produce a relaxation pressure well above the required 6–10 cm H_2O. Hence, at the start of the breath group, inspiratory muscles are used to check these forces (see shaded area in Figure 4). Later in the breath group, as lung volume falls, participation of these muscles becomes less and less necessary, and eventually, it is eliminated. Later

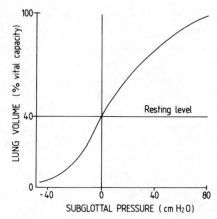

Figure 3.   Pressures developed as a function of lung volume when respiratory muscles are relaxed.

still, however, when lung volume decreases even further, relaxation alone becomes insufficient to produce the 6–10 cm H_2O pressure. The elastic recoil forces must then be supplemented by activity of expiratory muscles as shown in the stippled area in Figure 4 (Ladefoged, 1967). To complete a particularly long breath group, the individual may even continue to use expiratory muscles to bring lung volume below resting level to, say, 35% of vital capacity.

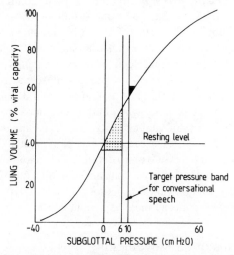

Figure 4.   Lung volume and pressure relationships during conversational speech. Initially, lung volume is high and inspiratory muscle checking (black area) is needed to keep pressure within target band. Towards the end of the breath group, expiratory muscle forces must supplement relaxation (stippled area) to ensure pressure remains within target band.

In conversational speech, tidal volume, maximum inspiration level, and the subglottal pressure representing the desired outcome of exhalation vary somewhat from breath group to breath group (Bouhuys, Proctor, and Mead, 1966). In singing, however, all these parameters show very considerable variation. The amount of air used for a breath group commonly varies between 20 and 50% of vital capacity, but phrases that are particularly long or require especially high air flows may use considerably more. Furthermore, although maximum inspiration level for many breath groups is very high, exhalation starts at quite low levels for some of them. This is because starting a second breath group at a lower maximum inspiration level than a first allows singers to minimise the inspiration time between the two breath groups. (Because of this variability in tidal volume and maximum inspiration level, virtually the whole vital capacity is in singing; Proctor, 1980). Finally, as a wide range of loudnesses is required in singing, the subglottal pressures that singers are required to produce also show considerable variation. Whereas the range used by speakers is restricted to the 6–10 cm H_2O mentioned, that employed by singers extends from about 5 cm H_2O for soft notes to 30 cm H_2O for loud and even 60 cm H_2O for very loud notes (Proctor, 1974). Furthermore, this increased range must not be attained at the expense of accuracy—quite the reverse.

Because of the variability in the maximum inspiration level (i.e., the initial condition from which exhalation starts) and in the required subglottal pressure (i.e., the desired outcome of exhalation), the muscle contractions required to exhale a particular tidal volume vary from breath group to breath group. This is illustrated in Figure 5. Figure 5a shows that exhaling 20% of vital capacity to produce a constant subglottal pressure of 15 cm H_2O requires a decreasing level of inspiratory muscle activity when exhalation starts at 90% of vital capacity, first inspiratory then expiratory muscle activity when exhalation starts at 65% of vital capacity and an increasing level of expiratory muscle activity when exhalation starts at 40% of vital capacity. Thus, the same required outcome necessitates different patterns of muscle activity when initial conditions are different. Figure 5b shows that exhaling 20% of vital capacity from a maximum inspiration level of 70% of vital capacity requires an increasing level of expiratory muscle activity when a constant subglottal pressure of 40 cm in H_2O is required, first inspiratory then expiratory muscle activity when a constant subglottal pressure of 20 cm H_2O is required and a decreasing level of inspiratory muscle activity when a constant subglottal pressure of 10 cm H_2O must be maintained.

Production of Exhalation Movements during Singing

It is clear from Figure 5 that the sort of simple motor program that would be adequate for producing exhalation in quiet breathing could not be expected to

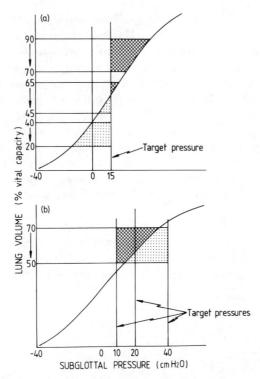

Figure 5.   Lung volume and pressure relationships during singing. Shaded areas show inspiratory muscle activity and stippled areas show expiratory muscle activity: (a) Breath groups starting from different maximum inspiration levels but requiring same target pressure; and (b) breath groups starting from the same maximum inspiration level but requiring different target pressures.

control exhalation for singing. The pattern of muscle contractions and, hence, the motor program would have to be different for every possible maximum inspiration level from which exhalation starts and for every possible subglottal pressure required. This means that a vast number of motor programs would have to be learnt and stored in the brain. It would also mean that singers would be able to sing only at the particular loudness for which they had received training. For other novel loudnesses, the appropriate motor program would not have been acquired, and hence, the appropriate pattern of muscle contractions could not be produced. These considerations lead to the conclusion that exhalation for singing is not controlled by a large set of separate simple motor programs.

One model of motor control that can account for the phenomena outlined (Figure 5) is Schmidt's (1975, 1982b) schema theory. Schmidt first argues that there are not separate motor programs stored for each of the movement variants observed in performance of a skill. Instead, a single generalised motor program produces the whole class of movements. However, parameters must be inserted into the program before it is executed. Different parameters produce the different movement variants. For example, these parameters could specify the initial levels of activity in inspiratory and expiratory muscles, together with their respective rates of change. Schmidt goes on to argue that, in learning a skill, individuals do not acquire separate sets of associations linking particular values of these parameters with particular initial conditions for each possible required outcome. Instead, they learn a rule or schema that relates the value of a continuously variable motor program parameter to continuously variable values that specify initial conditions and desired outcomes. Such a schema may be likened to an internalised multiple regression equation with a movement parameter as the dependent variable and initial conditions and desired outcomes as independent ones.

Figure 6a shows a hypothetical schema or rule relating a movement parameter (in this case, initial checking force exerted by inspiratory muscles) to movement outcome (i.e., subglottal pressure). In practice, the function is unlikely to be linear. This relationship between a movement parameter and desired outcome is

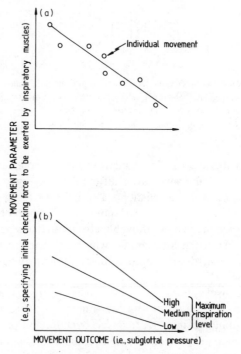

Figure 6. (a) Hypothetical parameter specification schema for exhalation; and (b) hypothetical parameter specification schema for exhalation showing dependence on maximum inspiration level.

expected to vary continuously with initial conditions (e.g., maximum inspiration level from which exhalation starts). In Figure 6b, the hypothetical relationship between initial inspiratory checking force and subglottal pressure is shown for three discrete maximum inspiration levels. Other exhalation parameters (e.g., rate of increase in force exerted by expiratory muscles) are related to desired outcome and initial conditions by similar schemata.

Maximum inspiration level from which exhalation starts was identified above as a particularly important initial-condition variable that affects the relationship between movement parameters and subglottal pressure. However, there are other variables that also affect this relationship. One such is the extent of resistance to airflow provided by articulatory and/or glottal constriction. Airflow increases and, without compensation, subglottal pressure drops when the vocal tract moves from a relatively constricted configuration (e.g., during frictive or stop production) to a relatively unconstricted one (e.g., during vowel production) or when the vocal cords decrease in tautness as pitch is lowered. However, as Warren (1976, 1982) points out, the level of airflow from the lungs does not appreciably affect subglottal pressure, because the respiratory muscles adjust the recoil forces to keep it constant. Thus, either planned articulatory and glottal changes must be entered into the exhalation schema as additional initial-condition variables, or else mechanisms sensing these changes are able to modify execution of the exhalation program.

As a regression rule, each schema should be viewed as a statistical relationship. That is to say that error variance ensures that any one exhalation a singer makes is unlikely to conform exactly to the rule. Sources of error variance include any aspects of the singer's body or environment that affect the relationship between movement parameters and desired subglottal pressure but that are not included with maximum inspiration level as initial-condition variables. Variations in bodily posture (Hixon, 1973), thoracic constriction by clothing (Proctor, 1980), and lung elasticity (e.g., after stage fright reduces tracheobronchial secretion) may be such factors. Because of this error variance, each exhalation produces a data point some distance away from the regression line derived from a whole set of such points (Figure 6a).

Within this framework, learning to sing must involve internalizing exhalation schemata. How is this done? Schmidt (1982a) argues that data points are stored for some brief period. In singing notes of different loudnesses, the novice singer uses different movement parameters that produce different subglottal pressures. Consequently, each one of these notes produces a separate data point. By some curve-fitting procedure, the individual extracts a preliminary schema from this initial set of data points. Once the schema has been extracted, the separate data points are lost from storage. However, each time the generalised exhalation program is executed, another new data point is produced. The point is used to make minor adjustments to the regression equation constants (e.g., the intercept and slope of the line in Figure 6a) but, once it has performed that function, it is not retained. The schema therefore becomes an increasingly accurate reflection of the underlying relationships among movement parameters, desired outcome, and initial conditions. The singer uses this rule, together with knowledge of the desired outcome and initial conditions, to identify the movement parameters to be inserted into the generalised exhalation program. This explains why practice enables the trained singer to control subglottal pressure with increasing precision. (With training, the singer may also identify more factors to be included as initial condition variables, thereby reducing the error variance associated with the schema.)

If schemata are to be acquired in this manner, individuals must be able to monitor both the initial conditions and the outcomes of their exhalation movements. Stretch-sensitive pulmonary mechanoreceptors may be expected to provide information concerning maximum inspired volume while vestibular and cutaneous receptors may provide information about the various other factors that could be included in the exhalation schema as additional initial-condition variables. Provision of an appropriate subglottal pressure head is the desired outcome of lung activity in singing. Wyke and Kirchner (1976) argue that subglottal mucosal mechanoreceptors provide information about this variable during singing.

The type of schema outlined allows the singer to specify movement parameters when desired movement outcome and initial conditions are known. I term it a "parameter specification schema." It serves to enable a singer to gain fine control over subglottal pressure. However, the singer must also ensure that the subglottal pressure head that is precisely produced in this way provides the particular sensory consequences (i.e., loudness) required by the music. For this, the performer needs to acquire two other types of rule, which I refer to as "outcome specification" and "sensation specification" schemata, respectively.

The outcome specification schema relates movement outcome (i.e., subglottal pressure) to the sensation of loudness experienced by the singer. Given that an individual knows the loudness he or she wishes to experience, it allows specification of the subglottal pressure that will produce that loudness. Figure 7a shows an outcome specification schema for exhalation, which is derived from individual data points in exactly the same manner as outlined for the parameter specification schema. (Again, it is most unlikely that any real schema would have the linear form shown in Figure 7). The point y on the ordinate indicates the subglottal pressure a singer must develop in order to experience a loudness level x.

Subglottal pressure is a major determinant of loudness. However, a number of factors may affect the precise nature of the relationship between these two variables. First, when articulators constrict the vocal tract, pressure builds up between the constriction and the glottis. This reduces pressure difference across the glottis so that vocal-fold vibration and, hence, emitted sound become less intense. This effect accounts for vowels involving considerable articulatory con-

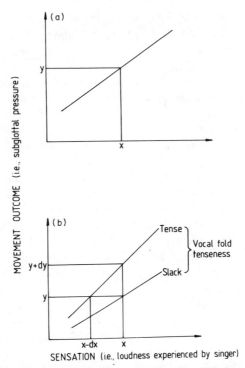

Figure 7. (a) Hypothetical outcome specification schema for exhalation; and (b) hyopthetical outcome specification schema for exhalation showing dependence on vocal cord tension.

striction (e.g., /i/ and /u/) being produced at an intensity 4–5 dB less than relatively open vowels (e.g., /a/) but with the same subglottal pressure. However, although degree of articulatory resistance to airflow affects the relationship between intensity and subglottal pressure, it does not appear to affect the one between loudness and subglottal pressure. This is because the auditory system appears to normalize differences that arise from this factor. An /i/ or /u/ that is 5 dB less intense than an /a/ is heard just as loud.

A second factor to be considered as one that may affect the relationship shown in Figure 7a is resistance to airflow (i.e., impedance) at the glottis. Higher notes are associated with greater glottal impedance because they are produced with tauter vocal cords. Because of this, a given subglottal pressure would produce a high-pitched note that is less intense than a low-pitched one. As there is no evidence that the auditory system normalises the loudness differences that would arise from this factor over the pitch ranges that are used in singing, it must be assumed that a soprano would hear her middle C as louder than her top C if she produced the two notes with the same subglottal pressure. Thus, vocal-fold tension should be treated as an initial condition for the outcome specification schema in just the same way that maximum inspiration level is treated as one in the parameter specification schema depicted in Figure 6b. It may be seen from Figure 7b that a subglottal pressure of y that produces a loudness level of x with relatively slack vocal cords only succeeds in producing a loudness level of $x - dx$ with tenser ones. To maintain a loudness level of x as vocal-fold tension increases, the singer has to increase subglottal pressure from y to $y + dy$. Both stretch-sensitive mechanoreceptors (i.e., spiral nerve endings and a few muscle spindles) and tendon organs are present in the intrinsic laryngeal musculature (Wyke and Kirchner, 1976), so means for monitoring overall vocal-fold tension does exist.

Another factor known to affect the relationship between one's own vocal loudness and subglottal pressure is level of background auditory stimulation. At a given intensity, one judges one's own voice as quieter when background noise level is higher. The Lombard effect is the classic demonstration of this. It occurs when an experimenter increases the intensity of a sound that a vocalizing individual is hearing through headphones. Observers, unable to hear the background sound, notice the performer's voice increase in loudness. The performer, in contrast, remains unaware of this increase. Of course, normally, a subglottal pressure increase such as this is adaptive. The vocal intensity increase resulting from it would stop the voice becoming inaudible to listeners as background sound level increased. Consequently, it would enable individuals in the same acoustic environment (unlike the performer and the observer in the demonstration) to communicate with one another at their preferred loudness level. Because singers are usually closer to instrumental accompaniment than listeners, they are normally in a slightly different acoustic environment from their audience and may, therefore, have to learn to modify the Lombard effect. Certainly, background sound level is a candidate for an additional initial-condition variable in the outcome specification schema.

Together, acquisition of the appropriate parameter and outcome specification schemata enables an individual to sing so as to experience the particular loudness he or she desires. This would be all that is necessary if the singer is performing solely for himself or herself. However, when performance is for the benefit of an audience, the singer must ensure that his or her own sensation of loudness is associated with listeners' sensations of loudness that are appropriate to the music. Acquisition of a sensation specification schema allows this to be done. Such a schema relates the sensation of loudness experienced by the singer to listeners' reports of the musical appropriateness of the loudness they experience. (It is the role of expert listeners, such as conductors or voice coaches, to provide these reports.) Figure 8a shows a hypothetical sensation specification schema for exhalation that is derived from individual data points in the same manner as outlined for the parameter specification schema. Point y specifies the loudness at which the singer must experience his or her voice for an expert listener to report

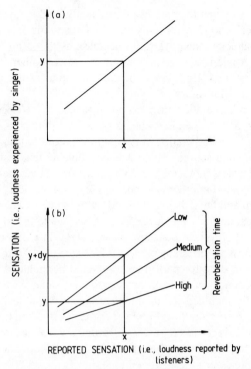

Figure 8. (a) Hypothetical sensation specification schema for exhalation; and (b) hypothetical sensation specification schema for exhalation showing dependence on room acoustics.

that the audience would hear the sung note at a loudness (x) appropriate to the music.

Certain factors are expected to affect the nature of the relationship between the loudness of a note as experienced by its singer and the loudness of the same note as reported by expert listeners in the audience. Prominent among these factors are the acoustic features of the room used for the performance. Reverberant sound reinforces direct sound and adds to overall loudness. Loudness of direct sound decreases as the distance between the sound source (i.e., the singer) and the listener increases. Reverberant sound level, however, is the same throughout the room. For a given sound source, it depends on the room's reverberation time. This is higher in higher volume rooms and in rooms with surfaces having lower absorption characteristics. Because the listener is farther from the sound source than the singer, reverberant sound contributes relatively more (and direct sound correspondingly less) to overall loudness for the listener than for the singer. Therefore, notes that are sung in rooms of different sizes so that they are heard equally loud by the singer would be heard by a listener as louder in larger rooms. Similarly, notes sung in rooms with surfaces of different absorption characteristics in such a way that they are heard as equally loud by the singer would be heard by a listener as louder in rooms with less absorbing surfaces. (Typically, the absorption characteristics of a room decrease as the size of the audience it contains drops). Air temperature and humidity are two other factors known to affect reverberation time. Both would be expected to influence the nature of the relationship depicted in Figure 8a.

Differences in reverberation time do not just lead to two performances perceived as equally loud by the singer being heard by listeners as having different overall loudnesses. Reverberation time of an auditorium usually varies with frequency of the sound source. Thus, it is conceivable that a singer could produce a high and a low note in one auditorium and have them perceived by listeners as equally loud but then produce them again in an identical manner in a second auditorium and have them perceived by the same listeners as differing in loudness. It is most unlikely that an expert listener would modify the criteria for what is musically appropriate to accommodate such venue-dependent changes in the relative loudness of different pitches. Consequently, reverberation characteristics of the room used for performances should be included as initial conditions in the sensation specification schema in the same way that maximum-inspiration level is included as an initial-condition variable in the parameter specification schema (Figure 6b). Figure 8b indicates how the loudness of a note as experienced by a singer has to increase from y to $y + dy$ as reverberation time decreases from a high to a low value in order to maintain loudness of the note as experienced by a listener at x.

I have argued that a singer has to internalize three different types of rule in order to be able to sing each of the notes in a piece of music at the appropriate loudness. However, this is not to suggest that these rules or schemata are actively used *during* the performance of a highly rehearsed piece. Ideally, training the voice, practice on a particular composition, and rehearsal in a particular auditorium should enable a singer to acquire and use the schemata. Thus, the parameters of the generalised motor program for exhalation can be specified for each breath group prior to performance. During the performance itself, the appropriate parameters are retrieved from store prior to each breath group and inserted into the program. During execution of the program, the only adaptive mechanisms to operate are reflex systems that ensure that the muscular changes specified by the movement parameters are carried out despite fluctuations in the condition of the environment or body (.e.g, due to fatigue). However, all performance is monitored by feedback processes. As this monitoring adds new data points that are incorporated into the schemata, it causes slight changes in the parameters inserted into the program for future performances. Figure 9 summarises how schemata are used to insert parameters into the exhalation program prior to a breath group (solid lines), how the exhalation program is then executed (double lines), and how schemata are modified in response to feedback arising from its execution (dotted lines).

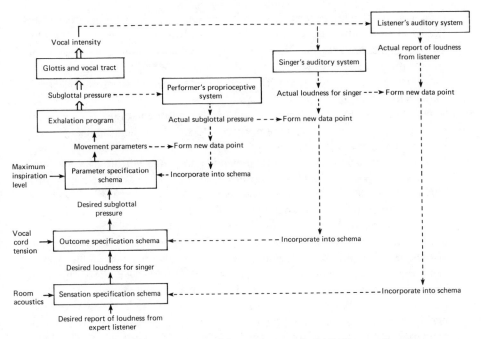

Figure 9.   Use of exhalation schemata prior to performance (solid lines); execution of program during performance (double lines); and modification of each schema in response to feedback (dotted lines).

Figure 9 shows how feedback processes are used to form new data points for schemata. They are obtained from various combinations of the movement parameters used, feedback of various types, and the initial conditions present when exhalation occurred. However, it is important to stress that feedback can have another role quite separate from provision of new data points for schemata and not depicted in Figure 9. By comparing the feedback concerning the actual value of some feature (e.g., loudness) with the desired value of that feature, the singer can determine whether an error has been made (i.e., the note was too loud or too soft). This type of error monitoring occurs after the program has been executed. However, it should be mentioned that reviews of work on motor control (e.g., Harvey and Greer, 1980; Kelso and Stelmach, 1976) include much discussion about whether this type of error monitoring can be used *during* program execution to modify ongoing movement. It is possible that the difference between the actual and desired value of some feature can be used to adjust the values of the parameters in the motor program while it is running. For instance, determination that loudness is greater than intended would result in an increase in the force exerted by inspiratory muscles (or a decrease in the force exerted by expiratory ones). Schmidt (1982a, 1982b) argues that error-based modification of motor program parameters during movement execution would be possible only for slow movements and that, even then, there is evidence that it does not take place (Kelso, 1977; Kelso and Stelmach, 1976; see also Howell, Chapter 11, this volume). According to this view, a singer would use only such closed-loop control for production of long sustained notes. (See Abbs and Kennedy, 1982, for a review of the role of feedback in the ongoing control of speech movements.)

What sort of practice and training does a singer require in order to acquire and use the schemata depicted in Figure 9? (By "acquiring" the schemata, I mean storing them in memory. By "using" them, I mean employing them to specify the movement parameters for each breath group in the performance of some particular composition in some particular room.)

Acquisition of schemata depends on acquisition of new data points. Because the factors included as initial-condition variables are different for each of the three types of schemata, the types of experience leading to new data points are also different for each of them. Practising singing notes to produce different subglottal pressures from different maximum inspiration levels contributes to the parameter specification schema. Practising using these different subglottal pressures under different conditions of vocal-fold tension so that the singer experiences different loudnesses contributes to the outcome specification schema. Finally, practising singing these different loudnesses in different venues so that different reports of loudness from expert listeners are produced contributes to the sensation specification schema. Thus, both the parameter and outcome specification schema can be acquired largely on the basis of vocal exercises that require notes of different intensities to be sung at different pitches from different maximum inspiration levels. Acquisition of the sensation specification schema further requires that these exercises take place with a coach in various different rooms.

It should be clear from Figures 6, 7, and 8 that if data points are all tightly clustered together, there is little certainty about the overall slope, shape, or position of the function. A rule or schema extracted from highly clustered data is weaker than one extracted from data spread throughout the range of the function. The more variety present in the exercises, the stronger the resulting schemata are. So, for optimum acquisition of exhalation schemata, it is important to include as many combinations as possible of maximum inspiration levels, loudnesses, pitches, and performance venues. (This prediction from schema theory concerning variability of practice has now been subjected to experiental test for a variety of different motor skills. Shapiro and Schmidt, 1982, have reviewed this work).

Use of exhalation schemata involves input of a desired report of loudness. Even if no actual reports from listeners are received after the performance, a desired report can still be input into the sensation specification schema. However, no errors in its use would be detected, and it could not be modified after performance. Use of the exhalation schemata must also involve input of the initial conditions for each one. The parameter specification schema requires input of the maximum inspiration level, which would depend on phrasing of breath groups and tempo. The outcome specification schema requires input of vocal-cord tension, which depends on the pitch of the note to be produced. Knowledge of these factors must be acquired from study and rehearsal of the particular composition to be performed. The sensation specification schema requires input of room reverberation time, which depends both on pitch of the note to be produced and on physical features of the auditorium. Knowledge of the factors relating to room reverberation must be acquired from study of and rehearsal in the room to be used for performance. So, in order to make full use of the schemata, the singer must learn about the musical features of a particular song and about the acoustic features of the particular auditorium in which it is to be performed.

A final issue concerns *when* the exhalation schemata are used. It is possible that during practice and rehearsal, the singer has been able to use the schemata to specify the exhalation movement parameters for all breath groups in the composition. These can then be retrieved from long-term memory and placed in working memory prior to the start of performance. During each inhalation within the performance, the parameters for the next breath group can be entered from working memory into the generalised exhalation program for immediate execution. However, there is a problem with this scenario: It does not allow flexibility within and across performances. Singers would not be able to respond to changes in initial-condition variables. (For instance, tempo may vary slightly from one performance to another—perhaps because a solo singer's accompanist changes. Alternatively, a change in size of the audience may affect room reverberation time.) Thus, it seems much more likely that practice and rehearsal are used to gain knowledge about initial-condition variables and that it is this information that is stored in long-term memory. It is then brought into working memory prior to performance, but modified slightly there if conditions on a particular occasion demand such adjustment. During inhalation prior to a breath group (or perhaps prior to small group of breath groups), this information, together with the desired report of loudness, is used as input into the exhalation schemata in order to specify movement parameters. These would then be fed into the genealized exhalation program for execution.

PHONATION

Borden and Harris (1980) succinctly describe the vocal folds as follows:

> The vocal folds are shelf-like elastic protuberances of tendon, muscles and mucous membrane which lie behind the 'Adam's apple' or thyroid cartilage and run in an anterior–posterior direction. Their tension and elasticity can be varied; they can be made thicker or thinner, shorter or longer, they can be opened wide, closed together, or put into

intermediate positions and they can be elevated or depressed in their vertical relationship
to the cavities above (p. 74).

When the vocal folds are apart (abducted), airflow through them is noiseless.
When they are placed together (adducted) tightly, no air flows through them, and
so, again, they produce no sound. However, when they are adducted less tightly
and subglottal pressure is sufficient to open and close them periodically, sound
results and is heard as voice.

The Movements Subserving Phonation

Perceived pitch of the voice depends largely on the frequency (F) with which
the vocal folds release puffs of air into the vocal tract. This can be expressed by
the equation $F = C\sqrt{K/M}$ (Proctor, 1980). C includes the resting dimensions of
the vibrating folds and the subglottal pressure to which they are subjected. K is
an elastic factor combining the natural elasticity of the folds with any added
elasticity. Added elasticity depends on the tone of the muscle (i.e., vocalis)
within the vocal folds and/or any stretching of the folds beyond their resting
dimensions. Muscles inside the larynx (i.e., intrinsic laryngeal muscles) can
stretch the folds longitudinally, whereas muscles affecting the height of the
larynx in the throat (i.e., extrinsic laryngeal muscles) can stretch the folds
vertically (Ohala, 1972, 1977). M is the mass per unit length of the folds. It can
be reduced by contraction of muscles (e.g., the cricothyroid) that lengthen the
folds and increased either by relaxation of these same muscles or by isotonic
contraction of the vocalis (Harvey and Howell, 1980).

Clearly, frequency of vocal fold vibration can be altered in a variety of different ways. For instance, it can be increased by co-contracting the vocalis and
cricothyroid so that the folds become more tense without any change in their
length; by raising the larynx in the throat so that the folds are tensed vertically; by
isotonic contraction of the cricothyroid (and/or certain other muscles) so that the
folds become longer, thinner, and tenser; by increasing subglottal pressure; or by
using the adductory muscles to increase medial compression of parts of the folds
so that the resting dimensions of the part of them that is free to vibrate are
decreased (Broad, 1973). Recent research has been devoted to investigating just
how frequency of vocal-fold vibration is actually altered. Although much work
remains to be done, certain generalisations can now be made with some degree of
confidence.

First, although subglottal pressure can affect F, individuals do not appear to
use it to control F. This is the subject of a review by Ohala (1978) so is not be
discussed in detail here. However, it is worth mentioning that findings show that
laryngeal paralysis produces defects in pitch regulation (Critchley and Kubik,
1925) but pulmonary paralysis does not (Peterson, 1958).

A second generalisation is that the means by which the larynx maintains or changes F depends on whether F is high, low, or in-between. Because the larynx is used in slightly different ways at different pitches, there are also differences in the harmonic spectra associated with pressure pulses resulting from phonation at those pitches. These differences in harmonic spectra are perceived as differences in vocal quality and referred to as differences in vocal register (Colton, 1973; Colton and Hollien, 1973). Thus, the different ways of using the larynx at different levels of F can be thought of as physiological correlates of vocal register. As a singer moves from the lowest to the highest note that can be produced, the voice shifts from register to register. However, the point at which a different way of increasing F comes into play is not fixed at a particular value of F but extends over a small range of F's. This overlap allows trained singers to phase out one means of changing F while phasing another in and, therefore, to switch from register to register in a smooth manner (Large, 1973; Russo and Large, 1978). This process of eliminating the perceptual demarcation line between registers is known as register-equalization.

The number of perceptually distinguishable registers and the details of their physiological and acoustical correlates are still the subject of debate. Although some authors hold that there are as many as seven registers, most are content with identifying just two (Vennard, 1967) or three (Folkins and Kuehn, 1982; Hollien, 1974; Marchesi, 1970). Hollien (1974) argues that a low frequency or pulse register is used to produce sounds below about 50 Hz. Within it, the vocal folds are short, thick, compliant, and highly medially compressed. Furthermore, x-rays have shown that the ventricular folds may be lowered onto the true vocal folds to add to their vibratory mass. As pitch is changed within this register, there appears to be no alteration in the length of the vocal folds (Allen and Hollien, 1973). During phonation, air leaks through the folds at irregular intervals. Such variability in the period of vocal pulses is known as "jitter" and is correlated with a perception of vocal roughness. This coarse quality of the voice in pulse register is sometimes known as "vocal fry" and may be one of the reasons that involvement of the pulse register in singing is restricted to certain specialized styles such as Tibetan chant (Large and Murray, 1981). The mid-frequency or model register is the chest voice that is used for speech and virtually all bass and contralto song. A wide range of frequencies (over one and a half octaves) and intensities (40–100 dB) can be produced. A rich spectrum of harmonics spanning over four octaves is present and jitter, low when the modal register is used for speech, is even lower when it is used for singing (Murray, Large, and Dalgaard, 1979). In this register, the whole of the vocal folds vibrate and most investigators have found that changing pitch is accompanied by a change in their length (Damaste, Hollien, Moore, and Murphy, 1968; Hollien, 1960; Hollien and Moore, 1960; Sonninen, 1954) and thickness (Hollien, 1962; Hollien and Colton, 1969; Hollien and Curtis, 1969). The high-frequency or loft register corresponds to falsetto voice. The range of intensities is lower than in modal register and the harmonic spectrum is not as rich (Russo and Large, 1978). Pitch change does not appear to involve an alteration in the length of the vocal cords. However, in loft register, all dimensions (lateral width, vertical thickness, and anterior–posterior length) of those portions of the vocal folds that are free to vibrate are smaller than they are in modal register and pitch may be increased by reducing them still further.

Mechanisms of pitch change (and, hence, the vocal registers to which they give rise) vary between untrained and trained singers and between trained singers performing in different styles. Untrained singers use vertical movement of the larynx in the production of pitch change. Trained singers, in contrast, tend to keep their larynx in a constant lower-than-normal position and to restrict their means of producing pitch change to mechanisms intrinsic to the larynx (Shipp, 1977; Shipp and Izdebski, 1975). This has the effect of maintaining the vocal tract at constant length and, therefore, of minimising source–tract interactions that would cause pitch-dependent vowel distortion (Izdebski and Shipp, 1979). It does, however, appear to be responsible for the appearance of the 'singer's formant' and the consequent change in vowel quality that generally distinguishes sung vowels from spoken ones (Sundberg, 1974).

Although all trained singers seem to use mechanisms intrinsic to the larynx to produce pitch change, the particular ones they employ depend on the style of singing they have been trained to adopt. For instance, in bel canto, high notes are produced in falsetto, and so equalization between loft and modal registers is necessary at some point in the pitch range (Russo and Large, 1978). In operatic singing, however, the highest notes are produced in a chest-related voice (called operatic head voice) by a mechanism that seems little different from the one used to produce lower notes (Large, Baird and Jenkins, 1980; Large, Iwata, and von Leden, 1972).

Production of Phonation Movements during Singing

It is clear that a variety of laryngeal mechanisms can be used to maintain and change the frequency with which air puffs are released into the vocal tract. However, following Schmidt (1975, 1982a), it can be maintained that the whole class of possible laryngeal configurations used for phonation is produced by a single generalised motor program operating in a manner similar to the generalised exhalation program outlined previously. Again, parameters would have to be inserted into the program before it was executed and differences in the parameters would produce differences in the laryngeal configuration resulting from execution. Parameters would, for example, specify the levels of activity in the various laryngeal muscles, together with their respective rates of change. Param-

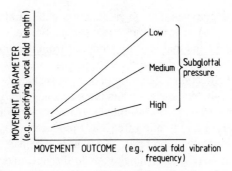

Figure 10.   Hypothetical parameter specification schema for phonation showing dependence on subglottal pressure.

eters inserted into the program would be derived from a parameter-specification schema. Such a schema is shown in Figure 10. It relates the continuously variable motor program parameters to the vocal-fold vibration frequency (*F*) desired as the outcome of phonation. (A singer able to sing in different styles would have a parameter specification schema for each one.)

Certain factors expected to affect the nature of the relationship between phonation parameters and the desired *F* would be included in the schema as initial conditions. Subglottal pressure is one such factor (Figure 10) because, although not used to control *F*, it does affect *F*. Studies in which care was taken to ensure vocal-cord configuration remained constant have shown that *F* increases by 2–5 Hz for every cm H$_2$O increase in subglottal pressure (see Ohala, 1978, for a review of this work). It is as a consequence of this that ''during a crescendo (produced by a rising subglottal pressure) the frequency of vibration would rise (and with it the perceived pitch of the voice) unless internal adjustment of elastic forces in the folds has occurred proportionately'' (Proctor, 1980, p. 58). This internal adjustment, enabling subglottal pressure and *F* to be altered independently of one another, is felt to be a hallmark of the trained singing voice (Daniloff, Schuckers, and Feth, 1980). Borden and Harris, (1980) suggest that it involves relaxation of the cricothyroid and, perhaps, vocalis muscles.

For a parameter specification schema for phonation to be acquired, singers must be able to monitor subglottal pressure and frequency of vocal-fold vibration. Wyke and Kirchner's (1976) view that subglottal mucosal mechanoreceptors provide feedback about subglottal pressure has already been mentioned. However, they also point out that the laryngeal mucosa contains glomerular, corpuscular nerve endings embedded in the submucosa. These receptors, which they suggest function as low-threshold mechanoreceptors, are well placed to provide feedback about vocal-fold movement during phonation and, hence, about its frequency. Proctor (1980) anaesthetized his own laryngeal mucosa and reported that, although he could talk intelligibly, he could no longer sing in an acceptable fashion. He argues that, in conjunction with similar experiments by Gould and Tanabe (1975), this signifies "that some more delicate control is used for singing than talking and that sensory feedback from the mucosa of the vocal folds is part of that control" (Proctor, 1980, p. 60).

The parameter specification schema for phonation enables the singer to specify laryngeal muscle activity parameters when the frequency of vocal-fold vibration desired as an outcome of phonation is known. However, the singer must be able to ensure that this laryngeal vibration frequency produces a sensation of pitch in the listener that is musically appropriate. Two more schemata must be acquired for this purpose. They are directly analogous to the outcome specification and sensation specification schemata described previously for exhalation. The outcome specification schema for phonation relates movement outcome (i.e., frequency of vocal-fold vibration) to the sensation of pitch experienced by the phonating individual. Given that the singer knows the pitch he or she wishes to experience, it allows specification of the vocal-fold vibration frequency that will produce that pitch. It is, in other words, the singer's internalized, psychophysical scaling of the subjective pitch of his or her voice against frequency of vibration of his or her vocal folds. It would be acquired from individual data points in the same manner as has been outlined for other schemata.

Factors affecting the nature of the relationship between a singer's perception of his or her own vocal pitch and vocal-fold vibration frequency would be included as initial conditions in the outcome specification schema. While few studies of such factors have been made, it is known that the pitch of a pure tone of given frequency depends on its sound level (Stevens, 1935). It should be noted, however, that the effect is considerably smaller than Stevens originally reported (Terhardt, 1979), that it is subject to variation across individuals (Ward, 1970), and that it has not been demonstrated for sounds produced by the subject making the psychophysical judgement. Pitch and other features of background sound are also candidates for initial-condition variables in this type of schema. Sapir, McClean, and Larson (1983) show that input of an auditory stimulus via headphones can alter the vocal-fold vibration frequency of phonating individuals. This phenomenon can be ascribed to a process of acoustic automonitoring and may be akin to the Lombard effect. Like that effect, it may be normally adaptive but, because of differences in the acoustic environment of performer and audience, may need to be modified by trained singers. According to Wyke and Kircher (1976), "In untrained speakers, the acoustic automonitoring process is largely unconscious (that is to say, it is reflex): but in trained speakers, actors and singers deliberate voluntary control of phonation of a high order of precision in response to acoustic automonitoring may be acquired by practice" (p. 564).

Acquisition of parameter specification and outcome specification schemata for phonation allows a performer to sing so as to experience the particular pitch he or she desires. However, when performance is for the benefit of an audience, the singer must ensure that this pitch is associated with listeners' sensations of pitch that are appropriate to the music. Acquisition of a sensation specification schema for phonation allows this to be done. This schema relates the singer's sensations of pitch to listeners' reports of their sensations of pitch of the same notes. Pitch sensations of singers and listeners are based on quite different auditory information. The singer's ear receives sound by both bone conduction and air conduction, but the listener receives the same sound by air conduction alone. The frequency of vocal-fold vibration is the fundamental frequency (F_0) of the sound generated at the level of the larynx. F_0 is the determinant of the pitch of a complex sound and is well represented in the spectrum of bone-conducted voice. Singers are thus able to perceive the pitch of their own voices—an ability crucial to the acquisition and use of phonation schemata.

In contrast to this, F_0 is weak relative to harmonics or even completely absent in air-conducted voice. However, listeners still report a sensation of pitch in the signal. They must use the information remaining in it to extract the pitch that would be perceived if the missing fundamental (Licklider, 1956) were present. Terhardt (1974) refers to this extracted pitch as virtual pitch and suggests that it is derived from the spacing of the remaining harmonics in the signal. Extraction appears to make use of the fact that the missing fundamental is given by the lowest common factor in the frequencies of these harmonics. (This is because partials must be harmonically related in order to contribute to virtual pitch.)

Because virtual pitch is extracted only when the missing fundamental lies within the frequency range of the human voice, Terhardt (1974) proposes that it depends on a learning process that takes place early in life and that relies on listening to the human voice. Fortuyn and Ritsma (1979) argue that this process is actually one of listening to one's own voice. Because this signal contains both the fundamental and harmonics that are spaced in such a way as to imply that fundamental, it can be used as a basis for forming an internal representation of the relationship between these two types of information. That this internal representation is a schema or rule rather than a set of stored associations between particular fundamentals and the resulting spacings of their harmonics is shown by the fact that people can extract virtual pitch from voices outside their own vocal range. Only a rule allows such extrapolation from experience. It is this schema— the sensation specification scheme for phonation—that allows the singer to produce a desired virtual pitch in the listener (and also, of course, to extract virtual pitch from notes produced by others).

Certain variables may affect the relationship between the fundamental present in the bone-conducted sound heard by the singer and harmonics in the air-conducted sound heard by an audience. For instance, anti-resonances (or "zeros" in filter terminology) present in the vocal tract may remove certain harmonics in such a way that the lowest common factor in the frequencies of the remaining ones is altered. To allow for this, filter characteristics of the vocal tract could be included as initial-condition variables in the schema. For sustained phonation, these characteristics reflect the vowel sound being produced.

Although the schema appears to be acquired early in life as Terhardt (1974) and Fortuyn and Ritsma (1979) suggest, there is no reason to suppose that it cannot be further refined in later life. (In fact, as the vocal-tract shape corresponding to a particular vowel when sung is different from that corresponding to the same vowel when spoken, inclusion of vowel-tract characteristics as initial-condition variables would necessitate refinement of the schema during acquistion of singing skills.) Schema modification would occur in the same manner as was outlined previously for exhalation schemata (Figure 9). Vocal exercises producing many data points across the widest possible range of pitches and vocal-tract shapes would provide the high-variability practice that an optimum strategy for schema refinement requires (see p. 304).

Figure 11 summarises how the three schemata just outlined are used to insert parameters into the phonation program prior to a breath group (solid lines), how

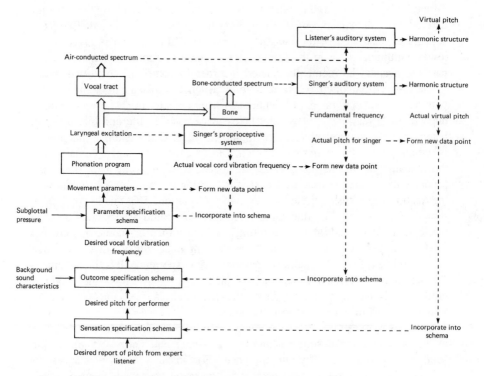

Figure 11. Use of phonation schemata prior to performance (solid lines), execution of program during performance (double lines), and modification of each schema after performance in response to feedback (dotted lines).

this program is then executed (double lines), and how the schemata are modified in response to feedback arising from execution (dotted lines). Considerations concerning error monitoring and conditions for acquisition and use of schemata are similar to those previously outlined for exhalation.

ARTICULATION OF VOWELS

The articulators (tongue, palate, lips, jaw, and pharynx), modify the shape, and hence, the resonant properties of the vocal tract. The different acoustic properties of the different vowels arise because each vowel is characterised by its own particular set of vocal-tract resonances and anti-resonances. Consequently, by altering the relative emphasis given to the harmonics in the glottal source spectrum, changes in articulator position can result in a change in the vowel that is produced.

The Movements Subserving Vowel Articulation

Vocal tract resonances or formants are labelled from the lower end of the frequency spectrum. Thus, the lowest formant is shown as F_1, the next as F_2, and so on. Although the particular frequency location of each one should be regarded as arising from the shape of the vocal tract as a whole, certain articulatory changes tend to be associated with movement of particular formants. Jaw lowering tends to increase the size of the constriction between tongue and palate, thereby increasing F_1. As a result of this, the F_1 of close or high vowels (e.g., /i/) is lower than that of the open or low vowels (e.g., /æ/). As the position of maximum contraction between tongue and palate moves forward, F_2 tends to rise. Thus, this formant becomes progressively higher as the vowel is changed from /æ/ through /ɛ/, /e/, and /ʊ/ to /i/. Both F_1 and F_2 tend to decrease in frequency as lip protrustions and/or larynx lowering increases overall vocal-tract length. Thus, they become progressively lower as the vowel is changed from /æ/ through /ɔ/ and /o/ to /u/. Nasalization, produced by lowering the soft palate and thereby opening the velopharyngeal port, results in a shift of vowel formants upwards and introduces anti-resonances and high-frequency damping into the spectra.

Production of Vowel Articulation
Movements during Singing

How are different vocal-tract shapes produced? If the movement parameters inserted into the generalized articulation program specify the forces to be exerted by the various articulator muscles, then those needed to produce a particular vocal-tract shape have to depend on the vocal-tract shape from which movement starts—to produce an /ɛ/ shape, the tongue is moved down from an /i/ shape, but up from an /æ/ shape. It is, of course, possible that the parameter specification schema for desired vocal tract shape includes current vocal-tract shape as an initial-condition variable. However, various other solutions to this problem of motor equivalence have been proposed. These have been reviewed by Howell and Harvey (1983), and so only two of the more important ones are discussed here. According to one view (MacNeilage, 1970), desired vocal-tract shape is first transformed into a set of desired muscle lengths. Because of the compensatory action of the alpha–gamma feedback system, commands for muscles to reach particular lengths are independent of their current lengths. Fowler, Rubin, Remez, and Turvey (1980) take a different approach. They view the articulators and their associated muscles as mass-spring systems. In contrast to MacNeilage (1970), they argue that the information sent to these muscles specifies new, unstretched lengths for them and that such speicfication enables desired muscle lengths (and hence, vocal-tract shapes) to be produced independent of current muscle lengths and without the use of feedback. The nature of the parameters inserted into motor programs has been discussed recently by Stein (1982) and is not pursued further here. For present purposes, what is important is that both MacNeilage's (1970) and Fowler et al.'s (1980) schemes allow specification of the movement parameters required to produce desired vocal-tract dimensions without the need to include current vocal-tract dimensions as initial condition variables.

Even within the framework adopted by Fowler et al. (1980), there are certain factors that must be included within the articulatory parameter specification schema as initial-condition variables. To examine these factors, it is worthwhile considering their notions in a little more detail. They argue that the parameter specification rule or schema is given by an equation like that of a vibratory system, such as that of a linear spring $F = -s(l - l_0)$. Here l_0 is the length of a spring when there are no forces acting on it, l is its current length, s is a stiffness parameter, and F is the force developed by the spring. The behaviour of a real spring is governed totally by the external forces $(-F)$ acting on it. In contrast to actual springs, muscle-system springs incorporate internal controls and are therefore not governed solely by the value of $-F$. In particular, the parameters l_0 and s can be altered. The importance of this can be seen by rewriting the equation as $l_0 = l + (F/s)$ and then representing it in a manner analogous to that previously employed for parameter specification schemata (Figure 12).

Figure 12 indicates that the equation for a linear spring is one possible parameter specification schema that enables a performer to specify the movement parameter, l_0, that must be inserted into a generalized motor program to produce a desired outcome (i.e., muscle length, l), given that a particular initial condition, F, is present. In other words, if Fowler et al.'s (1980) framework is

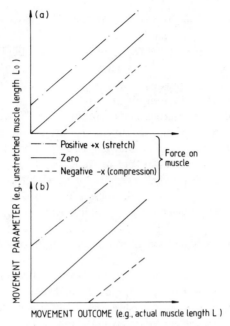

Figure 12.   Hypothetical parameter specification schema for vowel articulation showing dependence on force on muscles: (a) muscle stiffness high; and (b) muscle stiffness low.

adopted, the factors to be regarded as initial-condition variables within the parameter specification schema are the various forces acting on the articulator muscles in question. These forces have both external (e.g., gravitational) and internal (e.g., aerodynamic) origins. Forces due to gravity may vary because of changes in the bodily orientation of the individual. Lowering the velum to produce nasal sounds is aided by gravity when a singer is in a normal upright position but is not facilitated in this way when the performer's head is in a horizontal position. The l_0 parameters inserted into a generalised articulation program to produce nasalization by shortening the palatoglossus and palatopharyngeus (i.e., velar-lowering) muscles have to increase in value as the performer's head moved away from the upright position. Changes in supraglottal pressure also alter the resultant forces acting on various articulators (e.g., the velum and the tongue during retroflection). Thus, changes in this variable alter the l_0's required to produce the desired muscle lengths corresponding to the desired vocal-tract shape. Therefore, it should also be included as an initial-condition variable in the parameter specification schema for articulation.

The two panels of Figure 12 show the parameter specification schema when the stiffness parameter, s, is set at high (Figure 12a) and low (Figure 12b) values. It may be seen that the effect of the initial-condition variable, F, is scaled by the stiffness parameter, s. Specifically, the effect of F in altering the values of l_0 that must be specified to reach a desired l is reduced as s is increased. Why would a performer wish to control the stiffness of his or her articulatory muscles? One reason is to produce different frequencies of vibration of articulators. We have already seen how the frequency of vibration of the vocal cords depends on their stiffness. Frequency of vibration ·of the tongue during a trilled /r/ depends on stiffness in a similar way (Hardcastle, 1976; Harvey and Greer, 1982). Specification of tongue-muscle stiffness parameters to produce a trill at some desired frequency have to include supraglottal pressure as an initial-condition variable. As singers operate over a much greater range of supraglottal pressures than speakers, they have to learn to alter tongue stiffness over a much greater range to produce a trill of given frequency. Stiffness control also appears to be important in production of the lip movement involved in release of bilabial stop consonants (Sussman, MacNeilage, and Hansan, 1973). However, within Fowler et al.'s (1980) framework, it is not part of the mechanism of vowel articulation under consideration here.

The parameter specification schema for vowel articulation ensures that the articulators are positioned so as to produce the desired vocal-tract dimensions. However, the singer must also ensure that these dimensions are the ones that produce perception of the appropriate sound in the listener. Two more schemata must be acquired for this purpose. They are analogous to the outcome specification and sensation specification schemata previously described for exhalation and phonation. The outcome specification schema for vowel articulation relates movement outcome (i.e., a set of vocal-tract dimensions) to the formant frequencies of the vowel perceived by the singer. Consequently, given that the performer knows the vowel that he or she wishes to experience, it allows specification of the vocal-tract dimensions that will produce that vowel.

As noted previously, changes in vocal-tract dimensions produce changes in formant positions. Differences in formant positions are thus indicative of differences in vocal-tract dimensions. Studies by Sundberg (1975) on a trained singer and by Howell (1980) on untrained ones have demonstrated that vowel-formant frequencies change with the pitch at which the vowel is sung. Hence, the outcome specification schema relating the singer's vocal-tract dimensions to the formant positions of the vowel that he or she perceives includes pitch as an initial-condition variable (Figure 13). Sundberg (1982b) argues that this pitch-dependent articulation of vowels arises when fundamental frequency of the singing voice is higher than the F_0 of the spoken vowel. In these circumstances, information concerning F_1 would not be transmitted in song if the position it has in speech were to be retained. This would result in misinterpretation of F_2 as F_1, leading to the vowel sounding like one other than intended. To avoid this possibility, F_1 is raised to a frequency close to that of the fundamental. The increased jaw opening used to accomplish this also results in some (smaller)

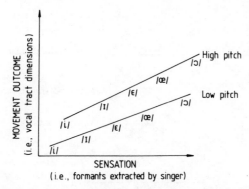

Figure 13. Hypothetical outcome specification schema for vowel articulation showing dependence on pitch for various vowels. In this example, movement outcome is a set of muscle lengths associated with jaw opening and the sensation is that associated with F_1.

changes in the position of other formants. Although the maneuvre allows F_1 to be transmitted in the signal, it also leads to an increasing similarity between the first and, to some extent, second formants of the various vowels as pitch increases. This, in turn, leads to decreasing discriminability between the vowels (Stumpf, 1926). However, Sundberg (1977) has shown that the reduction in discriminability is even more severe without pitch-contingent formant change.

The sensation specification schema for vowel articulation relates the formant frequencies of the vowel perceived by the singer to the formant frequencies of the vowel perceived by those listening. Whereas listeners must rely on air-conducted feedback to assess vowel quality, the performer has access to both air- and bone-conducted feedback. The transmission characteristics of air and bone conduction are not the same. As frequency increases, bone conduction becomes less effective than air conduction (Tonndorf, 1972). Howell and Powell (1983; see also Howell, Chapter 11, this volume) simultaneously recorded air- and bone-conducted productions of various vowels and showed that their spectra depended on transmission route. Typically, the bone-conducted spectra contain extra resonance in the 1.0–2.5 kHz region, and, at least for certain vowels, the formants appear lower than those of the corresponding air-conducted spectra (see, for instance, [i] in Figure 13, Chapter 11, this volume). The two transmission routes converge at the cochlea (Lowy, 1942; von Bekesy, 1932) where the spectra must be combined. Formant positions extracted from the combined spectrum lie between those extracted from the two separate spectra. Their exact locations depend on the relative amplitude at the cochlea of the air- and bone-conducted sound. Anything changing the relative effectiveness of the two transmission routes alters the formant positions in the combined spectrum. Occlusion of the external ear canals not only reduces masking from background sounds but also

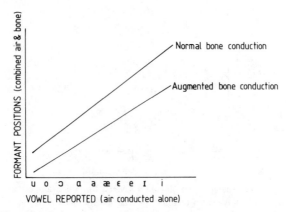

Figure 14. Hypothetical sensation specification schema for vowel articulation showing dependence on level of bone conduction. This shows the position of a formant in the combined air- and
bone-conducted sound spectrum of the singer against the vowel reported by a listener on the basis of
air conduction alone.

increases the relative effectiveness of bone conduction (Tonndorf, 1972). This
not only makes the voice boom (because of increased low frequency components) but appears to alter vowel quality (e.g., /a/ towards /ɔ/).

The sensation specification schema for vowel articulation relates the combined
spectrum formant positions of the vowel perceived by the singer to the formant
positions in the air-conducted spectrum responsible for vowel perception in the
listener. Various maneuvres by singers may alter the relative effectiveness of
their air- and bone-conducted feedback (see Howell Chapter 11, this volume),
and they would have to be included as initial-condition variables within this
schema (Figure 14). Some of these maneuvres may be performed for the express
purpose of increasing the level of bone-conducted feedback so that overall loudness of the voice is raised relative to that of background accompaniment. They
may or may not be employed throughout singing. Whether they are used may
depend on background sound level. Other maneuvres may be made for quite
different articulatory reasons and just happen to affect the relative effectiveness
of bone conduction.

Certain singers—particularly folk singers—are sometimes observed occluding one of their external ear canals. This increases the overall amplitude of the
auditory feedback they receive, but also, for the reasons outlined previously,
produces some qualitative change in it. (Of course, canal occlusion need not be
complete to produce a change in the effectiveness of bone conduction. Even
partial occlusion resulting from displacement of the head of the mandible (von
Bekesy, 1941) may alter it to some extent (Tonndorf, 1972).) Other singers may
have developed a rather different technique for increasing the effectiveness of
bone-conducted feedback, thereby raising the loudness of their voices relative to

the level of background musical accompaniment. Tonndorf, Campbell, Bernstein, and Reneau (1966) confirmed von Bekesy's (1932) and Groen's (1962) hypothesis that air enclosed within the middle ear acts as a compliance to reduce the effectiveness of bone conduction. In singers, this compliance may be reduced and bone conduction thereby increased by opening of the (normally closed) auditory tubes. It is a reduction in middle-ear compliance in this way that results in phonation during yawning sounding similar to phonation with the external ear canals occluded. If this manner of increasing bone-conducted feedback is used by singers, it should have effects on both the production and on the singer's perception of the vowel. The effect on production would arise from modification of the parameter specification schema to ensure opening of the auditory tubes. The contraction of the tensor palatini and the levator palatini required to accomplish this (Holmquist, 1976) also tends to raise and tense the velum (Hardcastle, 1976). This acts to increase the size of the oropharyngeal cavity and so lower the position of the second and higher formants of the vowel. In fact, Sundberg (1974) has confirmed that these formants are lower in sung than in spoken vowels (Fant, 1973). The effect on the singer's perception of the vowel would

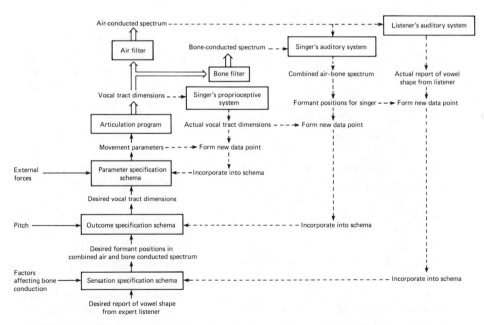

Figure 15. Use of vowel articulation schemata prior to performance (solid lines), execution of program during performance (double lines), and modification of each schema after performance in response to feedback (dotted lines).

arise from the shift in the position of the formants in the combined spectrum because of their extra weighting towards their positions in the bone-conducted spectrum alone (Howell and Powell, 1983). Together, these effects may be reflected in the instructions given by many singing teachers (e.g., Appleman, 1967) to their students that vowel quality should be modified in singing such that /e/ is shifted toward /œ/, /a/ towards /ɑ/, /i/ towards /y/, and so on.

The three schemata for vowel articulation enable singers to produce a vowel as close as possible to the one specified as musically appropriate by an expert listener. Of course, in different styles of singing, experts may require production of rather different vowel shapes (Miller, 1977; Miller and Schutte, 1983). Figure 15 summarises how the three schemata are used to insert parameters into the vowel articulation program prior to a breath group (solid lines), how this program is then executed (double lines); and how the schemata are modified in response to feedback arising from execution (dotted lines). Considerations concerning error monitoring and conditions for acquisition and use of schemata are similar to those previously outlined for exhalation and phonation.

COORDINATION

Previously, programs for exhalation, phonation, and articulation have been discussed separately. However, before the singer can perform, they must be integrated into an overall singing program. This is necessary to ensure that exhalation, phonation, and articulation are properly synchronized. Fowler et al. (1980) discuss problems of coordination such as this. They refer to generalized motor programs as coordinative structures. Coordination requires that lower level programs or coordinative structures (i.e., those subserving exhalation, phonation, and articulation) be functionally embedded or nested under a higher level program (i.e., one subserving vocalisation). They point out that this nesting process itself results in some modification of the lower level programs. This is because parameters in lower-level programs are interdependent and so must be simultaneously and optimally estimated when these programs are integrated under a higher level one for coordination. For example, parameters inserted into the exhalation program to produce a particular subglottal pressure depend on vocal-cord tension (Figure 9), but parameters inserted into the phonation program to produce a particular vocal-cord tension (and hence, laryngeal excitation pattern) depend on subglottal pressure (Figure 11). When these two programs are embedded within the higher level singing program, these mutually dependent parameters must be simultaneously and optimally estimated. To solve this problem, the internal regression techniques employed by the performer need to be akin to the multivariate regression methods devised by statisticians for simultaneous estimation of a number of parameters.

IMPLICATIONS

Collins (1983) points out that "vocal instruction is often based upon the experiences of the individual teacher rather than upon theories of learning" (p. 56). My aim has been to show that theories of motor learning and performance that have been recently developed within the cognitive psychology of motor control can be applied to the problems a singer has in communicating musical structure to listeners. Acquiring and exercising singing skill can be viewed as a matter of internalizing, using, and subsequently modifying rules or schemata. I have suggested that these rules are statistical in nature and that internal analogues of regression are used to extract them from the data that accumulate with every successive singing performance. Adoption of this approach would have various implications for the instruction and training of singers.

Effects of Conditions of Practice

According to schema theory, data useful for modifying and strengthening parameter and outcome specification schemata are gathered whenever a person sings. Even when the singing is very poor but the performer is not aware that it is poor, new data points contributing to these schemata are collected. All that is necessary is that the performer's brain, body, and sense organs be intact. In this sense, even bad singing can be good practice. If the individual also receives information about the performance from an expert listener, additional learning can occur. This extra information can be of two types, each important for a different reason: (1) The listener can describe *what* he experienced in an absolute fashion (e.g., middle C sung fortissimo) or in a relative one (e.g., a note a semitone sharper and twice as loud as sung the last time). This non-evaluative type of information contributes to sensation specification schemata independently of whether performance was good or bad. Again, even bad singing can be good practice. (2) the listener can label the performance as good or bad. Of course, such an evaluation may be implicit in the first type of information (as when the singer knows the correct note is B♯ but is told that a C was produced), but it need not be. (Often, a singer is told that he or she has sung loudly or twice as loud as before but still is not sure whether the loudness produced was musically appropriate.) The second evaluative type of information is important for specifying the goals that are used as input to the sensation specification schemata. Without knowing these goals, schemata can be acquired but cannot be used to perform a particular piece of music. Typically, there are many possible ways of singing a piece badly but only one (or, at least, relatively few) of singing it well. Thus, unless the expert listener can specify fairly precisely the degree to which an error has been made, goal learning should gain particular benefit from a combination of good performance and feedback specifying that performance was good.

Variability of Practice

It follows from the regression method that stronger schemata are acquired when the data points are spread throughout the range of the movement variables (see p. 304). The voice should be exercised not just throughout the its full range of pitches, loudnesses, and vowel shapes, but also under a full range of initial conditions affecting the production of those features. Furthermore, coordination of exhalation, phonation, and articulation would benefit from training and performing with as wide a variety of combinations of loudness, pitch, and vowel shapes as possible.

Use of Artificial Feedback Aids

Where expert listeners are unavailable, artificial feedback devices may act as partial substitutes and allow acquisition of data contributing to sensation specification schemata. The laryngograph (Fourcin and Abberton, 1971) is one such device that the author has found useful for providing singers with precise information regarding pitch. It may also be used to supply some information concerning jitter, the physiological correlate of vocal roughness that is diminished in singers relative to non-singers (Murray et al., 1979). Wilson (1982) describes another device that provides the singer with information concerning the singer's formant, an important indicator of sung vowel quality. However, though useful, these devices can be considered only partial substitutes for expert listeners. The goal of singing is to produce perceptions in people, not readings on machines. The devices cannot be regarded as full simulations of the human perceptual system. Many variables affecting the perceptions of listeners may not affect the readings on the devices.

QUERIES

The application of schema theory to singing raises a number of queries. Although I deal here with those that are obvious to me, there are, no doubt, others that have, as yet, escaped my attention.

Attentional Constraints

One may question whether it is reasonable to regard a singer as acquiring and using rules when so many different factors can be included in them. Inclusion of many initial conditions in the schemata may be expected to place a heavy attentional load on the singer during training and performance. In fact, the singer does not *have* to include some relevant factor as an initial condition in the rule. It is just that the singing would be better if it were included. Some factors may be relatively unimportant and add little to the error variance of the rule when they are not explicitly included as relevant variables. Other factors may be more crucial, and their exclusion from the rule would have more drastic consequences. The importance of a factor depends on how much it contributes to the variance of the independent variable constituting the output of the system applying the rule. Early in singing training, the individual can be expected to reduce the attentional load by analysing just the most important factors to determine how they should be included in the rule. Later, with the analysis complete and a preliminary version of the rule formulated, attentional capacity can be released to determine how else error variance may be reduced. Another factor can then be incorporated, the rule modified, and the process repeated. In this way, the singer would gradually learn how to reach performance goals more and more precisely. Of course, inclusion of particular factors in the form of the rule stored in long-term memory does not obligate the singer to include them all when the rule is used. Just monitoring for certain factors, such as reverberation time (Schneider and Fisk, 1983), may demand some attentional capacity. When this is at a premium because of simultaneous demands from other activities (e.g., acting or playing a musical instrument), attention-demanding inclusion of less important factors in the used form of the rule may be sacrificed.

Sensory monitoring and movement planning, together with learning about these processes, may not be the only demands on the trainee singer's attention. Executing the movements involved in singing and learning about this process may also require attention. For instance, in the section on "The Movements Subserving Phonation," many ways in which laryngeal muscle contractions can cause vocal pitch change were outlined. The larynx is a complex organ and there are many different ways in which it can move. In other words, it has many degrees of freedom. To use it to its full potential in singing, the singer must be able to exploit all these degrees of freedom. To the trainee singer, controlling and learning to control each degree of freedom requires attention. To reduce these processing demands, the trainee may first freeze most degrees of freedom and just allow a limited form of movement. (Freezing of degrees of freedom of intrinsic laryngeal pitch-change mechanisms may explain why untrained singers use extrinsic mechanisms producing vertical laryngeal movement to change pitch (Shipp and Izdebski, 1975).) Once learning about how this relatively simple movement affects pitch has occurred, attentional capacity may be released. Another degree of freedom can then be unfrozen and the available attention used to learn how it affects what is already known. As more and more movement parameters are specified by the parameter specification schemata, movement goals are reached more and more precisely. This process of gradually unfreezing degrees of freedom during movement learning has been summarised by Turvey, Fitch, and Tuller(1982):

> When you are just beginning to learn a skill, one of the first things you will notice is that you eliminate, as it were, some of your degrees of freedom—put simply, you keep a good part of your body fairly rigid. You do not exhibit the flexibility of a skilled performer. Watch a child learning how to hit a baseball. Initially, he or she stands quite rigid, facing the ball, holding most of the body stiff. This posture simplifies the problem, but it does not allow a very efficient swing. As the child gets slightly better, one of the things that he or she will do is allow shoulder movements into the swing. Several degrees of freedom are "unfrozen." . . . Why is the batter trying to regulate more degrees of freedom? Fundamentally, the skill demands it. A good baseball batter must allow flexibility of the hips, shoulders, and wrists. The additional degrees of freedom are important in giving power to the swing. In summary, acquiring a skill is essentially trying to find ways of controlling the degrees of freedom and of exploiting the forces made available by the context. (p. 251)

The Origin of a Generalized Motor Program for Vocalisation

Acquisition of schemata allows parameters to be inserted into a generalized motor program for vocalization (under which these for exhalation, phonation, and articulation are nested) so that it can be used for the exercise of singing skills. The question of the origin of this generalized motor program arises. Various lines of evidence suggest an innate basis for it. The earliest form of babbling in children appears to be universal across different linguistic environments (Nakazima, 1962; Weir, 1966), can be observed in deaf children (Mavilja, 1969) and seems unaffected by differences in learning opportunities (Lenneberg, Rebelsky, and Nichols, 1965).

Form in Which Goals Are Stored in Long-term Memory

Musical goals may not be specified in terms of the loudness, pitch, and vowel shape for particular notes but in terms of differences in loudness, pitch, and vowel shape between successive notes. For instance, input to the phonation schemata may be in the form of musical intervals rather than musical notes. This issue of whether locations (analogous to musical notes) or distances (analogous to musical intervals) are learned has been the subject of much research on the acquisition of limb movement skill. Most of the studies in which these cues have been separated have examined movement recall over relatively short periods of time. They indicate that location information is more precisely remembered but that, in some circumstances, distance information can also be retained (Diewert, 1975; Laabs, 1973; Martenuik, 1973). It would be rash to extrapolate from this work on limb movement: Cue-separation studies on singing need to be carried out. However, Shepard (1982a, 1982b) has shown that the extent to which pitch differences are perceived in terms of musical intervals depends on level of musical experience and training. Thus, goal specification in terms of musical intervals may be the prerogative of trained musicians. Hagerman and Sundberg's (1980) demonstration of systematic deviations from just and Pythagorean intonation in barbershop singing (apparently to avoid beats) implies that the actual intervals learnt vary with the style of singing.

The Effects of Consonant Articulation

Fowler et al. (1980) argue that the system responsible for production of vowels is separate from that responsible for production of consonants. The former process was discussed in the section on "Articulation of Vowels," but questions regarding the latter remain. Although there have only been a few studies of consonant production in singing, a little is known about how it affects other features of the voice. Scotto di Carlo (1979) found that exaggerated articulation of consonants reduces spectral homogeneity within a register, affects the appearance of the singer's formant and vibrato, and disrupts the accuracy of pitch production. At the beginning of a breath group, the extent of this disruption is related to the degree of occlusion of the consonant. She argues that there are detrimental effects of consonant production on the aesthetics of performance that can only be reduced by under-articulation of highly occluding consonants. There is a "precarious balance that the singer has to reach if he [or she] wants to preserve both the intelligibility of the text and the aesthetic value of the music" (p. 23).

Information Flow in the Singer

According to the model outlined here, the sensation specification schema, the outcome specification schema, and the parameter specification schema form a chain of command (Figure 16, Path a). A listener can specify some desired auditory perception (e.g., "I should like you to sing a note that I hear as middle C"). The performer uses this to specify a desired auditory perception of his or her own. This, in turn, is used to specify a proprioceptive target that will identify the movement parameters capable of producing the observed auditory perception in the listener. The question arises as to whether any of these stages can be skipped. For instance, can a listener's desired auditory perception be used to specify the proprioceptive target in the performer directly (Path b in Figure 16)? Observations on the speech of deaf individuals suggest that this cannot be done. Profoundly deaf children are unlikely to develop normal speech. Furthermore, although adventitiously deaf speakers suffer little immediate speech deteriora-

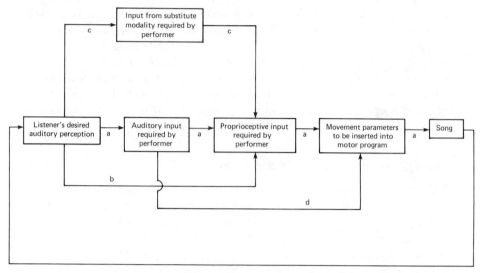

Figure 16.   Alternative paths for information flow in the singer.

tion, their intelligibility does become impaired after a period of deafness. This may be taken to indicate long-term forgetting of outcome specification and/or sensation specification schemata. Immediately after the onset of deafness, those schemata are still intact and can be effectively used to specify desired proprioceptive outcomes of movement. However, without auditory input, no new data points can be added to them. Long-term forgetting results in an increase in error variance so that they are less able to specify proprioceptive targets with precision. Because of this, movement parameters are less well specified, and a decrease in intelligibility occurs. This decrease would not be expected if schemata exist that enable proprioceptive targets to be specified directly without the mediation of internal auditory codes.

A number of sensory substitution techniques have been developed for the deaf (e.g., Fourcin and Abberton, 1971). The aim is to substitute an intact sensory modality for the absent auditory input. New sensation specification schemata between listeners' reports and the substitute sensory input and new outcome specification schemata between the substitute sensory input and desired proprioceptive outcomes of movement can be developed because new data points contributing to these schemata can be collected (Path c in Figure 16). These techniques are reviewed by Knox (1976) and Sherrick (1978).

A related issue is that of whether the performer's desired auditory perception can directly specify movement parameters without the mediation of internal proprioceptive codes (Path d in Figure 16). Unfortunately, longitudinal studies of the effects of acquired proprioceptive processing deficits on vocalization have not been reported. (It remains possible that certain dysarthrias have such an origin.) There is, however, some evidence that proprioceptive input can be important for specification of the parameters inserted into the motor programs for limb movement. Lashley (1917) examined a soldier 5 years after a gunshot wound had eliminated proprioceptive input from one of his legs. Its absence was indicated by the man's inability to detect the extent, duration, direction, or even the presence of passive movements of the limb. Without vision, he could still duplicate his own voluntary movement about the knee joint as accurately as a normal individual. Thus, proprioceptive input did not seem to be important for movement *control*. (As movement duplication may rely on repeated execution of the same movement plans, this finding cast no light on his ability to plan movements.) However, when asked to move a specific distance, his performance was inferior (although not greatly so) to that of a normal individual. This finding implies that proprioceptive input is important for the *planning* of limb movements. After the injury, schemata relating required movement distance (specified by the experiments) to required proprioceptive outcome of movement and relating this required proprioception to movement parameters had been subject to some decay in long-term memory. Without proprioceptive input from the limb in question, no new data points could be added to these schemata. Hence, movement parameters were less well specified and the observed decrease in accuracy occurred. This decrease would not have been expected if schemata exist that enable required movement distance to specify movement parameters directly without mediation by internal proprioceptive codes.

Acceptable Error Margins for Singers

As long as the singer can operate within the error bands determined by the resolving powers of the expert listener's auditory system, performance is regarded as satisfactory. How large are these error bands? For single tones, psychoacoustic studies show them to be relatively narrow. Even so, the barbershop-quartet singers studied by Hagerman and Sundberg (1980) produced fundamental frequencies to a given target with standard deviations "of the same order of magnitude as those obtained in psychoacoustic pitch matching and interval matching experiments" (p. 14). However, the ear is much less capable of tracking rapid changes in fundamental frequency (Sundberg, 1982a). This is just as well. It means that not only do many of the acoustically disrupting effects of consonants (discussed previously) go unnoticed, but so do the perturberations that naturally accompany rapid pitch changes of the voice. Mario Palencia and I have used a laryngograph to record these perturberations in a highly trained professional singer. Figure 17 shows typical oscillations after a rapid pitch change that were not perceived by listeners. Fujisaki (1983), who first documented perturberations of this type argues that they arise from the springlike

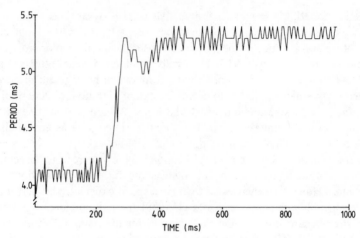

Figure 17. Largyngographic record of pitch change in a professional singer, showing lengthening of the period of the voice as pitch is changed from a high to a lower note. Note perturbations in record immediately after pitch change.

nature of the pitch change system (discussed previously). However, the extent to which this model fits the data remains to be determined.

REFERENCES

Abbs, J. H., and Kennedy, J. C., III, Neurophysiological processes of speech movement control. In N. J. Lass, L. V. McReynolds, J. L. Northern, and D. E. Yoder (Eds.), *Speech, language and hearing: Vol. 1. Normal processes.* London: Saunders, 1982.

Allen, E. L., and Hollien, H. Laminographic study of pulse register phonation. *Folia Phoniatrica,* 1973, *25,* 241–250.

Appleman, D. R. *The science of vocal pedagogy* London: Indiana University Press, 1967.

Bartlett, F. C. *Remembering.* Cambridge: Cambridge University Press, 1932.

Borden, G. J., and Harris, K. S. *Speech science primer.* London: Williams and Wilkins, 1980.

Bouhuys, A., Proctor, D. F., and Mead, J. Kinetic aspects of singing. *Journal of Applied Physiology,* 1966, *21,* 483–496.

Broad, D. J. Phonation. In F. D. Minifie, T. J. Hixon, and F. Williams (Eds.), *Normal aspects of speech, hearing and language.* Englewood Cliffs, NJ: Prentice-Hall, 1973.

Chomsky, N. *Aspects of the theory of syntax.* Cambridge, MA: MIT Press, 1965.

Collins, M. E. Goal identification and systematic instruction in private voice lessons. *Journal of Research in Singing,* 1983, *7,* 56–66.

Colton, R. Some acoustic parameters related to the perception of modal-falsetto voice quality. *Folia Phoniatrica,* 1973, *25,* 302–311.

Colton, R., and Hollien, H. Perceptual differences of the modal and falsetto registers. *Folia Phoniatrica,* 1973, *25,* 270–280.

Critchley, M., and Kubik, C. S. The mechanisms of speech and deglutition in progressive bulbar palsy. *Brain,* 1925, *48,* 492–534.

Damaste, P. H., Hollien, H., Moore, P., and Murphy, T. An x-ray of vocal fold length. *Folia Phoniatrica*, 1968, *20*, 349–359.

Daniloff, R., Schuckers, G., and Feth, L. *The physiology of speech and hearing*. Englewood Cliffs, NJ: Prentice-Hall, 1980.

Diewert, G. L. Retention and coding in motor short term memory: A comparison of storage codes for distance and location information. *Journal of Motor Behaviour*, 1975, *7*, 183–190.

Fant, G. *Speech sounds and features*. Cambridge, MA: MIT Press, 1973.

Folkins, J. W., and Kuehn, D. P. Speech production. In N. J. Lass, L. V. McReynolds, J. L. Northern, and D. E. Yoder (Eds.), *Speech, language and hearing: Vol. 1. Normal processes*. London: Saunders, 1982.

Fortuyn, D. J., and Ritsma, R. J. Virtual pitch and our own voice. In O. Creutzfeldt, H. Scheich, and Chr. Schreiner (Eds.), *Hearing mechanisms and speech*. Berlin: Springer-Verlag, 1979.

Fourcin, A., and Abberton, E. First applications of a new laryngograph. *Medical and Biological Illustration*, 1971, *21*, 172–182.

Fowler, C. A., Rubin, P., Remez, R. E., and Turvey, N. T. Implications for speech production of a general theory of action. In B. Butterworth (Ed.), *Language production: Vol. 1. Speech and talk*. London: Academic Press, 1980.

Fujisaki, H. Dynamic characteristics of voice fundamental frequency in speech and singing. In P. F. MacNeilage (Ed.), *The production of speech*. New York: Springer-Verlag, 1983.

Gould, W. J., and Tanabe, M. The effect of anaesthesia of the internal branch of the superior laryngeal nerve upon phonation. *Folia Phoniatrica*, 1975, *27*, 337–349.

Groen, J. J. The value of the Weber test. In H. F. Schuknecht (Ed.), *International Symposium of Oto-sclerosis, Detroit, 1960*. Boston, MA: Little Brown, 1962.

Hagerman, B., and Sundberg, J. Fundamental frequency adjustment in barbershop singing. *Journal of Research and Singing*, 1980, *4*, 3–17.

Hardcastle, W. J. *Physiology of speech production: An introduction for speech scientists*. London: Academic Press, 1976.

Harvey, N., and Greer, K. Action: The mechanisms of motor control. In G. Claxton (Ed.), *Cognitive psychology New directions*. London: Routledge and Kegan Paul, 1980.

Harvey, N., and Greer, K. Force and stiffness: Further considerations. *The Behavioural and Brain Sciences*, 1982, *5*, 547–548.

Harvey, N., and Howell, P. Isotonic vocalis contraction as a means of producing rapid decreases in F_0. *Journal of Speech and Hearing Research*, 1980, *23*, 576–592.

Head, H. *Aphasia and kindred disorders of speech* (Vols. 1–2). New York: Macmillan, 1926.

Hixon, T. J. Respiratory function in speech. In F. Minifie, T. Hixon, and F. Williams (Eds.), *Normal aspects of speech, hearing and language*. Englewood Cliffs, NJ: Prentice-Hall, 1973.

Hollien, H. Vocal pitch variation related to change in vocal fold length. *Journal of Speech and Hearing Research*, 1960, *3*, 150–156.

Hollien, H. Vocal fold thickness and fundamental frequency of phonation. *Journal of Speech and Hearing Research*, 1962, *5*, 237–243.

Hollien, H. On vocal registers. *Journal of Phonetics*, 1974, *2*, 25–43.

Hollien, H., and Colton, R. H. Four laminagraphic studies of vocal fold thickness. *Folia Phoniatrica*, 1969, *21*, 179–198.

Hollien, H., and Curtis, J. F. A laminagraphic study of vocal pitch. *Journal of Speech and Hearing Research*, 1969, *3*, 179–198.

Hollien, H., and Moore, P. Measurements of the vocal folds during changes in pitch. *Journal of speech and hearing research*, 1960, *3*, 157–165.

Holmquist, H. J. Auditory and tubal function. In R. Hinchcliffe and D. Harrison (Eds.), *Scientific foundations of oto-laryngology*. London: Heinemann, 1976.

Howell, P. Change in phoneme targets with different phonation. In G. E. Stelmach and J. Requin (Eds.), *Tutorials in motor behaviour*. Amsterdam: North Holland, 1980.

Howell, P., and Harvey, N. Perceptual equivalents and motor equivalents in speech. In B. Butterworth (Ed.), *Language production: Vol. 2. Development, writing and other language processes*. London: Academic Press, 1983.

Howell, P., and Powell, D. J. Hearing your voice through bone and air: Implications for explanations for stuttering behaviour from studies of normal speakers. *Journal of Fluency Disorders*, 1983, *9*, 247–264.

Izdebski, K., and Shipp, T. The effects of vertical laryngeal position on singers' sustained vowel formants. *Journal of Research in Singing*. 1979, *2*, 1–9.

Keele, S. W., and Summers, J. J. The structure of motor programs. In G. G. Stelmach (Ed.), *Motor control: Issues and trends*. New York: Academic Press, 1976.

Kelso, J. A. S. Motor control mechanisms underlying human movement production. *Journal of Experimental Psychology: Human Perception and Performance*, 1977, *3*, 529–543.

Kelso, J. A. S., and Stelmach, G. E. Central and peripheral mechanisms in motor control. In J. E. Stelmach (Ed.), *Motor control: Issues and trends*. New York: Academic Press, 1976.

Knox, E. Electroacoustic rehabilitation equipment other than hearing aids. In R. Hinchcliffe and D. Harrison (Eds.), *Scientific foundations of oto-laryngology*. London: Heinnemann, 1976.

Laabs, G. J. Retention characteristics of different reproduction cues in motor short term memory. *Journal of Experimental Psychology*, 1973, *100*, 168–177.

Ladefoged, P. *Three areas of experimental phonetics*. London: Oxford University Press, 1977.

Large, J. Acoustic study of register equalisation in singing. *Folia Phoniatrica*, 1973, *25*, 39–61.

Large, J., Baird, E., and Jenkins, T. Studies of the male high voice mechanisms: Preliminary report and definition of the term 'register'. *Journal of Research in Singing*, 1980, *4*, 26–33.

Large, J., Iwata, S., and Leden, H. von, The male operatic head register versus falsetto, *Folia Phoniatrica*, 1972, *24*, 19–29.

Large, J., and Murray, T. Observations on the nature of Tibetan chant. *Journal of Research and Singing*, 1981, *5*, 22–28.

Lashley, K. S. The accuracy of movement in the absence of excitation in the moving organ. *The American Journal of Physiology*, 1917, *43*, 169–194.

Lenneberg, E. H., Rebelsky, F., and Nichols, I. The vocalisation of infants born to deaf and hearing parents. *Human Development*, 1965, *8*, 23–37.

Licklider, J. C. R. Auditory frequency analysis. In C. Cherry (Ed.), *Information theory*. New York: Academic Press, 1956.

Lowy, K. Cancellation of the electrical cochlear response with air- and bone-conducted sound. *Journal of the Acoustical Society of America*, 1942, *14*, 156–158.

MacNeilage, P. F. Motor control of serial ordering of speech. *Psychological Review*, 1970, *77*, 182–196.

Marchesi, M. *Theoretical and practical vocal method*. New York: Dover, 1970.

Mavilja, M. P. *Spontaneous vocalisations and babbling of hearing-impaired, infants*. Unpublished doctoral dissertation, Columbia University, New York, 1969.

Miller, R. *English, French, and Italian techniques of singing*. Metuchen, NJ: Scarecrow, 1977.

Miller, R., and Schutte, H. Spectral analysis of timbre in a professional male (tenor) voice. *Journal of Research and Singing*, 1983, *7*, 6–10.

Martenuik, R. G. Retention characteristics of short-term cues. *Journal of Motor Behavior*, 1973, *5*, 312–317.

Murray, T., Large, J., and Dalgaard, J. Vocal jitter in sung and spoken vowels. *Journal of Research and Singing*, 1979, *2*, 28–43.

Nakazima, S. A comparative study of the speech developments of Japanese and American English in childhood: Part 1. A comparison of the speech developments of voices at the prelinguistic period. *Studia Phonologica*, 1962, *2*, 27–46.

Ohala, J. J. How is pitch lowered? *Journal of the Acoustical Society of America*, 1972, *52*, 124.

Ohala, J. J. Speculations on pitch regulation. *Phonetica*, 1977, *34*, 310–312.

Ohala, J. J. Production of tone. In V. A. Fromkin (Ed.), *Tone: A linguistic survey*. New York: Academic Press, 1978, 5–40.

Peterson, G. E. Some observations on speech. *Quarterly Journal of Speech*, 1958, *44*, 402–412.

Proctor, D. F. Breathing mechanisms during phonation and singing. In B. Wyke (Ed.), *Ventilatory and phonatory control systems: An international symposium*. London: Oxford University Press, 1974, 39–57.

Proctor, D. F. *Breathing, speech and song*, New York: Springer-Verlag, 1980.

Russo, V., and Large, J. Psychoacoustic study of bel canto model for register equalisation: Male chest and falsetto. *Journal of Research in Singing*, 1978, *1*, 1–25.

Sapir, S., McClean, M. D., and Larson, C. R. Human laryngeal response to auditory stimulation. *Journal of the Acoustical Society of America*, 1983, *73*, 315–321.

Schmidt, R. A. A schema theory of discrete motor skill learning. *Psychological Review*, 1975, *82*, 225–260.

Schmidt, R. A. The schema theory as a solution to some persistent problems in motor-learning theory. In G. E. Stelmach (Ed.), *Motor control: Issues and trends*. New York: Academic Press, 1976.

Schmidt, R. A. *Motor control and learning: A behavioural Emphasis*. Champaign, IL: Human Kinetics, 1982. (a)

Schmidt, R. A. The schema concept. In J. A. S. Kelso (Ed.), *Human motor behavior: An introduction*. Hillsdale, NJ: Lawrence Erlbaum, 1982, 219–235. (b)

Schneider, W., and Fisk, A. D. Attention theory and mechanisms for skilled performance. In R. A. Magill (Ed.), *Memory and control of action*. New York: North Holland, 1983.

Scotto, di Carlo, N. Perturbing effects of overarticulation in singing. *Journal of Research in Singing*, 1979, *2*, 10–27.

Shapiro, D. C., and Schmidt, R. A. The schema theory: Recent evidence and developmental implications. In J. A. S. Kelso and J. Clark (Eds.), *The development of movement control and coordination*. New York: Wiley, 1982.

Shepard, R. N. Geometrical approximations to the structure of musical pitch. *Psychological Review*, 1982, *89*, 305–333. (a)

Shepard, R. N. Structural representations of musical pitch. In D. Deutsch (Ed.), *The psychology of music*. London: Academic Press, 1982, 344–390. (b)

Sherrick, C. E. Language through alternative modalities. In J. F. Kavanagh (Ed.), *Speech and language in the laboratory, school and clinic*. Cambridge, MA: MIT Press, 1978.

Shipp, T. Vertical laryngical position in singing. *Journal of Research and Singing*, 1977, *1*, 16–24.

Shipp, T., and Izdebski, K. Vocal frequency and vertical larynx positioning by singers and non-singers. *Journal of the Acoustical Society of America*, 1975, *58*, 1104–1106.

Sonninen, A. Is the length of the vocal cords the same at all different levels of singing? *Acta Otolaryngologica* (Supplement), 1954, *118*, 219–231.

Stevens, S. S. The relation of pitch to intensity. *Journal of the Acoustical Society of America*, 1935, *6*, 150–154.

Stein, R. B. What muscle variable(s) does the nervous system control in limb movements. *The Behavioral and Brain Sciences*, 1982, *5*, 535–578.

Stumpf, C. *Die Sprachlaute* [The sounds of speech]. Berlin: Springer-Verlag, 1926.

Sundberg, J. Articulatory interpretation of "singing formant." *Journal of the Acoustical Society of America*, 1974, *55*, 838–844.

Sundberg, J. Formant technique in a professional female singer. *Acustica,* 1975, *32,* 89–96.

Sundberg, J. Vibrato and vowel identification. *Archives of Acoustics (Polish Academy of Sciences),* 1977, *2,* 257–266.

Sundberg, J. Effects of vibrato and the "singing formant" on pitch. *Journal of Research in Singing,* 1982, *5,* 3–17. (a)

Sundberg, J. Perception of singing. In D. Deutsch (Ed.), *The psychology of music.* London: Academic Press, 1982, 59–98. (b)

Sussman, H. M., MacNeilage, P. F., and Hanson, R. J. Labial and mandibular dynamics during the production of bilabial consonants: Preliminary observations. *Journal of Speech and Hearing Research,* 1973, *16,* 397–420.

Terhardt, E. Pitch, consonants and harmony. *Journal of the Acoustical Society of America,* 1974, *55,* 1061–1069.

Terhardt, E. Calculating virtual pitch. *Hearing Research,* 1979, *1,* 155–182.

Tonndorf, J. Bone conduction. In J. V. Tobias (Ed.), *Foundations of modern auditory theory* (Vol. 2). New York: Academic Press, 1972.

Tonndorf, J., Campbell, R. A., Bernstein, L., and Reneau, J. P. Quantitative evaluations of bone conduction components in cats. *Acta Oto-Laryngologica,* Supplement 1966, *213,* 10–38.

Turvey, M. T., Fitch, H. L., and Tuller, B. The Bernstein perspective: Vol. 1. The problems of degrees of freedom and context-conditioned variability in J. A. S. Kelso (Ed.), *Human motor behaviour: An introduction.* Hillsdale, NJ: Erlbaum, 1982.

Vennard, W. *Singing: The mechanism and the technic.* New York: Carl Fischer, 1967.

von Bekesy, G. Zur Theorie des Horens bei der Schallaufnahme durch Knochenleitung [On the theory of tone reception as a result of bone conduction]. *Poggendorf's Annalen der Physik und Chemie,* 1932, *13,* 111–136.

von Bekesy, G. Ueber die Schallausbreitung bei Knochenleitung [On the spread of tones by bone conduction]. *Zeitschrift Hals-, Nasen- und Ohrenheilkunde,* 1941, *47,* 430–442.

Ward, Music perception. In J. V. Tobias (Ed.), *Foundations of modern auditory theory: Vol. 1.* London: Academic Press, 1970.

Warren, D. W. Aerodynamics of speech production. In N. J. Lass (Ed.), *Contemporary issues in experimental phonetics.* New York: Academic Press, 1976.

Warren, D. W. Aerodynamics of speech. In N. J. Lass, L. V. McReynolds, J. L. Northern, and D. E. Yoder (Eds.), *Speech, language and hearing: Vol. 1. Normal processes.* London: Saunders, 1982.

Weir, R. Some questions on the child's learning of phonology. In F. Smith and G. A. Miller (Eds.), *The genesis of language.* Cambridge, MA: MIT Press, 1966.

Wilson, J. An electronic instrument for conditioning the singing formant. *Journal of Research in Singing,* 1982, *5,* 18–32.

Wyke, B. D., and Kirchner, J. A. Larynx-neurology. In R. Hinchcliffe and D. Harrison, (Eds.), *Scientific foundations of oto-laryngology.* London: Heinemann, 1976.

Index

A

Absolute judgment, 80
Absolute pitch, 189–208
 Gestalt qualities, 190
 identification strategies, 190–208
  anchoring, 192, 196
  colour hearing, 195
  pattern of errors, 201
  sequential effects, 192
  tinnitus, 195
 key identification, 202
 relativity, 190–208
 training of, 199–205
 verbal code, 204
Afghan music, 242–258
African music, 238–242
Agogic accentuation, 213, 228
Alphabets
 ad hoc, 30
 common, 30
Ambitus, 246
Amplitude response, 262–264
Analysis–resynthesis, 73
Antara, 245–246
Array
 linear/tiered, 244, 251, 258
Articulation
 of music, 212, 216, 229
 of speech, 289, 313–320; see also Vowel
  articulation
Articulator
 mandible, 265, 272, 275–276
Āstāi, 245–246, 255
Attentional streams, 47
Auditory corners, see Pitch
Auditory image, 257
Auditory nerve, 270, 275
Auditory stream segregation, 83, 104, 106

B

Bach, 90, 91
Bairami, 245–249
Barber shop singing, 325
Bars, 53
Beat, 53
 timing, 223
Beethoven, 169–170, 184
Bhog, 245–246
Breath analysis, 155–156

C

Cadence, 83
 authentic, 41
Cardinality, 12
Categorical perception, 203, 205, 220
Chord, 40, 111
Chord group, 40
Christian chant notation, early, 6
Chromatic scale, 76, 80, 124, 198
Chromatic set, 9–10, 13
Circle of fifths, see Fifths
Cluster pattern, 252–253
Cochlea, see Peripheral auditory system, Inner
 ear
Coherence, 11–12, 112
 of diatonic scale, 81
Composition, 40
Compound sequences, 25–26
Consonance, 79, 100; see also Dissonance
Constrained randomness, 73, 74
Contemporary music, 234
Contour, 76, 91, 96–110, 111
 features, 104–109
 melodic, 109, 110, 149–152, 169–186
 non-reversals, 104
 reversals, 85, 86, 93, 103–105, 106, 109

Contour *(continued)*
    transposed, 106–107
    untransposed, 104–106
Coordinative structure, 320
Cyclic alphabet, 18
Cyclic group, 10, 127

D

Damping, 273
Decision bias, 93
Deep structure, *see* Transformational grammar
Descriptive modelling, 31
Deutsch and Feroe, 23
Diatonic major scale, 6, 9–12, 87, 128
Diatonic scale, 2, 7–13, 76, 79, 80, 81, 88
    intervals, 78–79
Disruptive rhythm hypothesis and DAF, 284
Dissonance, 79; *see also* Consonance
Dominant leading note, 69, 129
Dominant root, 89
Duration ratios, 219, 223, 225
Dutār, 242–258
Dynamic, 212, 216

E

Elementary operators, 23–25
Equal temperament tuning system, 76
Equivalence, 10
    inversional, 12
    octave, 75, 97, 127
    transpositional, 11, 137
    transpositional–inversional, 138
Error monitoring, 303
Ethnomusicology, 237–258
Excitation of the vocal tract
    voiced, 259
    voiceless, 264
Exhalation, 289, 291–305
Expression, 209–236; *see also* Expressive
    variation
Expressive variation, 144–145

F

Feedback, 303
    and artificial aids, 322
    kinaesthetic, 285
    proprioceptive, 285

vocal feedback
    and amplification systems, 281
    auditory, 281, 282
    direction of sound, 281, 282
    in choir settings, 281
    middle ear muscles and, 280, 282
    reverberant sound, 301
    reverberation time, 302
    room acoustics, 303
Feroe, *see* Deutsch and Feroe
Fifths, 100, 112
    circle of, 27, 77, 88, 124, 126–129, 182
    progression, 41
    ratio, 79
    span, 78, 81, 89, 94, 95
Figural interpretations, 57
Filter, 260
Folk melody, *see* Melody
Formant, 262, 271, 279, 280, 289
    of a singer, 308
Frequency
    discrimination, 71
    fundamental, 74
    of a note, 74, 77
    ratio, 122–123
Fretting, 244

G

Gardenpath sentences and sequences, 61–62
Generative grammars, *see* Music modelling
Generator, 80, 112
Gestalt principles, 26–27, 47–48, 81, 84, 85
    closedness, 82
    common fate, 48
    figure/ground, 47, 82
    good continuation, 47, 82
    laws of organisation, 82
    proximity, 48, 82, 83
    regularity, 48
    similarity, 48, 82
    symmetry, 48, 82
Global precedence, 109
Group structure, *see* Group theory
Group theory, 10, 13, 80, 81, 100, 111–114
Grouping analysis, 34–36
    articulation of boundaries, 35
    parallelism in structure, 35
    symmetry, 35
    transformational rule, 35
Grouping structure, 217

H

Hair cell, 268
Harmonics (partials), 111
  analysis, 157–158
  complex, 74
Harmony, 78–79
  harmonic structure, 33–34, 37–43, 157–158
Hierarchical principles, 27–28
Hierarchically organised groups, 28–29
Hill-climbing progression, 71, 73, 74
Hocketing, 284

I

"Iliac suite", 87
Improvisation, 160
Information theory, 85, 89, 191
Intuition of experienced listeners, 161
Inversion, 12, 139
Ives, Charles, 185

J

Jackendoff, see Lerdahl and Jackendoff
Jazz, 42–44
  12-bar blues, 42

K

Key, 78, 81, 88, 91, 93–95, 96–104, 112, 127,
    171–172
  distance, 172
  establishment of, 184–186
Keynotes, see Tonic
Kalimba, 240

L

Leading note, 89
Lerdahl and Jackendoff, 35–39, 149, 161, 235
Licks, see Jazz
Logarithmic scale, 122
Lungs
  maximum inspiration level, 297
  subglottal pressure, 292
  vital capacity, 292

M

Macrocontours, 107
Macromelodies, 98–104, 107

Major scale, 198
Mass–spring systems, 314
Matrix of major and minor thirds, 27
Meatus, see Peripheral auditory system, outer
    ear
Mediant, 129
Mel scale, 122
Melodic accentuation, 86
Melodic patterns, see Melody
Melodious scaling, 90–92
Melodiousness, 90, 91–92, 94, 95
Melody, 43, 101, 143–167, 169
  approximation to, 73
  discrimination, 92
  dutār, 249
  familiar, 180–181
  folk, 143
  length, 172, 176–180
  novel, 178–180
  recall, see Recall of melodies
  rubāb, 249
Membrane
  basilar, 268, 270
  Reissner's, 268
  tectorial, 268, 270
Metre, 211–217, 220
  as generative grammars, 54; see also
    Metrical units
Metrical analysis, 34–36, 152–154
Metrical grouping
  accents and, 56
  note-length and, 56–59
  repetition and, 58–59
Metrical units, 53
Microcontours, 107
Micromelodies, 98–104, 107, 112
Microscales, 111
Microtonal systems, 111–114
Middle ear muscle
  stapedius, 266–267
  tensor tympani, 266, 267
Middle ear ossicle
  incus, 265–266
  malleus, 265–266
  stapes, 265–266, 268, 276
Mistuning, 96–103
Modality, 2, 7–8, 13
Mode, 6–8, 15, 76, 129, 245, 247
  major, 76
  minor, 76
Modulation, 78

Motor grammar, 242, 258
Motor program, 224, 230
  generalized, 295
  simple, 292
Motor learning, 321
Movement
  and music structure, 237–258
  in African music, 238–242
  nuclear patterns, 240
  parameters in speech, 296
Multidimensional scaling, 76, 81
Music modelling, 21–51
  generative grammars, 42–44, 233
  natural language grammars, 31–34, 42–43
  rewriting rules, 33, 43
Music theory, 1–4, 12
Musical aesthetics, 73
Musical memory
  structural knowledge, 143
  structural simplification, 157
Musical notation, 3, 84, 143–145
  sharpness value, 77

N

Naghme-ye kashāl, 244–247, 255–256
Natural language grammars, *see* Music
  modelling
New music, 97, 110–114
Notation, *see* Musical notation
Nursery tunes, 42–44

O

Octave, 79, 96, 100
  species, 6
Organ of Corti, 263
Overtones, *see* Harmonics (partials)

P

Paired comparison scaling, 90–91
Parsing, 41
PASS, *see* Auditory stream segregation
Pattern; *see also* Cluster pattern, Scalar pattern
  inherent, 240–242
  motional, 240–242
  sonic, 240–242
  uncertainty, 92, 94, 95
Perception
  of airborne sound, 265–270
  of bone-conducted sound, 274–277
  of contour information, 176–183
  of interval information, 176–183
Perceptual grouping, *see* Perceptual
  organisation
Perceptual organisation, 26, 81–84, 88, 102
Perfect pitch, *see* Absolute pitch
Performance, 237–238
  convention, 231
  motor control, 238
  musical, 209
Peripheral auditory system, 268; *see also* Hair
  cells, Membranes, Middle ear muscles,
  Middle ear ossicles, Organ of Corti,
  Pinna, Scala, Tympanic membrane
  inner ear, 265, 267–270, 275
  middle ear, 265, 267
  outer ear, 265, 268, 272, 275–276
Phase cancellation, 275
Phonation, 289, 305
Phrase, 53
  final lengthening, 213, 229
  structure, 44, 155, 156–157
Piano performance, 210
Pinna, 265
Pitch, 5–13, 74–76, 79
  chroma, 75
  classes, 10–11, 13, 75, 76, 113, 128, 137
  contour, 86, 109
  height, 75, 105, 106, 124
  identification, *see* Absolute pitch
  memory, 108
  paradox, 75–76
  perception, 74, 121–140, 145, 190
  reversals, 85, 104, 109
  virtual, 311
  voice, 102
Plagal cadence, 41
Plausibility value, 41
Pragnanz (law of), 71
Preference rules, *see* Grouping analysis,
  Metrical analysis, Prolongation reduction,
  Time-span reduction
Probability, 88
Problem solving, 72
Procedures, 224
Prolongational reduction, 34–38
  contrapuntal, directional chords, 38
  harmonic structural chords, 38
Prosody, 44, 101
Prototypicality, 13–19, 129

Psychophysical scaling, 90

Q

q values, 77–79, 87, 88

R

Reaction time, 172, 174–175
Recall, 146–147
  of melodies, 143–167
  musicians and non-musicians, 158–159
Receiver operating characteristic, 93
Recognition memory, 92–95, 146–147
Redundancy, 72, 89–90, 91–92, 94–95
Register equalisation, 307
Representation
  canonical, 211
  expressive, 211, 227
  structural, 211
Rhythm, 90, 185, 209–236; *see also* Rhythmic
  analysis, Rhythmic categories, Rhythmic
  organisation, Rhythmic reproduction
  perceptual representation, 220
  as tree structure, 90
Rhythmic analysis, 154
Rhythmic categories, 219–227
Rhythmic organisation
  dutār, 250
  rubāb, 250
Rhythmic reproduction, 154
Rubāb, 242–258

S

Same/next relationships, 28–29
Sanchāri, 245–246
Sawtooth, 262, 272
Scala
  media, 268
  tympani, 268
  vestibuli, 268
Scalar conformance, 130–140
Scalar pattern, 252–253
Scalar schema, 132, 135–138
Scalar structure, 130
Scale, 80, 87–89, 91, 92, 93–95, 96–104,
  112–114; *see also* Chromatic scale,
  Diatonic scale, Major scale, Scalar
  conformance, Scalar schema, Scalar
  structure

Schema
  outcome specification, 298, 310, 316
  parameter specification, 298, 310, 316
  sensation specification, 300, 311, 317
  theory, 290
Schemata, 287
Schenkerian analysis, 39; *see also*
  Prolongational reduction
  Ursatz, 39
Schubert, 186
Semitones, 76, 88, 89
Sensorimotor structure, 256
Sequence operators, 25
Serial position, 172, 176–179, 180–181
Signal detection, 93
Simon and Sumner, 28–31
Simple-ratio hypothesis, 96, 100, 111, 113, 114
Simplicity, 11–12
Singing, 147
Skull, bones of
  mastoid, 278
  temporal, 273, 276
Source-filter theory, 260–265
Spatiomotor representation, 252, 257
Spectrum
  amplitude, 262
  phase, 262
Speech
  intonation, 109
  phrase boundaries, 109, 110
  stress, 109
Staff notation, 4
Subharmonics, 79
Sumner, *see* Simon and Sumner
Surface structure, *see* Transformational
  grammar
Syllables, 284
Syncopation, 59–60
Systemic grammar, 40–42
  hierarchical levels, 40

T

Tablature, 4
Tegner, *see* Nursery tunes
Tempo, 217–220
Theme, 169–170, 184–186
Time
  perception, 145
  signature, 54
Time-span analysis, *see* Time-span reduction

Time-span reduction, 34–37
  cadences, 37
  structural beginnings and endings, 37
Timing, 210; *see also* Beat timing
  constraint, 223
  profile, 229
Tonal ambiguity, 185–186
Tonal context, 183
"Tonal" music, 32; *see also* Lerdahl and
  Jackendoff, Winograd
Tonality, 2, 5–8, 13, 40, 79, 81, 92, 101, 102,
  111, 127, 190
  melodic, 17
Tone sequences, perceptual organisation of,
  71–119
Tonic note, 129
  keynotes, 77, 81, 87, 88
Tonic root, 89
Tonic scale, 76, 81
Transcription, 72, 143–145
Transformational grammar, 33–34
  deep structure, 34
  kernel sentence, 34
  surface structure, 34
Transitional probabilities, 31
Transposition, 11–12, 71, 81, 84, 92, 101, 113,
  139, 171–172, 175–179, 181–182
Tree notation, *see* Time-span reduction,
  Prolongation reduction
Tree structure, *see also* Rhythm
  hierarchical metrical tree ¹60–161
Triads, 111
Tritone, 78
Tuning, 96–103, 107
Twelve-bar blues, *see* Jazz
Tympanic membrane, 265

                    U

Uncertainty, 71

Unique interval multiplicity, 12
Uniquesness, 11–12

                    V

Vibration
  forced, 271
  resonance, 271; *see also* Formant
Visual art perspective, 73
Visual perception, 102, 110
Vocal quality, 307
  and jitter, 307
Vocal registers, 307
Vocal tract shape, 260
Vocalisation
  and airborne sound, 259, 265, 311
  and bone-conducted sound, 270–273, 311,
    318
Voice coach, 300
Vowel articulation, 308, 312–320
  and front–back position of the tongue,
    260
  monophthongal vowels, 260
  tongue height, 260

                    W

Wagner, 185
Well-formedness rules, *see* Grouping analysis,
  Metrical analysis, Prolongational
  reduction, Time-span reduction
Well-formed sentences, 32
Whole-tone scale, *see* Chromatic scale
Window of inner ear
  oval, 268–269, 276
  round, 268–269, 276
Winograd, 40–42; *see also* Systemic grammar